Unscripted America

OXFORD STUDIES IN AMERICAN LITERARY HISTORY

Gordon Hutner, Series Editor

Unscripted America

INDIGENOUS LANGUAGES AND THE ORIGINS OF A LITERARY NATION

Sarah Rivett

OXFORD
UNIVERSITY PRESS

OXFORD

UNIVERSITY PRESS

Oxford University Press is a department of the University of Oxford.
It furthers the University's objective of excellence in research, scholarship,
and education by publishing worldwide. Oxford is a registered trade mark of
Oxford University Press in the UK and certain other countries.

Published in the United States of America by Oxford University Press
198 Madison Avenue, New York, NY 10016, United States of America.

Library of Congress Cataloging-in-Publication Data
Names: Rivett, Sarah, author.
Title: Unscripted America : indigenous languages and the origins of a literary nation / Sarah Rivett.
Description: New York : Oxford University Press, [2017] | Series: Oxford Studies in
American Literary History | Includes bibliographical references and index.
Identifiers: LCCN 2016051093| ISBN 9780190492564 (Print) | ISBN 9780190492595
(e-book) | ISBN 9780190492588 (e-book)
Subjects: LCSH: Native language—North America—History. | Languages in contact—
North America—History. | Indians of North America—Languages—History—17th century. |
Indians of North America—Languages—History—18th century. | Indians of North America—
Languages—Influence on English. | Language and education—North America—History. |
Language and culture—North America—History.
Classification: LCC P120.N37 R48 2017 | DDC 497—dc23 LC record available at
https://lccn.loc.gov/2016051093

3 5 7 9 8 6 4 2
Printed by Sheridan Books, Inc., United States of America

For Rhodri, Max, and Oscar

There are, it may be, so many kinds of voices in the world, and none of them is without signification.

—1 CORINTHIANS 14.10

Thou seest howe all thynges are renewed in Christe and howe the names of thynges are chaunged.

—DESIDERIUS ERASMUS, *ENCHIRIDION*

Sermo; audibilis ergo: at Deus, ut invisiblis est, ita et est inaudibilis... non igitur eiusdem essentiae sermo cum Deo.

—JOHN MILTON, *DE DOCTRINA CHRISTIANA*

Kummog kodonat toottumm ooetite aong annun nonash *is in English* our question: *but I pray, sir, count the letters! Nor do we find in all this language the least affinity to, or derivation from any European speech that we are acquainted with. I know not what thoughts it will produce in my reader, when I inform him that once, finding that the Dæmons in a possessed young woman understood the Latin, and Greek, and Hebrew languages, my curiosity led me to make trial of this Indian language, and the Dæmons did seem as if they did not understand it.*

—COTTON MATHER, *MAGNALIA CHRISTI AMERICANA*

A tongue will wrestle its mouth to death and lose—
language is a cemetery.
Tribal dentists light lab-coat pyres in memoriam of lost molars—
Our cavities are larger than HUD houses.
Some Indians' wisdom teeth never stop growing back in—
we were made to bite back—
until we learn to bite first.

—NATALIE DIAZ, "CLOUD WATCHING"

{ CONTENTS }

{ ACKNOWLEDGMENTS }

In the summer of 2006, I presented a paper on missionary linguistics at Harvard's Atlantic History Seminar that became the origins of this book. Several years passed before I could fully immerse myself in the topic, but I carried the folder containing my seminar paper and the useful comments that I had collected from seminar participants with me to Washington University in St. Louis, the Huntington Library, and then to Princeton University in 2009 where I turned to the topic in earnest; eventually, it would lead me to write this book.

My preliminary thinking about language encounters in colonial North America benefitted from conversations with scholars and colleagues at each of these institutions. At Princeton, I am fortunate to have received collegial and institutional support for the research and writing of this book. The Donald A. Stauffer Preceptorship gave me a sabbatical year (2013–2014) during which most of this book was written. I am very grateful to the D'Arcy McNickle Center for American Indian and Indigenous Studies at the Newberry Library in Chicago, where I held a faculty fellowship in the fall of 2011, and where I did a great deal of archival work for this project and received excellent feedback from other fellows and from Newberry Library staff. Princeton University's Committee on Research in the Humanities and Social Sciences provided generous support for this project. I thank Gordon Hutner for selecting my book for his Oxford University Press series, and my thanks to the press's editorial and production team, especially Brendan O'Neil, Sarah Pirovitz, and Gwen Colvin.

Since that Harvard seminar in 2006, I have presented work from this project and received probing questions and helpful feedback on numerous occasions. Colleagues from institutions and forums that have invited me to present my work and to which I am particularly grateful include the Mediascapes Conference at Duke University, Bates College Honors Program, the Newberry Library, the Heyman Center for the Humanities at Columbia University, the Center for American Studies at the University of Heidelberg, the American

Literature Seminar at the University of Oxford University, the Davis
Center Seminar at Princeton University, the Columbia University
American Studies Seminar, Rutgers University, the Rhode Island
Historical Society, the British Association of Nineteenth-Century
Americanists, the University of Nottingham, the University of
Amsterdam, Yale University Department of English, Notre Dame
University Department of English, University of Chicago Divinity
School, CUNY Graduate Center, and the McNeil Center for Early
American Studies. Earlier versions and sections from this book have
appeared in *The William and Mary Quarterly, American Literature,*
and in three volumes: *Early American Mediascapes, Cultures of
Translation and the Translation of Culture in Early Modern Europe,*
and *Translating Nature.*

The colleagues and friends who took the time to read drafts carefully and critically made this book stronger than it ever could have
been without them. I owe an immense debt of gratitude to Greg
Jackson and Fredrika Teute, who read every word and commented
on just about every sentence. I am deeply appreciative of their pains-
taking labors and efforts to grasp the meaning beyond the page.
Steve Thomas, Cristobal Silva, and Julie Kim are the fabulous three
comprising the NYC writing group that I was fortunate to become a
part of several years ago. They have patiently read drafts of my over-
sized chapters and offered extraordinary comments, criticisms, and
suggestions that have helped the project immeasurably. I also owe
special thanks to Sean Harvey, who invited me to collaborate on a
project that became our co-authored article in *EAS* and from whom
I have learned a great deal. Teresa Toulouse read drafts on numerous
occasions and gave characteristically insightful and challenging
feedback. Collaborative projects with Sophie Gee, Stephanie Kirk,
and Sally Promey helped to place this project in a broader context at
critical moments. Thanks also to Ralph Bauer, Anna Brickhouse,
Jason Bell, Jim Chandler, Matt Cohen, Chris Grasso, Rudolph Glitz,
Jeffrey Glover, Robert Gunn, Sandra Gustafson, Myra Jehlen, Laura
Knoppers, Andrew Lanham, Laura Murray, Drew Newman, Josh
Piker, Lloyd Pratt, Eric Slauter, Caleb Smith, Priscilla Wald, and
Michael Warner.

In an intensely archival project, I benefitted significantly from the
knowledge of archivists, scholars, and librarians I met at the American
Philosophical Society in Philadelphia, the Beinecke Library at Yale,
the Bodleian Library and Rhodes House in Oxford, Cambridge

University Library, the Lambeth Palace Library in London, the Massachusetts Historical Society in Boston, the Newberry Library in Chicago, the Firestone Library in Princeton, and the Watkinson Library in Hartford, Connecticut, just to name a few. For their knowledge and support, special thanks are due to Scott Stevens, Ken Minkema, Jim McClure, and Rick Ring. I have particularly enjoyed the excellence and intimacy that characterizes Princeton's Rare Books and Special Collections Department where I wish to thank Stephen Ferguson, Gabriel Swift, Paul Needham, and AnnaLee Pauls.

At Princeton, I am very lucky to have such fabulous interlocutors in English, American Studies, and throughout the university. Colleagues and graduate students far too numerous to name have shaped this project over the years. I greatly appreciate their support, collaborative thinking, criticism, and guidance. In particular, I would like to thank those who took time to read drafts or listen to talks from this project: Hans Aarsleff, Hendrick Hartog, Linda Colley, Bradin Cormack, Jeff Dolven, Diana Fuss, Bill Gleason, Claudia Johnson, Joshua Katz, Josh Kotin, Russ Leo, Meredith Martin, Deborah Nord, Lee Mitchell, Rebecca Rosen, Marni Sandweiss, Starry Schor, Nigel Smith, Vance Smith, Kelly Swartz, Wendy Warren, and Susan Wolfson. I feel fortunate to have such terrific graduate students to learn from. Thanks especially to the graduate students in my "Religion in the Atlantic World" seminar where many ideas related to this project crystalized. Andrew Ferris edited the entire manuscript, caught many errors, secured permissions, and straightened out my endnotes, greatly easing the challenges of the final stages of manuscript preparation. Sara Marcus helped me with the research for chapters 7 and 8. I am truly lucky to have had the opportunity to write this book among so many smart people and in such a constructively critical yet supportive environment.

Finally, thanks are due to my family. My sons, Oscar and Max, were born during this book's production. While they are too young to have a memory of the time I spent working on it, they each spent many hours asleep in a baby carrier as I wrote and edited. They were both excellent companions during this laborious process. My parents offer ongoing support and are devoted grandparents, which has allowed more time for writing. Finally, thanks to Rhodri Lewis for reading multiple drafts, sustaining me throughout this project's duration, and for giving this book its title.

Unscripted America

{ INTRODUCTION }

In 1664, French Jesuit Louis Nicolas arrived in Quebec. Upon first hearing Ojibwe, Nicolas declared that he had encountered the most barbaric language in the world. But after listening to and studying approximately fifteen Algonquian languages over a ten-year period in New France, he took a different view. Now, Nicolas wrote that he had "discovered all of the secrets of the most beautiful languages in the universe."[1] After a decade among the indigenous populations of the Great Lakes region, Nicolas's ear hears with pleasure the sound of a native speaker who, he explains, pronounces a word with the same refinement as a native speaker of Italian. "Savage" sounds transform into savage eloquence, Nicolas explains, so much so that there is even an Ojibwe word, *kanita iarimitagousitchik*, meaning "Beautiful Speakers," "Orators," or "Those who know how to talk."[2]

Despite the multitude of preconceived notions, conflicting theologies, and disparaging ideologies that Europeans attached to indigenous tongues, learning these languages required a cultural immersion and a thoroughgoing exchange of knowledge. The missionaries who became the most accomplished linguists sat in wigwams for hours and submitted to corrections by indigenous peoples; they abandoned what they thought they knew in order to learn a new system of language and of thinking. In the *Jesuit Relations*, this immersive process recurs as a trope intrinsic to the Jesuit spiritual experience in North America. This scene of linguistic encounter between Europeans and indigenous populations transformed understandings of language. Moreover, the knowledge exchanged in colonial linguistic encounters fundamentally altered the Euro-American perspectives on words, human origins, cosmology, history, and aesthetics, substantially affecting religious, Enlightenment, and literary history.

The pattern exhibited by Nicolas's missionary career repeats itself from early seventeenth-century contact through the antebellum period of American literary production: an initial perception that North American languages are barbaric, followed by inquiry and discovery of their beauty. Over these two centuries, Euro-American missionaries, philosophers, statesmen, and writers discovered an intrinsic beauty and aesthetic potential in the native languages in North America. In 1727, Experience Mayhew tells his readers that the Wampanoag spoken on Martha's Vineyard is "good and regular." While the "Terms of art," are not yet fixed, Wampanoag is certainly "capable" of cultivating them. Mayhew also notes the singularity to be found in the continent's indigenous words when he writes that the "Indians" are not as beholden to other nations as the English are for borrowed terms and concepts. French philosopher Constantin François de Chassebœuf, the Comte de Volney, notes an analogy between "the savages of North America" and the "ancient nations of Greece and Italy" and sees an intrinsic poetic capacity in indigenous words.[3] The novelist William Gilmore Simms advocates assembling the "crude ballads" of American tribes into a "symmetrical narrative, too beautiful for fact." Simms states that these ballads contain very little actual information but that they are "true to art."[4]

In recognizing an inherent beauty in indigenous tongues, seventeenth-century missionaries also believed that the languages of North America could be redeemed and fashioned into something useful. For Puritans such as Roger Williams and John Eliot, just as for Jesuits like Paul Le Jeune and Jean de Brébeuf, the incomprehensible tongues spoken by their proselytes were merely the remnants of the Tower of Babel. Missionaries believed that diligent efforts of transcription and translation, as well as submitting these languages to grammatical rules, would aid in the project of reconstituting language as an instrument of universal redemptive force. North American missionaries inherited this concept of a New World Babel from the Spanish who had been importing printing presses to New Spain since the 1560s and who had an erudite transatlantic discourse on language and Christian translation by the 1590s. Gonzalo Fernández de Oviedo y Valdés noted that the multitude of languages that Columbus encountered in the Caribbean islands was a sign of post-Babelian confusion that served as an aid to Spanish conquest. Oviedo concluded that linguistic diversity was a sign of sin that could only be remedied through evangelization.[5] In seventeenth-century North America, perceptions of indigenous languages followed this model. Efforts to learn indigenous languages were as important as the business of saving souls. Part of this had to do with the way that an Atlantic discourse on language fueled an interest in American tongues. The presentation copy of the Eliot Bible is perhaps the most famous example of the kind of status that Christian translations attained in the seventeenth century; the first edition of Chrestien Le Clercq's *Nouvelle Relation de la Gaspesie* (1691) in John Locke's library is a less well-known but telling instance of an Atlantic interest in New World missions.[6]

For most of the seventeenth century, North American languages figured in theological and philosophical conversations about natural and scriptural histories and in the construction of national genealogies. Yet Christian hermeneutics and Enlightenment taxonomies repeatedly failed to account for the data accrued through the language encounter. Rather than a peripheral colonial practice that produced a barely legible archive, missionary linguistics reveals the existence of an inseparable link between language encounters and American literary and intellectual history.

Comparative Colonial Linguistics

In *The Maine Woods,* Henry David Thoreau writes, "There was something refreshing and wildly musical to my ears in the very name of the white man's canoe, reminding me of Charlevoix and Canadian Voyageurs."[7] Thoreau was an avid reader of the *Jesuit Relations*. He came of age at a time when historians enshrined the image of New France on the minds of nineteenth-century American readers, most famously by his contemporary, Francis Parkman.[8] As this passage suggests, nineteenth-century Anglo-American writers often romanticized the French colonial presence in the North just as they did the vanishing American Indian. Deeming the demise of both as an inevitable means of paving the way for a great Anglo-American civilization, writers such as Thoreau nonetheless celebrated the proximity to nature to be found equally in indigenous words and French travel narratives. In his conflation of the indigenous word, "canoe" and the early seventeenth-century explorer, Charlevoix, Thoreau highlights the recursive nostalgia that many nineteenth-century writers ascribed to an otherwise inaccessible and vanishing past. The fascination with the poetic capacity of indigenous languages that persisted throughout much of the eighteenth century became a significant feature of nineteenth-century literary production, beginning in James Fenimore Cooper's *Leatherstocking Tales,* the author with whom this study ends.

Unscripted America compares the practice of missionary linguistics in New France and New England. This comparison is important to understanding the radically disruptive impact of colonial language encounters on seventeenth- and eighteenth-century European ideas about language. Differences of theology, colonialism, and imperialism impacted the ways that French Jesuits and Anglo-Protestants approached the transcription and translation of Algonquian and Iroquoian languages. Yet the outcome—specifically the challenges that the untranslatable phrase or concept presented to Christian and Enlightenment universals—was largely commensurate across national and linguistic borders. *Unscripted America* traces continuities as well as differences in French Jesuit and Anglo-Protestant missionary texts. This comparative study includes not only French and English colonial sources but a range of indigenous texts and languages; its geographic scope is limited primarily to the northeast of North America where Algonquian and a few Iroquoian languages such as Mohawk were spoken. The Euro-American written record of Algonquian is the most voluminous for North America, even though Algonquian language families are the most subject to prognoses of endangerment and extinction.

French and British missionaries had distinct ways of adjusting to the disruptive impact of untranslatable indigenous phrases and concepts on Christian and Enlightenment universals. French Recollect and Jesuit missionaries, Chrestien Le Clercq, Jacques Gravier, Sebastian Rale, Pierre Maillard, and Francois Picquet developed visual and mnemonic systems of representation, adapting the Catholic semiotics of communion to missionary settings. Jesuits ushered in an era of colonial anthropology that culminated in an attempt to control Mohawk and Mi'kmaq tribes through linguistic and cultural knowledge during the imperial wars that consumed the North American landscape for much of the eighteenth century. Starting in the early 1700s, knowledge of North American languages became intrinsic to French military strategy: Jesuit priests were called upon to cultivate strong American Indian alliances. During the Seven Years War (1754–63), François Picquet was highly valued for his fluent knowledge of Mohawk. He even marched with military troops and enacted scenes of ritual prayer before the French and their Mohawk allies went into battle against the British. Missionary linguistics remained a strategically important enterprise in Franco-America until the end of the Seven Years War.

Anglo-Protestants sought to collapse the linguistic differences they encountered on the missionary frontier into a millennial vision of their own divine right to the land. Building on the Protestant desire for co-substantiality between the word and the spirit, missionaries such as John Eliot, Experience Mayhew, Josiah Cotton, and David Brainerd attempted to Christianize Algonquian languages by making the words keys to divine truth. The British did not make missionary linguistics a part of their imperial project in the way that the French did. Moreover, the British Empire imposed a different model of allegiance, one that required higher degrees of conformity and uniformity with the Protestant faith and that often imagined English-language instruction as a key tool of civilization.[9] In Anglo-Protestantism, this shift toward the privileging of English-language instruction eroded the utility of linguistic knowledge as an instrument of colonization. Long after the Seven Years War ended the contest for North American dominion, indigenous words remained integral to Anglo-American identity as repositories of an ancient and sacred essence that underwrote a new national era of literary and scientific progress.

Unscripting American Literary History

The origins story is the *ur* genre of American literary history. A primary motivation for language collecting and linguistic study from the colonial period through the nineteenth century was a desire to construct new origin myths for the American Indian populations. Often, these myths functioned as explicit correctives to indigenous oral traditions. Writers of European descent had to create such fictions in order to account for alternate and competing histories as well as to give evidence of the Indians' relationship to the land and their projected disappearance. Missionaries who wished to place American Indians within Judeo-Christian history primarily espoused the Hebraic thesis. John Eliot claimed that Massachusetts resembled Hebrew and that the American Indians were one of the ten lost tribes. Though always marginal, this Hebraic thesis persisted well into the eighteenth century and beyond in Joseph François Lafitau's

Moeurs des Sauvages Américains (1724), James Adair's *History of the American Indians* (1775), William Robertson's *History of America* (1777), Jonathan Edwards Jr.'s *Observations on the Language of the Muhhekaneew Indians* (1788), Elias Boudinot's *Star in the West* (1816), and Joseph Smith's *Book of Mormon* (1830). Typically in these texts, the Hebraic thesis functions to offer evidence for scriptural history as being both rooted in and playing out on the North American continent. Though the authors of these texts presumed indigenous populations to be completely estranged from the scriptural roots of their languages, they also believed in their capacity to repair these fallen tongues. Missionaries believed that reparation would recover the sacred origins of Indian grammar that lay beneath what they took to be the new world of Babelian confusion.

The Hebraic thesis strikes our modern ears as strange, while modern science has given credence to the migration of indigenous populations across the Bering Strait from Asia.[10] We thus perceive proponents of the Asiatic thesis as more enlightened, or we see the emergence of this theory as representative of some form of intellectual progress. Yet it is important to keep in mind that the Hebraic thesis was perfectly in keeping with structures of reasoned discourse in the seventeenth century. As Eurocentric as this presumption seems to us today, it was entirely logical to mid-seventeenth-century missionaries and theologians who believed in an inherent link between biblical and natural history. Moreover, both are experienced as Eurocentric to indigenous populations who resist origins accounts that undercut their claims to belonging to the land as original people.[11] The Hebraic and Asiatic theses emerged simultaneously, with the Asiatic thesis dating as far back as Spanish Jesuit José de Acosta's *Natural and Moral History of the West Indies* (1590) and Dutch explorer Joannes de Laet's *History of the New World* (1625). Both of which made the case that American Indians migrated from Asia.

The Asiatic theory became more widely known and accepted in the eighteenth century as Enlightened ideas of natural history began to compete with religious modes of thinking. Jefferson and the Comte de Volney strongly critiqued the Hebraic thesis as religious nonsense, taking the Irish Indian trader and self-taught linguist James Adair as their primary target. In his *History of the American Indians* published in 1775, Adair claimed to hear within Chickasaw a "completion of the manifestations of God's infinite wisdom and power." According to Adair, nature exudes a sense of divine worship in Chickasaw, for the American Indian conception of God exists in smoke, fire, and clouds.[12] For Adair, the authentic sound of divinity comes through Chickasaw like music or poetry. While taking Adair as his object of critique, the Comte de Volney offered proof of a connection between Asia and Amerindians even as he heard the same mystical wholeness in Miami in his *View of the Climate and the Soil of the United States of America* (1804). Volney compared Miami verse to the songs of the bards Ossian and Homer and mapped sonic links between the Miami language and Greek, Arabic, and Hebrew. Written with the goal of encoding a renewable Eden in the very structure of an indigenous tongue, Volney describes Miami as regenerative. From it the divine art of poetry could be created for the present age.

Even though Jefferson and the Comte de Volney offered the Asiatic thesis as a secular replacement for the Hebraic idea, there was little difference in the values ascribed to each one. The Asiatic theory operated under the guise of empiricism to replace one ideology with another. As Vine Deloria Jr. concludes in *Red Earth, White Lies*, religious and scientific explanations of Indian origins were essentially commensurate. Both were parallel attempts to locate Indians within a primitive past, and then to prophesy the spread of Christianity or the rise of the new enlightened nation as an index and archive of that past.[13] Like the missionary proponents of the Hebraic thesis, Jefferson believed that authoritative knowledge of the indigenous past was the key to sovereignty in the present.[14] Jefferson's relentless quest for evidence of Indian origins disavowed the authority of Christianity in order to mask its residual structures. In American literary history, the Hebraic and Asiatic theses have had the effect of repudiating American Indian claims to being original peoples in the Western Hemisphere. Such dismissal became important to the contest over land claims and sovereignty in the early nineteenth century. Both myths of American Indian origins functioned ideologically to dismiss American Indian accounts of their origins as preposterous and to ensconce Indians within a primitive past that also prophesizes the rise of the new nation as an index of that past. Origin myths thus helped to legitimize the Anglo presence within the New World and to account for contemporary narratives of extinction. Yet even as Enlightened contrasts between the civilized and the primitive relegated the Indians to an ancient and unrecoverable past, notions of the sacred power of indigenous words persisted in American literature.

Far from a blanket endorsement of the hierarchy of the printed or written word, the purpose of Christian translation was to teach native proselytes to speak in the grammatically redeemed version of their own language. Missionaries understood the process of transcribing a primarily oral, indigenous language into a written form as an act of forcing the language to submit to European-derived grammatical rule. After doing so, they believed that the language would convey new spiritual truths once relearned and spoken by native proselytes. Missionaries believed that they were recapturing the sacred power of primitive tongues that had been diminished by the Fall and perhaps further damaged by the Babelian event and centuries or millennia of isolation from the Judeo-Christian redemption scheme. Inhering in this objective was the belief that these grammatically redeemed tongues were particularly keyed to the souls of their respective speakers, such that to recover the sacred power of the primitive tongue was to unlock its inherent evangelical efficacy, to awaken the native speaker's latent capacity to know with the brightness of inward revelation the true gospel of Christ.

What missionaries found through the process of Christian translation surprised them. Indigenous languages and speakers resisted the colonial scripts imposed on them and forced missionaries to confront the realities of multiple cosmologies and of language as a human construct. In John Eliot's Indian Library and in the *Jesuit Relations* "savage sounds" can still be heard through the Christian texts, not so much as instances of an indigenous voice but rather as the disruptive presence of a language, culture, and cosmology that could not be fully inscribed by or subjected to Christianity. Moreover, this failure had an unsettling impact on purportedly universal Christian truths. Missionaries knew that their records of colonial encounters and Indian conversion were not as hermeneutically closed as they wished them to be. The practice of scripting indigenous tongues thus had an unintended and disruptive impact on the pillars of North American colonization, namely Christianity and Enlightenment taxonomy. Early modern missionaries confronted Lockean linguistics in practice well before the publication of book 3 of the *Essay Concerning Human Understanding*, and they saw firsthand the insight of the twentieth-century linguist Benjamin Whorf who claims that "the picture of the universe shifts from tongue to tongue."[15]

Through these shifting cosmologies, indigenous languages resisted Christian translation. This resistance took a range of forms and was not necessarily always a conscious or coherent scheme. Practices of translation give the illusion of control through commensurate words and through the powers of communication. Yet, all languages also resist translation. As Lawrence Venuti writes, language is "a collective force, an assemblage of forms that constitute a semiotic regime."[16] Venuti goes on to explain that these forms are positioned hierarchically but this ordering is subject to constant variation. Therefore any language is a site of power relations. The act of translation itself can thus serve a disruptive function. Hierarchies cannot be maintained through translated words.

The "untranslatable" word or phrase that surfaces time and again in colonial-indigenous language encounters permits this process of survivance.[17] Jean de Brébeuf, a first-generation French Jesuit missionary who became a proficient speaker of Huron, notes that even the doctrinally elementary line, "In the name of the Father, and of the Son, and of the holy Ghost" proves quite difficult to convey in Huron-Wendat. Those who have no father on earth cannot say "Our Father," for to do so is an "insult" to "the dead whom they have loved."[18] Justifying his refusal to learn Mahican while at Stockbridge, Jonathan Edwards explains that the language is "very ill-fitted for communicating things moral and divine."[19] Thomas Jefferson found that his Indian agents often returned vocabulary lists to him with missing words. In the case of a Nanticoke list collected by Benjamin Hawkins, the broadside came back with an entire column crossed out with new words and their Nanticoke translation in its place.[20] In each case, untranslatability has a profoundly disruptive process on the form of Christian translation or knowledge acquisition taking place in the scene of linguistic encounter.

The untranslatable aspects of indigenous languages have a disruptive impact on universal truths of either Scripture or Enlightened taxonomies, the two predominant epistemological frameworks used to structure colonial investments in the New World. I refer to this disruptive impact as a process of unscripting. As a capitalized noun, Scripture refers to the sacred writings of the Old and New Testaments. As a lowercase noun, scripture refers to the action or art of writing. It also functions as a verb meaning to write, or place on record.[21] Scripting, lowercase noun and verb, is what the missionaries imagined they were doing when they undertook the hubristic task of translating the primarily oral indigenous languages of North America into a written form. The ideology structuring this process radically oversimplified the languages that they encountered. Dismissing the complexities of inflection that infuse oral languages with meaning, the missionaries recorded sounds phonetically, using the roman alphabet or some other system of notation and orthographic practices rooted in European languages.

Thomas Harriot offers a key early example of this practice of attempting to script indigenous languages. During his time in Roanoke, Virginia, present-day North Carolina, Harriot learned Carolina Algonquian and also taught English to two Algonquian men. He devised a strikingly novel phonetic orthography to capture Carolina Algonquian exactly as it sounded. Harriot's orthography derived from the system developed by the English spelling reformer, John Hart, as a means of figuring out how to record and print vernacular dialects.[22] The characters are systematic modifications of a dozen shapes that represent vowels. Harriot titled his alphabet "An Universal Alphabet containing six and thirty letters, whereby may be expressed the lively image of mans voice in what language soever; first devised upon occasion to seek for fit letters to express Virginian speech." Most of the papers recording this alphabet have been lost. Only a fragment remains. Yet the title reveals something of Hariot's understanding of the relationship between oral and written language. His alphabet was designed to contain universal symbols that could organize and adequately represent the diverse aural quality of Virginian speech. Visual character representation would encapsulate more than one sound so that the alphabet as a whole could be universal in scope. Harriot's manuscript neither enjoyed wide circulation nor became the practical tool for which it was intended. For those who did see the manuscript, the unfamiliar representation of Algonquian letters likely looked more like curiosities than vehicles for trade and diplomacy.[23]

Harriot's efforts to produce a "universal alphabet" that would function as a transferable linguistic guide to any Virginian (i.e., Algonquian) language is a good example of early modern attempts to comprehend the curiosities encountered in new worlds. Roger Williams's *Key into the Language of America* (1643) is another. The *Key* exhibits a fantasy that Narragansett could be scripted into Judeo-Christian history. The assumption structuring Harriot's "universal alphabet" and Williams's *Key* is that the world's linguistic detritus could be collected, reordered, submitted to rule, and assigned a different order within the universe.

This book demonstrates how the ideas about language the Europeans brought with them to the New World came up against the realities of how language functions. The Native American philosopher Viola Cordova describes the reality of language through the metaphor of a window. "Language is a window that frames a particular view of the world. Even when the window disappears, the view that it framed remains."[24] While Cordova builds on Whorf's linguistic philosophy, this description of language goes beyond the Whorfian concept of linguistic relativity. For Cordova speaks of a cosmological permanence that remains even after a language vanishes. This cosmological permanence is the core of what is preserved in indigenous language texts even as the colonial linguistics participated in the language's destruction. When Brébeuf complains to his superior that "Our Father" cannot be translated, the problematic untranslatability of the phrase represents a cosmological permanence that refuses erasure. To some degree, Brébeuf recognizes the permanence of an indigenous theology that is land-based. Yet Brébeuf cannot quite come to terms with the constructed nature of language as it revolves around a distinct cosmology because of the way that this realization conflicts with Christianity.

By no mere coincidence, instances of untranslatability then occur with the greatest frequency in Christian texts and in practices of Christian translation, when cosmogonies and epistemologies come into frequent conflict.[25] Religion assumes an intercultural commonality at the same time that the attempt to impose a belief system on another culture exposes the fissures in human interconnectedness; religious translations reveal the numerous ways in which the words and narratives used to express belief are radically incommensurate. Missionaries of North America were the first to discover that not only could indigenous languages not be managed according to the universal truths espoused in Christian doctrine, but that the very effort to translate Christian concepts exposed human difference and cultural relativity. This discovery did not necessarily lead to salutary results: the failure to encompass these languages within European taxonomies and epistemologies caused a crisis whereby entire systems of belief were called into question.

The colonial history of missionary linguistics precedes an early national philology in which Peter Du Ponceau and others developed an obsession with the literary value of indigenous oral languages.

Lenni-Lenape, according to Du Ponceau and John Heckewelder, contained a richness due to its oral power, a capacity to represent nature more symbiotically and an unparalleled propensity toward metaphoricity with its beautiful literary quality. James Fenimore Cooper attempted to absorb and channel these linguistic qualities into a new form of writing. Of course Cooper's perception of the sonic aspects of indigenous tongues was a romanticization, and one that has been written about extensively in the literature on the trope of the noble savage. Yet this perception is also not reducible to the trope of the noble savage. Missionaries such as Jesuit Sebastian Rale and Puritan Josiah Cotton recognized the aesthetic value of native words by studying and—most important—listening to the sounds spoken by indigenous people. Such encounters taught missionaries that ideologies of savage speech were false and that an autonomous syntactical and phonetic integrity existed in indigenous oral literary traditions. Ideologies of indigenous orality as beautiful but primitive or of these languages as naturally dying out tempered the more salutary insights made by missionaries who spent years in close ethnographic contact. Yet both the recognition of aesthetic integrity and the commitment—however displaced by imperialist tendencies—toward making America's oral literary heritage part of the literary nation stems from a sustained confrontation with the resilience and permanence of North American languages.

Erasure through Preservation

In focusing on the resilience and permanence displayed in scenes of linguistic colonialism, *Unscripted America* contests the long-standing narrative of indigenous language death. Algonquian and Iroquoian language groups demonstrate forms of survival in the two language families that are most subject to prognoses of endangerment and extinction. The written record of these languages is also among the most voluminous for North America. To be sure, the authors of this archive performed a kind of historical violence to the languages, transmuting and deforming them in destructive ways. Yet orality proves more resilient and permanent than written forms of manuscript or print. Oral languages are more fluid in some ways and more fixed in others. They are adept at dealing with the fluctuations of time and space in a way that print history is not. Song is a prime example of this facet of oral languages. English and French mission-aries admired the musical propensity of indigenous populations. Jesuit letters praise Mohawk, for example, for being particularly skilled at the mnemonic properties of song, reporting a high level of aural precision.[26] In part for this reason, hymnals became one of the main texts of Christian translation. Hymnals also represent a point of confluence between indigenous oral performance and Christian ritual worship. Such a confluence could emerge because the "song's sounding life" took on a particular shape within each iteration.[27] Song, even as it became an instrument for imposing Christianity, also permitted indigenous modes of worship, language, and perfor-mance to survive. Mohawk hymns survive decades after the Jesuit missions disappeared in North America. Even today, the Mohawk Choir of St. Regis sings Mohawk hymns.[28] If the singing of hymns and psalms was often part of an interfaith and intercultural exchange between Indian proselytes and missionaries, Glenda Goodman dem-onstrates how psalmody also became the center point of conflict in times of war such as when Praying Indians made a mockery of Puritan signing during King Philip's War.[29]

The oral and aural qualities of indigenous languages permitted forms of indigenous language survival in Catholic hymnals, yet the same facets of language that remain intact across generations also create problems of untranslatability in the eighteenth century. While Christian translators were invested in translating oral languages into an invented written form, they soon began by recognizing the complexity and power of oral traditions and the resistance of these traditions to tran-scription and transliteration. Missionaries accorded the indigenous words spoken by the converted Praying Indian the most redemptive power. This was a power inherent in indigenous languages themselves.

The myth of language death, still very much with us today, is per-haps the last horizon of the Enlightenment theory of American Indian natural extinction and the concomitant romanticization of an irrecoverable past. Scholars such as Jill Lepore, Walter Mignolo, and Stephen Greenblatt have amply established that Christianity dispar-aged and destroyed indigenous tongues.[30] The destructive forces of early modern colonization set into motion a process of linguistic de-cline that archaeologist Colin Renfrew describes as "elite dominance," the most drastic and rapid form of language loss.[31] According to Ives Goddard, northeastern Algonquian was the language group most thoroughly destroyed through colonization.[32] Contemporary language revitalization programs use recovery as a way of trying to heal the wounds of colonialism. The Myaamia Center in Oxford, Ohio, is working to transcribe and translate the contents of two Miami-Illinois dictionaries, Gravier's and that of his successor, Jean Baptiste Le Boulanger. The goal of the Center is to use linguistics to reverse language loss and ultimately reclaim the language for the people who originally spoke it. This goal has already been realized in the Wôpanâak Language Reclamation Project (WLRP), which began in 1993. Mashpee tribal member Jessie "Little Doe" Baird claims to have heard a sacred message and to have seen the faces of her ancestors in a dream that she had for three consecutive nights. Baird interpreted her dream as a sign that the ancient language of the Wampanoag tribe should be reclaimed. After receiving a degree in linguistics from MIT, she worked in collaboration with Kenneth Hale to reconstruct Wampanoag from the printed seventeenth-century colonial records. The WLRP's homepage prominently displays the first page of Genesis from Eliot's 1663 Bible, suggesting a commingling of origins stories, one Judeo-Christian and one from the recovered ancestral language of the Wampanoag.

Within these projects, language loss is a metonym for the destruction of identity, culture, and sovereignty. Yet as the Maliseet scholar and linguistic anthropologist Bernard Perley points out, these categories are themselves built upon Enlightened assumptions.[33] For what does it mean to say that these languages are extinct? What are we to make of the vast records of Iroquois and eastern Algonquian left by Jesuit and Protestant missionaries? Collated vocabularies, dictionaries containing thousands of indigenous words, and grammars compose an archive of European attempts to acquire knowledge of North American languages. From this linguistic base came a massive translation project. Scripture, catechisms, psalms, bibles, and prayer books appeared in print and manuscript form in Wampanoag, Mi'kmaq, Mohawk, Abenaki, Miami-Illinois, Delaware, and Mohegan. Laura Murray once identified the pervasive American Indian Vocabulary list as an "elusive" literary genre.[34] Her article evokes the contradictory facets of missionary linguistics. Indigenous tongues were not simply erased; they were also preserved. *Unscripted America* takes as its foundational question: how did erasure happen through a long history of colonial efforts to preserve indigenous languages? Misguided though their efforts may have been, missionaries struggled to find a way to transcribe and maintain living indigenous languages and amassed a vast archive in doing so.

When one looks closely at the scene through which Europeans and American Indians exchanged linguistic knowledge, the intricacies of erasure through preservation emerge. The scene of language/knowledge exchange reveals a much more complex portrait than theories of colonial linguistics and elite dominance lead us to believe. If we consider what Myra Jehlen once labeled "history before the fact" of colonization and language extinction, indigenous languages were not simply destroyed through this process.[35] While it is of course true that the linguistic diversity of North America and the numbers of native speakers have dramatically diminished from the mid-seventeenth century to the present day, these languages did not simply recede into the background of the historical stage. Rather, native speakers, interlocutors, and translators actively shaped an archive of manuscript and print language texts that had a dramatic impact on Christian cosmologies, Enlightenment taxonomies, and the rise of a national literary culture. Time and again, indigenous actors practiced forms of what the literary critic Scott Lyons describes as "rhetorical sovereignty" by conveying knowledge in such a way that native languages refused placement and compartmentalization within European systems and structures of organization.[36]

In place of the narrative of language death, we might instead ask, how did Indian languages transform the structure of European and Euro-American intellectual history? As Jesuit and Puritan missionaries struggled to map indigenous tongues to universal Christian truths, Algonquian and Iroquois resisted this form of translation through a syntax that sustained a completely different cosmology. David Murray, the scholar whose *Forked Tongues* introduced the concept of missionary linguistics to American literary critics in the early 1990s, examines in his more recent book, *Matter, Magic, and Spirit* (2007), the non-material power of objects in indigenous belief systems.[37] Anthropologists Irving Hallowell and Mary Black have explained that in Ojibwe, for example, plants and animals can take animate and inanimate forms.[38] This is represented linguistically. Verbs and nouns are conjugated and gendered to reflect whether the object is animate or inanimate. Animacy is a shifting phenomenon; sometimes it is present in an object and sometimes it is not. Imagine the confusion of a seventeenth- or eighteenth-century missionary who believed that all creation was reducible to Christian truths encountering this semiotic world for the first time. The indigenous cosmologies encoded in words forced missionaries to confront the particularity of language rather than its universality.

In addition to disrupting Christian cosmologies, the texts produced through colonial-indigenous language encounters had two lives. Take the famous example of the 1663 printing of the Bible in Wampanoag, known as the Eliot Bible. Eliot's translation efforts aligned with those of his patrons in London's Royal Society to serve the evangelical purpose of propagating the Protestant ideal of *sola scriptura*. Presentation copies of the Eliot Bible were sent back to England with the hope of garnering more support for the mission. Yet the Eliot Bible represents a fantasy, not the reality, of linguistic control. The transcription, translation, and production of the text itself depended on the labor and intelligence of indigenous contributors, as Philip Round demonstrates in *Removable Type*. The efficacy of the translation then rested on indigenous interlocutors—whether they read it, believed it, and acted on it in terms that the ministers would have found doctrinally sound. Contextual evidence suggests that reception was not quite as fixed as Eliot would have liked. The Massachusett word for "wind," for example, was "Waban."[39] Waban was thus used to translate the passage from Ezekiel 37:9–10, "by prophesying to the wind, the wind came and the dry bones lived."[40] This passage was known as a highly effective homiletic among native audiences in particular because of an Indian preacher named Waban who famously converted many native proselytes. The Puritan ministers read this connection typologically. Yet the description of God breathing life into Ezekiel's dry bones corresponds to Wampanoag belief in *manit*, the spirit power that can animate people and objects in the natural world. Waban attained Christian authority while also maintaining the power of the spirit healer within traditional indigenous systems of belief. Other examples of American Indians converting to Christianity while still maintaining indigenous beliefs abound, particularly in French Jesuit records. Not only did this multivalent meaning open up syncretic possibility, French Jesuit priests were fascinated by the animate and inanimate ontology of indigenous words.

Jacques Gravier's Dictionary of the Algonquian-Illinois Language is a massive 580-page book consisting of approximately 25,000 Miami-Illinois words recorded over several decades. In a list of Illinois words pertaining to the spirit world, "Manet8a" is translated as "esprit, Dieu, de la neige, medecine." *Manitou* could mean snow, spirit, medical remedy, or God himself. The word *medecine* refers to the shamanic doctors within the community. The translation of Manitou as snow registers the Illinois belief in animating elements within the natural world. The dictionary records the connection between the indigenous spirit world and North American nature. The list beneath contains multiple variations of the word. Each variant has been altered through prefixes and suffixes that convey a range of meanings: *it is not God, it is God, divine, he calls himself a spirit, I am not God, a spirit, and so on.* The word variants with their constantly fluctuating meaning represent a fluid cosmology. The word itself conveys the presence or absence of the spirit through an animate or inanimate ending. On the one hand, the dictionary serves its purpose as an instrument of empire, the power that Antonio de Nebrija originally ascribed to vernacular translations.[41] The dictionary records the linguistic knowledge necessary to communicate effectively with the local Illinois population in order to convert them and secure their alliance with the French in the ongoing imperial wars. Yet the specificity and breadth of the recorded words also undermine this purpose. Words recorded in Gravier's *Dictionary* not only salvage Miami-Illinois language, religion, and culture, they also imported aspects of an indigenous cosmology into Jesuit consciousness.

Indigenous languages existed and continue to exist as porous and malleable records of fluid historical interactions rather than remnants of an all-but-forgotten past. Language exposes the false binary of modernity as it has been constructed throughout US history and literature as a series of ruptures and changes set against a static aboriginal past. By connecting colonial linguistics to its broader intellectual and literary contexts, we see that these languages appear not to have been simply lost or destroyed but rather absorbed into the American literary imagination. Missionaries, philologists, and eventually American poets and novelists represented indigenous words as useless and decaying artifacts of a lost civilization at the same time that they also saw them as aesthetically pleasing, beautiful objects to be integrated into the fabric of American letters and American archaeology. Indigenous language collecting and study evolved over the seventeenth, eighteenth, and nineteenth centuries as a contested space, expressive of mechanisms for asserting control while also radically exposing colonialism's limits.

Indigenous Words and American Literary History

In his 1998 essay on the "Amerindian Atlantic," Ian Steele posited that an outmoded anthropological perspective on the disappearing American Indians still shaped the fields of early American history. The

long-standing presumption of indigenous language death is a key
example of what Steele was describing.[42] The new critical focus on
cross-cultural exchanges and literacies in indigenous language texts is
an attempt to revise this perspective by linking the history of ideas to
different forms of indigenous resistance, perseverance, and survival.
Work by Matt Cohen, Kristina Bross and Hilary Wyss, Brett Rushforth,
Germaine Warkentin, Drew Lopenzina, and Birgit Brander Rasmussen
shows that colonial encounters and texts coauthored by European and
indigenous peoples actively integrated indigenous sign systems into
the spread of Western literacy and its accompanying textual forms.[43]
Additionally, work by David Silverman, Glenda Goodman, Philip
Round, Patrick Erben, Tracy Leavelle, Margaret J. Leahey, and Linford
D. Fisher read these textual forms as productive of cross-cultural exchanges, either through the blend between Christianity and indigenous spirituality, or between Euro-American and indigenous material
cultures.[44] Finally, Anthony Wallace, Sean Harvey, Edward Gray, and
Bernard Sheehan have explored the accumulation of linguistic knowledge as anthropological data in relation to the acquisition of land in
the territories where Indian languages were collected.[45] The outmoded
anthropological perspective that Steele identified initially emerged as
part of Anglo-America's national and Enlightenment agenda. The formation of the United States depended on a mindset that ensconced
indigenous populations within a primitive past, while making that
past indexical of the rise of a new civilization.

From early contact to early nationalism, early American writers in-
vestigated and invented stories of American origins. Roger Williams,
Brébeuf, Lafitau, the Comte de Volney, Thomas Jefferson, and James
Fenimore Cooper each devoted significant amounts of their oeuvre
to theories of the origins of indigenous populations, whether understood scripturally or through natural history. After the Seven
Years War, the quest for origins becomes a refrain for the establishment of an Anglo-American presence on the North American continent built upon the legacy of a defeated French Empire and the
palimpsest of an American Indian past. Early American writers took
on the ideological burden of forging a new relationship to the land
and its inhabitants. They struggled to generate some form of historical
continuity that might assuage the violent ruptures with the indigenous
past and the Old World.

This intense quest for origins as a constitutive feature of American
literary history, particularly as it relates to the American Indian

presence, sits in uneasy contrast to the critique of the origins thesis that has been almost uniformly practiced by Americanists of the past several decades. As a field, we have rightfully corrected the false teleology of linear succession from the Puritans to the rise of mercantile capitalism to the new nation with transatlantic, transnational, and hemispheric frameworks.[46] Such approaches also resist the reproduction of ideologies of originalism and exceptionalism in our scholarship such that our own narratives of American literary history no longer culminate with the US nation-state as the beacon of modernity. This corrective has certainly been an important one, yet it does not erase the fact of a teleology of colonial exceptionalism and national triumph as the cornerstone on which Anglo-American identity has been conceived and sustained. The recursive nostalgia for Native American canoes and French explorers that I attributed to Thoreau toward the beginning of this introduction was by no means an isolated gesture. Many nineteenth-century authors struggled to find the ends of America in America's beginnings.

Early American missionaries, statesmen, novelists, and poets had their own extensive origins historiography that pertained to American Indian tribes through which to construct this narrative of national triumph. Indigenous tongues constituted the archive that Thomas Jefferson, Benjamin Smith Barton, and the Comte de Volney used to measure the antiquity of indigenous America. Ideas about indigenous words and the natural historical framework into which they were placed fueled Anglo-American notions of belonging to the land. As Indian Vocabularies and natural histories proliferated in the early republic, colonial ideas about indigenous words as signs of ancient and prophetic truth persisted and helped to legitimize the British presence within the New World. Even as Enlightened contrasts between the civilized and the primitive relegated the populations that originally spoke these words to an ancient and unrecoverable past, Indian words continued to function as an aesthetic supplement to nineteenth-century literature. In recasting the origins of a literary nation, this study enables us to see how the notion of "America" that emerges around the turn of the eighteenth century, depended on its authors' capacity to interrogate, translate, and appropriate the indigenous past.

The "Savage Sounds" of Christian Translation

MISSIONARIES CONFRONT THE LIMITS OF
UNIVERSALISM IN EARLY AMERICA

In 1632 the ship carrying Father Paul Le Jeune from France to Quebec cast anchor in Tadoussac village. According to Le Jeune, nothing was so strange to him as the language spoken by the aborigines he encountered. He writes that "their singing seemed very disagreeable to me; the cadence always ended with reiterated aspirations." Le Jeune even records these "savage" sounds in his *Relation*: "oh! oh! oh! ah! ah! ah! hem! hem! hem!" to reiterate his point about an unappealing and foreign tongue.[1] Yet Le Jeune soon concluded that gaining knowledge of this foreign language was key to his mission's success as well as to the French colonial endeavor more broadly conceived. Soon after his arrival, Jérôme Lalemant established a Jesuit headquarters at Sainte-Marie from which the core group of priests were to embark on their missionary efforts in Huron country. Among these men were Jean de Brébeuf, Pierre Chaumonot, and Paul Ragueneau. This early missionary establishment enjoyed a great deal of continuity. Several of the priests lived among the Huron for ten years or more, acquiring a vast amount of linguistic and cultural expertise.[2]

Le Jeune succeeded in learning Huron and Montagnais and then in teaching his proselytes in their own language. His colleague Father Brébeuf took this linguistic expertise even further. Brébeuf's education in the Society of Jesus prepared him to encounter the world's disparate cultures with scientific precision.[3] In the twenty years that he spent living in Wendake, he observed, recorded, and categorized the linguistic and cosmological differences of his proselytes. His annual reports to the ecclesiastical authorities display a heightened sense of ethnographic awareness that registered most markedly at the level of astute syntactical and grammatical notations. Brébeuf translated catechisms from French to Huron, compiled the first dictionary of Huron words, and is credited with translating a French hymn into a Huron Christmas carol in 1642, an instance of how translation was often implicated in the process of creating religious ritual and ceremony. Originally a French folk melody with Huron lyrics, this colonial artifact is still widely known and sung in Canada today.

The year before Le Jeune cast anchor in Quebec, Roger Williams came to the Massachusetts Bay Colony. Williams's theological differences with the Massachusetts Bay orthodoxy surfaced not long after his arrival. Upon learning that the Massachusetts Bay government was preparing to send him back to England, Williams fled southward to found the colony of Providence along the shores of the Narragansett Bay.[4] Desiring a more secure legal base, Williams left for London in 1643 to request a royal charter for Rhode Island. In this same year, his *Key into the Language of America* was printed in London.

Scholars often read Williams's *Key into the Language of America* as expressive of Williams's version of religious toleration—the concept of liberty of conscience—which is in turn seen as conducive to greater degrees of humanity toward the American Indians than his Puritan brethren in the Massachusetts Bay Colony seemed to have registered.[5] The *Key* is then interpreted as exhibiting an anthropological approach to the Narragansett that, by its tacit comparative cultural analysis, suggests some degree of intercultural parity.[6] Scholars have observed that Williams at least had the capacity, rare in his time, to recognize this indigenous people and community on their own culturally specific terms, even though—consistent with belief in the New World's millennial role—he refashioned them as an exemplar of spiritual brethren, a cultural mediation well before its time in England, Plymouth, or the Massachusetts Bay Colony. Yet reading Williams's theology alongside his ethnography reveals that while he believed in civility as a model for earthly cohabitation, he was, not surprisingly, ultimately fixed in the logic of the Christian mission to integrate all earthly societies into the domain of Christ's church, and thus his earthly kingdom. He did not, therefore, recognize the Narragansett as culturally autonomous or as partaking in a distinct set of religious practices. Instead, Williams viewed the Narragansett within his own Christian millenarian framework, which espoused

the Narragansett as worshippers of pagan idolatry and, as yet, spiritually unprepared for immediate conversion.[7] Thus, *A Key into the
Language of America* is designed as a hermeneutically closed text. It
is a language key but one designed to grant spiritual intelligibility only
at a foreordained time, when Christ would, like the shepherd who
left the many to find the one, gather the scattered flock into the one
true church. Yet, even as Williams attempts to collapse Narragansett
words into an overarching framework of his own reformed theology, he struggles with the Narragansett cosmology's resistance to
assimilation within the prescribed pattern of the Puritan cultus. This
cosmology comes into sharp conflict with Williams's millenarian
frame, ultimately resulting in a disjointed text that oscillates between
ethnographic constructs of Narragansett culture (and what at times
appears to be Williams's sympathetic ambivalence) and the theological scaffolding inflexible to the accommodation of any difference.
Ultimately, the *Key* fails to sustain scriptural order, resolving itself
instead into the depiction of the fractured spiritual world that emerges
from this particular colonial language encounter.

Brébeuf and Williams shared an unusual grasp of indigenous languages for members of their generation. Each individual's understanding of the relationship between the Word and the spirit had
an impact on his linguistic practices. While constrained by the limits
of their religious world views, both Brébeuf and Williams felt compelled to abandon some of the verities they held dear in order to
learn and understand Huron-Wendat and Narragansett, respectively.
Even in these early years of French Jesuit and Puritan colonial enterprises, language acquisition required a process of immersion that
was cultural as well as spiritual. Missionaries had to acquire knowledge of indigenous cosmologies in order to perform the act of
Christian translation. Consequently, the indigenous language texts
produced by each of these missionaries exhibit varying degrees of
knowledge exchange. Missionaries worked to translate Christian
knowledge into indigenous tongues, but they also sought to gather
cultural and linguistic information from native interlocutors that
could then be relayed to European audiences. Brébeuf's report on
the Huron-Wendat language, dictionary, and translational practices
and Williams's *Key* similarly struggle to maintain formal coherence
and religious order in light of this knowledge exchange. This struggle
reveals that despite their religious differences, the consequence of
indigenous language immersion for both Brébeuf and Williams had

the same dramatic result: a fractured spiritual identity, caught between the putative universality of their respective Christian beliefs and the realities of multiple cosmologies that they experienced through the practice of translation. Despite their efforts to contain the cultural encounter within a Christian framework, Williams and Brébeuf import indigenous cosmologies and evidence of epistemological convergences into their missionary tracts. These fragments of indigenous cosmologies approximate what comparative philology refers to as "alien texts." The presence of significantly contrasting cosmogonies in missionary texts had a disruptive impact on the missionaries' respective theologies.[8] The colonial texts produced out of these language encounters exhibit a dialectical process of indigenous and Euro-American knowledge formation. The multiple world views inherent in language put pressure on Christianity's universality, paradoxically causing missionaries to have to confront more secular understandings of language and culture.

Puritan Theology in an American *Key*

Jesuits and Puritans shared a fundamental belief in religious conversion as an inwardly directed process.[9] They differed, however, in their respective understandings of how to translate that inward knowledge to an external form. In North America indigenous people spoke a preponderance of languages within close geographic proximity. European missionaries who encountered this phenomenon struggled to identify ways to communicate inner experience of conversion through language. This struggle became a central component of indigenous evangelism. Jesuits and Puritans developed different ways of adjudicating the relationship between the Word and the spirit. Among the Puritans, words were largely read as types following Luther's scriptural theology. In his *Lectures on Romans*, Luther argues that the Bible must be first interpreted according to its literal-grammatical sense, such that the reader understands the ostensible meaning the syntax conveys. Only after exegesis should he attempt to ascertain the typological implication in order to uncover the prophetical-spiritual meaning of the Holy Spirit. Scriptural words and their accretion into narrative thus prefigured and foreshadowed the unfolding of events within scriptural history. Understanding scriptural history depended on a precise and literal interpretation of the

Word itself.[10] The essential problem of language for the Puritans was that it existed within the economy of a fallen world. Biblical interpretation had to pass through the alembic of the fallible human mind; words spoken—even by the godly—were signs, themselves the post-lapsarian residue of the first language, within a visible, material realm and therefore inherently unreliable.

Anglo-Protestants faced a conflict between their commitment to the fallen status of language and of human perceptive capacities and their assertion of language's potentially prophetic power. How could it be one and both at the same time? Even their ability to recognize the latter was at odds with the former, the basis of the whole of the Augustinian-Calvinist scheme. Theologians developed different ways of managing this conflict, which led to different ideas about the potential for language to be recuperative. To what extent could words regain the signifying power that they lost in the Fall? Much of the confusion and ensuing disagreement centered on debates about whether Christ's spirit was ascendant or descendant. If Christ descended to earth in each moment of conversion, then the perceptive capacities of the converted could be redeemed. If, however, his spirit remained ascendant, then words, like all visible signs, were only shadowy approximations of invisible truths and therefore never completely reliable.

This divergent perspective on the significatory power of words was integral to the famous dispute between John Cotton and Roger Williams. Cotton took the view that conversion ameliorated language's fallen status. As his sermon title "Christ the Fountaine" (1651) suggests, he was of the opinion that Christ's spirit descended in the moment of conversion and radically reconfigured the convert's sensibilities: "he that is borne of God to a Spirituall life, is become *a new Creature, and old things are past away*, 2 Cor. 5.17. He hath a new mind, and a new heart, new affections, new Language, and new employments that he was never wont to doe before; now he can read Gods Word, and conferre with Gods people about the things of God."[11] Cotton proposes a world in which conversion and the saving grace of God repairs, at least in part, the ruptured status of human intellect, emotions, and language to create a new spiritual aptitude. The theology Cotton espouses would be propounded in forthcoming generations, perhaps most significantly in Jonathan Edwards's explanation—rationalized through Lockean epistemology—that the elect have greater access to divine truths than the unredeemed, a thesis first ventured in his sermon

"Divine and Supernatural Light" (1734) and later developed in his *Treatise Concerning Religious Affections* (1746).

Williams, by contrast, did not believe that spiritual conversion renovated the soul in this way or to this degree. For him, the spiritual and the civil realm remained apart, such that even though a soul was regenerated, it remained trapped within a body disfigured by the imputation of Adam's sin. Just as Williams denied the possibility of the visible church that the Massachusetts Puritans aspired to create as an approximation of Christ's invisible church, he also vehemently rejected Cotton's view on language's capacity to be redeemed. Or, as in the case of the spiritual basis of the primitive tongue, to redeem. Along with the human intellect and civil structures, Williams believed that races would remain incomprehensible to each other until the return of Christ. Only then would "spiritual language" be realizable.[12] He, in fact, penned his *Key* with the goal of creating a millennial text for Christian posterity. With Christ's return, the *Key* could, he hoped, be the basis for rendering Narragansett and English mutually intelligible and equally capable of revealing spiritual truths.

Despite labors that would seem to suggest otherwise, Williams continued to believe that language was inherently fallen. While he optimistically held that the *Key* might pave the way for the collapse of cultural and linguistic difference, it was a consummation indefinitely to be deferred. In addition to his *Key into the Language of America*, Williams composed another text, primarily a theological tract, on American Indian conversion, titled *Christenings Make Not Christians* (1645). Whereas the theology structuring the *Key* is obscure, *Christenings* clarifies the link between Williams's doctrine and his perspective on, and the timing of, American Indian conversion. Central to the intersection between theology and evangelism for Williams is a spiritual and millennial framework that negates his stance on language. The first half of the text identifies and explains the etymology of the term "Heathen" as a synonym and Dutch cognate for nation. Williams arrives at this conclusion through a process of translation. The Dutch word *HEYDENEN* signifies "Heathen or Nations," he explains. Moreover, scriptural translation from Hebrew and Greek renders the terms "Gentiles, Nations, Heathens" equivalent categories, so that history, geography, and ethnicity divide into commensurately aligned groupings. Williams thus presents a world that does not divide according to a binary division between Heathens and Christians: the visible church divides the world between God's elect and the reprobate, regardless of whether or not they are faithful Christians. Because Williams believes that some "heathens" will number among those predestined for salvation, he instead divides the world according to truth versus error, labeled in the idiom of reformed theology as "hypocrisy."

For Williams, the "Christian World" includes "*Asia, Europe,* a vaste part of *Africa,* and a great part also of *America*." The second half of the essay takes up this point by addressing the question of when it is appropriate to convert the "naked *American*," which he ultimately determines is not until the onset of Christ's millennial reign on earth, heralded with his return.[13] In *Christenings Make Not Christians*, Williams explains that the fallen world is ill-equipped for evangelization. Visible signs are limited in their capacity to signify as spiritual truths in the postlapsarian world, such that:

> in matters of Earth men will helpe to spell out each other, but in matters of Heaven (to which the soule is naturally so averse) how far are the Eares of man hedged up from listening to all improper Language?[14]

While earthly matters can be conveyed through language, Christian truths cannot. The degeneration of the natural world makes visible things and the damaged capacities of human "eares" inadequate in the communication of heavenly truths. For Williams, as for reformed Protestants, the loss was accumulative: material objects in the fallen world were but shadows that, in turn, are represented by words, which are the signs of signs, leaving signification at a double remove. Williams goes on to explain that he views it as his divine "endeavou[r]" "to attaine a propriety of Language."[15] That is, he wrote his *Key* in an attempt to establish a way, however limited, of communicating with the Narragansett when the proper time came for their conversion into Christian faith.

"Heathens" are defined in this text as those nations whose members are spiritually unprepared to receive Christ in full knowledge of their duty. To convert American Indians in half measures, to bend or diminish spiritual truths to meet the limited apprehension to which all language—particularly one isolated from the "blessed Ordinances" of Christendom for centuries—further reduces humanity's fallen reason would be but to replace one form of false worship with another:

> Why have I not brought them to such a conversion as I speake of?
> I answer, woe be to me, if I call light darknesse, or darknesse light;

sweet bitter, or bitter sweet; woe be to me if I call that conversion unto
God, which is indeed subversion of the soules of Millions in
Christendome, from one false worship to another, and the prophana-
tion of the holy name of God, his holy Son and blessed Ordinances.
America (as *Europe* and all nations) lyes dead in sin and trespasses.[16]

To teach the American Indians in the subtleties and nuances of
Christian doctrine, to offer them what Christian Europe had accumulated through an unbroken lineage of Christ's blessed Ordinances,
handed down and safeguarded through time, was, Williams believed,
to do more harm to them than if he were to leave them in their present peril but with a rudimentary knowledge of the faith. Any
pretense to full conversion merely compounds the problem of false
worship. Catholicism is, of course, the principal target of his critique,
or at least it is the ostensible target until the other direction of his
critique comes into fuller view. The Catholic stance on conversion
was the polar opposite of that espoused by Williams. The mass conversions that had taken place at the hands of the Spanish, he explains,
happen under the "false head" of the "Antichrist" whose "body" consists of "faith, baptimse, hope…preachings, conversions, salvations."
Each of these aspects of Catholic evangelism shares the same
"false nature."

Here and throughout the essay, Williams contrasts this false nature
to "the living and true God" who will be revealed "in the Lords
time."[17] True conversion, therefore, does not come about through
any of the mechanisms of human influence listed above, but rather
through the "first pattern[s]" "prefigure[d] and type[d] out" in the
Old Testament and perfected in their historical fulfillment in Christ's
new dispensation recorded in the Gospels.[18] Williams's announcement of a true conversion, initiated only through the prefiguration
revealed in the Book of Revelation, discloses the *Key*'s real function.
It is not intended as a text to catalyze the conversion process, for
even if the text contains much "knowledge of the Country" and the
Narragansett culture, he explains, its service as a "key" to Narragansett
conversion would require a superior linguistic knowledge than is
presently available to bring about the "propriety of speech" required
to "open matters of salvation to them."[19]

In the preface to the *Key*, Williams informs his audience that he
"drew the *Materialls*" for this text "in a rude lumpe at Sea." He explains that he intended the *Key* as a "private *helpe*" to his "owne

memory." He wished not to forget what he has "so *dearley bought*" through recent years of hardship in the fledgling Rhode Island Colony and the hard-earned confidence of the Narragansett people.[20] He thus positions his own spiritual identity as caught between two worlds: the world of the Narragansetts with whom he had made his physical and spiritual home and the world of England, a country that was at once his home of origin and a space of deep spiritual alienation. Written during the six-week sea journey, the text attempts to bridge these two worlds.

Yet, the primary function of Williams's *Key* is theological. It is a text designed to acquire currency at a future moment that coincides with the second coming of Christ, when the homology between visible and invisible worlds would be restored. Before this time, Williams insists on the futility of translation. The separation of Narragansett and English words into separate columns registers the profound impenetrability between two distinct sign systems. Upholding what might be described as an intensified Augustinian Calvinism, in that Williams's adhered to a bleaker view of the world's postlapsarian corruption than his Puritan brethren in the Massachusetts Bay, Williams did not believe that the fallen world could be even partially redeemed before the fulfillment of types described in the Book of Revelation. Yet in the *Key*, he assures his audience that once this time comes, both Narragansett and English will be reinfused with spiritual plentitude, making them not only mutually intelligible but also fully capable of conveying spiritual truths. The point of the *Key* is not to make the reader proficient in Narragansett, but rather to prepare him or her for a future time when the *Key* will serve in a time of millennial evangelism. In the recovery of a sacred dialect, Williams hoped that the *Key* might better unlock the Narragansett soul and also collapse cultural difference through the revelatory power of the transcribed, translated, and printed word.

The *Key* begins with the following declaration: "This *Key*, respects the *Native Language* of it, and happily may unlocke some *Rarities* concerning the *Natives* themselves, not yet discovered."[21] Through the metaphor of a key unlocking the undiscovered, Williams's *Key* sets the stage for a sweeping history of language encounters by claiming that both the land and its inhabitants contain the potential for recapturing something rare, wonderful, and original in American Indian words. The *Key* is more a doctrinal refutation of his English brethren than a missionary pamphlet. Williams ventriloquizes that critique through the Narragansett. He begins by acknowledging that the Narragansetts are cultural outsiders to the English, repeatedly identifying them as "barbarians," an allusion to Paul's First Letter to the Corinthians (14:11) in which he defines the barbarian as one whose speech is incomprehensible to anyone unfamiliar with the "voice" of a particular people.[22] Because Williams aspires to bring human communication to a closer approximation of the prelapsarian Edenic state, he frames his successful Christian translation of Narragansett more as an obligation to the millennial conditions that will advance Christ's earthly kingdom, than a missionizing duty to save souls.

Williams presents a favorable link between Narragansett intellectual and spiritual capacity and the quality of their words:

> In the braine their opinion is, that the soule (of which we shall speake in the Chapter of *Religion*) keeps her chiefe seat and residence:
> For the temper of the braine in quick apprehensions and accurate judgements (to say no more) the most high and soveraign God and Creator, hath not made them inferiour to *Europeans*.[23]

Williams asserts that, like contemporary philosophers, the Narragansetts understood the mind and the soul to be essentially interchangeable entities. In contrast to Brébeuf's general assessment, Williams finds no difference between the intellectual capacities of the Narragansett and their European counterparts. They have, he finds, little trouble apprehending and discerning differences and extrapolating doctrinal and moral connections and in determining spiritual truths (to gloss the seventeenth-century definition of "judgements," which denotes a sophisticated chain of faculty operations).

While on the face of it, Williams's assessment of the intellectual aptitude of the native people provides a preface to a discussion of their language, he also refutes a commonly held assumption about the people of the New World for a political end. The inference often drawn from European encounters with New World peoples was that the "primitive" state of native cultures and the wilds of a landscape, which, in its untamed and unproductive state—unameliorated by Christian civilization—was an impediment to moral development, and thus a socially, intellectually, and spiritually regressive force to civilized prosperity. One only had to look to the Jesuit encounters or even the anti-Indian propaganda coming out of the Bay Colony for the confirmation of the native peoples' inferiority. In attacking that assumption, Williams both attempts to disabuse his audience of an ethnographic fallacy, and to lay his enemies low. Given the evidence of the native people's intellectual parity with Europeans, who would not rather live in the wilds of the New World, well away from the corrupting influences and Christian hypocrisy of the Old World that enchains the individual's conscience? He expresses this ideal in this rather well-known poem from the *Key*:

1. *The courteous* Pagan *shall condemne*
   Uncourteous Englishmen,
   Who live like Foxes, Beares and Wolves,
   Or Lyon in his Den.

2. *Let none sing* blessings *to their soules,*
   For that they Courteous are:
   The wild Barbarians *with no more*
   Then Nature, goe so farre:

3. *If Natures Sons both* wild *and* tame,
   Humane and Courteous be:
   How ill becomes it Sonnes of God
   To want Humanity?[24]

Concluding the chapter "Of Salutation," Williams's poem takes direct aim at his former Massachusetts brethren, who, through a tyranny that not only breaks faith and fellowship, but occupies even the private space of the individual's conscience, have proved themselves less civil or "humane" than "Natures Sons both wild and tame." Through the *Key*, Williams works within the English tradition in order to transform it. It is a text written from a consciousness altered through his personal experience of cultural difference. Ultimately, Williams strives to shore up this difference, to collapse the barbaric utterances with which his reflections began into a common root of humanity. After all, the Narragansetts are, Williams tells us, "wandring Generations of *Adams* lost posteritie."[25] In the affirmation of this biblical genealogy, Williams crystalizes the most significant goal of the *Key*, albeit one deferred to a future providence: by learning the language in the implicit and seamless mode of translation that Williams has set forth, he aims to translate the pagan tongue of barbarism into the Christian language of salvific transformation that would, through the coming kingdom it would help bring about, spiritually transliterate the English and the Narragansetts alike.

The product of years of study and intercultural contact but written, edited, and printed in a very brief space of time, Williams's *Key into the Language of America* proves difficult to categorize generically. It interweaves linguistic, ethnographic, and spiritual themes through three discursive forms: it is a phrase book, consisting of vocabulary lists; a promotional tract with topical organization; and an emblem book with concluding poems that propound spiritual lessons. While these frames best serve the interests of language analysis and thus the purposes here, the *Key* also evokes other early modern traditions: history, travel narrative, natural history, essay, sermon, social commentary, and primer. In the phrase book section, words are arranged in columns on opposing sides of the page. The organization suggests a one-to-one correspondence between a highly recognizable set of phrases that include salutations, eating and entertainment, keeping time, discourse and news, family matters, and so on. In the tradition of the promotional tract, words are also selected that pertain to the natural landscape of Narragansett country, including a list of fish and fowl, beasts and cattle, and earth and fruit.

Williams's purpose for *Key into the Language of America* was thus quite different from the linguistic and cultural expertise that Brébeuf and Le Jeune acquired as a means of affirming their authority over the conversion of the natives. He imagined that the *Key* would be of use to future Apostles as they traveled through the wilderness to spread the news among the Narragansett of the impending union between Jews and Gentiles. This future vision informs the chapter "Of Discourse and Newes," particularly the first observation: "Their desire of, and delight in newes, is great, as the *Athenians*, and all men, more or lesse; a stranger that can relate newes in their owne language, they will stile him *Manittóo*, a God."[26] Williams imagines that future Apostles will have the capacity to communicate in the language of the Narragansett, a capacity, he infers, in which the *Key* might play an important part. The phrases he collects function not as prompts for how to do this but rather as declarations that might preface the sacred veracity of God's word: "*I will tell you newes*"; "*I speake very true*"; "*I shall know the truth*"; and so on.[27] While the list suggests what the Apostles might say to convey the joy and solemnity of the "good news," it is evocative rather than proscriptive.

The vocabulary lists are not designed to reflect or provide linguistic expertise, as is the case with the Jesuit dictionaries. Rather the

words arranged into two columns serve the opposite purpose of reminding the reader of the fallen state of the world.

Katoû eneéchaw.	*She is falling into Travell.*
Néechaw.	*She is in Travell.*
Paugcótche nechaúwaw.	*She is already delivered.*
Kitummâyi-mes-néchaw.	*She was just now delivered.*[28]

A line divides each column, suggesting that even though there may
be a one-to-one correspondence between each Narragansett phrase
and English translation, there is also a sense of the impenetrability of
meaning across the linguistic divide. In contrast to Brébeuf, whose
Relations contain ample disposition on Huron-Wendat grammar,
particularly the ways that it accords or departs from modern and ancient languages, Williams includes little on Narragansett grammar,
an indication that the *Key* is aimed more at spoken—largely through
rote memorization—rather than written translation. It is as if *Key
into the Language of America* is not a text about language at all. For
the appropriate audience—that is an audience of the elect—Williams
should not have to explain the intricacies of the Narragansett tongue.
His own expertise is assumed. The intensive labor behind the text—
the acquisition of language, associative analysis, structural study of
grammar, hours of immersive conversation—is all but invisible. The
conveyance of certain key words is a humble exercise of spiritual devotion rather than a functional vehicle for evangelization. The arrangement of words into two separate columns registers the fallen
state of the world; like descending financial accounts flowing into
deficit, the columns are memorably emblematic of the confusion and
chaos that have befallen creation and humanity. Just as the human
body inadequately houses the soul, words are, as Augustine argued
in *De Magistro*, but arbitrary signs.[29] They cannot be redeemed or
made whole but must remain as divided from spiritual signification
as the worlds of flesh and spirit that epitomize Williams's infralap-
sarian theology and govern his premillennial vision.

Also like Brébeuf, Williams is a devoted ethnographer, yet in the
case of the *Key*, his is cultural knowledge produced for a much different purpose. Whereas Brébeuf accumulated cultural knowledge
as a means of refining his linguistic expertise and, one senses, as a
part of the Jesuits' early modern commitment to knowledge formation, Williams's ethnography is a means of studying difference in
order to then explain it away. In relation to the sequence of phrases

on labor and childbirth—even then evocative metaphors of the soul's regeneration—Williams observes that "it hath pleased God in wonderfull manner to moderate that curse of the sorrowes of Child-bearing to these poore Indian women: So that ordinarily they have a wonderfull more speedy and easie Travell, and delivery then the Women of *Europe*." This observation includes a cultural distinction, namely that "the hardnesse of... constitution" found among Narragansett women permits them to bear the pains of childbirth more easily. Williams also comments that the Narragansett "count it a shame for a Woman in Travell to make complaint, and many of them are scarcely heard to groane."[30] Whatever we make of this as a culturally inflected difference, it is finally subsumed into speculation about the overarching design of a Christian God who "moderates" the "curse" for this particular population.

Language thus provides a window into a different culture that once "unlocked" becomes a spiritual bridge. The Narragansett are refashioned as spiritual exemplars, recipients of divine favor to an English audience of whom Williams was deeply critical. Finally, the category of "General Observations" that concludes each chapter elevates the text beyond the linguistic and ethnographic particulars of these modes into evidence of providential design working among lost tribes, even at the farthest reaches of the world:

> God hath planted in the Hearts of the Wildest of the sonnes of Men, an High and Honourable esteeme of the Mariage bed, insomuch that they universally submit unto it, and hold the Violation of that Bed, Abominable, and accordingly reape the Fruit thereof in the abundant increase of posterity.[31]

In contrast to the Jesuit approach, the *Key* does not seek to manage cultural difference, but rather looks through the prism of Scripture for continuity. For Williams, the natives are atavistic "rarities" or New World curiosities; their simultaneously strange and familiar behavior is an avenue through which Christian phenomena might be more adequately understood.

In his chapter "Death and Buriall," Williams observes a cultural difference reflected in Narragansett and English modes of expression: death is so terrifying that the natives never "mention the dead by name."[32] This facet of Narragansett culture corresponds directly to the inability to name the dead that Brébeuf observed among the

Huron-Wendat. Whereas Brébeuf puzzled over how to accommodate this alternate cosmology in his translation, Williams explains this difference through the universal and natural terror of death to all men. Death marks a passage into the unknown, invisible domain of the spirit world. This is a passage that the Narragansett represent by rendering the names of those who have undergone this journey unspeakable. Williams's observation about Narragansett culture becomes a mirror through which the English might confront one of the great mysteries at the heart of Calvinism: the terrifying finality of death without salvation. With uncertain knowledge of election, the passage from earth to heaven is a traceless movement and vividly suggests the possibility of a formless soul lost in another world without hope of redemption.

The concluding observation and poem that ends this chapter proposes Christian conversion as the only solution to the universal terror of death because it transforms death into rebirth. The horror of death dissolves through the redeemed convert who confronts the passage from life to death and then death to life, a morphology explained in detail in Romans 6 and reiterated in 1 John 3:14. This, Williams tells us, is the "sweet Paradox" and impenetrable mystery of God that can both be found in Scripture and observed among Christian Indians, as the chapter's concluding poem suggests:

The Indians *say their bodies die,*
> *Their soules they doe not die;*
> *Worse are then* Indians *such, as hold*
> *The souls mortalitie…*
> *Two Worlds of men shall rise and stand*
> *'Fore Christs most dreadfull barre;*
> Indians, *and* English *naked too,*
> *That now most gallant are.…* [33]

Directing his message toward his English reader in this final poem, Williams moves from the chapter's former reflection on cultural difference to one of Christian universality. Indians also understand the soul's immortality. The *Key*'s linguistic explorations provoke the reconfiguration of the categories that shape English Calvinist thought, just as Williams's own thought is transformed by his encounter with the Narragansett people.

These entwined discursive modes—linguistic, ethnographic, and theological—combine to fashion the *Key* into a closed hermeneutical system that collapses cultural and linguistic difference into spiritual similarity, though some chapters are more successful at it than others. The chapter "Of Their Religion" fails to fully synthesize the Narragansett cosmology that Williams discovers through his dialogue with a native interlocutor into a Christian vision. This chapter tells us that "Heaven" translates as "ayre." The Genesis story includes a singular man called "Adam" who is made out of "red Earth."[34] A recorded conversation between a sachem and a praying Indian illustrates the debate on whether there is more evidence for the transmigration of souls to the southwest as in traditional Narragansett belief, or to heaven and hell, as Christians believe. Williams claims to have witnessed this dialogue on a night when he had already "discoursed" "as farre as [his] language would reach." Settling into a condition of linguistic liminality, Williams overhears the sachem and praying Indian discuss the inability to know the journey of the soul due to the limitations of human sight. Both concede that they have not seen a soul go either to heaven or to the southwest. The sachem compares the two sources of spiritual authority. The English have "books and writings," he observes, whereas the Narragansett "take all upon trust from our forefathers." While the sachem concludes that books and writing might give the English a slight advantage as to authority, it is ultimately a moot point, since neither can demonstrate the souls' heavenward journey.[35]

Williams hears this dialogue through the limitations of language. It sits uneasily within the text exposing a subtle tension between indigenous belief and cultural practice and the aim of substantiating providential design. As if registering this tension and struggling to stifle a competing cosmology, the concluding general observation critiques Narragansett religious practices rather than showcasing spiritual exemplarity:

> Having lost the true and living God their Maker, [the Narrangansett] created out of the nothing of their own inventions many false and fained Gods and Creators.[36]

When confronted by Narragansett religious practices that cannot be reconciled with Christianity, Williams reverts to the lost tribes narrative of a population still deceiving themselves in premillennial

times. His inability to hold the Narragansett up as spiritual exemplars in this case demonstrates a moment in which the *Key* fails to
make language a universalizing force across disparate cultures. In
the absence of parallel concepts, corresponding vocabularies also
failed to develop. Williams recognizes that he can only "discourse"
on Christian teachings "as farre as [his] language would reach." This
is a sobering restriction for the exponent of a belief system constel-
lated around faith precisely because its great truths were largely
beyond the human ken.

Jesuit Literacies among the Huron

In contrast to Williams's concerted efforts to encase the Narragansett
within a Christian frame, French Jesuits had a highly developed approach to cultural and linguistic difference. From its inception, the
Society of Jesus prized linguistic and ethnographic study as the most
efficient means of propagating their faith. The impetus behind this
was doctrinal, for Ignatius, following St. Paul, urged his followers to
practice cultural translation. Matteo Ricci, the Italian Jesuit who
taught himself Chinese, is a famous sixteenth-century example of
this. Consequently, the Society soon compiled many grammars and
vocabularies of non-European languages.[37] Early priests to New
France, including Recollect Gabriel Sagard, and Jesuits Paul Le Jeune
and Brébeuf, followed and perfected this tradition, rapidly under-
taking massive efforts to observe, learn, and analyze the languages of
North America.[38]

Jesuit theologians did not strive for the same millennial goal of linguistic transparency in which the use of words would ultimately dissolve into a revelation of the hidden truths of natural and spiritual
worlds. Jesuits placed more emphasis on words as mediators of the
spirit, and on this concept of mediation as necessary to the spiritual
truths expressed and enacted on earth. Shortly after his arrival, Le Jeune
composed the *Pater Noster* in Huron verse and claimed to have taught
the Huron how to "sing" it for the reward of a "bowlful of peas."[39] Puritan
anxieties about hypocrisy and false conversion are absent from this
scene, not because the Jesuits cared less but because they believed that
ritual ultimately helped to enact the inward transformation.

The *Jesuit Relations* comprise seventy-three volumes of the most
important source on Native America in the seventeenth and eighteenth

centuries. They began informally as a way to report to heads of orders back home. From 1632 to 1673, a volume printed in Paris each year contained essayistic letters replete with ethnographic information. Read by the likes of Rousseau and Voltaire for information on natural law and the savage state, the *Jesuit Relations* helped to propel new theories of humans and society.[40] Throughout the *Jesuit Relations* are assertions of claims to the development of linguistic expertise that allowed the Jesuits to control with increasing precision the interpretation of the Catholic word by their proselytes. As Le Jeune states in his "Brief Relation of the Journey to New France," "any one who knew their language could manage them as he pleased."[41] Proficiency in indigenous tongues becomes an ideal that the Jesuits promote as their contribution to burgeoning French imperial interests.[42] Inaugurated by Le Jeune and the Parisian printer Sebastien Cramoisy, the *Jesuit Relations* were a decidedly French enterprise, directed at an elite audience of wealthy Parisian financiers. They were written with the aim of soliciting financial assistance for the Jesuit mission, such that the Jesuits linked the religious purpose of their mission with interests of the state under Louis XIV. Designs to convert indigenous Americans to Catholicism served the broader goal of implementing French identity across the continent, in the form of civility, customs, and culture.[43] This was the twinned impetus behind the acquisition of a vast amount of ethnographic knowledge. Understanding North American populations was the first step toward ensuring French *and* Catholic control over them.

The codification of the French vernacular as the national language of France coincided almost perfectly with the inaugural *Relations* as Cardinal Richelieu and others founded the French Academy of Language in 1635.[44] Somewhat paradoxically, this tightening of linguistic control through the church and the state increased the nationalization of Catholicism that would eventually lead to the suppression of the Jesuits in the Americas. Yet the establishment of French as an official, national language also allowed for more creative translations among Jesuit missionaries in New France. In other words, the stronger the hierarchy and national bureaucracy surrounding language, the more relaxed colonial missionaries could be about taking artistic liberties with Christian translations. Fluidity of meaning in a missionary context was less of a threat to religious and national enterprises with a strong ecclesiastical structure. By contrast, the Protestant ideal of *sola scriptura* permitted the dissemination of the Word into the vernacular, as evidenced by the wide Puritan support for Eliot's Massachusett Bible, but also led to greater anxiety about how words could be manipulated to obscure rather than reveal religious truths. By contesting state power through a nonconformist faith that elevated the authority of an individual's relationship to God, Puritans made vernacular worship more democratic while also tightening the need to control the precision of translation and the uses of language among lay populations. Sermons written in the characteristic Protestant plain style idealized the redaction of Scripture in universally intelligible terms as ministers eschewed Roman Catholic reliance on ecclesiastical hierarchies as a mediating force behind the Word.[45] Distinct French Jesuit and Anglo-Protestant theologies influenced not only doctrinal understandings of the relationship between word and spirit but also the designs that New World missionaries placed on the representational power of the words spoken by their converted proselytes.

Williams's critique of Catholicism in *Christenings Make Not Christians* is, finally, well-thrashed straw. His real target was the Massachusetts orthodoxy whose "hypocritic[al]" practice of "externall conversion" brings "men … into a *Church-estate*" as if they were a "Christian people"; for Williams, this resembled Jesuit practice and pedagogy.[46] The alignment of a critique directed at both the Massachusetts orthodoxy and Catholicism on the topic of conversion is, in fact, telling. At least for the forms of conversion practiced among the Jesuits in the Americas, there is a great deal of similarity with Puritan conversion—however else we have been taught to think of Reformed Protestant and Jesuit conversion practices. Like Williams, historians have attributed the disproportionate success of the Jesuits to a theology that is more adept at acculturation and syncretism. Yet at its core, conversion theology among the Jesuits and the Puritan orthodoxy share a great deal. John W. O'Malley argues that inner understanding and the call to inwardness was fundamental to the Jesuit spiritual journey. The Jesuit understanding of conversion largely followed the first week of St. Ignatius's *Spiritual Exercises*, which advocates a quotidian reflection on Original Sin. The spiritual exercises for the week involve a profound inward turning, a meditation on the powers of the soul, and a realization of the soul as imprisoned within a corruptible body. St. Ignatius encourages communicants to ask for forgiveness from sin by God's saving grace and warns against speaking idle or hollow words.[47]

The Jesuit Relations penned in New France adhere to a narrative structure patterned after the first week of the *Spiritual Exercises*, which also accords in some fundamental ways with the Puritan concept of justification: inward turning, reflection on one's implication with Original Sin, and a recognition of the material body as the corrupt prison house of the soul. Where the Jesuits and Puritans depart from each other is not in fact on the question of conversion but rather on how the experience of inner transformation is communicated to the external world. Disagreements over the shift from inner to outer, justification to sanctification, spanned a range of seventeenth-century theological controversies from the Antinomian Controversy, to *The Bloody Tenant of Persecution* (the quarrel between Williams and Cotton), to Puritan perceptions of false Catholic conversions. In his critique, Williams emphasizes the problem of externalization by focusing on the "reports" Catholic historians have written on American Indian conversion.

> If the reports (yea some of their owne *Historians*) be true, what monstrous and most inhumane conversions have they made; baptizing thousands, yea ten thousands of the poore Natives, sometimes by wiles and subtle devices, sometimes by force compelling them to submit to that which they understood not, neither before nor after such their monstrous Christning [*sic*] of them.[48]

Jesuits and Puritans agreed that the crux of the conversion experience involved an inward transformation of the soul. They disagreed on the capacity of language to adequately convey the spiritual meaning required to effect a spiritual transformation. For Williams, the misuse of language to instigate conversion has led to rampant anti-Christian hypocrisy. Language cannot be trusted to properly convey spiritual meaning, he insists. In fact, language's failure to signify enough meaning is the root cause of the proliferation of false Christianity in the world. Words, the hollow signs of spiritual concepts themselves already diminished in their capacity to convey to humanity's fallen reason, were, for Williams, the tried weapons of Satan's arsenal in his apocalyptic battle against God.

In their preaching and verbal instruction, Jesuits were more adept at using words to create verbal imagery of Catholic mysteries through more creative acts of translation. Take, for instance, this scene of catechistical composition and instruction described by Le Jeune:

I began to compose something in the way of a Catechism, or on the principles of the faith. Taking my paper in hand, I began to call a few children by ringing a little bell. At first I had six, then twelve, then fifteen, then twenty, and more. I have them say the *Pater*, the *Ave*, and the *Credo*, in their language. I explain to them, very crudely, the mysteries of the Holy Trinity and of the Incarnation, and at every few words I ask them if I speak well, if they can understand perfectly; they all answer me: *eoco, eoco, ninisitoutenan*, "yes, yes, we understand." Afterwards I ask them whether there are several Gods, and which of the three persons became man. I coin words approximating to their language, which I make them to understand.[49]

Le Jeune describes a scene of creative, though he might have said inspired, translation. His composition feeds off of the increasing numbers of children in attendance for the spiritual lesson, and he looks to them for affirmation of his pronunciation. The precision of Le Jeune's translation is, however, largely beside the point. Rather, conveying some sense of the "mysteries of the Holy Trinity," however "crudely," leads to "perfect understanding." The account of this scene raises the question of how such an approximate translation can possibly lead to perfect understanding, and how this understanding can be verified. For Le Jeune, perfection is simply a matter of recitation. The Huron-Wendat children say "the *Pater*, the *Ave*, and the *Credo*" in whatever "approximation" Le Jeune has been able to "coin" for them. As long as he hears the words echoed back to him with emulative, rhetorical accuracy, he feels assured that the Indian proselytes have understood perfectly. Le Jeune's description of this scene reveals a technique practiced broadly among Jesuits in their missionary work in the Americas. Echoing the words of the divine orator led the audience toward a particular interpretation.[50] The missionary arena heightened the need to avoid the misinterpretation of religious imagery among audiences deemed ignorant by virtue of being less educated.[51]

Cataloging the differences between Huron, French, and Latin, Brébeuf explained the challenges of orthography in the creation of written catechistical texts: "they have a letter to which we have nothing to correspond . . . the greater part of their words are composed of vowels." As with Greek, verb tenses vary somewhat, Brébeuf observes, to signify the agency or action of animate and inanimate life. Yet there are also "double conjugation[s]," which are unique to "American languages."[52] In contrast to many of his contemporaries, Brébeuf did not see the differences between European and American

Indian languages as signs of Amerindian degeneracy but rather of a different syntactical order. Today, linguist John Steckley affirms this portion of Brébeuf's assessment in his *Huron/English Dictionary*. This modern dictionary identifies verb conjugation as the "grammatical heart of the language."[53] Yet while Brébeuf appears to adopt a more enlightened linguistic approach, this did not necessarily translate into a more culturally relational interaction with indigenous converts, for language was a means of reinforcing what Jesuits deemed the doctrinal truths that transcended cultural and social identities. For Brébeuf, the acquisition of unprecedented levels of linguistic expertise was in proportion to the dissemination of this knowledge within the community. In line with Catholicism's ecclesiastical hierarchies as the mediating force behind the Word, Brébeuf maintained power by guarding his linguistic knowledge in order to select which spiritual message to redact through the Word.

Repeatedly in his translational practices, Brébeuf looked for commensurability between Huron-Wendat and Catholic concepts, but also observed how similarities broke down at the level of language itself. The Lord's Prayer was one example discussed at length in Brébeuf's 1636 *Relation*. He worked out one possible approximate translation of the first line through possessive pronouns, but then observed to his superior that there were still limits even with this adaptation. Huron-Wendat words carried with them aspects of the Huron-Wendat cosmology. Translating Christian texts, as Brébeuf complains, was not a straightforward business. In the first line of the Lord's Prayer, for example, "they can not say simply, Father . . . but are obliged to say one of the three, my father, thy father, his father." Consequently, the simple line "*In the name of the Father, and of the Son, and of the holy Ghost*" proved quite difficult to convey in Huron-Wendat, particularly since the syntactical meaning of "Father" here would denote all three meanings of father at once and in the same personage. Brébeuf asks his superior whether it might be okay to express the line as "*In the name of our Father, and of his Son, and of their holy Ghost?*"[54] Yet the issue is even more complex for it is not simply syntactical but rather linked to a cosmology underlying the syntactical ordering of possessive proper nouns. Those who have no father on earth cannot say "*Our Father*," for to do so is an "insult" to "the dead whom they have loved." Brébeuf supplements this rule with an anecdote of a Huron-Wendat woman who had recently lost her mother and almost refused to be baptized after she was catechized in the commandment, *"Thou shalt honor thy Father and thy Mother."* [55]

Achieving a high level of linguistic expertise obviously required deep cultural knowledge, which makes Brébeuf's 1636 *Relation* an invaluable ethnographic resource. From it, we learn of the Huron-Wendat feast of the dead, as well as the tribe's origin story, despite Brébeuf's dismissal of both as superstitions, which he editorializes with "astonish[ment]" that so much "blindness" can exist "in regard to the things of Heaven." This is particularly surprising, Brébeuf tells us, because the Huron-Wendat typically display "judgment and knowledge" in reference to things of the "earth."[56] Yet he discerns that such judgment is absent in the story of "Aataentsic," a female god who fell from heaven to serve as the head of the Huron nation.[57] According to Huron oral tradition, Aataentsic is the mother of humankind. She lived in the sky among the other Huron spirits, above a world covered entirely by ocean, until one day she slipped and fell through a hole. Seeing Aataentsic falling, a great tortoise gathered soil onto his back from the bottom of the ocean in order to cushion her landing. Landing on the soft mound of earth, Aataentsic soon gave birth to two boys, Tawiscaron and Iouskeha. Iouskeha became the protector of humankind. He built lakes and rivers, raised up crops of corn, and released animals to hunt. Tawiscaron and Aataentsic, however, had evil qualities and took pleasure in undoing his work. Eventually falling out, the brothers part, and Iouskeha takes Aataentsic to live with him. In the creation myth, Iouskeha symbolizes the sun and Aataentsic the moon, and as such are recognized, respectively, as creator and destroyer. Brébeuf's assessment notwithstanding, folklorists have suggested that the cohabitation of good and evil in the myth might have helped the Huron-Wendat people reconcile contradictory dimensions, not only in the creative and destructive forces of nature but also in the rapprochement of Euro-Indian interactions and male and female properties in their culture and cosmological belief.[58]

In Huron-Wendat belief, the natural, spiritual, and human-made worlds were entirely permeable. Spirits, referred to as *aki*, resided in forests, lakes, and rivers, and their agency shaped all human experiences, from travel and war, to ceremonial customs and interpersonal relationships.[59] While the Huron-Wendat did not assign the role of priest to individuals of their society, they nonetheless identified specific individuals with unusual qualities, including those of shaman and witch.[60] In addition to the challenge of learning Huron-Wendat with adequate proficiency, the French Jesuits faced the challenge of understanding and then penetrating a cosmology radically different from their own, one that was encoded by narrative mythologies they did not recognize as sacred and that, in any event, would not have corresponded to their own divine narratives. Steckley analyzes the impact of various Huron-Wendat words pertaining to constructions of the self—and thus especially representative of Huron cosmology—on translation. The definition of the word *aki* provides a salient case in point. Because the term could signify either good or bad spirit and represent a range of natural and supernatural forms, such as devil, demon, spirit, snake, witch, and warlock, it proved to be a particularly thorny problem when Brébeuf attempted to translate Ledesma's *Doctrine Christiana* (1573), a standard teaching text, into Huron. While some parallels existed between *aki* and the Catholic idea of angel, *aki* included a greater diversity of animate phenomena and therefore could not be adequately shaped to fit Catholic meaning without attaching to the translated term a catalog that negated all that *aki* did not mean in the context of angel. Such qualifying clauses would hardly be conducive in a textbook articulating new, complex, and foreign concepts for which distinctness and clarity were essential and misprisions came at great price.[61] The Jesuit commitment to ethnographic knowledge meant that translations had to maintain a cautious balance between the dangers of misinterpretation and the need for flexibility.

The challenge of finding correspondence between certain key concepts in Huron and French for the purposes of making catechistical instruction posed not only a practical problem but also a larger theological issue: the fundamental incompatibility between Jesuit and Huron religious world views reflected linguistically as well as narratively, as in the creation myth of Aataentsic contrasted with Genesis. In character with his Jesuit faith, Brébeuf dismisses the Aataentsic origin story as an example of the ignorance and "blindness" of Huron belief about the "things of heaven." Yet, despite his easy dismissal of its spiritual significance, the disproportionate amount of narrative space he commits to the "astonish[ing]" story in his 1636 *Relation* suggests that he detects in it some key, however faint or beyond his ability to discern, to unlocking some vital aspect of the Huron cosmogony. Brébeuf's chapter "What the Huron Think of Their Origin" begins with the conventional disclaimer that he is

investigating their "fables" for evidence of "forme[r]" "natural knowledge of the true God."[62] There are, he tells us, certain similarities
between the story of Aataentsic's husband eating fruit and Adam.[63]
He also draws a parallel between the fight between Tawiscaron and
Iouskeha and that of Cain and Abel.[64] These narrative parallels initially seem to reveal more about the analogical imagination at the
center of Catholic hermeneutics than they do about common narrative structures embedded in two disparate cosmogonies. Elsewhere
in the chapter, Brébeuf reveals a supplemental interest that is less
about finding evidence through which to construct parallels with
Christianity and more about an ethnographic fascination with a cosmology that not only departs so radically from scriptural history but
may also supply answers to mysteries within the Jesuit cosmos.[65]
Shortly after his opening with a conventional disclaimer of Huron
ignorance, Brébeuf states, "They think the Heavens existed a long
time before this wonder; but they cannot tell you when or how its
great bodies were drawn from the abysses of nothing."[66] Yet Brébeuf's
assessment of Huron faith is also an assessment of his own. It indicates a line of inquiry about phenomena to which there is no response, either in Huron belief or Catholicism. Further on in the
chapter, Brébeuf points out that, in terms of the origin of the heavens, the Huron account of the formation of "rivers, lakes, and seas"
might offer a "subtle solution of the question of our Schools upon
this point."[67] Embedded toward the end of this chapter is a sugges-
tion so subtle that it is easily missed, for Brébeuf offers no elaborating explanation of his meaning. But he seems to suggest that the
Huron account of Ioushekha's creation of bodies of water out of an
otherwise arid earth adds a missing element to Jesuit teachings.

Throughout the chapter, Brébeuf gradually softens his stance
toward the reality of truths that might be available through Huron
cosmology. Given the conventions of the genre in which he is writing, the intended audience, and his own role as religious authority,
this softening is muted and barely perceptible. Perhaps it was so even
to Brébeuf himself. Yet something of the Jesuit's own inward transformation comes across in the chapter's penultimate sentence: "If it
should please the divine Goodness to prove these false Prophets
untruthful, it would be no small advantage to add authority to our
faith in this Country, and to open the way for the publication of the
holy Gospel."[68] At the beginning of the chapter, Brébeuf unequivo-
cally declares the Huron origin story an untruthful "fable."[69] By the

conclusion, he seems increasingly less sure, finally resigning the burden of proving the "Prophets untruthful" to "divine Goodness." At least tacitly, he seems to have become aware of a built-in doctrinaire bias behind the project of gathering empirical information: the authority of the Jesuit system is predicated upon its ability to discredit competing world views. It is in this moment of realization that the text betrays itself, in the divided impulse that exposes how the comparative cultural ethnography so easily upstages the study's purportedly missionary-linguistic function. Brébeuf seems to be nearing a realization of the conflicting interest built into the Jesuit quest for knowledge that effectively puts spiritual validation at odds with rigorous scientific inquiry.

However broad ranging it might be, Brébeuf's ethnographic knowledge of the Huron-Wendat produced one of the first Huron dictionaries, which set the foundation for a thriving genre among French Jesuits in the New World.[70] The production of dictionaries required prolonged periods of linguistic immersion and a deep familiarity with the linguistic context of native terms, as well as the syntactical arrangement of words and the unique sound of letters. Accounts of language acquisition recorded in the *Relations* follow a predictable pattern. Le Jeune exemplified the experience: "On the 12th of October, seeing that I made very little progress, learning a few stray words with a great deal of trouble, I went to visit the cabins of the Savages, with the intention of going there often, and accustoming my ear to their tongue."[71] It was only through this process of immersion, repetition, and submission to the indigenous teacher that Jesuits had hope of making any progress in the language at all. Through this experience the Jesuits learned something of the intimate and inextricable relationship between language and culture. In spending time in "the cabins of the Savages," they came to know the intricacies of meaning and expression that would otherwise escape observation. Le Jeune observes:

I shall say here that the Savages are very fond of sagamité. The word "Sagamiteou" in their language really means water, or warm gruel. Now they have extended its meaning to signify all sorts of soups, broths, and similar things. This "sagamité," of which they are very fond, is made of cornmeal; if they are short of that, we sometimes give them some of our French flour, which, being boiled with water, makes simple paste. They do not fail to eat it with appetite, especially when we place in it a little "pimi;" that is to say, oil, for that is their sugar. They use it with their strawberries and raspberries when they eat them, as I am told, and their greatest feasts are of fat or of oil.[72]

This exposition on the meaning of "sagamité" in Huron takes up a fair amount of narrative space in Le Jeune's *Relation*. In contrast to religious terms, which often confound the Jesuits by presenting an alternate and potentially irreconcilable cosmology, secular terms are embraced for their cultural diversity. As Le Jeune explains, direct translation of "sagamité" is impossible, for the word refers to a variety of foods composing the Huron diet. He familiarizes the term by drawing an analogy with French flour, while he is also careful to explain distinct uses of Huron cornmeal. Food is an aspect of Huron culture that could be unthreateningly recognized as different. This passage serves to demonstrate the role reversal typical of the *Relation* where Le Jeune becomes the student rather than the master. He learns not only of linguistic nuances in spending hours in the "cabins of the Savages" but also of cultural insights that may indeed work in the service of Jesuit survival in the New World, or, failing that add to the archive of cultural knowledge for which the Jesuits were justly famed.

Food, particularly that which was derived from natural resources, constituted an important knowledge base that might help future Jesuit missionaries to navigate the environs upon which they, too, were dependent. Brébeuf's report contains one of the more striking summations of the necessity of inhabiting the position of student for the purposes of language acquisition:

The Huron language will be your saint Thomas and your Aristotle; and clever man as you are, and speaking glibly among learned and capable persons, you must make up your mind to be for a long time mute among the Barbarians. You will have accomplished much, if, at the end of a considerable time, you begin to stammer a little.[73]

The apparent humility expressed in this passage is striking. To his audience of wealthy donors back in Paris, Brébeuf not only advertises his proficiency in Huron but also proclaims the spiritual and intellectual edification that comes with such knowledge. "Mute among the Barbarians," Brébeuf discovers that studying an indigenous tongue is coterminous with studying God. Yet in addition to augmenting one's own inner spirituality—an important aspect of this role reversal from master to student—it was also a necessary step in establishing colonial dominance. The Jesuits asserted and maintained control by knowing the populations that they wished to dominate. By becoming students, Brébeuf and Le Jeune aspire to the "truth" that "any one who knew their language could manage them as he pleased."[74] Closer analysis suggests that as a part of and distinct from language acquisition, cultural knowledge in general also played an important part of that management. Whatever else could be said of the accounts of early modern Jesuit and Protestant missionaries, one detects in the Jesuit genre not only an attention to even the most mundane domestic, political, and ritual practices but also a close inquiry into motive and meaning of a given practice, and, often, where those inquiries failed to return a satisfactory explanation, a speculative discourse followed.

The Jesuit production of language texts mimicked this approach to colonial domination. Jesuits became devoted students of indigenous tongues in order to amass a knowledge base that proved to be their greatest asset in controlling North American native populations. This knowledge base proved extremely useful in the Anglo-French imperial conflict that would consume much of the eighteenth century. Despite the marked discrepancy between numbers of Anglo and French colonists, the French retained a stronghold in North America as a result of the Indian alliances they formed through language networks. This is not to say that this power dynamic was not ever or often inverted. The colonial language encounter also had the effect of unmooring words from their intended meaning through the circulation of indigenous language texts that could be reinterpreted by native proselytes.

Yet the Jesuits tried to guard against this inversion of authority by creating two economies of indigenous language texts: dictionaries designed for augmenting the expertise of the priests and catechisms designed for ritual use and spiritual edification of indigenous communities. Neither literary economy purported to collapse cultural difference. Indeed, the generic structure of dictionaries produced in New France suggests that the Jesuit approach to remedying the Babylonian Confusion of New World tongues was to embrace it. By cultivating a high level of linguistic expertise, French Jesuit missionaries were able to assimilate cosmological conflicts. As students of the Huron spirit pantheon, they were free to engage in creative acts of translation that made them more adept at developing mnemonic devices to instigate conversion.

Brébeuf's Christmas carol, penned in the Huron language in the 1640s—allegedly 1643—told the story of Christ's birth. In contrast to the point in time when he translated the Ledesma catechism, Brébeuf was fluent in Huron when he composed the carol. Perhaps inspired by this success, he also drew on his cultural knowledge of the rich song tradition in Huron to develop music as a strategy for teaching Christian doctrine to the Huron-Wendat. The Ledesma translation, for example, included thirty newly coined Huron nouns to express Christian concepts. Almost all were ungrammatical in Huron. The Christmas carol, by contrast, is a verb-driven creative translation. By 1643, Brébeuf had recognized that Huron was more verb-based than European languages and integrated his advanced linguistic knowledge into the Huron carol. Additionally, Brébeuf drew on his deep cultural knowledge of Huron-Wendat. He used the term *aki* to refer to the Huron concept of spirits rather than Catholic angels, and he spoke of Jesus as having compassion in the same manner that the Huron expected from their spirits. The Christmas carol not only became emblematic of French Jesuit success among the Huron-Wendat, it also survived for centuries as a facet of Huron culture, due in part to Brébeuf's capacity to successfully create a document of acculturation.[75]

By the 1640s, the Jesuit production of indigenous language texts exhibited a marked difference between the acquisition of linguistic expertise in dictionaries and the catechistical-ritual culture circulating in French missionary settlements. Jesuit priests maintained power by simultaneously guarding their linguistic knowledge from both their communicants and broader non-Jesuit audiences and by choosing what spiritual truths, church doctrines, and Christian narrative traditions to redact through the Word. Catechisms circulated among indigenous proselytes but, as noted, dictionaries did not. Because the Word itself was believed to carry spiritual truths, Jesuit missionaries restricted access to it, both in carefully selecting material for translation and in limiting access to their native-language compendia. It had been a tried and true church practice since the influential Council of Toulouse in 1229. In an attempt to stamp out heresy and avoid demystifying the Word, the council made it a punishable sin for the laity to possess the Bible and to read the psalter or even the Breviary in the vernacular. The requirement of Latin education also sufficiently reduced access.[76] In the case of Jesuit missions, conversion could be verified verbally, through the communicant's recitation of the Lord's Prayer or his or her singing a Catholic hymn in the space carved out for communal ritual worship. A native proselyte's ability to discuss the intricacies of his or her own experience of faith was not a prerequisite for Catholic conversion as it was for the American Puritans. Rather, regular ritual worship could stand in for an experience—or the inability to articulate it—that was presumed to come later.

From Mystical Linguistics to Millennial Fervor

In the later years of his missionary career, Brébeuf seems to have lost much of the animated curiosity and detailed rational empiricism that drove his early linguistic study. His increasing refuge within a fervent mysticism in the 1640s corresponds to an alarming rise of a number of violent visions recorded in his spiritual journal, including "stains of red and purple blood on the clothes of all [Jesuit] Fathers." While Brébeuf struggled to interpret these visions within the context of biblical prophecy, particularly attuned to the Book of Revelation, the source of his apprehension lay near at hand.[77] After 1640, mounting resistance among the traditionalist non-Christian Wendats spread intracultural tension and fear, and finally escalating violence. The conflict took on the overtone of a psychomachia. Traditionalists began making competing claims to spiritual visions as supernatural evidence of the destructive presence of the "Black Robes" and their religious and cultural indoctrination. Abetted by their Iroquois allies, the traditionalists fomented violence against the French Jesuits and Christian Huron-Wendats. In March 1649, they captured, tortured, and killed Brébeuf, bringing the Jesuit scheme for Huron literacy and conversion to an abrupt end in the same decade that millennial fervor percolated in England.[78]

In 1643, the year of the publication of Williams's *Key*, England plunged into greater and greater political and religious strife. When Williams returned, Parliament was already aligned against Charles I in a civil war that would eventuate in regicide and the rise of the commonwealth, further fanning the flames of millennialism. Within the context of an actual and symbolically apocalyptic battle unfolding around them, mystical ideas of the power of language would

flourish for the next two decades in Britain, infusing an acute interest in the occult into the period's philosophical tradition. Following
the publication of the *Key*, missionary linguists continued to combine theological purpose with philosophical inquiry. Anglo-American
missionaries developed a linguistic practice based on a Protestant
millennial frame. The mystical ideas of language that circulated
in missionary communities ensured that definitions of language
remained deeply contested in the philosophical context of mid-
seventeenth-century England.

This debate about languages' form and function in the world corresponded to the dramatic rise in linguistic activity in North
America. Missionaries sought to contribute their work on Indian
languages to the mystical strand of seventeenth-century philosophy.
While ascribing empirical value to Indian words as visible signs,
Protestant missionaries also sought to account for the role language
would play in the imminent advent of the millennial kingdom. There
was little contradiction between Protestant missionary theology and
mystical ideas circulating in England and on the European continent.
The Protestant mindset of *sola scriptura* blended seamlessly with the
vision for an ideal, spiritual ur-language where words signified their
referents with an adamic purity. The mutual goal of missionaries and
philosophers was to repair the ruins of Babel by restoring language
from its fallen status to a purer connection between the word, the
object signified in the natural world, and its corresponding referent
in the invisible world. As words became more closely aligned with
their natural and divine referent, language, they believed, would
become increasingly transparent and spiritually resonant.

Many New World missionaries participated in Menasseh ben
Israel's attempt to locate the lost tribes in his *Hope of Israel*, first
printed in 1650, a mythology that would, two centuries later, directly
inspire Joseph Smith's millennial visions of the American Indians
as descendants of one or more of the lost tribes of Israel. A rabbi in
a Sephardic community in Amsterdam, Menasseh believed that
Israelites survived on every continent, including the Americas, and
in the 1640s began propounding his messianic theories in texts
embraced by the New World adherents of Christian millenarianism.
His work was popular at mid century among the Hartlib Circle and
also among language mystics, associated with the learned occultists
Thomas Vaughan and Henry Reynolds, particularly in their search
to recover the key to noumenal knowledge believed to be unlocked

through the translation of ancient symbols and rituals. It was the adherents of linguistic mysticism who first advocated for the repatriation of Jews to England, which Cromwell sanctioned in 1656. This was not entirely a gesture of British toleration, but at least in part was rooted in a financial motivation for new trading contacts. Yet the increasing certainty that Jews would play a vital role in the advent of Christ's return—though the specifics, ranging from chiliasm to immediate Judgment, were much contested—was an emerging theme of Anglo-American millennialism. The religious deference and authority with which Anglo-American Protestants treated Jews, albeit largely in their absence, had been foreshadowed in the first decade of the century when, under the auspices of King James, the Church of England heralded the arrival into London of more than thirty Jewish rabbinical scholars to oversee the Hebrew translation of the Old Testament for the 1611 Authorized Version. (When one recalls that the King James Bible was believed even by the episcopacy to have been divinely "conserved"—and thus retained its authority as the inspired Word of God—it becomes apparent that the Jewish translators' expertise was deemed to be much more than technical.)

Appearing the same year as *Hope of Israel*, Thomas Thorowgood's *Jews in America* made two remarkable claims for the messianic potential of Puritan evangelization: that the Massachusett language approximated Hebrew, and that the North American natives were descendants of the ten lost tribes of Israel. Building their own sectarian vision for Christian universalism, many Puritan missionaries believed that the Christian translation of indigenous words could mitigate the effects of God's imposed linguistic diaspora. By the 1640s and 1650s, nearly two decades after the settlement of the Massachusetts Bay Colony, the Puritan mission was finally gaining momentum. Missionaries like the famed John Eliot and the father-and-son team Thomas Mayhew Sr. and Thomas Mayhew Jr. embraced the millennialism they found in mystical theories of language. Each instance of Christian conversion narrated by an Indian proselyte in a redeemed Algonquian tongue would bear witness to the descent of the Holy Spirit and the gradual reparation of the divine blight of Babylonian multilingualism.

The linguistic interventions of Williams and Brébeuf caused religious strife, revealing the complexities of Christian translation. Learning another language required each missionary to come into intimate contact with another people and required unprecedented degrees of understanding. The act of translation in one respect show-cased the commensurability of words, thoughts, and feelings but it also led to an uncomfortable recognition of difference and compet-ing world views. Ironically, during the second half of seventeenth century, Jesuit and Protestant writings on American languages cata-lyzed the rise of more secular understandings of language as a human construct.

But this proto-secular philosophy also led to an uncomfortable recognition of difference and the dangerous presence of competing world views, where none had been presumed. The cultural threat was only part of the danger posed by the linguistic encounter. Of even greater concern to Williams and Brébeuf was the fact that these linguistic interlocutions began to break down the programmatic nature of Christian faith. Ethnographic recognition chipped away at Christian verities. The millennialism that surfaced in the 1640s, in the writings of Brébeuf and Williams signals an attempt to contain the chaos produced by the coexistence of disparate systems of belief. Over two centuries of missionary linguistics in North America, a version of this pattern recurs, from the myth of the ten lost tribes to the regenerative violence of Cooper's novels. Language demanded a form of recognition that was at times absorbed into intercultural modes of communication and at times experienced as a profound threat to rhetorical and cosmological sovereignty.

Learning to Write Algonquian Letters

THE INDIGENOUS PLACE OF LANGUAGE
PHILOSOPHY IN THE SEVENTEENTH-CENTURY
ATLANTIC WORLD

Among his substantial library of seventeenth-century travel narratives, John Locke owned a first edition of Chrestien Le Clercq's *Nouvelle Relation de la Gaspesie* (1691). Le Clercq's *Relation* recounts his experience in the 1660s and 1670s as a Recollect missionary among the Mi'kmaq people of Nova Scotia, or, as Le Clercq refers to them, the Gaspesian people.[1] The book is partly an ethnography designed "to give the public a picture" of the customs and religion of the Mi'kmaq and partly a record of missionary success, with Le Clercq attributing the latter to his system of hieroglyphs, ostensibly based on a Mi'kmaq system of writing and tailored as a mnemonic aid for Catholic prayers.[2] On the back inside cover of Locke's copy of the *Relation*, he marked in pencil a series of pages that describe the Mi'kmaq view of the soul's immortality. This was the very same topic that Locke engaged in his *Essay Concerning Human Understanding* (1690), *Reasonableness of Christianity* (1695), and debate with Edward Stillingfleet.[3] His page marks suggest that Locke viewed Le Clercq's *Relation* as a source of ethnographic information relevant to contemporary debates about matter and spirit.

In addition to observing the Mi'kmaq religion, Le Clercq describes his own experience of trying to learn the "Gaspesian" language, which, he reports, has "nothing at all in common...with the languages of our Europe." For Le Clercq, the numerous Indian nations of New France constitute an intensified version of Babylonian confusion due to the "infinity of different tongues which prevail among all these peoples." Eschewing any belief in language's biblical origins, Locke would not have agreed with Le Clercq's assessment

that the multiplicity of New World "tongues" reflected the extension
of the curse of Babel to the New World. Yet he would have found that
the practical dilemma Le Clercq faced as a missionary resonated
with his own philosophical interest in the relationship between revealed religion and language as a system of representation. Le Clercq's
work among the Mi'kmaq invites the question of whether the cosmology of a Franciscan Recollect could be successfully translated
into a language that was exceedingly difficult to learn, that bore no
resemblance to European tongues, and, perhaps most important,
that espoused a very different understanding of the relationship between matter and spirit. After expending much "trouble and labour"
to learn the "Gaspesian tongue," Le Clercq realized that the transliteration of key Christian concepts was not phonemically possible in
the roman alphabet. He came up with a creative solution, devising a
system of "characters," which he claimed were based on Mi'kmaq
hieroglyphs; these characters were refashioned to accord with
Catholic prayers and written on birch bark in charcoal.[4]

In contrast to Le Clercq's efficient use of Mi'kmaq hieroglyphs
hand-drawn on birch bark, Puritan missionary John Eliot struggled
with an expensive forty-year project of Christian translation.[5]
Listening to indigenous words, Eliot attempted to understand an entirely foreign syntax, to transform an oral language into a written
one, and then to translate Christian sermons, primers, Bibles, and
conversion tracts into Wampanoag.[6] His aim was not simply to make
these Christian texts intelligible to his native proselytes but also to
transform the language itself from what Eliot perceived as its fallen
and savage status into a redeemed Algonquian language capable of
conveying Christian truths in a new form. By the end of Eliot's life,
Wampanoag was proving no more malleable to this purpose than it
had in his earlier and more optimistic years. The combined force of
King Philip's War, of a missionary enterprise that became in the
1680s too costly to sustain in relation to its achieved results, and of a
Wampanoag-English Christian world of fluctuating rather than fixed
meaning caused Eliot to enter into a state of near despair.[7]

While the Eliot Tracts do not appear in the "Voyages and Travel"
section of Locke's library, Eliot's linguistic work also enjoyed a transatlantic reach. Eliot corresponded extensively with Royal Society
member Robert Boyle, and his missionary work was also known to
mystical linguists such as Samuel Hartlib and John Dury. This transatlantic network reveals that Eliot's transformation from millennial

missionary motivated by Wampanoag's ostensible proximity to Hebrew to linguist despairing at the irreducible materiality of Wampanoag words in the 1680s had a clear analog in the broader intellectual currents of the mid-seventeenth-century Anglosphere. Mystical theories of language characterized some of the central philosophical tenets of the Hartlib Circle, the Cambridge Platonists, and the founding members of the Royal Society.[8] Leading up to the publication of Locke's *Essay Concerning Human Understanding*, these theologically inflected notions of words as keys to metaphysical truth came increasingly into conflict with understandings of language as a human construct. Language encounters in the Americas revealed language to be more private, fluctuating, and contextually specific.[9] By the late seventeenth century, book 3 of Locke's *Essay Concerning Human Understanding* would effectively end the vogue for mystical and biblical ideas about words. Translated into French in 1700 before eliciting a response from Locke's French student Étienne Bonnot de Condillac, the *Essay Concerning Human Understanding* had a clear and lasting impact in the British Isles, on the Continent, and in the American colonies.[10]

Mi'kmaq and Wampanoag language texts exist today due to indigenous contributions to missionary linguistics. As a partial consequence of these surviving texts, Mi'kmaq is one of the few remaining eastern Algonquian languages still spoken, with an estimated three thousand native speakers. Wampanoag, though one of the first eastern Algonquian languages declared dead, is currently undergoing a massive project of revitalization. Both the survival of Mi'kmaq and the revival of Wampanoag have been facilitated by the archive of language documents coauthored by seventeenth-century missionaries and American Indians[11]

Yet despite the facet of cultural effacement involved, the impact of Mi'kmaq and Wampanoag on intellectual history in the seventeenth century offers another perspective on Algonquian language survival. Though espousing theologically disparate approaches, Le Clercq's and Eliot's attempts to translate Christian texts into indigenous languages contributed to the late seventeenth-century philosophical recognition of words as the fabric of human society. Eastern Algonquian languages are commonly believed to be the language group most permanently destroyed through European contact. Whereas scholars have amply documented the catastrophic impact of linguistic colonialism in North America, the inverse perspective holds that indigenous languages worked to transform the structure of European thought: Mi'kmaq and Wampanoag had lasting consequences for seventeenth-century European language philosophy's foundational assumption that all languages adhered to universal truths.[12] Both of these languages facilitated the realization that language was best understood as a social construct comprising a system of arbitrary signs. While useful as a means of communication, words themselves did not provide human access to either divinity or the invisible ideas existing within the human mind. The limitations of translation realized within each missionary setting ultimately curtailed the reach of Christianity's purportedly universal scope, making religion appear instead as a material record of a finite system of signification. Late seventeenth-century missionaries and philosophers had to accept language and belief as contingent entities, dependent on the practices and contexts of individuals and communities.

Seventeenth-Century Linguistic Theologies

As the vehicle for the transmission of the divine word and the particularity of the human experience of divinity, language resided between natural and supernatural, visible and invisible realms among early modern Christians. Seventeenth-century theologians believed that all languages had fallen away from the Edenic ideal represented by Adam's power to name, where sign and signified shared a seamless semiotic link and a common essence.[13] Following the destruction of Babel, words became imperfectly joined to their referents. Matching the visual or auditory signifying entity to the mental or material signified image depended, from Babel forward, on arbitrary systems of representation. Ancient as well as early modern theologians and philosophers struggled to understand and at times overcome three major world historical consequences that resulted from this myth of linguistic fragmentation: irreparably fallen human speech fell short of adequately representing the visible world of nature, words resembled but could no longer act as metaphysical keys to the invisible world of God, and nations would not understand the "meaning" of one another's "voice."[14] Across the British Isles and the Continent, seventeenth-century philosophers strove to find solutions to this problem.

For Protestant reformers, whose millennial fervor intensified during the English Civil War, language was the key to increasing

Christian knowledge. A mystical language movement originated in the sixteenth-century teachings of Jakob Böhme, the German theologian who believed in the possibility of a language of nature that would regain Adam's power to name. For Böhme and other sixteenth-century reformers, language and nature were considered avenues to divine truth. Consequently, remedying the effects of Babel required both studying the ancient scriptural languages of Hebrew and Greek and sanctifying vernacular languages so that they could be put on the same footing as the traditionally understood sacred languages. In the 1640s Czech educator and writer Johann Amos Comenius, as well as English promoters of Comenius such as Samuel Hartlib and John Dury, perpetuated this vision. Hartlib and Dury both felt that humanity could partially recover from the linguistic consequences of the Fall by recuperating the sense and usage of this original Adamic language. Since for Adam language and knowledge were one, the reclamation of this lost but perfect and sacred tongue would eliminate the profound epistemic rupture that had occurred as a consequence of Adam and Eve's expulsion from the garden of Eden and the subsequent collapse of the Tower of Babel.[15] Eliot placed Wampanoag directly within this mystical language scheme, observing that this strange language carries mystical power.[16] The quest for the reparation of the word was made manifest through a global interest in Babylonian confusion. All languages were considered to have the potential, once sanctified, to be spiritually equal, which placed the vernacular on par with Hebrew and Greek.

In the fourth chapter of *Leviathan* (1651), Thomas Hobbes challenged this philosophy of language's Adamic origins, describing speech as a predominantly social invention. Speech, according to Hobbes, "consist[s] of Names or Appellations, and their Connexion." It is used "to transferre our Mentall Discourse, into Verbal; or the Trayne of our Thoughts, into a Trayne of Words," which provide "mutuall utility and conversation; without which, there had been amongst men, neither Common-wealth, nor Society, nor Contract, nor Peace, no more than amongst Lyons, Bears, and Wolves." For Hobbes, speech is the central ingredient of the social contract because it allows a means of communication that separates humans from their natural state. While Hobbes acknowledges that language comes from "Adam and his posterity," he explains that language has become a predominantly human invention as more names have been added over time to match circumstances and experiences. Language,

for Hobbes, then, is a social construct. Therefore it is variable, condi-
tioned by the experiences and circumstances of a given time
and place:

> When we conceive the same things differently, we can hardly avoyd
> different naming of them. For though the nature of that we conceive,
> be the same; yet the diversity of our reception of it, in respect of dif-
> ferent constitutions of body, and prejudices of opinion, gives every
> thing a tincture of our different passions. And therefore in reasoning,
> a man must take heed of words; which besides the signification of
> what we imagine of their nature, have a signification also of the
> nature, disposition, and interest of the speaker.[17]

Hobbes's statement about the mutability of words and referents made
the Bohemian and Comenian vision for a seamless correspondence
between language and nature increasingly difficult to imagine. If
there was no constancy to words across different "constitutions of
body, and prejudices of opinion," there was no possibility of realizing
the state of semiotic perfection on which mystical linguistics
depended.

Henry More responded to Hobbes almost immediately with
his *Antidote Against Atheisme* (1653) and then more fully in his
Immortality of the Soul (1659). Both texts attempt to rescue belief in
the Platonic possibility of words to signify the spirit. In his *Essay
Towards a Real Character and a Philosophical Language* (1668), John
Wilkins elaborated the idea of a universally comprehensible language that would facilitate commerce, improve natural knowledge,
and spread awareness of Christian religion. In 1690 Locke rounded
off a century of schism and debate over the significatory power of
words, largely by reiterating the Hobbesian position in the expanded
form of book 3 of the *Essay Concerning Human Understanding*.[18]

During the mid- to late seventeenth century, part of missionaries'
spiritual commitment was to try to recover some of this lost potential for words to signify divine truth. In a 1645 letter to Hartlib, Dury
established the philosophical hope for such missionary work by explaining his "motion for the Conversion of the Indians." Dury went
on to describe the "Law written in the Hebrew language" that could
be discovered among Israelite descendants in "Asia & Turkie" as well
as in northern "America."[19] Twenty-five years later, Wilkins transformed this millennial aspiration into a commercial and political

one. Invoking the legacy of Mithridates, who knew twenty-two languages, Wilkins reported on the vast discovery of "varieties of Tongues...in Asia, Afric, or America."[20] Anticipating this connection five years before the publication of Wilkins's text, Eliot wrote to Richard Baxter in 1663 to acquire more information on the "universal Character and Language" and its usefulness in promoting the "great Design of Christ."[21] Anglo-Protestant missionaries responded to this philosophical movement through a desire to create a porous world where both language collecting and mastery became the keys to Christian universalism and imperial dominance.

In the Catholic context, theologians did not strive for the same millennial goal of linguistic transparency where the use of words would ultimately dissolve into a revelation of the hidden truths of natural and spiritual worlds. They placed more emphasis on words as mediators of the spirit, as necessary to the spiritual truths expressed and enacted on earth. This theological difference in their approach to language stemmed from the Counter-Reformation insistence on an ecclesiastical hierarchy, which maintained authority through its own power to redact spiritual truths carried through the word. Central to the Protestant attack on the Catholic Church was the notion that this hierarchy interrupted faith in a way that prevented revealed truths from transcending language and becoming manifest on earth to each repentant individual.[22] Reformed theologians idealized the transparency of the word based on the assumption that all humans receive the key of knowledge, stipulating that truth came from within and could not be conveyed merely through the symbolic register of the word or thing. Catholics dwelled within the textured meaning of the word itself, while Protestants strove for a utopian state in which the necessity of the word would disintegrate entirely.

This broad theological distinction affected English Puritans and French Jesuits and Recollects as each missionary group negotiated their relationship to their respective crowns and to the circumstances of proselytizing among American Indian communities. Seeking a form of religious autonomy from England, the Puritans inculcated the practice of *sola scriptura* (by scripture alone) and *sola fides* (by faith alone) within their missionary communities. Literacy was a prerequisite for conversion within the missionary towns of Natick and Martha's Vineyard. Modeling a form of faith more beholden to ecclesiastical hierarchies, Chrestien Le Clercq and his successor, Pierre Maillard, actively discouraged indigenous literacies and favored mnemonic techniques for inculcating conversion.[23] Eliot worked ardently to translate the Bible into the Wampanoag vernacular.[24] His efforts followed closely on the heels of the Malay Bible, which was the first Bible printed in a non-Western language. Given that Roman Catholics carefully guarded against the dissemination of the Latin Vulgate Bible in the vernacular, scriptural translation was not a priority among the French Jesuits and Recollects. During the reign of Louis XIII and his first minister, Armand-Jean du Plessis, Cardinal Richelieu, French bishops sought to solidify episcopal discipline, primarily by shoring up control over penitential practice and worship. Though bringing Catholicism to the masses was a primary concern of the Counter-Reformation movement in seventeenth-century France, the clergy accomplished this goal by maintaining a sharp distinction between the educated and literate religious authorities and illiterate French peasants. Consequently, throughout the French countryside, clergy designed oral catechisms, pictures, religious paintings, and other forms of visual and material culture as indispensable components of a universal and uniformly imposed faith. Described as "the largest laboratory in early modern Europe for the politically supported replacement by Catholicism of the Protestantism that had been implanted in the sixteenth century," France was an apt training ground for the Recollect and Jesuit missionaries who would heed the call to go to the New World.[25] Perhaps due to the mechanisms already in place for converting French peasants, early Jesuit missionaries to North America compared the "Savages" to "French beggars who are half-roasted in the Sun."[26] This comparison suggests a parallel project of fashioning national subjects, making peasants and American Indians into Frenchmen in France and New France respectively. While the finely honed techniques of conversion transferred seamlessly to the North American context, the Jesuits maintained an uncertain relationship to the crown, also seeking a form of religious autonomy through their New World sojourns.[27] The monarchy struggled to maintain control by refusing to send a printing press to North America despite requests from Jesuit priests. This refusal to send a printing press to the New World stemmed from the Roman Catholic tendency to centralize and standardize religious practice as well as from the culture of Catholic Gallicanism in seventeenth-century France.[28]

In keeping with the political tenor of Gallican religion in the seventeenth century, between 1629 and 1635 Cardinal Richelieu founded the Académie Française, which included a component of linguistic unification. The crown sought to extend control over disparate regions of France, thus unifying the country under one monarchy. This demanded a common French language instead of distinct and mutually incomprehensible regional languages and dialects. The purity of the French language and high standards of eloquence became priorities of the Académie: it sought to delineate clearly the rules of the French language so that French would become the most perfect modern language possible. Such efforts developed alongside commensurate changes in early modern dictionaries and grammars. Increasingly, dictionaries depicted French in relation to other living languages, as in Randle Cotgrave's *A Dictionarie of the French and English Tongues* (1611). Early historians of the Académie Française assigned to the division on language began to compile dictionaries of regional dialects, such as Jean Doujat's *Dictionaire de la langue toulousaine* (1638). The Académie's texts began to exhibit increased attention to grammatical rules, a trend visible in Claude Favre de Vaugelas's *Remarques sur la langue françoise* (1647) and famously culminating with the Port-Royal *Grammaire* in 1660.[29]

The standardization and purification of an elite French language, coupled with an ecclesiastical hierarchy maintained through varying degrees of literacy, meant that the millennial impulses of mystical linguistics did not evolve in the same way in the Francophone world as they did in the Anglosphere. There was less linguistic diversity in seventeenth-century England, and the Protestant emphasis on the printed word worked to homogenize the English vernacular. In part as a result of the discrepancy between language, nation, and print, French Jesuit and Recollect missionaries were more accepting of linguistic diversity, more willing to cede the fact that indigenous words would not become transparent vessels for the spirit but were simply the tools used to translate key Christian concepts and elicit conversion. Le Clercq replicated in Nova Scotia the division between the literate clergy and the illiterate proselytes by making himself a "dictionary" in order to master Mi'kmaq while only instructing native people in the "characters" that made up the birch-bark prayers.[30]

As Le Clercq and Eliot soon learned after beginning their linguistic studies, Wampanoag and Mi'kmaq resisted adaptation to a Christian cosmos. Differences between European and indigenous syntax, cosmology, and semiology presented insurmountable challenges. In Wampanoag and Mi'kmaq, there is no sense of the word as an arbiter of the spirit. Because neither Wampanoag nor Mi'kmaq cosmology separates the invisible from the visible world, each language demonstrates continuity between animate and inanimate creation. In Mi'kmaq animate beings include humans, animals, trees, distinct features of the landscape, and material objects such as canoes or decorative hair strings. A specific animate ending denotes the material quality of these objects. Animate beings are not inert. They have *mn'tu*, or power, an inanimate force underlying the whole world. This power can take on the conscious pattern of animate forms.[31] The Wampanoag embraced a similar belief in *manit*, a spiritual power that could be manifested in any form. Manit expressed itself in "the appearance, behavior, or strangeness of animals, plants, people, and things, both Indian and European."[32] This indigenous American cosmology exhibited a world of complete interpenetration of animate and inanimate forms. According to the Wampanoag world view on Martha's Vineyard man, flora, fauna, and all elements were related as kin and of one nature.[33] Given that Christian and European cosmologies depended on a strict division between matter and spirit, this conflation of animate and inanimate properties inevitably led to misunderstandings. Roger Williams and Eliot often mistook manit for a god, when in fact it denoted any form of spiritual power.[34] Le Clercq concluded of the Mi'kmaq, "From these false premises, based upon a tradition so fabulous, they have drawn these extravagant conclusions,—that everything is animated and that souls are nothing other than the ghost of that which had been animated."[35] Le Clercq recognizes aspects of Mi'kmaq cosmology that are fundamentally different from French Catholicism. While portray animism as false, he nonetheless recognizes a coherent indigenous belief system.

Indigenous cosmologies reflected a different way of thinking about one of the constitutive features of seventeenth-century Christianity, namely, the strict division between the visible and invisible worlds. This division circumscribed human knowledge of the divine to a limited sphere. While on earth, Christians resigned themselves to living with the condition of a divine presence that was largely unknowable. The Mi'kmaq and Wampanoag sense of the permeability of animate and inanimate forms flew in the face of this belief as a form of blasphemy. Yet the native belief in a fundamental ability to discern the spiritual power inherent in material forms may have also had a certain illicit appeal to Eliot and Le Clercq as doctrinally forbidden knowledge. Both missionaries believed they were entering into situations where their task would be to rectify a postlapsarian relationship between visible and invisible realms. They viewed these savage worlds as having fallen further and further away from an original spiritual truth, which, once discovered, could be repaired.[36] What they found instead was that indigenous languages confounded the distinctions between matter and spirit in which they believed.

Both Le Clercq and Eliot aimed to secure more productive avenues to divine truth while also affirming the canopy of Christian millennialism, but the linguistic work produced in each case was more philosophically akin to Locke's notion of the finite and contingent status of language. Colonial language encounters thus compounded the philosophical insecurities of a century consumed with the representational dilemma of linguistic signs severed from their referent. As early modern grammar books emphasized the ordering of signs themselves as the key to rhetorical eloquence and meaning making, the interposition of words and variable syntactic structures among many Algonquian language groups heightened the counternarrative of linguistic disorder, of words as tenuous and potentially insufficient points of reference for making and maintaining order in the world.

Anglo-Protestant Pedagogies of Translation

In 1663 Eliot printed the first edition of *Mamusse wunneetupanatamwe up biblum God*, which has become known as the Eliot Bible and is one of the first complete Bibles published in a non-Western language. Eliot's efforts toward scriptural translation were very much in line with the interests of his patrons in London as Royal Society members worked to produce Gaelic, Lithuanian, and Turkish Bibles as well.[37] Though presentation copies of the Eliot Bible were sent back to England with the hope of garnering more support for the New England mission, the evangelical purpose of the text was to propagate knowledge of Scriptures based on the *sola scriptura* ideal. Scriptural knowledge required literacy, prompting Eliot to commission the printing of the *Indian Primer* six years after his Bible. Speaking to the significance of literacy as a prerequisite for implementing Protestantism in the indigenous community, the *Indian Primer* first appeared in 1669, several years before the *New England*

Primer, which is believed to have begun circulating in the 1680s.[38]
The *Indian Primer* partook of a long tradition of Protestant primers
and catechisms, which sought both to inculcate a personalized faith
by teaching Protestants how to read the Bible and to instill uniformity
by uniting creed and alphabet. Yet because the print production of
this particular text preceded that of the *New England Primer* by more
than a decade, Eliot also broke new pedagogical ground in 1669.

The *Indian Primer* promotes a circular model of language acquisition and pedagogical practice designed to underscore and secure the
epistemological certainty attached to each linguistic sign. The *Primer*
enacted a transformation at the level of language acquisition itself
with the aim of reconfiguring the mind of the native proselyte as a
tabula rasa, ready to receive the salvific light of Christ in the moment
of conversion. Unselfconsciously redacting Wampanoag into specific arrangements of alphabetical writing, the *Primer* seeks to make
the word on the page transparent so it would seamlessly convey universal Christian truths. In so doing, Eliot expanded on the mystical
language philosophers' vision by seeking to bring his native proselytes closer to his own linguistic ideal as expressed in the *Communion
of Churches* (1666): "I will turn to the people a pure Language: And
when Egypt is converted it is expressed by this, that they shall speak
the Language of Canaan, Isa. 19.18."[39] This universalizing goal of
evangelization also describes the pedagogy of the *Indian Primer*.

Simplifying the Algonquian language into the basic elements of
the Roman alphabet, the *Primer* begins by enumerating the vowels
and consonants that would aid native children in learning written
Algonquian words. A description of lowercase and capital letters introduces the reader to the typeface intended to be the naturalized
medium through which Wampanoag natives would learn to read
Algonquian-Christian texts. Moving on to syllables, the *Primer* then
teaches the basics of pronunciation by introducing the reader to sections of words from one to fifteen syllables, so that compound words
could be correctly read and pronounced from the printed page. The
Primer's spelling and pronunciation lessons culminate with the
Lord's Prayer, translated directly so that each English word had an
explicit corresponding word in Algonquian (see Figs. 2.1 and 2.2),
with certain exceptions, such as God. The Protestant promulgation
of faith depended on maintaining uniformity of language.

In the *Indian Primer*, the translated words of the Lord's Prayer
adapted a word within the Wampanoag language to the explanation

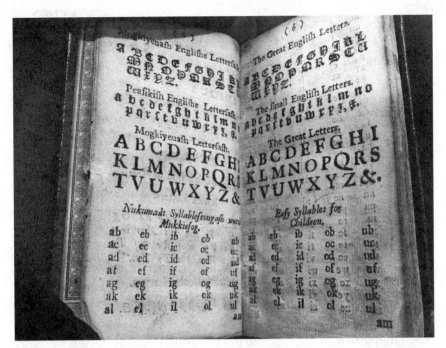

FIGURE 2.1. *The Indian Primer, or the Way of Training Up Indian Youth in the Good Knowledge of God*, p. 6. 1720. Photo courtesy of the Newberry Library, Chicago (Vault Ayer 421 M343 E43).

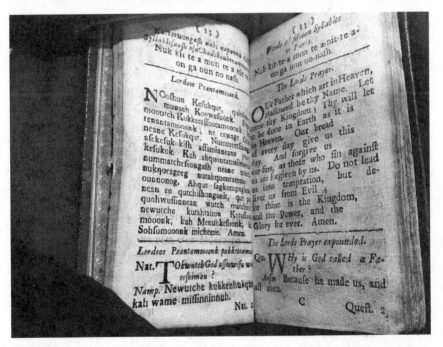

FIGURE 2.2. *Indian Primer*, p. 13. Photo courtesy of the Newberry Library, Chicago (Vault Ayer 421 M343 E43).

of a Christian phenomenon. For example, in Figure 2, "Lords" has been translated as "Lordooe"; "Prayer" as "Peantamooonk." According to Ives Goddard and Kathleen J. Bragdon, who draw their linguistic expertise primarily from native writing in Massachusett, "peahtam-mooonk" means "religion," while "peahtammauwonat" means "to pray to him." Assuming the words even predated Eliot's translation of the Lord's Prayer, the meaning does not translate precisely. Additionally, the two variants on this word were not common—they were seemingly used only once in 1766 by Zachary Houssueit, an Indian preacher in Martha's Vineyard—in all of the collected native writings in Massachusett. *Lordooe* does not enter into the written indigenous vocabulary at all, yet *Lord* appears multiple times.[40] This seems to suggest that *Lordooe* was an invented word that Eliot created because it sounded more in keeping with the Massachusett lexicon than the English word *Lord*.

Yet even a word with as privileged a sacred status as *God* is not translated into a superimposed or re-signified Massachusett vocabulary but retained in English. This is somewhat surprising given that both James Hammond Trumbull's *Natick Dictionary* and Goddard and Bragdon indicate that the word *manit* would make an acceptable translation for "God."[41] Another possibility might have been the word *Kautántowwit*, which although Narragansett in origin also occurred in Wampanoag and meant "the great Southwest God, to whose house all souls go."[42] Other untranslated words include *Amen*, the names of chapters in the Bible, and even certain instances of the word *Lord* that are embedded in the text. Perhaps feeling that these words were too closely associated with indigenous religion, Eliot did not include an Algonquian version in Christian pedagogical texts, reflecting the limits of syncretism in the Anglo-Protestant context.[43] Replacing the word *manit* with the English and Christian word for God was an important step in reorganizing the cosmos of the native proselytes in order to prepare them for Christian conversion. Each case of a Christian-English word introduced to the written version of Massachusett, or a Christian-Massachusett word imported into the indigenous language, demonstrates the missionary process of crafting a newly Christianized Algonquian language. Additionally, both the typeface and the roman alphabet in which Massachusett words were set reflected the crossover quality of Anglo-Algonquianisms designed, as they were, to realign the cosmological perspective of the native children and potential converts reading from the *Primer*.

Through the *Indian Primer*, Eliot sought to regulate and impose a Christianized version of Massachusett on the ears and tongues of indigenous children while also giving them the tools to elicit their own unique response to the Bible and to the inward transformation of their souls through the grace of God. Christianized Massachusett words functioned as a mediating frame and measure of the success of the mission, for it was only through a "believing speech" and Algonquian "prayer" that the progress of the gospel could be gauged.[44] Words mattered, but only for the divine knowledge that they were believed to represent. When spoken by native proselytes, Massachusett went a long way toward recapturing the lost language of Adam, revealing new spiritual truths that could only be gleaned within this New World context.

The *Indian Primer* calculates human understanding in Aristotelian terms, very similar to what John Locke would codify in his *Essay Concerning Human Understanding* as the impression of simple ideas within the human mind.[45] While the Puritan theological notion of Original Sin presented a contradiction to Locke's philosophy of the *tabula rasa*, Eliot believed in a complete rescripting of the relationship between words and Christian cosmology. Sign and referent could be configured to produce a thorough reorganization of innate knowledge. The *Logick Primer* (1672) carries this process of a totalizing mental reconfiguration one step further, as indicated by a title page that promotes the tool as an "Iron Key" designed to "open the rich Treasury of the holy Scriptures." The tract is written in English with the Massachusett word underneath in order to make every "thing" as well as every aspect of "speech" "open to be known." Moving sequentially, the logic of this primer begins with single notions or words such as "God, created, in beginning" in a section explaining Genesis 1:1–2.[46] The second part consists of instruction on how to combine single notions in order to make useful propositions, while the final section teaches the composition of propositions to make a speech. The idea behind the *Logick Primer* was to instruct native children in the proper elements of speech, so that when they recounted their own personal experience of salvation, the spoken Massachusett achieved the status of a new, redeemed form.

A 1673 letter written by Thomas Shepard Jr. to a minister in Scotland presented the successful implementation of this method of Christian instruction in the best possible light by describing scenes of scriptural reading by praying Indians. Shepard enclosed a copy of the *Indian Primer* and the *Logick Primer* so that the Scottish minister could see Eliot's evangelical approach. In five praying towns scattered throughout New England, Shepard described how Eliot "began his prayers in the Indian's language." In Natick the son of Waban, one of the more active native proselytes, read the Proverbs from Eliot's Indian Bible, "which [according to one account] had been printed & was in the hands of the Indians." A native named Job prayed for half an hour in "the Indian Language" and then preached from Hebrews 15:1. Several praying Indians stood up and read from the *Primer* or from Eliot's Bible. Shepard's goal in describing these scenes in such explicit detail was to depict a divinely redeemed Algonquian language. He explained that Eliot had made much progress in aligning this language with "the Hebrew character," understood as the ursacred language.[47] Through Eliot's translation, the sacred essence of Algonquian words had been unlocked. His Indian library represented for Shepard substantial progress toward the reclamation of a primitive Christian language and the reunification of the disparate Reformed churches into one mystical body. For Shepard, as for Eliot, evangelical efforts served the purpose of both converting the American Indian and affirming the imminence of the Protestant millennium.

Despite the almost singular idealism of this letter, this vision was never systematically realized in practice. The reception of words among Wampanoag and English audiences was much less fixed than Eliot and Shepard imagined. The Massachusett word for "wind," for example, was "Waubon" (Waban). There was some speculation that the name conveyed particular resonance among native proselytes when Eliot preached about the dry bones in Ezekiel 37:9–10. Dury wrote a letter to the New England ministers conveying his own observations on the significance of the name. He explained that the scriptural passage, which states, "*By prophesying to the wind, the wind came and the dry bones lived*," might have had special meaning for the native proselytes, many of whom were converted by Waban. According to Dury, this link between the figure Waban and the dry bones of Ezekiel was "ground for a very weighty thought; that that portion of Scripture should be first of all openned to them, which clearly foretold the conversion of *Israel*, i.e. The 10. Tribes universally understood, and peculiarly meant by the name or notion of *Israel*."[48] Committed to Protestant unity and a believer in the ten lost tribes theory of American Indian origins, Dury shared the same vision of

New England evangelism as an index of millennial promise. Waban, both the figure and the indigenous word, was what opened Scripture to the Indian proselytes, making them receptive to conversion by him rather than Eliot. The word speaks the truth of the gospel, according to Dury, while also foreshadowing the descent of the Holy Spirit.

Read through the reverse angle of the native perspective, the spiritual leader Waban was endowed with a particular capacity to heal, placing him on an equal if not superior level to Eliot himself. Waban famously converted many native proselytes who were drawn to his power to heal both within this Christian cosmos and through their own concept of a healing spirit. As other critics have commented, the passage about Ezekiel's dry bones was particularly significant for native audiences because it carried the literal meaning of healing from physical sickness as well as the spiritual prophecy of healing the sick soul. This passage may also have resonated because the description of God breathing life into Ezekiel's dry bones corresponds to Wampanoag beliefs in manit, the spirit power that can animate people and objects in the natural world. Based on this conflation of the literal and the spiritual, Waban possibly attained authority within a Christian cosmos while also maintaining the power of the spirit healer within more traditional indigenous systems of belief. In an exchange with his uncle, Nishoukou, during which Waban encouraged Nishoukou to convert to Christianity as preparation for death, Waban emphasized the power of God over both body and soul. Waban explained that "food" strengthens body and soul alike. By drawing an analogy between the physical nourishment of the body through food, and the spiritual nourishment of the soul through grace, Waban managed to convince the elder sachem Nishoukou of the salvific power of Christ without requiring that Nishoukou relinquish his own system of belief in the division between matter and spirit.[49]

The conversation between Waban and Nishoukou appears in Eliot's 1671 tract, *Indian Dialogues*. Modeling this text after the philosophical genre codified by Plato in the fourth century B.C.E., Eliot intended the *Dialogues* to be "*Instructive*" rather than didactic so that the Anglo reader would learn on reading the text "what might or should have been said." Immediately, this tract introduces the ambiguity of meaning intrinsic to the process of translating Christianity to indigenous communities. Through a series of dialogues staged between praying Indians and their unconverted kin, readers learn that the resistance to Christianity often comes in the form of confusion over the relationship between matter and spirit: "If your praying to God do indeed teach you the true way of being rich, as you say, how then cometh it to pass that you are so poor still?" Piumbuhhou, the "Learned" Indian within the "*Indian Churches*," explains to his congregation that there is a difference between earthly and heavenly riches and that knowledge of God, grace, and Jesus is the greatest attainable wealth. Piumbuhhou conveys this meaning by separating the Anglo-Protestant interpretation of Scripture from the knowledge that may be gleaned through the autonomous interpretation of the Christian reader: "The Book of God is no invention of English-men, it is the holy Law of God himself, which was given unto man by God, before English-men had any knowledge of God." Piumbuhhou describes the Bible as a repository of ancient Christian wisdom, bespeaking a truth that transcends national as well as linguistic affiliation. While the Algonquian Bible had been gifted to the Indians by the English, providing them with "great cause to be thankful to the English," it was also, according to the teachings of Piumbuhhou, believed to have released the greater truth of a universalizing spirit among these New World proselytes.[50] In the Sabbath Meeting, Piumbuhhou makes an even stronger case for the interpretive autonomy that comes from reading the word of God: "This Book was written long before the English-men prayed to God, and English-men have learned all their wisdome out of this Book, and now they have Translated it for us, and if we attend unto it, it will teach us wisdome, as it hath taught them."[51]

The *Indian Primer* and *Logick Primer* were pedagogical texts designed to secure linguistic meaning, yet the native description of the Eliot Bible as recorded in the *Indian Dialogues* reveals a world of meaning in flux. Piumbuhhou presents a more fluid dynamic of interaction between the material and spiritual world than Puritan theology would traditionally grant. He describes a Christian God that "provides Flesh" through a cyclical process of growth and regeneration as grass and herbs feed the beasts that feed humans, strengthening the "blood, flesh, sinew[s] and bones in us." In a passage that echoes the language of Ezekiel 37, Piumbuhhou describes a Christian world that emulates the indigenous concept of permeability between animate and inanimate realms. God turns "Leaves" of grass into "blood, flesh, sinews and bones."[52] The portrait of nature described here is one in which the spirit animates matter, making it powerful and connected to a greater whole. Eliot's translational efforts were effective in creating a true form of *sola scriptura*, but not to the ends that he intended. The interpretive liberty implemented in the native community did not unleash Christian primitivism but rather revealed some of the discrepancies between Wampanoag and Christian cosmology.

Letters exchanged among Robert Boyle, Eliot, and other commissioners of the United Colonies in New England, such as Harvard president Charles Chauncey, Simon Bradstreet, and Thomas Danforth, from the mid-1660s to the 1680s reflect increasing despair on the part of Eliot and others over the progress of Indian conversion and the limits of translation. The reason for this was partly financial, since the translation and print production of texts in Eliot's Indian library cost enormous amounts of money, time, and labor. Yet it was far from a mere material concern, as Chauncey's letter to Boyle in 1669 reveals. Chauncey began by thanking Boyle for the "press & types &…skilled printer" sent to New England in order to ameliorate the Commissioners' financial "straits" and allow the Scripture and other pedagogical texts to be "printed in Indian." What was at stake here was more than just the well-being of the mission; it was also the validation of the Protestant vision: "For we fear (alas!) that if the printing press fall to wreck… America [will] be without printers, & the Academy with its scholars suffer damage." The print production of Indian-language texts, evangelization, and the very quality of learning at Harvard were all interconnected for Chauncey. Without the press, characters, and type, American Protestantism stood in imminent danger of collapse.[53] The demands of the material history of Eliot's Indian library, the need to constantly appeal to Boyle for more money, printers, and material, stood in marked contrast to the original idealism of accessing spiritual truths hidden within Wampanoag words.[54]

Correspondent descriptions of native conversion focused increasingly on external markers of ritual worship or civility rather than the inward quest for evidence of the workings of grace on Wampanoag souls that we see in *Tears of Repentance* (1653).[55] In a 1684 letter to Boyle, Eliot shows his appreciation for a monetary gift by cataloging ritualized forms of worship: "the officer begineth with Prayer…they call forth such as are to answer the catechise…a chapter is read…a psalme is sung." Besides the rather un-Puritan focus on the more formalized aspects of worship, this passage is remarkable for its repeated qualifications: sometimes an "officer" is not ordained, sometimes "there is not yet a church gathered," sometimes the catechistical lesson is omitted when none are qualified to answer questions.[56] Eliot describes a landscape of depleted spiritual resources despite his best efforts to convey the ways in which the progress of the gospel was still taking hold. The shift from an earlier 1650s phase of Wampanoag linguistic idealism and Puritan *sola fides* to external forms of worship and civility was as much a consequence of the limits of translation as it was of the more familiar causes such as the impact of King Philip's War and the gradual transformation of Puritan theology.[57] Not only had Eliot exhausted the financial and intellectual resources necessary for achieving his millennial aspirations for the Christianization of Wampanoag words, but there were very few, if any, missionaries with comparable expertise to carry on with his work. As the New England Commissioners confessed, "Wee must needes owne that wee now finde it very difficult to procure an addition of fit persons to labour in that worke of the Lord." Rates and quality of conversion as well as knowledge of Wampanoag among Puritan missionaries declined during Eliot's lifetime.[58]

Indigenous-Catholic Ideograms

Like John Eliot, Christien Le Clercq went to tremendous "trouble and labour" to acquire knowledge of Mi'kmaq. He "even made a dictionary" of the "Gaspesian tongue," building upon the linguistic work of his Recollect predecessor Gabriel Sagard, who developed the first published account of Huron in 1632.[59] Just as John Locke owned and read Le Clercq's *Relation*, he also read Sagard's *Dictionary* and remarked in his notes that it was "very good."[60] Yet despite the inroads that Le Clercq made in mastering Mi'kmaq, he recognized the limitations of Christian translation. Guarding his knowledge from his native proselytes, Le Clercq, rather than attempting to seamlessly translate Christianity into indigenous words, struggled to develop a catechistical translation that his proselytes would comprehend and remember without ambiguity of meaning. Eventually, he found a solution by conveying Catholic catechistical teachings through ideograms, which he claimed to have derived from Mi'kmaq culture. His ideographic prayers eschewed efforts to translate Christian truths into representations of Mi'kmaq configured through the Roman alphabet. Instead, Le Clercq sought to accomplish his missionary goals through a visual system of translation.

By 1675 Le Clercq lamented what he saw as the Mi'kmaqs' utter incapacity to grasp Christian spiritual meaning through language in their current spiritually depleted state: "These poor blind creatures hear as songs what we say of our mysteries; they take only what is material and meets the senses; they have their natural vices and un-meaning superstitions, savage, brutal, and barbarous manners and customs; they would willingly be baptized ten times a day for a glass of brandy and a pipe of tobacco."[61] In this text, *First Establishment of the Faith in New France*, Le Clercq relates his failure to effectively communicate the depths of Christian mystery to a population too wedded to the material meaning of words. Noting a profound dif-ference between the expression of the Gaspesian language and the languages in Europe, Le Clercq reflected on the impossibility of con-veying Christian hymns as transparent signs of the spirit in Mi'kmaq. The depths of spiritual meaning that Le Clercq felt himself to be possessed of could never be adequately related to a population that insisted on a sensory and material encounter with the words them-selves. What Le Clercq represented as the Mi'kmaq failure to grasp spiritual meaning stemmed from two different ways of understand-ing the relationship between word and spirit. In Mi'kmaq, as previ-ously discussed, nouns fall into animate and inanimate categories, with animate indicating a connection to a greater whole. Verb end-ings tie into this cognitive system as well. Rather than a tense-based structure, Mi'kmaq verbs relate to how speakers and listeners con-nect to each other based on shared understanding. Speakers nar-rate events according to how they have experienced them. The very structure of the language itself adheres to a part-to-whole relation-ship. Objects, ways of knowing, and experiences connect to a broader spiritual cosmology that exists throughout the natural world. Power underlies the entire world in the Mi'kmaq cosmology. Every form is a manifestation of power.[62]

American Indian philosopher V. F. Cordova describes language as "a window that frames a particular view of the world."[63] Le Clercq understood that the structure of the Mi'kmaq language differed from those of Europe, but he failed to grasp the Mi'kmaq view of the world. Intent on finding Mi'kmaq equivalents for the concepts of value within a Christian cosmology, Le Clercq could not perceive the conceptual frame reflected in the structure and syntax of Mi'kmaq words. Consequently, he reduced a fundamentally different understanding of the relationship between word and spirit to a base materiality measured by Euro-Christian values. Recognizing the challenge that this material linguistics presented to New World conversion endeavors, Le Clercq reflected on the difficulty of adequately conveying meaning. He noted his frustration that the children were "'slow to memorize' scripture."[64] Because it was hard to translate Christian concepts into Mi'kmaq, Le Clercq observed that the "method" by which he attempted to "teach the Indians to pray to God" was cumbersome and largely ineffective. Eventually, however, Le Clercq discovered that the Mi'kmaq understood picture symbols much more readily than words, and, in doing so, appears to have discovered an indigenous form of literacy.

> I noticed that some children were making marks with charcoal upon birch-bark, and were counting these with the finger very accurately at each word of prayers which they pronounced. This made me believe that by giving them some formulary, which would aid their memory by definite characters, I should advance much more quickly than by teaching them through the method of making them repeat a number of times that... which I said to them. I was charmed to find that I was not mistaken.[65]

Le Clercq set out to record Mi'kmaq symbols in charcoal on sheets of birch bark. In doing so, he adopted a system of writing that he claimed to have observed in use among the native inhabitants of the Gaspé.[66]

Whether or not there is some truth to this claim, ideographs, pictographs, and hieroglyphs played powerfully in the cultural imaginaries of seventeenth-century travel writers and philosophers who associated these systems of communication with more primitive, prelinguistic, and even childlike populations. Jesuit José de Acosta's *Historia natural y moral de las Indias* (*Natural and Moral History of the Indies*), first published in 1590, explains that "no nation of Indians discovered in our time uses letters or writing." Citing Aristotle as his authority, Acosta explains that "letters" signify words, which in turn represent "men's concepts and thoughts." Pictographs or signs, by contrast, even though they may be written, are not letters. According to Acosta, "a picture of the sun cannot be called writing, or letters representing the sun, but is simply a picture." Acosta's elevation of the letter above other systems of communication reflects a widespread Renaissance belief in the superiority of the alphabet.[67] In his

Nieuwe wereldt, ofte, Beschrijvinghe van West-Indien (History of the New World), the Dutch geographer Joannes de Laet maintained a similar hierarchy of language in order to trace the "savage" state and origins of the inhabitants of New France.[68]

This early modern refusal to recognize pictographic systems as forms of writing, letters, and language persisted throughout the seventeenth century, eventuating in the hierarchy most clearly defined by Giambattista Vico in his *New Science* (1725). Referring to the vast philosophical literature on the origins of languages and letters, Vico presents the accepted idea that "the first pagan people conceived ideas of things using imaginative archetypes of animate beings, or personifications." He gives the example of the Scythian king in Asia using five objects to denote his system of communication.[69] Yet even as images and pictures were seen by writers from Acosta to Vico as primitive and prelinguistic, they were also believed to enjoy a greater degree of semiotic integrity. Letters depended on representational abstraction in order to convey human concepts and thoughts, whereas pictographs directly represented the objects themselves, thereby collapsing the relationship between vehicles of communication and objects within the natural world to a far greater degree than more advanced systems of writing could. Non-alphabetical and non-phonetic modes of representation were thus often idealized throughout the seventeenth century as the basis for creating a common and universally intelligible system of writing. Moreover, as Thomas Browne proposed in his *Pseudodoxia Epidemica* (1646), an alphabet of things rather than words might reverse the confusion of Babel by exhibiting a more natural mode of expression that could evade the inevitable problem of human fallibility encoded in all linguistic systems.[70]

In inventing or adapting Mi'kmaq pictographs as Catholic catechism, Le Clercq drew on these early modern beliefs. He reinforced a fundamental hierarchy between refined letters and primitive modes of expression, echoing Acosta's sentiment through his own proclamation that the Gaspesians "have no knowledge of letters." Yet like Browne and in anticipation of Vico, Le Clercq also mapped a nostalgic yearning onto the symbols of communication that the Mi'kmaq did have, imagining at once both a higher mnemonic potential for conveying Christian truths and the pictographs as keys that might potentially grant access to a lost Eden. Though it was enshrouded in secrecy that obscured the origins of the Mi'kmaq even—or especially—from themselves, Le Clercq contended that encoded within the pictographs was "some dim and fabulous notion of the creation of the world, and of the deluge."[71] They worshipped the cross without knowing what they were worshipping. But if one discovered the true meaning latent within these signs, as Le Clercq claimed to have done, one could unlock the secrets of an innate Mi'kmaq proclivity toward Christianity. Remapped within a Christian cosmos, the symbols transformed from the marks of a non-alphabetic, childlike society into the signs of a lost Eden, newly recuperated in the New World.

While the precise nature of the relationship between Le Clercq's birch-bark ideograms and indigenous systems of writing is unclear, two glyphs have been discovered in the hills of Bedford, Nova Scotia, that resemble one of Le Clercq's symbols. One consists of a circle enclosing an eight-pointed star, while the second is a stick figure of a hunter preparing to throw a spear. The glyphs date from 1500 C.E. and are believed to be the oldest in Atlantic Canada. A common motif in Mi'kmaq art to the present day, the star glyph is of particular significance because it represents the sun, which is the most power-ful god in Mi'kmaq cosmology. According to Le Clercq, seventeenth-century Mi'kmaq addressed the sun through prayer every morning, referring to it with the same honorary title given to a chief. The sun, in the Mi'kmaq cosmology, created the universe and divided the earth into parts.[72]

Le Clercq blamed this symbol on indigenous paganism but then used it to begin Christian translation, a process through which in-digenous signs were assigned a new Christian meaning. A Mi'kmaq creation story relayed to us by Le Clercq has clear allusions to Genesis, indicating the missionary's attempt to suture two cosmolo-gies. The sun created a man and woman who bore numerous chil-dren. Soon the children started to kill one another, and the sun wept with grief. The tears created a flood over earth that destroyed all but the good relatives, who then received from the Sun God basic sur-vival skills for living on earth.[73]

Le Clercq made frequent use of the star glyph in creating his ideo-grams, which would then be used to translate Christian prayers (see Fig. 2.3). The star appears in the text as a symbol of heaven, though it is also distinguished from the symbol for God. Just as the word *Waban* functioned for the Wampanoag as a means of translating in-digenous perspectives on the animate and inanimate quality of sub-stances into Christian terms, the Mi'kmaq sun functioned to imbue catechistical symbols with spiritual meaning. The appearance of a

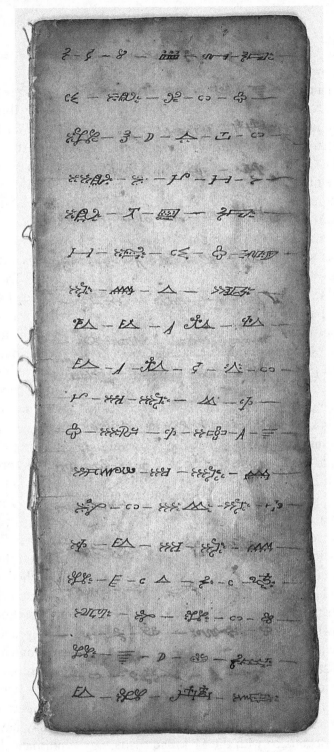

FIGURE 2.3. Manuscript book of Micmac ideograms. Invented by the Recollect Father Chrestien Le Clercq, missionary to the Indians, 1675–1687. Princeton University, Department of Rare Books and Special Collections.

sun in a Christian catechistical text infused the textual object with divine power.

Referring to his leaves as instructional papers, Le Clercq recorded his ideograms on sheets of birch bark, which were distributed to Mi'kmaq families in much the same manner that the *Indian Primer* was distributed to Wampanoag families. On these instructional sheets, Le Clercq arranged the symbols in accordance with the simple narrative placement of words in the Catholic prayer books, creating an ideographic translation of the Lord's Prayer, the Angelical Salutation, and the Apostles' Creed (see Fig. 2.4).[74]

Le Clercq reported that the Mi'kmaq treated the instructional papers as sacred texts, generating—through practice as much as through word—a pidgin form of Mi'kmaq Catholicism. "They preserve these instructive papers with so much care, and they have for them so particular an esteem, that they keep them very neatly in little cases of birch-bark bedecked with wampum, with beadwork, and with porcupine quills. They hold them between their hands, as we do our prayer-books, during the Holy Mass, after which they shut them up again in their cases."[75] Le Clercq marveled at the success of his ideographic system that allowed his proselytes to so "readily grasp this kind of reading that they learn in a single day what they would never have been able to retain in a whole week without the aid of these cards." He described Mi'kmaq children "making marks on birch bark with coal" in order to recopy the ideograms according to their prearranged sequence in the formation of the Lord's Prayer, and then pointing a finger at every picture as they pronounced it. An image that appeared in the first edition of Le Clercq's *New Relation* in Paris in 1691 illustrates this scene (see Fig. 2.5). Le Clercq imagined that this system would advance the spread of the gospel more rapidly than any other, and he advocated that any missionary "who wishes to produce a great deal of fruit in a short time" should employ this method.[76]

Borrowing cultural symbols as well as the material practice of writing with charcoal on birch bark, Le Clercq created a catechistical culture that drew on Mi'kmaq spiritual belief and meaning. Birch bark was everywhere in Mi'kmaq culture, from canoes to scrolls of pictorial mnemonics. The instructional tablets developed by Le Clercq functioned within this mnemonic frame and may have unwittingly dovetailed with the Mi'kmaq cosmology as animate objects. Both the birch bark and its charcoal ideograms were infused with the spirit. The birch bark forged continuity between the Mi'kmaq

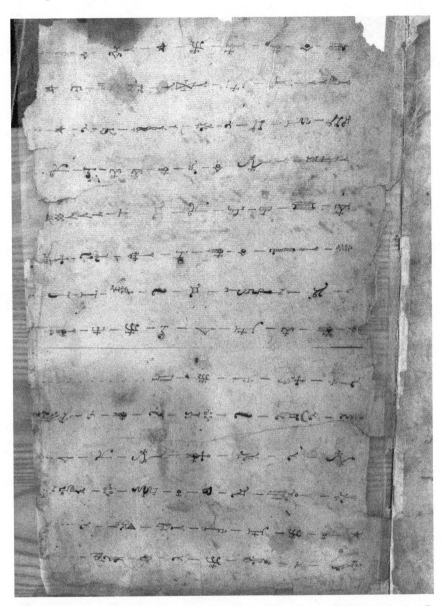

FIGURE 2.4. Manuscript of Catholic prayer book from 1848, including the Lord's Prayer, using Le Clercq's Micmac ideograms. Photo courtesy of the Newberry Library, Chicago (Ayer MS 627).

conception of the spirit residing within matter and the Catholic belief in the sacrament as a symbol of the body and blood of Christ, where the symbol also contains divine power. The instructional tablets implanted faith into the hearts and speech of Mi'kmaq proselytes, not through the alphabetic rearrangement of thought that we

This picture, which faces page 140 in the original, obviously represents the use of Father le Clercq's characters, or hieroglyphics, in teaching the prayers of the Church to the Indians. The priest may be intended to represent Father le Clercq.

FIGURE 2.5. Le Clercq, from *New Relation of Gaspesia*, published with an original 1691 edition. Photo courtesy of the Newberry Library, Chicago (F82. 157, p. 140).

see in the case of Eliot but rather through a symbolic system that conjoined the Catholic religion with Mi'kmaq material and spiritual practices.[77]

Affirming Le Clercq's desire to find Catholic equivalents among the Mi'kmaq was the presence of a cross. The cross predated Le

Clercq's arrival, possibly by one hundred years, though it was a post-contact phenomenon. Beginning in the sixteenth century, cross-bearing Europeans started traveling to the banks of Maritime Canada for fishing and trade. During these years, the Mi'kmaq did not convert to Christianity, so the cross took on an entirely different meaning within their culture. By the time Le Clercq settled in Gaspé, the cross had been fully incorporated into Mi'kmaq shamanistic and diplomatic rituals. Among the Mi'kmaq, the cross had the status of a shamanistic fetish with a supernatural origin. Yet it also functioned as an important object of diplomacy, much like wampum did among the native populations of the Saint Lawrence River. Seeming to straddle utilitarian and non-utilitarian functions, the cross existed in Mi'kmaq culture as an object whose value had been reassigned, much like the French goods among the Ojibwa and Dakota in the early colonial period. Given the multivalent use of the cross, the object might have functioned as a substitute for other objects that were in the culture prior to contact.[78]

Le Clercq made much of the cross, citing the object as evidence that the Mi'kmaq were "worshipping without knowledge thereof." He writes that they both drew and wore the cross "religiously upon their bodies and their clothes." Le Clercq explains that the cross served as a focal point of social organization and religious worship that even made Gaspesian cemeteries appear more like those of Christians than of "barbarians," sprinkled as they were with crosses placed over the tombs. The Gaspesians were, Le Clercq exclaimed, "the Athenians of a new world."[79] By typologically associating the Gaspesians with an ancient civilization, Le Clercq identifies a form of virtuous heathenism that would culminate in Christianity. Early Christian fathers such as Origen and seventeenth-century theologians such as Robert Boyle and Cotton Mather made similar observations about non-Christian cultures. This portrayal of Christian inevitability extended to linguistic observations as well. Ancient Greek was believed to carry the kernel of a sacred essence that could be activated once infused with the light of the gospel through the New Testament translation. Mi'kmaq ideographs similarly contained a sacred power, capable of signifying Christian truths once newly rendered in a distinct and otherworldly symbolic and syntactic idiom.[80]

For Le Clercq, the authentic sign of conversion consisted of the rearrangement of symbols to accord with the Gallic-Catholic sense of *translatio-imperii*. In his *New Relation of Gaspesia*, Le Clercq used his own discovery of the symbol of the cross among the Gaspesian Indians as evidence that France's New World conquest was providentially designed. Le Clercq reported that the cross "presided over their councils, their voyages," and "their cemeteries" and took this as proof that the Gaspesians, like the Greeks before them, "were rendering their homage and their adoration to the Cross of an unknown God." The sign of true conversion among the Gaspesians happened not through the complete erasure of native forms of worship but rather through the realignment of the significance of the cross to accord with Catholic values. Accessing the Gaspesian belief that the cross was passed down from their ancestors, Le Clercq reported "melt[ing]" the hearts of the "Cross-bearers" into "tears" by explaining its proper symbolic purpose. The Gaspesians repented and asked forgiveness before reorienting their worship of the cross toward the proper use just taught to them by Le Clercq:

> The night passed with these sentiments of devotion, and the next day, at daybreak, the father had his altar erected in a special wigwam, which the Indians had arranged very suitably with branches of fir, and there he celebrated the Holy Mass, after which, all clothed as he was in his priestly robes, he distributed Crosses to all the Gaspesians present, even to the children. These Indians, by a holy emulation, which indicated visibly the approbation they gave to the zeal of their missionary, each and all prepared several fine Crosses, which they ornamented with beadwork, wampum, and their usual painting; and they attached them at the two ends of their canoes in which they embarked, chanting devoutly the *Vexilla regis*.[81]

This scene reveals the palimpsest-like layering of French Catholicism over a civilization that—as Le Clercq informed the reader—already contained the incipient form of this Christian translation (see Fig. 2.6). Symbols remain of primary importance to the scene: the cross is ornamented with beadwork and wampum, just as the Lord's Prayer, rendered in hieroglyphs, was inscribed with charcoal on birch bark in the manner of writing already in use within the community.

Missionaries John Eliot and Chrestien Le Clercq discovered in practice that words could not be collated as codes to a larger metaphysical truth. Giving up on his initial attempts to translate Catholicism into Mi'kmaq, Le Clercq found success in the use of an alternate system of representation where Mi'kmaq symbols of the cross and the sun became catechistical tools. Eliot's Indian Library

This picture obviously represents the celebration of the Holy Mass beside a river which must be that of the Cross-bearer Indians, *i.e.* the Miramichi. Although inserted opposite page 146 in the original, it seems certainly intended to illustrate the incidents described on pages 194–198, in which case the priest may be intended to represent Father Jumeau.

FIGURE 2.6. Le Clercq, from *New Relation of Gaspesia*, published with an original 1691 edition. Photo courtesy of the Newberry Library, Chicago (F82. 157, p. 146).

proliferated translation as material practice rather than reducing the Wampanoag word to a transparent vessel of the spirit. In each of these missionary contexts, indigenous languages remained wedded to indigenous cosmologies, creating hybrid forms of spiritual practice that refused to yield completely to the framework of Puritan or

Jesuit Christian orthodoxy. Indigenous words maintained their own autonomy as well as their own hermeneutic frame, despite the irreversible permutations they underwent through the process of translation. In their attempts to overcome linguistic difference, mid- to late seventeenth-century missionary linguists produced a body of texts that set into practice a new philosophical perspective on words. Rather than serving as paths to higher religious truths, indigenous words ultimately fractured the millennial vision operative within each respective missionary movement. At the turn of the eighteenth century, the secularizing force of an ethnographic perspective would require missionaries, theologians, and philosophers alike to acknowledge that human diversity as well as the natural world exhibited evidence from a prehistoric past that could not be entirely assembled into the biblical framework of Mosaic history.

Shortly after Le Clercq's and Eliot's respective projects in missionary linguistics, John Locke published his *Essay Concerning Human Understanding* (1690), a text that would famously thwart philosophical efforts to approach language as a metaphysical code for discovering divine truth. To believers in the mystical power of words, Locke announced the mere materiality of the linguistic sign in a way that posed a problem for the Protestant millennial project as well as for Roman Catholics who imagined that the spirit inhered in the sign itself. Before the publication of the *Essay,* missionaries grappled with the problem of the materiality of language in practice. They discovered that the linguistic sign could not become a transparent vehicle for the communication of the spirit. Attempts to spiritualize language ended up proliferating signs rather than securing new avenues to God, thus rendering the secular dimensions of language more apparent.

Book 3 of Locke's *Essay Concerning Human Understanding* famously prompted an epistemic transformation in language philosophy toward emergent ideas about words as human constructs rather than manifestations of divine revelation. Yet the impact of Locke's philosophy stemmed more from the questions ensuing from the epistemological possibility that the *Essay Concerning Human Understanding* struggled to foreclose than from the philosophical discoveries made therein. At times, Locke himself poses these questions, as in a section of book 3 where he imagines what would happen if the "inquisitive Mind" tried to alter the substance of the essence that the biblical Adam named. The desire to know is a linguistic endeavor, driving further and further investigation into the "endless"

"Properties" of substances.[82] Locke's *Essay Concerning Human Understanding* ultimately presents a portrait of human language as a sequence of archetypal representations of complex ideas that could only ever be mere shadows of the things they meant to represent. The *Essay* represents a contemporaneous intellectual struggle to reconcile the empirical evidence and systems of knowledge. It thus philosophically reinforces the staunch division between visible and invisible worlds that Calvinist theologians long before him struggled to maintain.

His own construction of a world that was only empirically knowable within a finite material domain perhaps was the reason that Locke felt drawn to the passages of Mi'kmaq language and religion in his copy of Le Clercq's *Relation*. The passages that Locke marked in this text concern Mi'kmaq belief in the transmigration of souls, superstitions, and ideas of the souls' immortality. It is as if the curiosities encountered through travel literature allowed Locke to enter into an alternate philosophical world, one in which symbols of communication and sociability maintained a more permeable relation between matter and spirit than his own take on the finite and relative nature of words would ever allow. Francophone writers inhabited a world view that was more conducive to recognizing linguistic and cultural difference than their Anglo contemporaries, and Locke's reading interests tilted in this direction. His library contained a vast array of French travel literature, including Jacques de Bourges's *Relation Du Voyage Monseigneur l'evèque* (1666), Isaac de La Peyrère's *Relation de l'Islande* (1663), Gabriel Dellon's *Nouvelle Relation d'un voyage fait aux Indes Orientales* (1699), and Louis Le Comte's *Lettre a Monseigneur le duc du Mayne sur les ceremonies de la Chine* (1700), among many others. Given the extent of Locke's own literary journeys through France in an attempt to entertain a world beyond the epistemological limits imposed in the *Essay Concerning Human Understanding*, it stands to reason that the *Essay*'s most thorough response would come from Locke's French student Etienne Bonnot De Condillac, whose *Essay on the Origin of Human Knowledge* (1746) attempted to reintroduce a metaphysical basis to Lockean theory.[83]

Locke drew equally from Anglo sources as well, most notably for our purposes here Robert Boyle, who seemed to have entertained an analogous philosophical curiosity in the Wampanoag and whose own copy of *Indian Grammar Begun* (1666) was in fact dedicated to him by Eliot. Given the extensive biographical and methodological overlap between Boyle and Locke, it is not difficult to imagine a certain degree of epistemological convergence in their fascination with American Indians. Locke not only assisted Boyle at an early stage in his own career but also modeled many of his ideas on Boyle's corpuscular philosophy. Collaboratively, Boyle and Locke built a new vision of nature that advanced the empirical knowledge accessible therein at the same time that it also foreclosed the possibility of knowing the world beyond. For each philosopher, indigenous cosmologies of the spirit residing within matter, of linguistic signs that conveyed animate as well as inanimate forms, took on new appeal in proximity to a more mechanistic if materially knowable universe. As the missionary impulse to assemble Mi'kmaq and Wampanoag words into a coherent Judeo-Christian frame exposed the power of the words themselves to resist that structure of representation, Locke found that the fragile, corruptible, and tenuous nature of words compelled further inquiry into the very things the words were meant to represent.[84]

From the seventeenth to the twenty-first centuries, Eliot's Indian Bible and the Mi'kmaq prayer book have existed within a system of philosophical and anthropological circulation that came to view the languages of North America as curiosities or as measures of the mental capacity of the populations that originally spoke them. By the nineteenth century, Indian vocabularies, grammars, and philosophical debates about Algonquian's metaphysical potential increasingly rendered native languages relics of an ancient and unrecoverable past. Yet these texts also contain another kind of knowledge that has proven usable for another audience. For tribal descendants as well as scholars of indigenous history, they exemplify "native survivance" through the forms of alternate worlds encoded in the very colonial archives that set out to efface these histories.[85] Indigenous language intractability to Christian cosmologies not only set into motion a new philosophical realization of the relation between words and things but also marked the refusal on the part of the indigenous speaker's maintenance of her language outside of purportedly "universal" early modern or Enlightenment scheme. American Indian language texts contain a contested history of modernity's own legacies of loss as well as a record of the challenges posed by language survival and revitalization being practiced among Mi'kmaq and Wampanoag descendants today.

Indigenous Cosmologies of the Early
Eighteenth-Century Atlantic World

Housed in the Watkinson Library is a 580-page tome, measuring twenty-nine centimeters, bound in marbled leather, and containing over 22,000 Illinois-Algonquian words listed alphabetically. The dictionary is the work of Jesuit Jacques Gravier. His small penmanship economizes space. Words are crossed out and corrections made, sometimes in Gravier's hand and sometimes in that of his successors. The result of two decades of work, the dictionary was most likely completed in the 1710s.[1] By the looks of this artifact, the Jesuits had made great strides in learning North American Indian languages since Father Paul Le Jeune declared in 1635 that he was making little progress and could only "lear[n] a few stray words [in Montagnais] with a great deal of trouble."[2] As the first two chapters have recounted, learning indigenous languages was one of the most difficult challenges that a missionary faced upon arrival in North America. Missionaries often had to abandon what they thought they knew about languages in order to parse through what sounded to them like unfamiliar savage sounds.

Gravier's *Dictionary* bespeaks a colonial world in which this was no longer the case. The manuscript volume reflects a vast amount of expertise that stands in striking contrast to records of the fumbled linguistic efforts of earlier generations.[3] This dictionary and others like it suggest that the colonial language encounter was qualitatively different for third-generation missionaries such as Anglo-Protestants Josiah Cotton and Experience Mayhew and French Jesuits Sebastian Rale, Jacques Gravier, and Antoine-Robert Le Boullenger. In contrast to their predecessors, these missionaries either had generations of knowledge at their disposal, or they learned American Indian languages as young children. Experience Mayhew writes in his *Observations on the Indian Language* (1722), "I learnt the Indian language by Rote, as I did my mother Tongue, and not by Studying the Rules of it as the Lattin Tongue is comonly Learned."[4] This heightened ethno-linguistic knowledge directly led to the emergence of unprecedented Euro-American insights into indigenous linguistic structures and their accompanying cosmologies around the turn of the eighteenth century. A sizable manuscript archive from this period remains the most lasting evidence of indigenous languages that purportedly "died" around this same time, including Illinois, Wampanoag, Massachusett, eastern Abenaki, and Huron-Wendat.[5]

The linguistic knowledge developed out of a specific time and place to which its accuracy is indebted. In the early eighteenth century, American Indian languages outgrew their usefulness, for both Christian cosmologies and Atlantic networks of philosophical exchange. The inutility of American Indian languages to broader religious and Enlightenment epistemologies permitted the dictionaries produced in this period to absorb and preserve an indigenous perspective on words. From this emerged an appreciation of indigenous languages as syntactically autonomous, expressive of an entire cosmology, and aesthetically beautiful. This sense of indigenous languages recorded in the dictionaries stands in sharp contrast to contemporary European philosophical and political understandings of North American languages, most of which viewed them as deficient or irrelevant in contrast to European languages. Early eighteenth-century missionary linguistics thus made remarkable strides toward recognizing the cultural relativity of language at precisely the moment that the philosophical value of this knowledge decreased in Atlantic economies of exchange.

Comparing third-generation French Jesuits and Anglo-Protestants highlights an important facet of the colonial language encounter: despite their theological and imperial differences, both groups acquired similarly localized and often salutary insights into North American languages while also accumulating a vast paper and print trail of dictionaries, translated catechisms, and sermons written in Abenaki, Massachusett, and Wampanoag.[6] In their transcriptions and record keeping, French-Jesuits and Anglo-Protestants came to disparate though simultaneous recognition of the semantic dimensions of the indigenous languages of North America in contradistinction to European ideas of American linguistic savagery. Such recognition happened through the active and integral presence of indigenous interlocutors in the production of these texts. While rendered useless in the contemporary framework of Atlantic intellectual history, the voluminous writing served to perpetuate indigenous language systems and to make lasting advancements in indigenous linguistics. At the same time, the spatial split between localized knowledge of indigenous languages and more sweeping Atlantic epistemologies had consequences for long-standing divisions between indigenous and Atlantic histories.[7]

A pivotal historical moment in which the division between localized indigenous knowledge in North America and broader Atlantic epistemologies occurred. Previous attempts to enfold American Indian languages into Christian cosmologies and scriptural history broke down irreparably. Biblical linguistics had long served as a compelling resource for understanding the dispersal of peoples and nations throughout the world. Yet the material realities of colonial encounters and concomitant advancements in natural philosophy that took place from 1680 to 1720 put increased pressure on scriptural history.[8] Philosophers, theologians, and missionaries confronted the enormous difficulty of constructing a coherent map of human origins and population dispersal out of the numerous "barbarous" languages of North America.[9] Indigenous tongues fell out of sync with modern time.[10] With the localization of indigenous linguistic knowledge its relevance to Enlightenment epistemologies was dismissed.

Indigeneity in Anglo- and French-Language Philosophy

As eighteenth-century comparative philology fashioned language into an effective tool for constructing a national genealogy, it was increasingly seen as too unstable to reliably account for human origins on a global scale.[11] The increased awareness of the unreliability of philology as a measure of human populations around the globe had a parallel development in natural history. From the 1670s through the early eighteenth century, fossil shells produced evidence that earth was older than Mosaic creation, which fixed all species in a limited time period. As evidence of a world of nature that exceeded that recorded in the Bible, fossils represented ancient curiosities and natural mysteries that philosophers had to account for. Mathew Hale and Thomas Burnet did so by bifurcating the origins of the earth into antediluvian and post-diluvian phases. Hale's *Primitive Origination of Mankind* (1677) placed human origins 2,460 years after the divinely inspired writings of Moses, thus allowing Mosaic history to remain the oldest history on earth.[12] In his *Theory of the Earth* (1684), Burnet advanced this perspective of a "Primigenial" and "Postdiluvian" earth that allowed for commensurability between biblical history and natural evidence that was much older than the Bible.[13]

In his lectures on earthquakes and sea fossils in the 1680s and 1690s, Robert Hooke disrupted this antediluvian perspective by making the controversial case that not all of natural history could be reconciled with the Bible. Hooke did so not by denying Mosaic history but rather by debunking the use of natural evidence to affirm that history. For Hooke, the Flood was one of many natural catastrophes, each of which contributed to the "Transpositions and Metamorphoses" that had been altering the material composition of the natural world for centuries. Consequently, fossil shells could be found all over the British Isles, even in "the most In[l]and Parts."[14] In counterpoint, John Woodward's *Essay Toward a Natural History of the Earth* (1695) reconstructed the antediluvian earth that was dissolved at the time of the Flood. Fossils were merely a vestige of the former.[15] Woodward took great interest in the mysteries of ancient archaeological monuments, such as the remains found at Stonehenge and Avebury, proposing that these sites were the key to understanding both human history and the history of Britain.

In his *Magnalia Christi Americana* (1702), Cotton Mather presents a different perspective on American Indian tongues as indices of degeneration. Having fallen to a point of unrecognizable debasement, indigenous words were, for Mather, notable only in the sense of their difference from European tongues. Within the providential framework to which Mather ardently clung, this difference could only be understood as a mark of utter savagery:

> Kummog kodonat toottumm ooetite aong annun nonash is in English our question: but I pray, sir, count the letters! Nor do we find in all this language the least affinity to, or derivation from any European speech that we are acquainted with. I know not what thoughts it will produce in my reader, when I inform him that once, finding that the Dæmons in a possessed young woman understood the Latin, and Greek, and Hebrew languages, my curiosity led me to make trial of this Indian language, and the Dæmons did seem as if they did not understand it.[16]

Mather made no attempt to actually learn Massachusett. As a linguistic outsider, he could only "count the letters" and conclude that the sheer length of the words themselves indicated a tongue that had been falling since the destruction of Babel. Arriving at a point of utter misrecognition, indigenous words exhibited a complete fracturing of the relationship between sign and referent. Not only does Mather find the language lacking all "affinity" with European speech, the devil himself who could understand Latin, Greek, and Hebrew could not make sense of this "savage" idiom. The contradictory nature of Mather's perspective on Massachusett betrays his bewilderment. A language that has continued to devolve since Babel should be comprehensible to demons, and yet even the demons affirm the linguistic alienness of the Indian tongue. Mather's commentary on Massachusett is precisely the opposite of what fascinated his contemporary philologists Edward Lhwyd, Richard Baxter, and William Stukeley about ancient Briton, where words exhibited an idealized onomatopoetic relation to the natural world, where short syllables corresponded to the sounds of a flowing river, or visually echoed balanced architectural forms.[17] From this perspective, the civilized languages lost their poetic proximity to nature. Mather and Lafitau present the opposite scenario. Indian words were believed to be so fallen as to have become out of sync with their environment.

Mather's rant about the degeneracy of North American indigenous words reflects his own philosophical uncertainty about the place of these languages within Mosaic history. His rather specious theological argument masks the limits of knowledge about American Indian origins and the problem that this question poses for scriptural authority. The origin of Indian tongues had to be understood by eighteenth-century natural historians hoping to uphold Moses's account. Moreover, as comparative etymologies of Briton gradually replaced biblical accounts of linguistic dispersal, the indigenous languages spoken in North America lessened in relevance to Anglo-Protestants writing national and world history on the other side of the Atlantic. As Mather would write in his massive *Biblia Americana*, "The *American* Languages, can as yett have but little Account given of them."[18] As any natural historian wishing to develop a theory of the earth's origins knew, the peopling of North America had to be accounted for. But because it was too problematic, too fraught within internal inconsistences, and complex external realities of migration and conquest, the Babylon account seemed specious to any serious empiricist or rationalist. Consequently, language was not seen as the best means of accounting for American origins.

Residing between the naturally discoverable and humanly formed, words became fossils to a host of early eighteenth-century philosophers, offering insight into the history of Britain through the legacy of Celtic origins. A desire to discover the primitive roots of an untouched ancient language as a supplement to natural history and antiquarianism thus emerged in the work of Lhwyd, the Scottish Presbyterian minister and philologist David Malcolm, Richard Baxter and his nephew William Baxter, Woodward, the physician and naturalist Martin Lister, and others. Through the study of primitive Briton linguistics, this natural philosophical coterie sought to make the chronology of the nation more thoroughly understood.[19]

This mode of philological inquiry as the key to Britain's ancient roots was not without precedent. Richard Verstegan's *Restitution of Decayed Intelligence in Antiquities* (1605) went into six editions by 1673. Verstegan first identified the Anglo-Saxon race as descendants of the Celts and Celtic as the original language spoken before the fall of Babel. Over the course of this text's publication history, this biblical chronology would become more difficult to maintain. Yet, the idea of Celtic as the original language of Britain and one of the most ancient languages of the world set the tone for early eighteenth-century Anglo-Saxon studies and for a new linguistic genealogy of the nation that would effectively replace Mosaic ethnology while absorbing one of its central tenants: languages and people formed the basis of nations; to reconstruct their genealogy was to bring one closer to the purity of an original connection between words and nature and to recapture a primordial sense of the world as it once was. While operating through the rational framework of comparative etymology, linguistic nationalism imported a biblical form into a secular frame.

As philology thrived as a field of study in the British Isles, those immersed in the field became increasingly dismissive of the philosophical value of American languages. Lhwyd reframed prior beliefs in Adamic languages with a secular chronology of the nation in his *Archaeologia Britannica* (1707). A comprehensive study of British languages including their etymologies, customs, and traditions, pre-Roman monuments, and Roman and Welsh monuments with their inscriptions, the *Archaeologia Britannica* has very little to say about linguistic roots in North America.[20] While Lhwyd acknowledged that the languages of America and Asia were interesting as points of intellectual comparison, of how name and sound are aligned in purportedly ancient tongues, they bore little relation to Briton's genealogy. Lhwyd and his coterie parsed the script of ancient Celtic, read the Irish Bible, and measured inscriptions above church doors to discover the ancient roots of Britain's mother tongue. As they did so, philological study became more concerned with questions of national origins. Consequently, North American missionary linguistics all but disappeared from the transatlantic network of information exchange that had characterized Anglo-philosophical relations only a generation before.[21]

Not quite ready to embrace this secular understanding of comparative etymology, Lhwyd's contemporary, the Bretagne philosopher Paul-Yves Pezron, wrote a five-volume study of the *Antiquities of Nations* (1706) to chart the "Historical, Chronological, and Etymological discoveries" of ancient Britain in order to describe the dispersal of people and tongues *prior* to the linguistic confusion that ensued from the fall of Babel. His goal was to create an antediluvian linguistic world such that the genetic account of population dispersal could be maintained alongside more secular developments in historical linguistics. Taking care to present Britain as one of the more ancient nations in the world, Pezron's primary evidence for this claim comes through a systematic study of Celtic, which he shows to have generated Greek, Latin, and German words.[22] Though widely read by Lhwyd's coterie, Pezron's *Antiquities* was soon considered a specious scheme. The science was believed to be overshadowed by Pezron's commitment to the genetic account of nations to the point of becoming a "Mixture of Truth and Fable."[23] The mixed reception of Pezron, whose work was sound enough to be taken seriously yet ultimately tainted by an unyielding biblical framework, illustrates the almost complete dismantling of Noetic genealogy in early eighteenth-century linguistic studies.

Lhwyd developed a method of studying words in relation to the specificity of place, namely the landscape of the British Isles. In light of this new focus on the etymology of nation, missionary linguistics lost some of its momentum as an integral component of philological study in the Anglosphere. Lhwyd's approach posited word fragments as emerging from the earth, and in certain corners of the British Isles, where they had remained untouched for centuries. Discoverable throughout the farthest reaches of Britain, ancient writing, in particular writing on stones, provided telling evidence of a language frozen in time. During his fieldwork, from 1697 to 1701, Lhwyd made numerous sketches of inscribed stones and stone sculpture in Wales and other Celtic areas. Frequently dating to the ninth century, such monuments served as material remains of ancient Britons.[24] A two-volume set of sketches of antiquities and inscriptions, believed to be copied directly from originals made by Lhwyd and his assistants by the British antiquary John Anstis, are housed in the British Library (see Fig. 3.1). The volumes catalog Druidical stone monuments from different regions in England, Wales, Scotland, and Ireland. Druidical spirituality and biblical time are recorded through these stones.[25] Old Testament patriarchs were believed to have erected such monuments. They were used to mark districts even through the early years of Christianity when they also became repurposed as objects of worship with representations of Christ's crucifixion cut on them.[26] An index of time and place, the stones marked the landscape with Christian beginnings.[27] They were used by British antiquaries to make sense of the transition from the earliest fragments of Druid culture through early Christianity. Historical layers emerge across the landscape in palimpsestic synchronicity, as with the crosses that become repurposed from boundary markers to objects of worship. The stones often contained the earliest records of writing through hieroglyphic figures believed to be of pagan origin. Lhywd thus posited that language was born out of a connection to the land, as immovable as ancient stones.

Lhywd's etymological work served as a new heuristic for the dispersal of people and the peopling of nations. His Scottish correspondent, David Malcolm, used this heuristic more emphatically than Lhwyd as a way of rejoining biblical time and natural history. "Languages are in a great Measure the Keys of Knowledge," Malcolm wrote.[28] By uncovering linguistic roots in their simple and unmixed form, one could treat words as fossils, applying the study of the ancient past to contemporary debates about world and biblical history. Malcolm proposed St. Kilda in the Outer Hebrides, "the most remote" of all places "belonging to *Great Britain*," as the ideal place to do this. Describing the paucity of alphabetic letters and the simplicity of sound spoken there, Lhwyd asserts that the "simplest Shape of Language

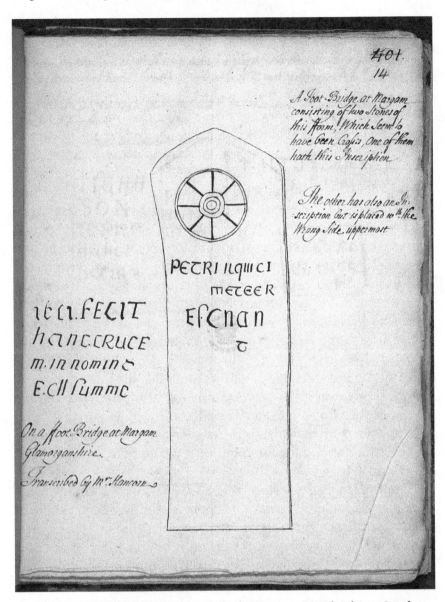

FIGURE 3.1. Image from Stowe manuscript 1023–1024, British Library, London.

may be found in the remotest Places from the Center of the Dispersion of Mankind," thus making the island an apt laboratory for observation and study.[29] Words function on St. Kilda as a kind of time capsule, each one an encoded remnant of centuries past. To perceive this, the natural philologist had to begin to capture language in its simple and unmixed state, prior to linguistic relativism or separation from the natural world.

Stones engraved with hieroglyphs, fragmented words, and "primitive" tongues survived as the detritus of a post-Lockean world that beckoned new fantasies of prelapsarian synthetic wholeness through poetry and national affiliation. This was the past brought forward into the present.[30] The "Commendatory Poems" included in the *Archaeologia Britannica* reveal a form of poetic compensation for the shattering of biblical linguistics and the slow pace of the science of comparative philology struggling to take its place. Composed in Latin, Scots, Gaelic, and Welsh, the poems, written in praise of Lhwyd, draw their inspiration from the "ancient rusticity" and "rugged fragments of words which were once heard on these native mountains by [the authors'] forefathers and ancestors." The poems formally embody what Lhwyd sought to accomplish linguistically, "making languages speak their ancient forms, to declare their truth." The poems chart a circular process of rejuvenation and renewal as Lhwyd's search for the "origins of words" has "blunted the teeth of time" and permitted "dead tongues to rise again."[31] Briton's Muse comes from the resurrection of dead tongues, as the poems present a secularized aesthetic mirror of the previous generations' theological quest for the lost language of Adam. Alongside his contributions to historical linguistics, Lhwyd's *Archaeologia* also prompted Thomas Blackwell, Richard Lowth, and Anne-Robert-Jacques Turgot to posit a "harmonic" convergence among Celtic languages, reflecting a sacred, poetic primitivism at the forgotten yet still faintly recoverable heart of the British tongue.[32]

Primitive languages accord with natural law, or so went the belief of numerous Enlightenment philosophers. The syntax was thought to emulate the natural order of ideas, an order that was both poetic and divine. Primitive languages were thus closer to nature than those that had evolved through the layers of civilization that philosophers such as Vico, Adam Smith, and Adam Ferguson speak of. Civilization came at a cost, and the cost was the proximity to nature to be found in indigenous languages. And alongside this connection between language and nature was a sense of being rooted to a place and as emerging organically from the earth that gave birth to original tongues and the bodies who spoke them. In addition to conveying the vestiges of historical time, language derived from place and from nature, according to an insight that Vico made that was quite similar to that of Lhywd. "Different climates," Vico writes, produce "different customs," which in turn produces "different languages." Languages are most beautiful when "faithful to their origin."[33] This is because the place of origin retains the sense of myth and divinity encoded in the first languages. Language thus evolves as the repository of knowledge of the body and of the body's interaction with the natural world. Philosopher David Abram places Vico at the beginning of phenomenological theories of intersubjective knowledge, where language is rooted in a nonverbal exchange between the body and the world. For Abram, as for Vico, a language that remains faithful to its origins carries with it knowledge of a "primordial world."[34]

Incontrovertibly, Vico tells us, "The world of nations is in fact a human creation."[35] Languages formed by a "mixture of many barbarous languages" contained unclear origins and were therefore "more likely to deceive and mislead."[36] Divine and conceptual languages, along with their natural etymological order, evolve into the "articulate speech" employed by "all of today's nations."[37] Genealogy was important to understanding both the word and the nation. When "articulate speech" seemed too much a mix of barbarous tongues, the means of national communication became confusing and deceptive. For Vico, a national language of articulate speech came at the cost of the language's poetic origins. The balance between language and power had to be carefully maintained as the laws of civil nature demand that people maintain sovereignty over their language and letters. When states deprive the people of this sovereignty, societies grow corrupt and the "barbarism of antiquity" recurs.[38] Language in Vico's *Scienza Nuova* (1725) serves as the catalyst to the rise as well as the decline of nations and civil society. Nations thus depended on an account of linguistic origins, even though such stories were invariably built on imagined foundations, a means of imposing the past on the present. R. G. Collingwood's notion of the past as an object governed by the relationship that contemporary thought brings to bear on it is useful for understanding the philosophical desire for linguistic origins as ancient, original, pure, and distinctive.[39]

As British philological interests became more centered on the specificity of place and notions of Celtic as the primitive antecedent to modern English, missionary knowledge of North American languages faded into the background of Anglo philosophical interest. However, despite Lhwyd's construction of a secular, national genealogy of Briton and the simultaneous abandonment of wide-scale efforts to translate the gospel into indigenous tongues by early eighteenth-century missionary organizations, Anglo missionary linguistics persisted and even thrived. French natural philosophers, by contrast, remained more engaged with the linguistic discoveries of the Americas and, particularly, the ethnological data produced therein. The Society of Jesus continued to value linguistic knowledge. Consequently, third-generation Jesuits demonstrate high levels of proficiency. A cohort of Jesuit missionaries, including Rale, Le Boullenger, Gravier, and Gabriel Marest worked among the Abenaki and the Illinois from the 1690s to the 1720s. As self-described arduous students of native teachers, they developed an unprecedented level of linguistic expertise.

Indian Teachers among the Jesuits

Jesuits placed a primacy on learning native languages.[40] This ideal is woven throughout the *Jesuit Relations*, as in Julien Binneteau's letter of praise for Gabriel Marest. Binneteau describes Marest in terms idealized by the Society. We learn that Marest has an innate talent for languages, such that he has learned Illinois in "four or five months," and a relentless work ethic: "he works excessively during the day, and he sits up at night to improve himself in the language. . . . He lives only on a little boiled corn, with which he sometimes mixes a few small beans."[41] Zealous to the point of placing his own life in a precarious position, Marest exemplifies the ardor of language study as the first phase of the Jesuit's vocation in North America. This narrative motif, which derives from St. Ignatius's *Spiritual Exercises* (1548), recurs throughout the *Jesuit Relations*.[42]

Take Sebastian Rale's arrival in Quebec in 1689. Rale reported on his deep sense of isolation and alienation to the Society. He describes New France as an Antipodean world full of animals rather than men. Yet he also understood his safe arrival in Quebec as divine dispensation, fastening him to his godly purpose. The first order of fulfilling his divine duty involved mastering the language of the Abenaki. He explains that he has been able to produce a "dictionary, which is quite thick and very useful." Based on the words recorded in this dictionary, Rale penned a catechism that, he reports, amply describes "the mysteries of our religion."[43]

Rale spent thirty years on the outskirts of Quebec, working on his *Dictionary of the Abnaki Language in North America*. In a letter reflecting on his efforts, Rale comments on the specific manner in which one must learn the language: "it is not sufficient to study the words and their meaning, and to acquire a stock of words and phrases." Sufficient knowledge of Abenaki required a deep familiarity with the customs of the native speakers in order to acquaint oneself with the arrangement of words as well as with the unique sounds of certain letters. During his residence in Norridgewock Mission, Maine (Kennebec), Rale conceded that the French alphabet did not adequately represent the range of sounds in spoken Abenaki. In lieu of French letters, the "figure 8" is used to signify a certain sound that is made "wholly from the throat without any motion of the lips."[44] The pronunciation approximates the French word *huit* and represents the phonemes *o*, *oo*, and *w*. This orthographic variation reflects Rale's attempt to record the aural sound of Abenaki in his *Dictionary*. His method of doing so involved a reverse scene of catechistical instruction. Rale reports spending hours "in [Abenaki] huts to hear them talk." He would then select some native speakers whom he felt had "the most intelligence and the best style of speaking." Before this group of assembled speakers, Rale would express some of the articles of the catechism in his own broken Abenaki and then hear their corrections. He remarked on the "turn and genius of their language" and of the way that it is "altogether different from European languages."[45] Listening carefully to the delicate expression, he would then record the sound immediately. The dictionary is entirely phonetic, an attempt to visually capture and accurately record a series of sounds. The tension between a desire for control through linguistic mastery coupled with the subversions of authority that invariably happen through bidirectional knowledge flow and translational practices is replete throughout the archive of indigenous language texts, and particularly pronounced in relation to the early eighteenth-century dictionary projects.

Father Jacques Gravier enjoyed success as a missionary through his mastery of the Miami-Illinois language, for which he wrote a *Kaskaskia-to-French Dictionary* over a period of two decades. Encoded within the dictionary is Gravier's ethnography of Illinois practices of hunting, love, competition, and medicine. In his journal, Gravier makes the point that such cultural knowledge is rare, commenting that the Illinois "are so secret regarding all the mysteries of their Religion that the Missionary can discover nothing about them." One of his Jesuit reports describes these mysteries unfolding through a young woman of seventeen who refused to marry and then became a spiritual exemplar and an instructor within the community. After experiencing the "displeasure" of her family over her decision not to marry, the young woman underwent a practice of intense mortification by wearing a "girdle of thorns... for two whole days." Gravier supposes that she might have crippled herself with this practice had he not been informed, whereupon he "compelled her to use it with more moderation." The colonial violence inscribed on the body of this young Illinois woman notwithstanding, the autonomy ascribed to her is striking. She veers from the path expected of her by her parents and her community by telling them that "she did not wish to marry; that she had already given all her heart to God." She then chooses the form of fleshly mortification appropriate for this action.[46] The severity of her self-flagellation is haunting. The girdle of thorns reflects a desire to confine her young, still developing body and sexuality. It also stands out as an intensified form of the already severe Jesuit asceticism recounted in the *Relations*. As a reward for surviving this display of austere piety, Gravier makes the young woman a translator and instructor of Christianity. She demonstrates an intense desire to teach the children, spending hours listening to their catechisms and answering questions. The reward for such extreme asceticism is a greater degree of spiritual authority than this young woman might otherwise have enjoyed.

This incident suggests multiple levels of mediation operating through the translation of Christianity from one language to another and from one community of believers to another. The young girl embodies a certain spiritual ideal for Gravier and for her community. While obviously an asset to the fluency of catechistical instruction, once the young woman begins her instruction, meaning automatically becomes less fixed. The copper-plate engravings that Gravier designed with the intent of imprinting a certain mental image upon the Indian mind are replaced by a lively question-and-answer period, orchestrated by the young girl rather than Gravier. While third-generation Jesuits gained more colonial control through higher degrees of linguistic and cultural knowledge, successful conversion and higher degrees of fluency among indigenous proselytes also decreased the fixity of meaning through which Christian truths were conveyed.

Gravier's successor, Antoine-Robert Le Boullenger, arrived at the Illinois mission in 1719, when the study of Miami-Illinois was already fairly advanced. When Le Boullenger began his French-Illinois

Dictionary in 1719, he combined the genres of phrasebook and hymnal (see Fig 3.2). The lexical section consists of more than three thousand words. It is remarkable for the Illinois variants given under many of the French key words. For example, the verbs *voir* and *aller* contain multiple variants, many more than in Gravier's *Dictionary*. This is likely due to the evolution in understanding of Illinois verb configuration. At the beginning of his dictionary, Le Boullenger lists all of the possible combinations of verb inflections. He also understood the importance of intonation in Illinois more thoroughly than his predecessors. Pre-aspiration is marked in Le Boullenger's dictionary such that the word for grandmother, *noohkoma*, was written as *nohc8ma* and *nocc8ma*, while Gravier transcribed it as *n8c8ma*.[47] Alongside the nuanced lexical portions of Le Boullenger's dictionary are multiple religious texts in Illinois, which are not translated. Hymns, sacraments, the Ten Commandments, and the history of Genesis all appear in Illinois with French titles. The contrast between these two sections reveals the discrepancy between an advanced level of linguistic expertise on the one hand and the creativity of the translator on the other. The number of variants offered for a simple verb such as *voir* reflects the impossibility of precise translation. Consequently, Le Boullenger does not aspire to create the appearance of transparency between Illinois and French. Rather, he permits the lexicon to embody the striking differences between each language. Yet in the ritual space of the hymn, or sacrament, or even in the narrative retelling of the Fall, Le Boullenger drew upon his knowledge of Illinois phonetics to write an oral text designed to deliver an unequivocal spiritual message. In the oral ritual space, the religious text elided linguistic difference, once words were lifted off of the page. Le Boullenger's devotional section suggests that when enacted through the song or sacred text, the spirit infused the material word. The mysteries of Christianity could thus be conveyed across the cultural and linguistic divide.

Designed to produce more efficacious missions, dictionaries produced by Jesuits enhanced colonial control on the one hand, but they also opened up lines of communication between Indians and priests on the other. Both populations came to understand the flux of metaphysical meanings that resulted from the confluence of two distinct world views. Thus while the Society of Jesus envisioned linguistic mastery as a means of more uniformly implementing Jesuitical doctrine, within the local communities themselves, language often became

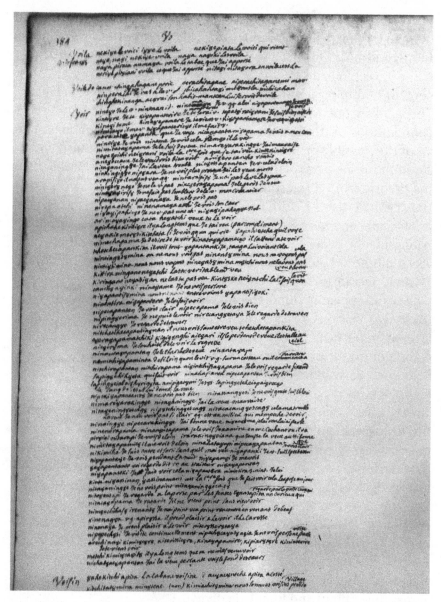

FIGURE 3.2. Antoine-Robert Le Boullenger, *French and Miami-Illinois Dictionary*, John Carter Brown Library, Providence, Rhode Island.

generative rather than prescriptive. Hybrid forms of worship emerged out of the confluence of competing world views.[48] The practices of linguistic immersion that Jesuits had to undergo also often led to unanticipated forms of conversion, as when Rale remarks that Abenaki "has its perfects," that it is a "grand" language, especially

"when one considers its economy." Giving an ample and unprecedented perspective on the subtleties of indigenous tongues, the
dictionaries permitted the original Christian message to change in
content as well as form through the process of translation. Yet the
tensions traced in this section between the priests' efforts to maintain colonial control and local indigenous subversions of it were
elided through a broader emergent discourse of language as a measure of savagery rather than the bidirectional exchange of concepts, as
illustrated through Lafitau's writing. The Jesuit dictionaries, many of
which existed only in manuscript until the twentieth century's language revitalization efforts, record forms of knowledge that were
rejected by a broader Enlightenment discourse that increasingly relegated Huron and Iroquoian populations not only to a primitive but
also to an untraceable past.

Father Joseph-François Lafitau spent five years in North America
conversing with Jesuit missionary Father Julian Garnier and studying the Iroquois custom and language before writing *Moeurs des
Sauvages Ameriquains comparees aux moeurs des premiers temps*
(1724). Also drawing on an extensive archive of travel and philosophical texts from Homer to Pliny to Acosta to his contemporary,
Bernard Le Bovier de Fontenelle, Lafitau's *Moeurs des Sauvages*
addresses some of the central philosophical issues of his time. The
study begins and ends with the claim about the futility of seeking
"connections" between "the barbarous languages and the learned
ones."[49] Despite the numerous "conjectures" that have been made,
linguistic relations are too numerous to trace, too confusing to be
used as a method of tracing genealogies of nations and civilizations
or patterns of population dispersal.[50] Thus, while Lafitau takes the
ample linguistic knowledge ascertained by his missionary brethren
into account, he also eschews the possibility of using language as a
heuristic for reconstructing the history of the world.

A chapter on "Language" concludes Lafitau's *Moeurs des Sauvages*.
Despite Lafitau's fairly substantial knowledge of Iroquoian grammatical and syntactical structure, he dwells in generalities in this chapter,
invoking more questions than he answers. Toward the end of the
chapter, Lafitau laments that he did not give a more thorough-going
account of Iroquois structure, if only as a corrective to "travellers"
who "have contented themselves with giving some imperfect vocabularies consisting of a few deformed words which are in most
common use."[51] Proper treatment, Lafitau insists, would take too

much narrative space, though it's hard to imagine this as a central concern when it comes at the end of a work over six hundred pages long. The "barbarous terms," Lafitau speculates, would be "disagreeable to the public." Perhaps most significant, "scholars themselves cannot gain much enlightenment" from these words other than to show how "very far from those known to us" these languages are.[52] Lafitau articulates a dynamic of philosophical exclusion and a new principle of polite sensibility that precludes eastern Algonquian and Iroquoian from early eighteenth-century networks of language-knowledge exchange. Despite his status as a competent Iroquoian and Huron linguist in his own right, despite the five years spent in North America where the Jesuits had accumulated vast knowledge of indigenous tongues, Lafitau dismisses the languages as too "barbarous," structurally different, and "deformed" through years of colonial interactions to be of much use to anyone, particularly scholars.

What is puzzling about this sentiment is that Lafitau knows better. Indeed, within this same passage he writes that Iroquois and Huron "are rich in spite of the poverty attributed to them…although they have a different structure from ours, they have great beauties."[53] In a pattern that we see with many Jesuit priests, once Lafitau knows Iroquois, it transforms from a "barbarous" compilation of deformed sounds to a pleasing system of beauty. Lafitau hints at an aesthetic potential for Huron and Iroquois, yet he fails to see any philosophical or scientific merit. His reflections add up to emphatic statements of fundamental difference: "Not only do the American languages have no analogy with the Hebraic language, the Oriental, Greek, and Latin languages, and all those which pass as learned, but neither do they have any with the modern European languages and the others known to us." Just as Lafitau's ethnographic descriptions ensconce the Indians within a primitive past, his remarks on language isolate this population from the rest of the world.[54] Yet the contact that has taken place over the nearly three hundred years of American "discovery" has made communication a necessity, "forc[ing]" the Iroquois and the French to speak in order to engage in trade or common defense. Lamentably, according to Lafitau, this contact has led to the further degeneration of Iroquois tongues, producing "gestures" and "corrupt words" that do not belong to either language and "a speech without rhyme or reason."[55] There is nothing pure or original to be found in indigenous tongues. Instead, one finds barbarity unlike anything that the European ear is accustomed to, further degenerated through the force of contact.

While language was not the place where he hoped to discover it, the recuperation of a divine original among the Iroquois and Huron populations of America was central to Lafitau's purpose. His *Moeurs des Sauvages* joins a chorus of philosophers, from Hugo Grotius and Laet to Cotton Mather, in an attempt to reconcile the peopling of the Americas with Mosaic history. Lafitau runs through the catalog of possibilities that have been proposed since Grotius's controversial claim in *The Dissertation on the Origin of the American Races* (1642) that America was peopled from Scandinavia, the Yucatan from Ethiopia, and Peru from China. All that is known to date, Lafitau states, is that "America could have been reached from different places and thus peopled on all sides."[56] Evidence remains inconclusive. In light of this, Lafitau made an interesting philosophical move: he proposed that in fact what philosophers should do is to consider the Iroquois creation story.

Upon recounting the story of Turtle Island, Lafitau immediately states that it is so "absur[d]" as to "arous[e] pity." However, he quickly counters, "it is no more ridiculous than some of those invented by the Greeks who were such ingenious people." He partially legitimates the creation story in order to cull Christian truth from it: "across this fable, ridiculous as it is, we seem to half-see the truth, in spite of the thick darkness enveloping it." Through Lafitau's divinely inspired pen, darkness surrounding these half-truths recedes to reveal in Christian light: "the woman in the earthly paradise, the tree of the knowledge of good and evil, the temptation into which she had the misfortune to fall... the wrath of God driving our first ancestors from the place of delights where he had placed them... [and] the murder of Abel killed by his brother, Cain."[57] The story of Turtle Island becomes a degenerate form of Judeo-Christian history in Lafitau's hands. The "half" truths of the fable in which it is told are a shadow of a lost original connection to the one true God. The revelation of this truth becomes Lafitau's reason for doing ethnology. Through the study of native customs, these degenerate forms of Mosaic history can be newly brought to light. The peopling of the Americas, which had so puzzled natural philosophers since the discovery of the continents and presented others with a fundamental challenge to biblical chronology, can be resolved by looking to the populations themselves. Among North America's indigenous population, Lafitau finds "knowledge of the flood" and "traces of a very ancient belief (by which they are persuaded) that, just as the world was submerged by the waters of the deluge, it must also perish at the end of time by fire which will entirely consume it."[58] Embedded within Lafitau's retelling of the Iroquois creation story is a glimmer of Christian truth, obscured by centuries of degeneration.

To Speak in Broken Indian

In contrast to the Jesuitical ideal of language learning, early eighteenth-century Protestant missionaries in North America began to elevate the importance of English as the one true tongue and instrument of nation-building. The Society for the Propagation of the Gospel (SPG) and the Society for the Propagation of Christian Knowledge (SPCK) increasingly took over from the Puritans as the engines of Protestant conversion.[59] In its initial 1701 proposal for "Propagating the Gospel in All Pagan Countries," the SPG began with the noble intention of "educating a competent number of young students of theology in those foreign Languages." However, this goal soon seemed impractical and inefficient. A proposal written the following year observed that the "multitude of pagan tongues" was a "Barr to the Propagation of the Gospel in any pagan country," but "particularly North America." The proposal imagined "removing that Barr by extirpating the various Dialects of the Indian Jargon, and establishing in its place the knowledge of the English Tongue." This "one Step," the proposal imagines "would facilitate the great design of civilizing and converting that part of the Heathen world." And thus began a new era of Anglo-Protestant missionary progress, one characterized by a desire for uniformity through the growth of the "English Tongue," rather than the translation of the word of God into a multiplicity of vernaculars.[60]

Even an organization such as the Society for the Propagation of Christian Knowledge (SPCK), which specialized in biblical translation, eschewed the significance of North American languages. Focusing on massive efforts to translate, print, and distribute copies of the Bible in Welsh, Portuguese, Arabic, and Irish, members of the SPCK were dismissive of the value of conveying Christian truths in American Indian languages. Indeed, one letter addressed to a minister in New England supposed that even though Mayhew knew Massachusett, he instructed his proselytes "in English" on Martha's Vineyard since this "seems to be the shortest way of conveying divine Truths into the minds of a people whose native Language is barren of all polite Expressions." So impoverished was the Massachusett language, this letter claimed, that it was woefully inadequate to sustain "ordinary ocurrences [sic] of Life and Body," and therefore must be "infinitely defective for what relates to the Soul."[61]

Despite the SPG's and SPCK's preference for Christian instruction in English, however, localized missionary efforts to learn indigenous languages certainly persisted well into the eighteenth century. The Dutch Reformed minister Bernardus Freeman, who was both a pastor in Schenectady and a missionary to the Indians in the Mohawk Valley, was the first Protestant to learn Mohawk and to transcribe it into the Roman alphabet.[62] In a letter to the SPG, dated May 31, 1712, Freeman explains that his method involved working closely with an interpreter to discover the "16 Alphabetical Letters" applicable to this language. From this transcription, he translated the "Gospel of St. Matthew from the beginning to the End, and the 1,2,3, Chapters of Genesis." Additionally, Freeman translated several of the psalms, the English Liturgy, and the Lord's Prayer. He claims to have "taught the Indian to read & write perfectly."[63] Freeman's linguistic work was necessary, for he discovered upon arriving in the Mohawk Valley that the Mohawks were completely opposed to learning English.[64] Freeman worked to translate and print Christian texts in Mohawk. His letters to the SPG suggest a high level of language proficiency and a concerted effort to translate the gospel into Mohawk such that standard Christian texts became integrated within the Mohawk community. Yet the goals of the SPG did not accord with Freeman's efforts, reflecting a high influx of English texts, including Bibles, Common Prayer Books, and catechistical lectures, into the community. Within the Christian community, Mohawk survived despite efforts by the SPG to eradicate it.

Analogous to the Mohawk case, the Wampanoag spoken among Christian Indians on Martha's Vineyard and in Plymouth has been preserved through the localized efforts of early eighteenth-century missionaries Experience Mayhew and Josiah Cotton despite mounting pressure to instruct Indian proselytes in English.[65] Mayhew revealed his own particular expertise of the language spoken on Martha's Vineyard in a 1722 letter to Royal Society member Paul Dudley, who wrote a request for "accounts of the Peculiarities & Beauties of the

Indian Language, and wherein they agre or differ from the Europians."
A response came in 1722. Mayhew reported that he was ill-equipped
to answer this question, for he was "no Gramarian."[66] In this letter,
Mayhew registers the limits of his own expertise. He engaged in a
form of direct, linguistic observation that was in practice much like
the Jesuit technique. Despite his evangelical investments, he was not
compelled by an overweening need to reintegrate Massachusett into
a coherent Christian cosmology. Rather, his letter to Dudley catalogs
a sequence of linguistic anomalies in relation to European languages.
Noun variations occur based upon whether the word is "animate or
inannimate" and whether "Their Magnitude" is "great or small." In
contrast to English words, Mayhew tells us that "the names of persons and things" in Indian words is "very significant." Mayhew explains that word length often indicates the significance of a place. For
example, a place called Nempanicklickanuk would be translated into
English as "The place of Thunder-clefts."[67] He informs the reader
that the place name derives from the historical occurrence of lightning striking a tree in this place, breaking it into pieces. Word length
gives the word a more precise signification. Often this signification
records the history of the land on which the natives dwell. Similar to
Lhywd's insight into Celtic and Welsh, Mayhew records a deep connection between word and place as constitutive of Massachusett.

A contemporary of Mayhew's, Josiah Cotton compiled an extensive
manuscript vocabulary of the Massachusett language and composed
several sermons in Massachusett while ministering in Plymouth.
Like their French Jesuit counterparts whose linguistic knowledge
spiked during this period, these missionaries acquired admirable
linguistic skills by working in relative isolation. Missionary linguists
of the Protestant persuasion were intellectually as well as physically
isolated, cut off from broader networks of meaning, be they Christian
or philosophical, such that their knowledge of indigenous tongues
had no context in which it could be understood other than the local
Christian community to whom they ministered.

Even though missionary linguistics was all but entirely excluded
from philological study in early eighteenth-century Britain and received
a paucity of support from missionary organizations, a sustained language encounter not only flourished among Anglo-Protestant missionaries but also led these missionaries to insights that were aston-
ishingly commensurate to indigenous cosmologies. Mayhew makes
a case for language as constituted by time, place, and people. These

observations are not only similar to Lhywd's; they also veer toward a hybrid cosmology that is both indigenous and Christian. In learning Massachusett as he did his own mother tongue, Mayhew could not help absorbing aspects of the world view encoded in the structure of the words. Nouns are animate; therefore nature is animate. Place names wield a special significatory power that is often a record of the animate history of that land, of interactions between worldly and other-worldly forces such as lightning and a tree.[68]

Yet despite the specificity of time and place, Mayhew tells us that Indians from Canada to Virginia, consisting of vastly disparate populations, "speak what was *Originally* one and the same Language."[69] Condensed within this word *originally* is a recognition of the structural similarities governing languages within one family. It is also a subtle illusion to the lost language of Eden, referring to an ongoing belief in a biblical past. For Mayhew, Massachusett represents a hybrid cosmology that is at once associated with biblical accounts of disparate tongues and syntactically representative of indigenous cosmologies. Through this hybrid cosmology, Mayhew observed Massachusett words to be a rich source of aesthetic potential. The language is "good and regular" he tells Dudley. While the "Termes of art are not yet fixed," Massachusett is certainly "capable" of cultivating them. Additionally, Mayhew senses an opportunity for a uniquely American aesthetic because the "Indians" are not as "beholden to other nations" as the English are for borrowed words.[70] Mayhew's observations foreshadow the Anglo-American literary fascination with the aesthetics of indigenous words to come.

Like Mayhew, Josiah Cotton built on the work of John Eliot, using both the Bible and the *Indian Primer* in an attempt to learn the rules of Indian orthography.[71] Yet Cotton also transformed Eliot's work through a more nuanced focus on Wampanoag's structural particularities. Also like Mayhew, Cotton was the descendant of three generations of missionaries. As the son of John Cotton Jr., who was himself a student of Wampanoag, Cotton grew up with a more subtle sense of the intricacies of the Indian tongue and the ways in which it differed from English. However, despite his native knowledge, Cotton encountered some difficulty in comprehension among his proselytes. A recorded dialogue vividly recounts the imperfections in the transmission of knowledge across missionary generations, while also revealing the profundity of local variations of the Wampanoag tongue.

The dialogue begins simply. Josiah Cotton asks, "How shall I learn Indian?" The praying Indian replies, "By talking with Indians, and minding their words, and manner of pronouncing." The dialogue begins by inverting linguistic authority. Rather than assuming the position of ministerial expertise, Cotton asks an Indian proselyte for advice. The indigenous perspective confirms his own suspicion that Indian is a "very difficult" language. Additionally, Josiah Cotton learns that one of the reasons that he is having difficulty preaching in "Indian" is because his father, John Cotton Jr., learned the language on Martha's Vineyard, or "Nope" as the island is called in Wampanoag. The knowledge passed down from father to son is imperfect, according to this native informant, because the language spoken on Martha's Vineyard is in fact quite different from the language spoken within the Plymouth community. When Josiah Cotton asked his interlocutor to explain the difference between "the language of the Island, and the main" he could not do so entirely but explained that "these Indians" (of Plymouth) "dont understand every word of them Indians." Due to this apparent miscommunication between missionary generations, Josiah Cotton can only speak "broken Indian." While phonetically and orthographically similar, the intonation is quite different. Consequently, the Indian proselyte tells Josiah Cotton that in his sermons, he doesn't "put the tone in the right place." Because this leads to comprehension that is fragmentary at best, the Indian proselyte advises that it would be better to "preach to the Indians in English" than in "broken Indian."[72]

Significantly, the difference between the Wampanoag spoken in these two locales is a consequence of oral expression. Indigenous speakers highlight the integral aural quality of their language. Syntax and orthography might be uniform but intonation makes all the difference in expression and comprehension. This indigenous perspective calls into question John Cotton Jr.'s linguistic expertise in a fashion that contradicts not only the testimonies of contemporary Puritan ministers but also the assumption among scholars that the languages spoken in Plymouth and Martha's Vineyard were mutually comprehensible.[73] Cotton Jr. did in fact learn Wampanoag on Martha's Vineyard in 1665, when he was sent there to redeem his name following a local scandal.[74] After an intensive year of linguistic study, he returned to a church of more than forty praying Indians, gathered between Sandwich and Plymouth. Here he continued his study of Wampanoag, composing his own manuscript notebook of Indian

Vocabulary. Josiah Cotton inherited his father's linguistic work, but also realized that he had to improve upon it, perhaps in light of the discoveries revealed in this dialogue. Pouring over his father's records, but also following the advice of the Indian proselyte that he "tal[k] with the Indians," Cotton composed his own vocabulary list. In a small manuscript notebook, he transcribed approximately three thousand translations of Massachusett words and phrases, producing what is, as far as I can tell, the only text in the early eighteenth-century Anglo-Protestant canon that comes to mirroring the achievements of the French Jesuits with their massive dictionary projects.

The vocabulary list shares with Mayhew's *Observations* a recognition of the autonomy and intrinsic beauty of Indian words. While Mayhew imagines the potential for developing terms of art for Wampanoag, Josiah Cotton does so, as he begins his list with a section on the arts that includes such phrases as "a comedy, or witty thing," "a tragedy, or sad thing," "an act," "a history," "melody," "a trumpet or music," and "inspiration." The list complements Mayhew's recognition of aesthetic potential encoded in Indian words. Conveying a hybrid cosmology like Mayhew's *Observations*, Josiah Cotton's vocabulary is replete with Christian terms and concepts: "heavenly," "hell," "predestination," "psalmist," "idol," "state of innocency," "corruption of the flesh," "incarnation," and "marrow of divinity."[75]

This hybrid cosmology of Wampanoag Christian words survived the journey from Martha's Vineyard to Plymouth. The list of Christian concepts also has meanings that bespeak some aspect of the indigenous spirit world. According to James Hammond Trumbull's *Natick Dictionary*, *Kēsuk*, the translation for heaven, means "the visible heavens, the sky," or "light" or, in some dialects, "the name of the sun as the source of heat."[76] The word for hell, *chepiohke*, means "the inclosed place of separation, hades, hell."[77] "The misery of hell" translates as *Awakompanaonk chepiohkomuk,* meaning "complaining, expressing of suffering, 'groaning.'"[78] A creative stretch at best, "predestination" translates into a phrase meaning something to the effect that "he thirsts after the 'old, ancient and so first in the order of time.'"[79] The generic form of the vocabulary masks the thematic variation on theological terms by appearing to present a one-to-one correspondence between English and Wampanoag. This collaborative project between father, son, and indigenous teachers attains linguistic expertise through flexible forms of faith. In relinquishing the Protestant insistence upon literal translation from the word of God to the vernacular, Josiah Cotton's vocabulary allows for a more fluid tool of cultural translation.

Josiah Cotton and Experience Mayhew were two of the last Puritan missionaries to learn indigenous languages with any degree of proficiency. They both had the advantage of familial knowledge of the language, knowledge either acquired through childhood interactions with native children on their father's mission or information passed down through generations. Mayhew and Cotton are notable not only for their proficiency in indigenous languages but also for their observations about the intricacies and particularities of the languages on their own terms. Both Cotton and Mayhew understood that the aspects of Mashpee and Wampanoag grammar that did not fit within the syntactical order of European languages nonetheless exhibited a logic of their own. Rather than viewing linguistic peculiarity as a mark of savagery or postlapsarian disorder as their predecessors had, Cotton and Mayhew made remarkable insights into the structure of a language as embedded within a speaking community. Unfortunately, they did so at the same moment that Massachusett speakers were on the decline due to nearly one hundred years of colonization. Even though missionaries had participated in the destruction of the language, Eliot's belief in the functional purpose of missionary linguistics also had led to efforts of linguistic preservation. Previous generations of missionaries had prized hearing testimonies of faith in a redeemed Algonquian tongue, but even with perfected dictionaries and increased missionary expertise, there were fewer American Indians who could speak the language.

Imperial Millennialism and the Battle
for American Indian Souls

One cold winter day in January 1722, Colonel Thomas Westbrook led one hundred British troops and their American Indian allies to surround the missionary village of Norridgewock, Maine. Most of the Catholic Abenaki residents were out hunting. Warned of the attack just in time, Sebastian Rale narrowly escaped into the forest. Storming Rale's house, the soldiers then carried off his strongbox, which contained correspondence and his manuscript dictionary of the Abenaki language.[1] Housed today in Harvard's Houghton Library, the dictionary chronicles its tumultuous history on the inside front cover, noting that it was "taken after the Fight at Norridgewock."[2] Rale posed a grave threat to the English because his superior linguistic knowledge helped to secure native allegiance and alliance. Capitalizing on the Abenaki's long history of conflict with the British, beginning with the First Abenaki War in the 1670s, Rale enlisted Abenaki support to further anchor the Franco-Catholic presence in North America. By taking the Abenaki dictionary, the British troops stole a key instrument of imperial war strategy.

From the Glorious Revolution in 1688 to the conclusion of the Napoleonic Wars in 1815, France and Britain were at war for the majority of the time. The colonial setting exacerbated these conflicts as New France and New England battled for dominion of North America.[3] Acadia, the territory between the Kennebec and St. Croix Rivers, was the site of an ongoing bloody contest. Between 1632, when it was first ceded to the French, and 1713, when the British ultimately gained control of the region through the Treaty of Utrecht, Acadia had passed back and forth between the French and the British no less than six times.[4]

Set on an international stage, Jesuit priests and Puritan ministers experienced the colonial wars as an intensification and renewal of

Reformation and Counter-Reformation struggles, understood as the great apocalyptic battle between God and Satan. At the core of colonial conflict was a nearly two-hundred-year-old religious battle, repackaged as national affiliation. A millennial zeal pitted Jesuit and Protestant forces against each other with renewed fervor. Language became key to consolidating British and French nationalism among colonial powers and indigenous populations alike.[5] As colonial powers, France and England both saw their American Indian proselytes as such raw material, ripe with potential in the service of their own ends. The British sought national uniformity by imposing English-language instruction, while the French continued to augment their own indigenous linguistic skills through a proliferating culture of dictionary compilation. Linguistic knowledge among Jesuits reached new heights and achieved greater stability through massive dictionary projects, even though only a fraction of this knowledge was used to raise literacy rates among indigenous populations.[6] Meanwhile, Anglo- and Dutch Protestant efforts expanded beyond the Puritans to include Anglican missionaries commissioned by the Society for the Propagation of the Gospel (SPG) to implement the uniform faith of the Church of England in America.[7]

France's military success depended on the priesthood's ability to form American Indian alliances. Alliances required the intimacy gained through conditions of relative trust, the strategic use of the knowledge acquired through years of missionary activity living among the Abenaki, the Mi'kmaq, and the Miami-Illinois people. The hope of Germain, Rale, and others was to translate linguistic knowledge and the capacity for communication into a protective shield of indigenous warriors that would fend off the British. Yet, linguistic knowledge facilitated a fantasy of colonial control that was often undermined through the very translation practices enacted in specific missionary communities. American Indians maintained autonomy through both their integration of Christianity and their alliances with European powers. Part of this autonomy came from the ways that Abenaki, Illinois, Mohawk, and Mi'kmaq languages themselves resisted generalized meaning.

Due to the larger Anglo-American population and the marked growth of colonial industry and commerce, native alliances were important but less essential to the British colonies strategic defense. The rise of the British Empire required conformity and uniformity with the dictates of the Protestant faith and necessitated the implementation of English language instruction. Anglo-Protestant missions neither had nor sought the Euro-indigenous intimacy required to forge strategic alliances. Instead, the SPG grew in prominence, importing *Common Prayer Books*, and a range of primers, and other such missionary texts that would aid in Christian conversion and foster Anglo-linguistic and Anglo-colonial affiliations. By contrast, and partially in response to the SPG's mandate for uniformity, which further alienated these Puritan missionaries from their own faith and country, few Anglo-Protestant missionaries achieved the indigenous linguistic expertise that Josiah Cotton and Experience Mayhew enjoyed.

Language seemed to Jesuit priests as well as Anglican and Puritan ministers the best way to control the indigenous populations upon whom this apocalyptic battle depended. Language was believed by priests, ministers, and statesmen to unite faith and nation during a time when divisions and alliances between the two were a matter of life, death, and sovereignty. Yet if language could unite, it could also divide. Colonial missionary practices did not always align with imperial goals. While the Anglican missionary William Andrews's attempt to maintain Mohawk in his Christian community in New York in response to indigenous demand might seem a prudent goal for mission outreach, Building a bulwark of religious knowledge and experience around the use of native languages could also subvert the trade and legislative interests of a burgeoning colony that ultimately relied on a model of community assimilation. As Puritan missionaries were increasingly relegated to the margins of the British world, ministers such as Experience Mayhew made unprecedented achievements mastering native languages despite the Crown's efforts to impose uniform English-language instruction.[8] In contrast to the SPG's program for linguistic conformity, the Wampanoag world view seeped through the pages of Mayhew's *Indian Converts* (1727), showcasing a local, Christian community on Martha's Vineyard that was at least partially at odds with the British imperial one. If language comprehension engendered the fantasy of seamless communication, it also heightened an awareness for and, in many cases, an acceptance of cultural difference. Rale recounts numerous instances of this: "what we understand by the word *Christianity* is known among the Savages only by the name of *Prayer*."[9] Indigenous language philosophers taught Rale, Gravier, Experience Mayhew, and Josiah Cotton the relativity and aesthetic value of North American tongues. Indigenous language epistemology persistently undermined the imperial script that each European power was at pains to inscribe upon the land and its inhabitants. Across a broad range of colonial indigenous language encounters, including Anglo-Wampanoag and Mohawk as well as Franco-Abenaki and Miami-Illinois, language remained elusive, multivalent, and locally resistant to any one formula of theological or national indoctrination.

Colonial Conflict and the Cauldron of Divine Wrath

In the decades following King Philip's War (Metacomet's Rebellion) (1675–1676), the English had good reason to fear the French and Indian alliance, for such alliances thrived as an integral component of France's survival in North America.[10] Boston alone had more than half of New France's entire population.[11] Primarily missionary communities or fur trading networks, French colonial outposts were not nearly as politically articulate or as communicative with their home government as the English. Meanwhile, by the end of the seventeenth century, with the consolidation of power under Louis XIV, France had become the strongest nation in Europe.[12] Partly out of the necessity of New World survival and partly as an extension of centralized authority back home, missionaries in New France became increasingly attentive to their rapport with American Indians as an indispensible political component in securing, managing, and protecting the French Empire.

Pierre Joseph de la Chasse's *Relation inédite de la mort du P. Sebastien Rale, 1724*, memorialized Rale as a martyr who died in the service of God protecting the souls and bodies of his Abenaki proselytes. Vividly re-creating the scene on August 23, 1724, when eight hundred British and three hundred American Indian soldiers surrounded the village of Norridgewock, La Chasse describes Rale's heroic actions in ushering women and children toward a protected riverbank where the British could not find them. In an attempt to represent Rale as a type of Christ, La Chasse focuses on the sacrificial details of his fate. Following the crucifixion of his biblical predecessor, Rale's body, La Chasse emphasizes, was, quite literally, riddled with bullets, his scalp taken, and his skull crushed by multiple hatchet blows, his mouth and eyes filled with mud, and leg bones broken and mutilated. This particular form of inhumanity, La Chasse reports, can only be the work of the "Savage allies of the English." In the great apocalyptic battle between God and Satan, the "Savage allies" embody the most satanic earthly forms.[13] La Chasse's *Relation* works rhetorically to paint them as such so that Rale's saintly goodness appears illuminated by "divine majesty" in contrast. Rale is either a godly saint or a traitor to the British Crown.[14] This bifurcated configuration of God versus Satan, Protestantism versus Catholicism, docile Indian ally and demonic "savage," was integral to the colonial script used by French Jesuits and Puritan ministers alike in an attempt to write the history of North America in a light favorable to their cause.[15] Missions worked with varying degrees of success relative to the goal of the European power.

Written at a moment of intense escalation of colonial conflict that would contribute to Dummer's War, Cotton Mather's 1707 publication *Another Tongue Brought in, to Confess the Great Saviour of the World* attempted to revitalize the Puritan mission by ironically emulating Franco-Catholic success. *Another Tongue* proposes to facilitate the transmission of the "Christian Religion" by transcending the problem of linguistic diversity. The new tongue to which the pamphlet refers was Iroquois, the language of a confederacy of tribes residing in the land between New England and New France. The Iroquois divided New France and New England and consisted of a "Covenant Chain," or trading alliance, that linked the Mohawks to the Dutch of New York. Despite British efforts to secure an alliance through this trade network, the Iroquois favored a policy of strict neutrality. That neutrality prompted Britain and France to increase efforts to assert sovereignty over the Iroquois. British officials sought to impose political and religious unity in Iroquois territory, while the French fortified their trading posts.[16] By the time *Another Tongue* appeared, the French had already penetrated deep into Iroquois territory through intricately connected and highly efficient fur trading networks, giving them a decided advantage in the acquisition of Iroquois culture. Mather, for instance, notes the grave threat represented by the French knowledge of Iroquois and, thus, the greater appeal of their particular Christian message. He explains that the Jesuits have already "Penetrated so deep West-ward in our North-*America*, as to Address the *Iroquois* Indians, with some Instructions of that *Christianity* which has been debased and depraved by their commixed *Popery.*" Moreover, Mather asserts in his report, the Jesuits have composed a catechism "in that very *Language*" that is "full of Gross Things, which were to be Expected from the Men of their

Intentions."[17] His solution was to counter the corrupting French influence with a Protestant catechism that fur traders could carry with them during their travels. He did so in hopes of providing native populations with a simple mnemonic device capable of countering the spread of Catholicism and its ritual heavy liturgy.

The dangers lurking on the northeastern borderlands were clear. The Jesuits had made significant advances into the territory, learned the language, and developed an evangelizing tool that communicated their version of the Christian message effectively. Without ministers in the region, without a working knowledge of the native tongue, and without a system of proselytization reducible to the formulation of a clear, concise Christian message, Mather feared that the Protestant cause was all but shut out in vast areas of the New World. In an ironic confluence of missionary strategy, Mather's catechism emulates Catholic catechistical texts. Questions are succinct; words and concepts are easy to remember. This is not a catechism that would work within the rubric of a standard Puritan approach to conversion where the transformation of the soul depended on an independent relationship to God. Rather, in the interest of creating a Protestant model that could compete against Catholic catechisms among the western Iroquois, particularly in the absence of a real mission presence, Mather fashioned a Catholic evangelical tool to mirror the success that he perceived on the other side of the theological divide. In a war-ravaged Northeast, the need to convert the Iroquois to Protestantism was a necessary strategy, not only in the allegorical "battle of the Antichrist" but also in the political battles fomenting between the two European powers. The fight for American Indian souls became an integral component of military strategy at this time, especially because conversion secured alliances. The previous generations' theological dichotomy of separating American Indians was now transformed into the more pragmatic distinction of mortal enemies and protective friends. The frontier became a space of dynamic and often violent cultural clashes and interactions based more on political rather than religious exigencies. Religion was left to align itself with the political as a necessary means of securing safe zones for missionary operations and less formal modes of evangelizing.

The son of the famous Northampton minister Solomon Stoddard and maternal uncle of Jonathan Edwards, John Stoddard commanded Deerfield's militia, formed to repel French and Indian raids, such as the one that nearly decimated the community in 1704.[18] Solomon Stoddard thus had vivid, firsthand exposure to the topic of his 1723 jeremiad, *Whether God is not Angry with the Country for doing so little towards the Conversion of the Indians?* In a fashion typical of the genre, Stoddard folds the "expensive, and bloody" wars that have left "many Towns desolate" into God's providential design. Since "*Philips* Wars," Stoddard recaps, the Indians have joined increasingly with the French as a perpetual scourge to English villages. Sometimes, he explains, "by the *Punishment*...Men may learn the Sin." In this case, he argues, if the Indians have been converted into agents of death, it is because we "have not done our duty to them." Although there was no Old Testament precedent for Jewish conversion of the Gentiles by the Jews, which was the typological model that the Puritans used to structure their relation to American Indian conversion, the times, according to Stoddard, had changed. Now it is the duty of the ministers "to Teach all Nations."[19] Language was the key not only to salvation but also to empire.

Stoddard begins with a simple humanitarian aim: "It is very great kindness to help Men to Heaven." This humanitarian aim was a rhetorical ploy designed to exacerbate the sense of shame that Stoddard intends to evoke in his audience in the ensuing section. "*The Examples of Others*," he states, "*may make us Ashamed*." The English, Germans, and Danes, he explains, have had great success in the East Indies, where the Bible has been printed in the local language and "the People that have been in Darkness, have seen great Light."[20] The passage confirms Stoddard's awareness of the activities of the Society for the Propagation of Christian Knowledge (SPCK), under whose auspice in the early 1700s Anglican ministers were being trained in Germany and then sent to the East Indies. They built churches and preached in either Malabarick or Portuguese. By 1710, there were 160 converts and 2 charity schools in India. The ministers involved persisted in their efforts to learn the local language and translate the New Testament into Malabarick and Portuguese.

By the early eighteenth century, British missionary efforts and linguistic training in the East Indies had surpassed such activity in North America, even though those missions began at a later date. The SPCK strongly backed translation efforts in the East Indies, while dismissing the necessity for Christian translation in North America. Native words were valued differently in each place. With regard to the New England missions, the SPCK exhorted that

English-language instruction was the best method of "conveying divine Truths," for the "native Language is barren of all polite Expression."[21] Ministers in the East Indies received the opposite message, as the Society invested money for the printing of the New Testament in multiple East Asian vernaculars.[22]

Stoddard's sermon conveys the peripheral place of New England within the British imperial imaginary. As Britain became increasingly a global empire through the efforts of the East India Company, North America became relegated to the status of just another colonial outpost among many.[23] Clinging to religion as the means to counter this peripheral status, Stoddard imagined augmenting missionary efforts in order to gather more bodies and convert more souls to British allegiance. Against the backdrop of their own anxieties surrounding the shortcomings of the Protestant mission in North America, the Puritans bore witness to the Catholic threat embodied in the guise of pagan savagery. The Abenaki frontier where the Jesuits had worked to build religious and political alliances with the Abenaki epitomized the threat, particularly because the British were constantly on the brink of violent disagreement with the Abenaki nation. The Jesuit alliances paved the way for the backing of the French state, which only compounded the Abenaki threat by escalating it the level of national and political animus.[24]

The *Relations des jésuites* (1632–1672) and *Lettres édifiantes et curieuses* (1702–1776) composed during the reign of Louis XIV reflect the integral role that the missionary enterprises played in helping to secure Louis XIV's imperial vision.[25] Covering China, the Middle East, and India, the *Lettres édifiantes* differ from the *Relations*, which primarily concern New France. For the Jesuits in North America, missionary reports to the Crown or to Rome had to compete with a worldwide network of missionary activity. Through this network, France began a serious scholarly engagement with the Ottoman world, India and China. As Britain and France each consolidated their colonial powers in these areas, European orientalism underwent a philosophical renaissance with articles published on Hebrew, Syriac, Arabic, Persian, and Turkish in the *Journal des Scavans* and the *Philosophical Transactions of the Royal Society*. French intellectual culture looked to primitive eastern Christian churches as Counter-Reformation evidence against the Protestant accusation that certain Catholic doctrine was a medieval invention. The linguistic and proselytizing work coming out of New France entered into the milieu of this intellectual debate about the status of these languages in the history of biblical criticism but without contributing oriental manuscripts to the Bibliothèque du Roi for Louis XIV's national project.[26]

Published in 1691 and attributed to Christian Le Clercq, *The Premier establissement de la foy dans la Nouvelle France* may be read as one attempt to contribute missionary discoveries in North America to the culture of orientalism in Louis XIV's court.[27] The *Premier establissement* is a retrospective account of Canadian history, from the colony founded by Champlain through the Recollet and Franciscan fathers to Father Christian Le Clercq's work on the coast of Gaspé, beginning with his 1673 arrival. The text recounts Le Clercq's attempt to learn the Mi'kmaq language by studying the "hieroglyphs" that "are still in use among the Micmacs."[28] These hieroglyphs may have been loosely based on Nova Scotian petroglyphs, but they are also presumed to be Le Clercq's creative adaptation of an indigenous sign system for catechistical purposes.[29] Written in a retrospective mode while recounting the glories of France's contemporary conquests—including Jacques Marquette and Louis Jolliet's exploration of the Mississippi Valley alongside Le Clercq's missionary success in the Gaspé—*the Premier establissement* details the imperial landscape of Louis XIV's vision for French ownership of the Ohio Valley. Le Clercq's hieroglyphs may well have been an attempt to fuel the king's orientalist desire for primitive signs of Christianity, offering "sufficient evidence to make us conjecture…that these people have not been wholly deaf to the voice of the apostles."[30] Wielding the key to this hieroglyphic knowledge, Le Clercq positions himself within the text as an agent of Louis XIV's imperial vision. His missionary success promises the permanent residue of Franco-Christianity in Nova Scotia and of M'ikmaq allegiance to the French Crown.

A sizable portion of Louis XIV's military power derived from his missionaries' rapport with American Indian tribes. Several installments of the monthly and annual *Relations* and *Lettres* written between the War of the League of Augsburg (1688–1697) and the War of Spanish Succession (1701–1714) frame colonial conflict as a transatlantic analog to the events on the continent. *Jesuit Relations* and *Lettres* also draw increased attention to the military potential of indigenous populations. A teacher of theology at the Jesuit College in Quebec and superior of the Canadian missionaries, Father Joseph Germain's letters establish a clear link between the Iroquois missions of his order, linguistic knowledge, and the politics of imperial conflict. He organized his Iroquois missions in accordance with the perceived threat the British posed to the south of New France.[31] A 1711 letter reports of a "well founded" "rumor," garnered from indigenous informants, that Britain was preparing a great naval expedition for the purpose of taking Canada. Germain reports on the geography of the North American colonies, describing the position of the five Iroquois nations between southern New England colonies and northern New France. Describing the power of the Iroquois alliance, Germain explains that they sided with the British. Britain assembled a fleet of twelve ships, "well loaded with munitions of all kinds and with troops inured to war." Joining with another fleet from Boston, the naval expedition alone consisted of eighty ships. Germain conveys the immediate problem that the British pose for the French militarily: "The English colony is, beyond comparison, more populous than the French." Yet, Germain continues, despite the odds stacked against them, the governor of Canada, Marquis de Vaudreuil, took the precaution of increasing French forces by gathering more than twelve hundred American Indians, allies carefully cultivated by French Jesuits living among them. Around rural settler communities near Quebec, stockades were erected to protect livestock, women, and children. Despite the odds, the British were defeated.

The Theological Possibility of Indigenous Words

When Rale first arrived in Acadia in 1690, he encountered a population already accustomed to the Jesuit presence. Beginning in the early seventeenth century, around 1611, black-robed priests arrived in native villages in canoes. They sought to discredit Abenaki shamanic beliefs, but were otherwise perceived as peaceful and sincere and, on those grounds, were accepted into the community. The Wabanaki, the local tribe among the eastern Abenaki to whom Rale primarily ministered, were familiar with Christianity from Father Gabriel Druillettes's mission in the 1650s. The Abenaki alliance formed midcentury gave the Wabanaki exposure to Christian natives throughout the St. Lawrence Valley, which intensified their exposure. Although no Jesuit priest lived among the Wabanaki from Druillettes's tenure in the 1650s through Rale's arrival in the early 1690s, the Wabanaki continued to practice the forms of worship that they had learned from Druillettes, adapted to their traditional belief system.

The Wabanaki saw Christianity as a potential solution to a period of social unrest between 1640 and 1670 that caused traditional faith in shamans and other spiritual leaders to ebb. Jesuits offered remedies for what they perceived as the limits of the shamans' capacity to heal post-contact phenomena such as illness. The communal acceptance of Christianity, however, did not necessitate the decline of Wabanaki belief systems. The resurgence of belief prompted by Jesuit teachings seemingly revitalized Wabanaki belief systems, leading to the creative adaptation of post-contact life. In this way, Wabanaki Catholicism proved a syncretic system that ultimately deepened their ancient religious life.[32] Throughout the seventeenth century, mission chapels became a fixture of native towns. Christianity was grafted onto Abenaki religious belief, and so the two spirit worlds coexisted.[33] The linguistic expertise acquired by third-generation Jesuits made this syncretic mission culture possible.

In Norridgewock, Rale encountered a language that seemed to have the capacity to overcome the representational limits of words. He gleaned this insight at the same moment that European linguistics became consumed with the constructed nature of words and their limitations—not simply to reveal divine truths but even to adequately reconstruct human history. Part of Rale's fascination with Abenaki was as a language that bore no trace of this representational trauma and that seemed syntactically adept at displaying a more intimate link between word and spirit.

Contrasting Abenaki expression favorably to the French, Rale admires the power of concrete injunctions rather than speculations. Translated Abenaki phrases mimic the style of a biblical command: "let them know me, let them love me, let them honor me." This list of injunctions inverts the subject and object, as if the Great Spirit answered the question rather than the believer. Through this inversion, the responses condense the distance between religious subject and the Great Spirit much more thoroughly than in the European rejoinder. The European manner of speech reinforces the division between the natural and the divine. Additionally, the European rejoinders remain bound within the limits of human knowledge. Creation serves the purpose of faith, the aspiration to know and to love. The Wabanaki manner of expression, by contrast, surpasses human limits to conjecture on what the Great Spirit communicates as the purpose of creation. Rale does not quote the Wabanaki language in this letter but many of the phrases recorded in his *Abenaki Dictionary* echo this expressive power through compound words and what may well have been Rale's likely awareness of the forceful nature of animate verbs.

For the verb *connoitre* (the seventeenth-century form of the word *connaitre*, "to know"), for example, "Je le fais connoitre" is translated as one declarative word *nesesiharan*. According to Henry Lorne Masta, a nineteenth-century Abenaki chief who wrote a grammar in order to ensure the continued cultural transmission of Abenaki children, transitive Abenaki verbs are either "strong" or "weak" depending on whether they refer to an animate or inanimate object.[34] The expression "Let them know me" would, in this way, have taken the strong conjugation of the Abenaki verb, "to know." Verb and object are conjoined within the recorded word. Additionally, in Rale's French encapsulation of Abenaki expression, the Wabanaki speaker translates the individual voice into a collective one, implying a communal rather than singular religious identity. The compound word registers an integral link between the communal knowledge and the subject of worship. The phrase "loving him" or *l'aimer*, as written in the Jesuit letter, appears in the *Dictionary* through several iterations of the conjugated noun and direct object: *nem8ssantzin, nem8ssanran, nem8ssantzitehanman*. The latter two recorded instances of the verb "to love" appear to be strong verbs, attached to an animate object.[35] Compound Wabanaki verbs convey power by taking on the object's animacy and collapsing the distance between the verb and object. In the case of Rale's recorded phrase, object and subject are also interchangeable. The expressive force that Rale finds in the phrases "Let them know me, let them love me" comes from the communal voice that appears to be answering the questions and from the Wabanaki method of suturing speaker to object and syntactically linking verb and object. "Believer," "act of faith," and "Great Spirit" are linguistically coextensive in an interchangeable space. Through this knitting together of subject, verb, and object, Rale discerns the "real beauties" of "the language of the Savages." Individual believer, communal ritual worship, and the Great Spirit conjoin in one synthetic whole. Knowledge of the divine is thus imminent in language as it is in nature and in creation. The divine exists within the spoken word; it is not partially and fragmentarily revealed through the word as seventeenth-century Christians believed. At the level of syntax itself, Abenaki connotes a more permeable boundary between the human and the divine.

Despite its antipathy to Christian doctrine, the continuity of natural and divine order in the Abenaki cosmos seems to have a certain allure to Rale. Given the stark separation between these realms within the Jesuit cosmology, and the difficulty of withstanding the world of the living for the promise of the invisible world to come, it is not difficult to imagine why. Rale lived according to the Society of Jesus's doctrine. His ascetic existence, far away from the comforts of his homeland, the ongoing warfare, and harsh conditions of survival in southern Maine were sufferings necessitated by his faith in Jesus. Following the dictates of St. Ignatius of Loyola's *Directorium exercitiorum spiritualium* (1522–1524) (Spiritual Exercises), Rale's New World journey was an allegorical preparation for the journey of his soul in the afterlife. Suffering weaned earthly affections. Self-devotion was Rale's ongoing reminder of the difficulty of entrance into the eternal life to come. Such entrance was hard won, requiring retreat, devotion, service, and trial. Following this template, Rale relinquished all comforts and safety to live the life of a martyr.

In light of this arduous path to eternal life, the expressive manner of Wabanaki speech, refashioned to convey Christian truths, offered a refreshing degree of spiritual security by conveying a sense of providential fulfillment. Rale interpreted the syncretic words of the Christian Wabanaki as echoes of an idealized link between humans and the divine spirit. Reveling in the expressive power of the indigenous Christian voice, he quotes the sacrament sung at the beginning of Mass in Abenaki, Huron, and Illinois. The actual meaning of the words spoken is unimportant; what matters is their formal significance. Spoken at Mass, the words consecrate the Host. The ritually chanted phrase enacts transubstantiation, such that the bread becomes Christ's body. By quoting the different phrases used to this end in sacramental practice among the Abenaki, Illinois, and Huron, Rale draws an analogy between the Catholic belief in transubstantiation and indigenous syntactical expression. In the moment of communion, the bread becomes the body of Christ. The separation between matter and spirit collapses within a moment of ritual worship, just as it does repeatedly through Algonquian syntax, designed to describe the permeable borders between matter and spirit, animate and inanimate objects. The very practices of translation that permitted the Wabanaki to conjoin Christianity to their traditional belief system appeared to Rale as an idealized form of faith.

The Illinois mission served as a training ground for Rale, for he spent time there before Frontenac called him to the Kennebec Valley. Rale's colleague, Gravier, grew this mission to a sustainable state after

several less than successful attempts. His linguistic knowledge sublimated admiration for Illinois cosmology, and his value to the French
imperial endeavors was commensurate to Rale's. The Illinois be-
longed to the eastern Great Lakes group of Algonquian. Therefore,
when the Jesuits pushed into the Great Lakes region in the 1660s,
they encountered a native population speaking a language for which
they had reasonable familiarity.[36] Claude Allouez is thought to have
produced the first manuscript in Miami-Illinois, a prayer book that
Jacques Marquette carried with him on his travels.[37] Settling into
residence among the Illinois tribes in 1689, Gravier vowed to continue the mission begun by Allouez and Marquette nearly two decades prior to his arrival.[38] Despite the various forms of "corruption"
that he found among the Illinois, their pervasive refusal to let him
baptize their children, and the rampant presence of shamans, which
he disparaged as "jugglers," within the community, Gravier reports
success as early as 1694: "My sins and the malice of men have not
prevented God from pouring down abundant blessings on this mission of the Illinois. It has been augmented by two hundred and six
souls whom I baptized between the 30th of March and 29th of
November, 1693."[39]

Despite the numerous challenges, Gravier's mission soon settled
into a routinized pattern of ritual practice. Whether he was there or
not, Gravier reports, the Illinois meet morning and night to pray to
God in their Chapel. So "much less barbarous" do the Illinois seem
compared to "other Savages," that Gravier soon comes to rely on native
spiritual leaders to instill and maintain Christianity within the community.[40] Gravier maintained a malleable position on the role that traditional Illinois beliefs might play in new forms of Christian worship.
On the one hand, he criticized chiefs and jugglers who "strongly opposed the christian faith." On the other hand, he freely entertained the
presence of shamans "who nevertheless manifested a very zealous
desire that his people should honor and attend catechism twice a
week."[41] This malleability evolved through Gravier's linguistic exchanges, which revealed to him the spiritual potential of Illinois words
and engendered a culture of exemplarity among Christian Illinois.

Gravier occasionally used young Illinois women as exemplary
saints or martyrs. One young Illinois girl defied her family by refusing to marry. To signify her celibacy and devotion to Christ, she wore
a girdle of thorns.[42] Elsewhere, Gravier reports on a young Christian
Iroquois woman named Marguerite who, along with her one-year-old

baby, was captured by non-Christian Iroquois and brutally tortured "while she uttered not a groan." Her thoughts of heaven and prayers to God grew stronger as she was "tied to the stake" while heated irons were applied to her body. A cry from a spectator that "Christians could not be killed" as "they were *only* spirits" intensified the efforts of the torturers, burning the woman's flesh away and stabbing her in the stomach with a bayonet. Ultimately, she died a martyr, proving the resolute faith of the godly Christians. Her young child, whom the Iroquois were not "barbarous enough to burn" cried for his mother until they "broke his head" and the child's "soul soared with his mother's to Heaven," in a final act of redemption that Gravier interprets as far preferable to a "wicked" life "among the Infidels."[43]

Common to each of these instances of extreme female ascetic and pious devotion was an intensified version of faith that, from Gravier's perspective, emerged from the interwoven spiritual and material realms accessible through the Illinois words spoken by Christian Indians. Gravier expresses an attraction to this interrelation between matter and spirit in Illinois culture, just as his colleague Rale had for Abenaki culture. During the torture of Marguerite, the spectator's cry that Christians could not be killed because they were "only spirits" is revelatory given that in indigenous religions, spirits were considered "living things," just as were humans, animals, and plants. Rather than transcending the human through a purely metaphysical ontology, the "living spirit" in an indigenous cosmology was not simply another living thing, but rather one that exuded more power and thus could not be physically overpowered by humans.[44] The spectator's explanation for Marguerite's resilience implies a hierarchy of animate forms in which Christianity comes out stronger than many living things to be found in nature. By including this detail in his official report to the Society, Gravier highlights indigenous recognition of Christian spiritual authority, perhaps suggesting that it was a feeling of inferiority regarding this power hierarchy that incited such a brutal attack upon Marguerite. Gravier's reports contain several other incidents of what he perceives as a jumbled indigenous perception of material and spiritual domains: the toad with the poisonous fumes to ward off Christianity; Manitou taking the form of a bird, an ox, and a bear; serpent skins hung up with painted feathers; and a sacrificial dog.[45] At times Gravier embraced this dense connection between matter and spirit, seeming to view it as a means of augmenting his own proselytizing efforts. At other times, the connection became a perceived source and symbol of the failure of evangelization, particularly at those times when traditional Illinois beliefs appeared to be an obstacle to Christian conversion. The quandary that Gravier found himself in, whether to permit or quash the persistence of traditional Illinois belief reflects the growing awareness of the specter of syncretism among Jesuit priests, a suspicion Protestant ministers had long harbored to a greater degree.[46]

Rale and Gravier were born and educated in France and therefore connected to French letters. Their massive dictionary projects make sense in this context. *Le dictionnaire de l'Académie Françoise* (1694) is a momentous text culminating over fifty years of work within the l'Académie founded by Cardinal Richelieu in 1629 (officially in 1635). *Le dictionnaire* was a massive collaborative attempt to account for the evolution of the French language while also codifying grammar, pronunciation, and orthography. *Le dictionnaire* built upon the work of Claude Favre de Vaugelas, one of the founding members of l'Académie whose *Remarques sur la langue Françoise* (1647) contained lengthy observations on the French language and attempted to arrange in a precise order the pronunciation, morphology, conjugation of verbs, orthography, gender of nouns, and idiomatic expressions. Vaugelas devoted himself to identifying "le bon usage" of French based on the spoken language of noble Parisians.[47]

A royal project undertaken during the rule of Louis XIV to whom *Le dictionnaire* is dedicated, the text contains the approximately eighteen thousand words (significantly less than those in Gravier's *Dictionary*). Through lexicography, the text purports to describe the quotidian language of gentlemen. Terms of art and science are also included as well as archaic words no longer in use and neologisms, though the Academy specifically forbade the formation of new words. The purpose was to establish precisely good and poor uses of French, including orthography as well as the choice of words.[48] As Jonathan Swift remarked in his *Proposal for Correcting, Improving, and Ascertaining the English Tongue in a Letter to the Earl of Oxford* (1712), "the *French* for these last Fifty Years hath been polishing [their language] as much as it will bear."[49] Influenced by the French model, Swift's letter was one of the early texts advocating British efforts toward standardizing English through the British Academy, founded in 1712.

Although distinct endeavors, there are several important parallels between Franco-European and Franco-American lexicography. Like

Le dictionnaire de l'Académie françoise, Jesuit dictionaries were intended to record proper usage, as heard by the priests through their engagement with local indigenous speakers. There is thus a replication of the idea of correct speech as proceeding from the oral to the written form. Additionally, Jesuit dictionaries often highlight similar aspects of language, including orthography, good usage, the order of words, and grammars. Jesuits also created the dictionaries as part of a continually evolving project in which they would constantly add to or refine what had already been written. The biggest difference between the two projects was that the Jesuits had to manage what linguistic anthropologist Michael Silverstein calls "ethnographic lexicography," or the means by which the anthropological study of language involves the collapse of the signifier/signified relationship.[50] In the missionary settings of New France, this collapse of the representational value of words meant that these dictionaries bore the additional theological burden of managing the overlap between language and cosmology.

Gravier authored what is perhaps the largest Jesuit dictionary from this time period. Containing more than 25,000 entries over 580 pages, Gravier compiled his Miami-Illinois–French Dictionary across many years (see Fig. 4.1).[51] In addition to the lists of words, Gravier's *Dictionary* includes observations on grammar, customs, mores, and religious beliefs. The artifact has grown in prominence as one of the most significant early records of Miami-Illinois.[52] One of Gravier's innovations was to record the syntax of compound words by demonstrating the translation of an entire expression in one Illinois word. For instance, *kitatanacans8nihire* translates as "je te donne sure quoy te coucher." Additionally, Gravier marks the root of a word and then gives the variations. For instance, "*ata8e*" is the "racine qui marque la parole"; "*nitate8ata8e*" translates as "je parle plus bas"; *nic8ec8etata8e*, "j'essaye de parler"; *nitac8ata8e*, "je parle une langue etrangere." In highlighting this element of Illinois grammar, Gravier reveals not only his comprehension but also his admiration for the same syntactical element in Miami-Illinois that appealed to Rale in Abenaki: the collapsing of the object and verb into one compound word.

In tirelessly working on such an opus, Gravier aimed to attain colonial control through linguistic knowledge. Unlike Rale, Gravier did not enjoy the same level of intimacy with his Christian-Indian community. In contrast to Rale's refusal to leave Norridgewock,

Gravier made frequent trips to the New French territory of Louisiana during his tenure at the Illinois mission. His reports from these trips conveyed his commitment to extending the boundaries of the French Empire. In a letter to Jesuit missionary to the Mohawks' Father Jacques de Lamberville, dated 16 February 1701, Gravier composed a *Survey of New France*. From the confluence of the Ohio, Mississippi, and the Arkansas Rivers, through Fort Bilocchi and the Spaniards of Pensacola to the mouth of the Mississippi River, Gravier describes a landscape that is rife with disease and hardship, but nonetheless full of potential for imperial expansion for those with expertise on the territory.[53] Oscillating between such surveys of the territory in New France and detailed ethnographic accounts of the Illinois people, Gravier's reports reflect his dual commitments as devoted missionary and diplomatic agent within the French Empire. He collects indigenous remedies for curing the French of New World diseases and records the iconography of war among the native populations that he encounters throughout his travels: "there is one Calumet for Peace and one for war, and they are distinguished solely by the Color of the feathers that adorn them. Red is the sign of war."[54] Gravier's reports offered useful information for developing military strategy as well as reporting on the spread of Catholicism among the indigenous inhabitants of the New World.

Recorded Illinois words convey both a sense of the indigenous spirit world and the natural world of North America, conveying a kind of natural knowledge that would fascinate missionaries, naturalists, and writers for decades to come. The page from his dictionary featured here offers a list of Illinois words pertaining to the spirit world. "Manet8a" is translated as "esprit, Dieu, de la neige, medecine." An odd array of variant meanings, the word most closely approximates Manitou with Gravier's unique orthography that could mean snow, spirit, medical remedy, or God himself.[55] The word "medecine" indicates the high degree of power that the Illinois accorded the shamanic doctors within the community. The same word, "medicine," appears in Gravier's reports to the Society where he quotes a conversation between the Kaskaskia chief and his medicine men, arguing against tribal recognition of the Catholic God:

> After speaking of our medicines and of what our grandfathers and ancestors have taught us, has this man who has come from afar better medicines than we have, to make us adopt his customs? His Fables are

good only in his own country; we have ours, which do not make us die as his do.[56]

The exchange rejects this power on the ground that it is only appropriate in the country to which it belongs. The recorded dialogue calls into question whether such knowledge coming from afar and from a different country is in fact adaptable in Illinois country, particularly when the Illinois people are dying from the Jesuit presence.[57] The translation of Manitou as snow registers the Illinois belief in the personal Manitou animating an element within the natural world. Here Gravier exposes the confluence between spiritual and material worlds. Finally, Manitou can be either God in the Christian sense of a supreme God or a more minor spirit that exists within the Illinois cosmos as part of an integral and ongoing interaction with nature. The list beneath the word "Manet8a" contains multiple variations of the word, altered through prefixes and suffixes that convey a range of meanings: it is not God, it is God, divine, he calls himself a spirit, I am not God, a spirit, and so on. The length of the list of word variants pertaining to "Manet8a," the variation recorded within that list, and

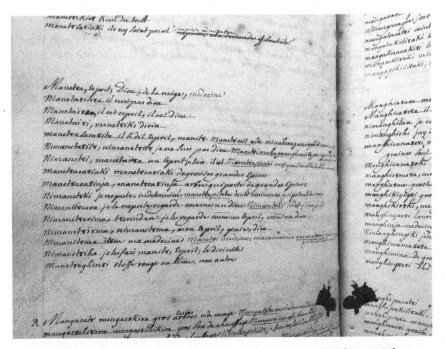

FIGURE 4.1. Jacques Gravier, *Kaskaskia-French Dictionary*, Watkinson Library, Trinity College, Hartford, *Conn.*

their constantly fluctuating meaning bespeak a linguistic world that represents a fluid cosmology. Word ending denotes an animate or inanimate quality to the noun. The word itself conveys the presence or absence of the spirit. The dictionary serves its purpose as the instrument of empire, recording the linguistic knowledge necessary to communicate with as well as convert the local Illinois population, the "Mase8tea," as Gravier identifies the Illinois people. Yet the precision and breadth of the recorded words also undermine this purpose, as the words themselves salvage and carry into Jesuit consciousness indelible aspects of an indigenous cosmology that would remain a part of Illinois Christianity. The enhanced understanding of the proximity between linguistic and spirit worlds led Jesuit priests to realize that the very act of translation itself folded traditional indigenous belief into a Christian frame. The better the linguist, the more apparent the interwoven world of word and spirit became.

Anglo-American Religious Conformity and Indigenous Communities of Resistance

Though the British had a long history of recognizing aboriginal land rights, during the Treaty of Utrecht (1713), the Mi'kmaq and Abenaki tribes were presumed part of the property exchanged and were denied a voice.[58] From a European perspective, conquest was primarily a question of sovereignty.[59] The Treaty of Utrecht that ended the War of Spanish Succession "yielded" the "Dominion, property, & possession" of Nova Scotia, formerly belonging to the "Crown of France" to "the Queen of Great Brittain & to her Crown forever." Dominion included "Islands[,] land[,] and places and the Inhabitants."[60]

While neither as assiduous in their endeavors nor as successful in their results, Anglo-Protestants also believed that the spread of the gospel among North America's native inhabitants would be advantageous to their imperial interests. Foreseeing this need for a cohesive religio-national identity abroad as well as at home, King William III founded the Society for the Propagation of the Gospel in Foreign Parts (SPG) in 1701. The Society exported missionaries, interpreters, and schoolteachers to North America. Their aim was to "instruct [the Indians] in the true Religion, and confirm them in their Duty to Her Majesty."[61] Protestant conversion was a tool for ensuring loyalty to the British Crown and winning indigenous souls away from French

Catholicism. After the 1707 Act of Union that formally linked Scotland, England, and Wales, Protestant identity was perceived as one of the primary facets of shared culture that drew disparate peoples together and united them under one God.[62] As Minister Thomas Barclay urged in his 1711 letter to the Society: "I hope the Society will send missionaries that have zeal and courage, for the French Indians are become very bold & commit bloody murders."[63] French priests directed their linguistic knowledge toward the transformation of the ritual space of worship into hymns sung and catechisms recited in indigenous tongues. The largely Anglican Society, by contrast, promoted the gospel through the religious word written in English. Large numbers of prayer books and catechisms were distributed throughout New York in the hope of teaching the "young People to understand *English*."[64]

In 1710, Peter Schulyer, first governor of Albany, sailed to England with five Mohawk sachems. He hoped to make a strong impression on the British Crown in order to strengthen the Anglo alliance with the Iroquois. One sachem died en route. The remaining four were outfitted by a theatrical dressmaker upon their arrival in London and presented to Queen Anne as foreign ambassadors. The leader, Thoyanoguen, was presented to the queen as the emperor of the Mohawks. These sachems were brought around the sites of London. Their visit was made famous and immortalized in a series of paintings by the Dutch artist Jan Verelst, who captured the odd attire fashioned for them by a London dressmaker. The Mohawk sachem made no small impression on the queen. The royal audience led her to send missionaries to the Iroquois. As "Frontier Nations" bordering the fledgling New York colony and the French settlement in Quebec, the Iroquois warranted the Society's particular attention on two counts: civil and religious. Protestant conversion was seen as a means of "prevent[ing] the Influence of the French Missionaries among them, (and thereby more effectively to secure their Fidelity)."[65] The difficulty was in finding missionaries prepared to take on such a task, missionaries who had adequate language skills to communicate with this indigenous population and the fortitude to live under purportedly harsh wilderness conditions.[66]

As we have seen, William Andrews stepped into this role in 1712, taking on the position of new missionary to the Iroquois. His letters, written regularly to the SPG during the relatively short duration of his tenure (1712–1718), reflect the Anglican emphasis on education as

a prerequisite for conversion. In the first letter written back to the
Society after his arrival at the Mohawk Castle (the term used for the
Mohawk village near the St. Lawrence River in upstate New York),
Andrews writes of his determination to teach the Mohawks to read
and write and asks the Society's preference as to whether they would
prefer that the children were taught in English or Mohawk. He
does, however, recommend "keep[ing] them to their own Language,"
for he observes that the Mohawk who learn English and Dutch are
prone to corruption—including "Swearing & prophane Discourse"—
through interactions with traders and soldiers.

Andrews built upon his own cursory knowledge of Mohawk by
working with an interpreter, Lawrence Claessen, to translate the
prayer book into Mohawk. Claessen was a Dutchman who had been
captured by the French-allied Iroquois in 1690 during a raid on
Schnectady. He was raised among the Caughnawagas for ten years.[67]
Andrews assessment of the superiority of Claessen's linguistic skills
is reflected in a number of his letters. Initially, Andrews mistook
Mohawk for a language that was entirely different from other
Iroquois nations, reporting that it was "most difficult to be learnt."
Typical of other disparaging remarks about indigenous languages at
the time, Andrews's grievance focuses on the length of the words.
Additionally, he seems to understand something of the aural quality
of the language when he explains that "understanding" had to be
"supplyed" by the "hearer." This was due to the "Narrowness" of
Mohawk, "imperfect" as it was in "Adverbs[,] conjunctions[,] inter-
jections."[68] In contrast to Rale, who after spending decades among
the Abenaki learned to hear beauty in their words, Andrews fixates
on the language's deficiencies.

Yet with the help of a manuscript compiled by his predecessor
among the Mohawk, Bernardus Freeman, and Claessen's efforts as
interpreter, Andrews made remarkable strides as a translator.[69] He
produced a Mohawk edition of the Lord's Prayer and the Apostles'
Creed shortly after arriving and then printed an entire prayer book
within three years. Most of his work was a compilation of the efforts
of Bernardus Freeman, the first Protestant to learn Mohawk and to
transcribe it into the roman alphabet.[70] By the time Andrews arrived, Freeman had already translated the Liturgy of the Church of
England, the Gospel of Matthew, several chapters of Genesis and
Exodus, several psalms, part of 1 Corinthians, and an explication of
the Ten Commandments. Freeman implies that he did this in order

to rewire the theological connections that the French Jesuits had already made among the Iroquois. He explains to the SPG that his translations accord with the "order of the Dutch Church," also included is "a short system of theology in which I take notice of the Errors of the Church of Rome, this I did because of the Errors the Jesuits had initiated them in."[71] He felt that the translation of Christian truths into Mohawk via the correct theological idiom was crucial to the difficult task of winning native souls in this imperial borderland.

The Morning and Evening Prayer, containing litany, church catechism, and family prayers, along with several chapters of the Old and New Testaments, was printed in New York in 1715. Entirely in Mohawk with the exception of English titles to guide the missionary toward the appropriate litany or prayer, the text is a remarkable record of the Mohawk language in the early eighteenth century. In his letters back to the SPG, Andrews emphasized that he did take care in communicating the Society's evangelizing instructions. He explained that he has translated the "manuscript copy of prayers" verbatim but that he also added "some other prayers & sentences of scripture, which we thought would be very useful for the Indians morning and Evening family prayers." Some changes had to be made to accommodate the language. For example, "the family prayers are abridged because they would have been too long for the Indians in their own Language." This explanation suggests that Andrews adapted the translation slightly for ease of use in Mohawk, to make the prayers easier to say and to remember in his proselytes' native tongue.[72]

Eager to prove the success of his mission, Andrews's letters were often accompanied by lists of baptized Indians. The lists include the Christian name of the baptized Mohawk, age, and date.[73] He emphasized the conversion of children, seizing upon their facility for learning to read and write in Mohawk and also on their desire to attend school in order to receive the "victuals" that Andrews would readily supply them with.[74] He sent translated texts back to London with the hope of garnering support for the educational portion of his mission: "I sent home the common prayer, the church catechism, several chapters and psalms in the Mohawk language to be presented if the Honorable Society approved of it."[75] Yet the SPG offered little in the way of material support for this endeavor. Despite his repeated recommendation that the Mohawk retain their native language, the SPG encouraged English instruction. Andrews repeatedly reports back on his dismal attempts to teach the Mohawk English: "I have prevailed with the parents of three or four boys to let them learn English. Two of them I have taken into my house."[76] His successes toward this end were few and far between. Perhaps due to the SPG's lack of support for a Mohawk library, Andrews printed his *Morning and Evening Prayer Book* in New York. Since the SPG's inception, numerous English texts had already been sent across the Atlantic for evangelizing purposes.[77] The organization was reluctant to open up another book market for Indian language texts.

Despite the SPG's encouragement, efforts toward English-language instruction proved futile, as Andrews complained in a letter to the SPG written four years after his arrival at Mohawk Castle:

> Sir I received yours about ten days since dated October 19th last, whereby I understand the Honorable Society would have the Catechism & a Vocabulary of English and Indian printed for the use of the Indian Children to learn English, but they are utterly averse to the Learning any other Language but their owne.[78]

While Andrews encouraged Mohawk as the lingua franca of his mission in order to protect the natives from outside corrupting influences, he had little choice. The Mohawk community actively resisted English-language instruction. David Humphreys reported on this resistance to learning English, explaining that "since they could by no Means prevail on the *Indians* to learn *English*," the Society had to consent to having some portions of Scripture translated into Mohawk.[79] The English interpreted this resistance as a willful recalcitrance and a moral failing. Of Henry Barclay, missionary to the Mohawk in Albany, Humphreys reports, "He tried all Methods he could think of, to engage them to be instructed in our Language and Religion, but with very small Success." They would convert and then return to "Savage Life."[80] The SPG noted that Barclay had more success among peoples of African descent, without seeming to realize that many of the Christian Africans were slaves rather than members of a sovereign Indian nation and thus had less autonomy over themselves and their descendants.[81]

Missionaries and members of the SPG interpreted the Mohawk resistance to learning English by placing the Mohawk within a stunted phase of stadial history. The *Historical Account* compares the Mohawk unfavorably to "the once mighty Empires of *Mexico* and

Peru." In contrast to the "stately Cities and Towns" and "Arts of Government" that these civilizations excelled in, the "*Northern Americans* bordering on the *British* Colonies were utterly *Barbarian.*" Lacking "cities," "cultivated...Ground," and "Morality," these "small Tribes, wandred naked in vast Desarts and Woods, leading a Bestial Life, in perpetual Wars with each other." Similar to the romanticized theories of American antiquity, which speculated that a "race" other than the American Indians built the mounds in the western prairies of what is today Missouri, the SPG subordinated Mohawk civilization to what they believed to be the more advanced cultures of the Mexicans and Peruvians Indians. According to the *Historical Account*, the difference is as great as that between "the Hords of *Siberia* and *Tartary*" from the "Elegance and Civility of the *Southern* Nations of *Europe.*"[82] By attributing the refusal to learn English as a sign of obstinate savagery, the Society refused to see the Mohawk actions as conscientious resistance to the Anglo-Protestant colonizing program.

The Mohawk's staunch refusal to have their children instructed in English as a prerequisite for Christian conversion was a refusal to have their language and culture stamped out by the SPG's colonizing interests. Children could attend school, but they could not be treated harshly. They could receive "victuals" as an incentive for attending school, but they were to keep their own mother tongue. As Christianity was incorporated into the community, the Mohawks also worked to guard the integrity of their own culture. That they ultimately forced Andrews out of his missionary post also speaks to their resistance to SPG strategies of religious and cultural assimilation. After the Tuscaroras were pushed out of their native Virginia by Anglo settlers in 1713, they migrated north. Members of the immigrant tribe ended up in New York and warned the Oneida and Mohawks that they had been "most barbarously used, and drove out of their Country, and that the *English* watched only for an Opportunity to extirpate them too." At this point, the SPG efforts became ineffective in North America. Andrews reports that the Mohawk had "reverted" to hunting, refusing to settle and cultivate the land and raise cattle. His letters adopt a tone of despair and he asks that his mission be disbanded. Reluctant to do so based on his account alone, the SPG wrote Robert Hunter, the governor of New York, who corroborated the story, explaining that Andrews's efforts were "fruitless" in regard to that "miserable Race of Men."[83] While interpreted by the SPG as a sign of meanest savagery, the Mohawk by all accounts determined both the terms and the duration of this early Anglo-Protestant foray into their country.

Due to Mohawk insistence in Christian instruction in their mother tongue, *The Morning and Evening Prayer* (1715) stands as an enduring printed record of their language, despite the context of early SPG efforts at linguistic erasure. The Mohawk Prayer Book was reprinted in 1763, 1769, and then again in 1787 by Joseph Brant, the famed Mohawk preacher. Joseph Brant became a staunch convert to Anglicanism. A protégé of William Johnson, the British superintendent for American Indian Affairs, Brant fought strenuously for the British during the Seven Years War and received his education at Moor's Indian Charity School. An English speaker with a native fluency in the languages of the Six Nations, Brant translated the Gospel of Mark into Mohawk. It was the only complete book of the Bible available in the Mohawk tongue in the eighteenth century.

The Wampanoag Influence on American Protestantism

From their first settlement on the Vineyard in 1642, the Mayhew clan worked assiduously to learn Wampanoag for the purposes of communication and homiletic instruction. They set up schools in order to teach Wampanoag children how to read and write in their own mother tongue, and circulated such texts as the Indian Bible, the *New England Confession of Faith*, several catechisms, *The Practice of Piety*, Shepard's *Sincere Convert*, a popular Psalter, the Gospel of John, and Baxter's *Call to the Unconverted*. Although Experience Mayhew complained in his *Brief Account of the State of the Indians on Martha's Vineyard, 1694–1720* about the scant supply of Indian Bibles on the island, the record of Wampanoag Christianity on the Vineyard suggests an impressive record of literacy.[84] Reading and writing are repeated and powerful themes in the Indian biographies of the period.

As the fourth generation of a missionary lineage, Experience Mayhew maintained and improved upon his own linguistic expertise and the thriving culture of Wampanoag Christianity. His biography notes that "The *Indian Language* has been from his Infancy natural to him."[85] Commissioned to translate a new version of the Book of Psalms and the Gospel of John, Mayhew made these texts integral to the aural culture of Vineyard Christianity culture. These texts regulated spiritual services on the island, which consisted of "meet[ing] for the Worship of GOD twice a Day on the Sabbath," "Prayer," psalm-singing, and then sermon preaching. For each of the island villages, Mayhew appointed an Indian preacher to conduct the sermons in the event of his absence.[86] Because he had developed a fluency in childhood, he achieved a level of Wampanoag mastery that far exceeded that of his predecessors or his SPG contemporaries. The intergenerational lineage of missionary lives within the Mayhew clan bequeathed to Experience Mayhew an extraordinary level of cultural understanding and communal intimacy. With that linguistic and cultural intimacy, Mayhew recognized fundamental cultural differences that made the precise translation of particularly colonial Puritan theology difficult. Implicitly acknowledging these differences, hybrid forms of Christian worship appear in *Indian Converts*, conveying the existence of an Indian community on Martha's Vineyard that had more in common with the Jesuit communities than the Anglican efforts at Mohawk Castle, which even then were tarred by the Mohawk perception of British imperial interests.

Mayhew's superior knowledge of Wampanoag garnered new linguistic insights that he recorded in the *Observations on the Indian Language* (1722). His later *Indian Converts*, a 1727 missionary tract intended to celebrate a typological triumph of Protestantism over Catholicism, also registers his awareness of language as a rich index of cultural difference. Both texts indicate how his superior linguistic knowledge permitted a greater incorporation of Wampanoag belief systems into standard Christian texts. As with the forms of syncretism and hybridity that we see in French Jesuit contexts where the duration of sustained contact is comparatively greater, Christianity in early eighteenth-century Martha's Vineyard was a blend of syncretic beliefs—a kind of nurtured island of Protestant heterodoxy—transmitted through a nuanced culture of language exchange.

In *Indian Converts* (1727), Mayhew aligns himself with Eliot's legacy. He makes the case in this tract that much mission work in Christian millennial history propagated the gospel among the "*uncultivated Souls*" of the New World's "*howling* Wilderness."[87] Testifying to this united front of Protestantism, the preface begins by underwriting the text with signatures from the most prominent ministers in Boston, not least among them Cotton Mather, Benjamin Colman, and Thomas Prince.[88] The witness of these ministers as to the legitimacy of the conversion experiences recorded therein places *Indian*

Converts within a long Puritan tradition of evangelizing success. By giving the text the characteristics of one of the Eliot tracts, Mayhew sanctions the tract as one of the most renowned in New England history. Following his association with a predecessor revered as much for his linguistic skill as his godly devotion, Mayhew leverages the authority of this tradition while departing from it.

In her introduction to *Indian Converts*, Laura Arnold Leibman describes Mayhew as "an odd mix of orthodoxy and innovation."[89] This "odd mix" consists of a contrast between an old-fashioned genre and a method of compilation that integrates indigenous narrative tradition and belief systems. Announcing the text as a "Historical Essay," Mayhew explains that "the Preaching of the Gospel to the *Aboriginal Natives* of this Land, has not been in vain," and that the essay stands as testimony of the continuation of a venerable ministerial tradition. Yet the author's preface also explains that the recorded narratives are comprised of oral, written, and printed accounts of Indian conversion left by his "Father, Grandfather, or others." Some of these "others," Mayhew tells us, include unnamed Indian preachers and lay ministers. All "oral Relations" come from "Persons worthy of Credit, whether *English* or *Indians*."[90] In *Indian Converts*, Mayhew creates a political and orthodox bridge that connects seventeenth-century Indian converts to eighteenth-century British imperial authority.

Disclosing the archival sources for his compilation as comprising a mixture of media forms, oral histories, private family writings, records preserved in both Wampanoag and English, and printed texts, Mayhew introduces *Indian Converts* as a hybrid text. He suggests that legitimate oral history exists as much within the English community as it does within the Indian community. He emphasizes the way in which stories and knowledge have been passed down from father to son for generations, gilding the Mayhew clan with Wampanoag gold. "Credit worthy" persons can, moreover, be found on either side of the cultural divide. Mayhew's disclosure that his archive is rooted in oral as well as written histories and composed by both Indian and English voices suggests a significant departure from the model set forth by John Eliot. "Worthy creditors" in the Eliot tracts are on the side of the ministerial elite who preface each tract with a statement about the document's authenticity. Additionally, Eliot drew a strict division between the practice of listening to oral testimonies of conversion and the work of transcribing them. In

Tears of Repentance (1653), for example, Eliot's most complete account of Natick conversion, the preface details the practice of listening and the attention paid to recording the spoken words as clearly as possible. Whereas the authenticity of the Eliot account depends on an explicit hierarchy between the oral and written work, Mayhew blurs the two such that they become almost indistinguishable. For Mayhew, the written word is not accorded the singular privilege that it is for Eliot.

Divided into "Ministers," "Men," "Women," and "Children," each section of Mayhew's *Indian Converts* comprises "examples" of faith among the Christian Wampanoag of Martha's Vineyard. Narrating the faith of Elizabeth Pattompan, a young woman who died at the age of seventeen in July 1710, Mayhew explains that "Some Days before she dy'd, she earnestly desired her Father to commit to writing, for the Benefit of her Relations, some things which she then uttered."[91] Her father, Josiah Pattompan, who was himself a professing Christian Indian, copied his daughter's dying words and presented them to Mayhew, who in turn published the dying girl's advice and observations in his missionary tract. The narrative included the daughter's exhortation that her father "*write these Words for the Use of my Brethren and Friends.*" Yet we also learn further on in the example that after having neglected to do so for some time after his daughter's death, Josiah witnessed her "Spectre." Confirming her appearance by familiar details—including the clothes that she often wore and, more intimately, even the visible appearance of the warts on her feet—Josiah identifies the apparition as his daughter and immediately sets out to "fulfil the Will of his Daughter, by committing her Words to Writing as she had desired him to do."[92]

Elizabeth's specter wields power in this scene not according to Protestant custom but according to the traditional Wampanoag belief in the "god of the dead," which was the most powerful spirit in Wampanoag visions and dreams.[93] Several aspects of this example stand out as remarkable: the inversion of a gender and age hierarchy that enables a young woman of seventeen to command her father to write, the appearance of an apparition as legitimate evidence of godliness in a Puritan conversion narrative, and the encomium on her godly behavior that Elizabeth pleads with her father to commit to writing. Perhaps most remarkable is the authority a dying young Wampanoag woman accords written word even on her deathbed. Elizabeth seems to have understood that this was the way to create a lasting record of her faith. Her agency and legacy draw upon her recognition of writing as the prescribed means of communicating Christian truths, while also depending on a more traditional Wampanoag belief in the afterlife and in the permeable boundary between visible and invisible.

Indian Converts contains multiple examples of the blurred boundary between the oral and the written, between the Christian valuation of the written word and the Wampanoag belief in the permeability of matter and spirit. Sarah Coomes, who died in Chilmark on March 10, 1723, just a few months before her seventh birthday, received instruction in "the things of God" from her mother and her grandmother. Mayhew reports that "when she asked her Grandmother to instruct her, she usually did it in these Words, *Kukkootammah Mannit;* that is, *Teach me God,* or instruct me concerning him."[94] *Mannit* (or *manit*) is the Wampanoag word for spiritual power. It connotes the traditional Wampanoag cosmology where the spirit flowed through topography, meteorology, and all the forms and elements of the natural world. In Wampanoag oral history, humans existed in a symbiotic relationship to manit. Mayhew's decision to first record Sarah's request for her grandmother's instruction in Wampanoag before translating it into English suggests the blurred distinction between these worlds. As a force present throughout all of nature, *manit* in the Wampanoag sense is different from God in the Christian sense. It refers to "he who (or that which) exceeds or passes beyond the common or normal, the preternatural or extraordinary." Kukkootammah (kuhkootamau) is a transitive, inanimate verb meaning "he points (it) out to, shows, makes known to."[95] That Sarah received this instruction from her Wampanoag grandmother reflects a telling inversion of the gender and racial hierarchies typically operative in recorded Puritan conversion narratives and deathbed confessions. This scene of instruction reflects a world in which knowledge passes from mother to daughter, for generations; it reflects a world in which women are as much the conduits of spiritual knowledge as men. Mayhew notes that as Sarah "increased in Knowledge," "she appeared to be more and more affected with a Sense of the Reality and the Importance of the Truths wherein she was instructed."[96]

While the narrative does not relate precisely what this "Sense of…Reality" consisted of, it is not a phenomenological state that one would typically find in Anglo-Puritan conversion narratives. In the

Puritan cosmos, "reality" resembled little more than the unchanging fallen world against which the faithful pinned their hopes for the afterlife. Sarah's "affecting" "Sense of…Reality" suggests a different experience. Her reality seems to change, perhaps with her own increasing awareness of the omnipresence and power of *manit* to permeate all aspects of the visible world around her. Her improved acquaintance with the nature of her own reality becomes a repeated theme in the text, not least through Mayhew's observation of her expanding awareness of "Truths," of "Belief," and "bare and naked Knowledge." He does not specify what this knowledge or belief consisted of and informs us that, while Sarah "could not her self express them, yet she firmly believed them."[97] Through this subtle affirmation of the godliness of Sarah's experience but ambiguity surrounding the precise definition of what this consists of, Mayhew allows for the coexistence of two entirely different cosmological worlds. Even as the framework of the text upholds the Eliot tradition by providing a "Historical Essay" from which the reader can bear witness to the "Fruit and Effect" of the "Preaching of the Gospel to the *Aboriginal Natives*," the contents of the examples themselves reveal a world of Wampanoag Christianity that departs significantly from prior missionary tracts.[98] This departure was the result of Mayhew's knowledge of Wampanoag, a language that he knew far better than his predecessors. While trying to integrate this knowledge into a Christian millennial frame, he also idealized certain aspects of the language, praising it for the poetic potential that he saw through his translation of the psalms. Both extolling its virtues and recognizing fundamental syntactical differences, Mayhew saw that in order to integrate the Wampanoag world, Puritan theology would have to become more elastic than it had traditionally been. Not only would a hybrid faith ingrain itself more firmly within the Martha's Vineyard community, it would also sustain and even improve the quality of religion itself.

Mayhew arrived at a realization comparable to Rale's as he recognized the poignancy of Wampanoag words. Given the nature of this particular work of translation, Mayhew began to contemplate the poetic potential of Wampanoag to convey Christian truths. As Cotton Mather says of the 1718 translation of the *Psalterium Americanum*, the psalms themselves convey a "rare part of the Christian *Asceticks*," of "the more Fine, Deep, and *Uncommon Thoughts*." The psalms, Mather tells us, "are *Golden Keys*, to the Immense Treasures of

Truth." Through them, the Reader begins to see "a Bright Light" and, expanding this reading experience to other parts of Scripture, can attain "a greater satisfaction of mind, than ever he had before." Important for accessing these higher Christian truths through the psalms was the work of translation, itself a poetic act, but one that did not merely "preserv[e] the *Clink* of the *Rhime*" but that rather elevated "those rich things, which the Holy SPIRIT of GOD speaks in the Original Hebrew."[99] In Mather's theory of translation, which he expounds at some length in the introduction to the *Psalterium Americanum*, poetry was a mere vessel for the spirit, a form through which the word of God could take shape. Working from the purity of this internal spiritual essence to the external vehicle of expression, the translation of the psalms emulated the Puritan semiotic of conversion that moved from the inward experience of assurance to the outward manifestation of the sanctified saint. As such, the functions of the psalms was to "dictate" a "method of *Singing*" "*filled with the Spirit*." The form of the sung psalm replicated the precision of the translation itself. In each case, Mather explains, "all True PIETY is begun by the Enkindling of these *Affections* in the Soul."[100] Correctly translated, the psalms ensure an enclosed circuit of ritual worship that moves from the "Holy Spirit of God" to the "Original Hebrew" to the "pure offering" of "blank verse" in his translation to the "enkindling" of the soul to the sung psalm that literally lifts the "hidden" scriptural "treasures" from the page.[101]

Although Mayhew completed his *Massachusetts Psalter* nine years before Mather's *Psalterium Americanum*, this logic of translation, the aesthetic importance accorded to making the word a vessel for the spirit, would not have escaped him. Mather's theory of psalms translation would have been all the more prescient because Mayhew was working with what was believed to be a language that was possibly as ancient as Hebrew and that conveyed a comparable sonic resonance. As Mayhew explains in his *Observations on the Indian Language*, "Indian words, especially, the names of persons and things, are generally very significant, by far more so than those of the English, as the Hebrew also are."[102] He imagines a resonance between nature and word that is common to both Wampanoag and Hebrew but less so in English. This observed connection of the closer relationship between word and nature in Wampanoag words would have taken on special meaning for him as he translated passages such as Psalm 1:3: "And he shall be like a tree planted by the rivers of water."[103]

Significantly, Jonathan Edwards bases his 1751 sermon to the Stockbridge Indians on this same passage, "Christ Is to the Heart Like a River to a Tree Planted By It." His doing so is just one example among many of the recycling of key spiritual and sermonic tropes in missionary texts. Yet the citation of Psalm 1:3 by both Mayhew and Edwards also indicates a recognition of certain aspects of Wampanoag and Mohican belief. A tree planted by a river figures prominently within the Mohican origins story. It is for this reason that Mayhew uses the same image to indicate the confluence between spirit and nature in Wampanoag belief.[104] The goal of the translated psalm was to capture this idea through the word, something that Mather tries to envision through blank verse and that Edwards and Mayhew do through their idealization of indigenous belief. Reflections on the aesthetic potential of Wampanoag follow from the Massachusetts Psalter. As Mayhew writes in his *Observations*, the Indian language is "good and regular" but that the "Termes of art are not yet fixed on."[105] Recognizing the particularities of aesthetic difference in Wampanoag, he hones in on the language's capacity to become a vessel for the truths of nature and of the spirit. He then incorporates into the millennial frame of *Indian Converts* hybrid forms of oral history, indigenous writing, as well as Wampanoag expressions that are both translated and untranslatable. Forms of Christian Wampanoag expression that he recorded in the text testify to the entrenchment of Protestantism in North American indigenous communities and to the effects of the colonial language encounter on the shifting landscape of Anglo-Protestant religious practices and genres.

Despite his celebrated mastery of Wampanoag, Experience's intimate knowledge of language did not necessarily translate into intellectual knowledge. Except for his *Observations on the Indian Language*, written at Paul Dudley's request, Mayhew wrote very little about the nature, grammar, or contents of Wampanoag. He announces in this letter to Dudley that "there is yet no good Gramer made for [the Indian language]," a remark that is at least implicitly dismissive of Eliot's *Indian Grammar Begun*.[106] And yet in contrast to Rale's and Gravier's work, Mayhew did little in his lifetime to produce a comprehensive study of the language. Fluency made him an exceptionally good missionary, but the transmission of his linguistic knowledge was never a priority, a feeling for the most part shared by his contemporaries and the British imperial network to which he was at least tangentially connected through his involvement in the

SPG. In many ways, the missionary community of Martha's Vineyard resembled those of Mayhew's Jesuit contemporaries: through the missionary idealization of Wampanoag, the facility of the *Massachusetts Psalter's* verse translation, and through the syncretic forms of Wampanoag Christianity incorporated into *Indian Converts* (1727). Yet because this linguistic knowledge was not valued within a broader network of imperial power as it was in the case of the Jesuits, Mayhew's language skills were not easily transferable into academic study nor was his ease of communication used to forge alliances during the wars.[107] Instead, *Indian Converts* combines Mayhew's attempt to uphold New England orthodoxies with the simultaneous challenge to those orthodoxies brought about through the translation of Christian truths into Wampanoag words.

This tension between the traditional Puritan genre of the missionary tract and the new forms of faith that surface in the narratives recorded in *Indian Converts* indicates the subtly shifting terrain of Protestant theology in colonial New England. As the descendant of a lineage of Congregational clergymen stretching back to the Bay Colony settlement, Mayhew came of age in a traditional Calvinist environment. During his missionary career, he saw tremendous theological change on the mainland. Solomon Stoddard ushered in what has long been seen as a more tolerant era of church membership by abandoning the testimony of faith as a prerequisite for communion. A series of "harvests" or mini-revivals took root throughout the Connecticut River Valley in the 1710s and 1720s, foreshadowing the transatlantic awakenings to come in the 1730s and 1740s.[108] By the early eighteenth century, it became apparent that Calvinism, as it had been practiced in New England for almost a century, would have to change to keep pace with the momentum of modernity. Harvard curriculum and ministerial training incorporated Lockean psychology and natural philosophy more fully than ever before, necessitating a change in previous theological conceptions of divine knowledge.[109] On the practical level of experiential Christianity, not even Jonathan Edwards's conservative reform of his grandfather's pulpit could stem the tide of the near arrival of Wesleyan and low-church evangelical "synergism"—the belief that the would-be convert works together with God to instigate the conversion process. On the broader economic and social levels, Boston, Philadelphia, New York, Charleston, and Newport experienced rapid urbanization beginning in the mid-eighteenth century, as public highways, wharves, and infrastructure were built to keep up with expanding populations. International trade brought unprecedented commercialism to the Atlantic seaboard cities.[110] As an island, Martha's Vineyard had the geographical advantage of at once positioning itself as isolated from these modernizing forces, the landscape of a spiritual refuge set against a tumultuous mainland, and as a beacon to the world, a new city on a hill that might set the religious tone for the next generation.

At least from Mayhew's perspective, Calvinism's response to modernity would have to take up the Indian question. This involved not only shifting the terrain of Protestant theology to find a way to accommodate Indian proselytes more effectively but also reimagining the Anglo-American Protestant relationship to the indigenous populations upon whose land Christian millennialism depended. The decline of the New England Way, traditionally conceived, left a gap in place of traditional ways of imagining the purpose on North American soil. If New England was not to be the spiritual model for the world, a way of reclaiming God for England, what were the Calvinists, whether Old Light or New Light, doing there? What purpose did the land serve in the fulfillment of providential design and biblical typology? Such questions had surfaced as early as the rise of the "Puritan" Commonwealth under Cromwell. But they had been renewed again and again, from the spiritual expediency that required the Halfway Covenant to King Philip's War to the Andros regime to the most significant epistemological crisis of colonial America, the Salem witchcraft trials. It was the culmination of all of these events, the ultimate disintegration of any coherent Puritan canopy in the wake of Salem that reinvigorated these questions with unprecedented force in the early eighteenth century.

With its 1727 publication date, smack in the middle of both Mayhew's career and the burgeoning theological crisis, *Indian Converts* attempted to answer these questions. Absorbing the lessons that Mayhew learned from his own indigenous language encounter, the work recasts the shifting framework of American Protestantism in a flexible frame. Rather than recognizing difference, the ability to accommodate the syncretic blend of traditional native beliefs and Catholicism that we see in the case of the Jesuits, Mayhew's *Indian Converts* embodies an assimilating impulse. This is not the SPG brand of assimilation, in which the Mohawk were to learn English, read *The Book of Common Prayer*, and practice the uniform faith of the Church of England. Such a model would never have worked in the Calvinist tradition, for New England theology was, at its core, schismatic. A dissenting religion lacking a clear formula for political or ecclesiastical hierarchy has to court orthodox conformity in order to ensure survival. Yet with each iteration, orthodoxy contained the seeds of its own undoing, for the rites of dissent composed the theological core of Puritan faith. It is, therefore, both a consequence of historical crisis and entirely predictable that *Indian Converts* fuses innovation with an orthodox form, for it is by that means that American Protestantism not only survived but also persisted in new forms. Mayhew's innovation was to align the oral history of his clan with that of the Wampanoag such that the two become one. The assimilating impulse of *Indian Converts* is based on reciprocity rather than conformity. The theology of revivalism to follow shortly on the heels of this work compounded this textual tendency of a theological identification between Anglo-Protestant America and its indigenous inhabitants. The Great Awakening recast America's origins and eschatological myth through the linguistic authority and power of the continent's original inhabitants. Increasingly, indigenous words were seen as repositories of an ancient prophetic wisdom of contemporary millennial unfolding.

The Nature of Indian Words in the Rise of Anglo-American Nativism

During his tenure as a missionary in Stockbridge (1751–1758), Jonathan Edwards often proved to be a good advocate for American Indian affairs. He urged the Massachusetts Assembly to honor land treaties to the Housatonnuks. He obtained indemnity money to pay a grieving family after one of its members was killed by two white settlers. He also wrote to the Boston commissioners to secure more blankets and food for his Indian scholars. By the standards of his day, Edwards was an able and committed advocate for Indian rights. Yet despite the sympathies for the plight of Indians in western Massachusetts and on the frontier, which he shared with his would-be son-in-law, David Brainerd, Edwards could be remarkably insensitive to indigenous cultures, an intolerance epitomized in his refusal to learn the language of the people he served.[1] In a letter to one of the mission's sponsors, Sir William Pepperrell, dated November 28, 1751, Edwards explained his reasons for this refusal: "Indian languages are extremely barbarous and barren, and very ill-fitted for communicating things moral and divine, or even things speculative and abstract. In short, they are wholly unfit for a people possessed of civilization, knowledge and refinement."[2] Edwards's letter gives voice and credence among many of his educated peers to the emergence and popularity of a pernicious ideology about American Indian languages. While largely still inchoate here, a colonial mentality of indigenous languages as a mark of savagery, and thus a barrier to civilization, would in the decades to follow, become a full-fledged ideology and eventually a tenet of national education policy. By the nineteenth-century, state, federal, and Bureau of Indian Affairs regularly mandated linguistic isolation and English-language instruction as the core of Indian boarding school curricula.

Among Jonathan Edwards's contemporaries, the perceived value of teaching American Indian proselytes how to read and speak in their own native tongue was on the decline by the mid-eighteenth century. Efforts to learn Mohegan, Mohawk, and Delaware were sporadic. Henry Barclay, for example, spent a year and a half among the Mohawk in an attempt to learn their language, but then confesses in a letter to John Sergeant that he "almost despair[s] in obtaining a perfect *Knowledge* of their Language" and still relies heavily on the use of an interpreter.[3] Gideon Hawley devised a cursory and functional list of Mohawk vocabulary, but his knowledge of and facility with the language was significantly less advanced than that of either of his immediate predecessors, Experience Mayhew and Josiah Cotton, or his French contemporaries (see Fig. 5.1). Sergeant made some effort to learn Mohican but always relied on the help of an interpreter and eventually began taking young Mohican children to Yale with him for the winter to "lead them into some Acquaintance with the *English* Language and Manners" and to draw on their cultural and linguistic knowledge to further his aspirations for a more adaptable system of Indian education.[4] Sergeant must have thought the arrangement reciprocal in another important way, for it is how he eventually learned to speak Mohican. Part of the reason for this decline in missionary linguistic skills was that it was simply easier and more economically feasible to teach American Indians English rather than to master multiple complex indigenous tongues. English-language instruction also eased the finance of printing and made it easier to maintain syllabaries, dictionaries, and grammar books. From the early eighteenth century on, the Society for the Propagation of the Gospel and the Society for the Propagation of Christian

FIGURE 5.1. Gideon Hawley, *Journal and Letter Book, 1753–1806*, Congregational Library, Boston, Mass.

Knowledge de-emphasized linguistic knowledge as a missionary crite-
ria and increasingly advocated English language instruction, facilitating communal, imperial, and diplomatic goals.

The practical concerns of early eighteenth-century missionary
organizations coincided with ideologies of indigenous languages as ir-
redeemable. Whereas Eliot's generation believed that Massachusett
could be reformed and reinfused with the sacred qualities of an original biblical language, Sergeant and David Brainerd's generation of
New Light theologians did not share this same millennial schema.
Thus, despite Sergeant's and Brainerd's expertise in indigenous languages, learning such languages was no longer driven by theological
purpose in the Anglo-Protestant world. The purported civility that
missionaries assumed English would bring to indigenous populations
outweighed the intellectual interest in the spiritual value of Indian
tongues. Moreover, the New Light theology around which ministers of
the First Great Awakening built their revivals decreased the symbolic
value of words in the moment of conversion. The emerging low-church
Methodism of the followers of Whitefield and Wesley, despite their
differences, veered in the same direction. Affective performance replaced redeemed speech as an integral sign of visible sainthood.

Jonathan Edwards's hagiographic *Life of Brainerd* (1746) details
Brainerd's circuit tours throughout New Jersey and Connecticut and
his highly successful American Indian revivals as evidence of "true
religion" when set in contrast to the fears of hypocrisy that plagued
Edwards since the Northampton revivals received criticism in the
mid-to late 1740s. For Edwards, the inward transformation of Brainerd's
soul and the confirmation of his election on his deathbed established
the authenticity of the new evangelical-inflected Congregationalism.

Edwards aspired to emulate this embrace of "true religion" when
he arrived in Stockbridge in 1751, two years after Brainerd's and John
Sergeant's deaths. Edwards's theological work at Stockbridge arose
partly as a response to the frustrations facing missionaries of Brainerd
and Sergeant's generation. From the 1730s–1750s, Brainerd and Sergeant
struggled with a transitional phase of colonialism, one rapidly moving
past a century of settlement and occupation toward mid-eighteenth-
century pressures for political domination through Anglo-Protestant
conversion.

A colonial outpost largely isolated from the formal institutions of
the Congregational Church, Stockbridge was a place where Edwards
could reinvigorate the meaning of true religion, both at the level of

individual conversion and on a broader world-scale, as he redefined the role of American Indians within global history. Putting the observations he had collated from Brainerd into practice, Edwards used Stockbridge as a laboratory for testing out his millennial theory in what he viewed as its most elemental form—the Indian proselytes in the Stockbridge congregation. In his Stockbridge sermons, Edwards renewed several key theological concepts, refashioning forms of nature and grace through his indigenous encounter. Indigenous means rooted to a sense of place, a way of belonging to the land's particular topography and its long-standing cultural developments and inhabitants. Edwards's writing during his Stockbridge years reflects a commingling of Calvinist and indigenous cosmologies. He sought to reinfuse a contested and practically impossible theological system with fresh insights derived from his sense—real or imagined—of the beliefs of the land's native inhabitants. This is not to say that Edwards had a salutary perspective on Anglo and American Indian coexistence. There is not much evidence in his Stockbridge writings that he was amenable to notions of American Indian sovereignty, autonomy, or rights, even though he both defended individual Indian rights and made efforts to improve the living conditions of his congregants. Rather, Edwards understood in this latter phase of his life that the Calvinist system of election and covenant were in decline and that cosmologies and epistemologies of nature and the supernatural absorbed from American Indian culture offered a method of salvaging American grace and millennial purpose. A central facet of this reconfiguration of American millennialism was the devaluation of indigenous languages as repositories for spiritual truths. Edwards performed his missionary work in the context of heightened advocacy for acculturation through English language and English civilization that arose in response to contemporary French Jesuit missionary practices. From Edwards to Thomas Jefferson, many theologians and philosophers viewed indigenous words as remnants of an unenlightened past. Indigenous words functioned increasingly as keys to an American antiquity that was archeological rather than biblical.

Hebrew Lexicons and the Solitude of Nature

Jonathan Edwards was a reluctant missionary.[5] His contemporaries, Sergeant, Gideon Hawley, Brainerd, and Henry Barclay were much more committed to the missionary cause.[6] Yet Edwards worked for seven years (1751–1758) as pastor at the Stockbridge mission. Even though the unexpected change in his pastoral duties was a result of his dismissal from his Northampton pulpit, Edwards was still reluctant to leave Stockbridge in 1758 to accept the Princeton presidency, the privileged bastion of Reformed faith. He framed this reticence in terms of his commitment to his theological reflections. While at Stockbridge, he spent thirteen hours a day in his small study writing. His time in Stockbridge produced a form of uninterrupted seclusion that enabled him to focus on what would become his greatest philosophical works: *Freedom of the Will* (1754), *Original Sin* (1758), and *The Nature of True Virtue* (1765). Yet, to dismiss Stockbridge merely as a writing retreat misses a larger point about a profound connection between the evangelizing mission and the transformations taking place in Edwards's philosophical writings and preaching practices.

At least two years before his move to Stockbridge, Edwards published *The Life of David Brainerd* following his protégé's death from tuberculosis in Edwards's home. *The Life of David Brainerd* is a composite text, assembled from Brainerd's journals, oral revelations, and letters. The voice of Edwards and Brainerd blurs past the point of distinguishability, while still offering a striking account of Brainerd's missionary ethnography and Edwards's adulation of his protégé. Through his efforts on the missionary circuit, Brainerd displayed a pattern of wilderness sojourning that corresponded with an inward transformation of his soul. In observing and writing Brainerd's *Life,* Edwards witnessed confirmation of his own theology. The degree to which he both venerated Brainerd and saw his faith and his mission as a kind of model for revivalism comes across clearly in the *Appendix* to *The Life of David Brainerd*. Edwards sees the revivals that Brainerd initiated among the American Indians in Long Island, New Jersey, and Pennsylvania as a kind of litmus test for the revivals that took place under his own supervision in Northampton and surrounding environs in 1734. The Indian revivals, according to Edwards, were strikingly different than those that took place among white colonists, or, as Edwards puts it, "amongst the English" in "both essence and fruits."[7] More akin to the "religion of the Separatists" due to their autonomous existence, the Indian revivals escaped the dangers of hypocrisy, representing instead "genuine and incontestable" expressions of faith.[8] Through Brainerd, Edwards models a saintly life. Moreover, *The Life of David Brainerd* displays a form of conversion and evangelization that reconfigures the symbolic importance of words, at once revitalizing and contesting an older linguistic philosophy that privileged the mythic import of the indigenous words spoken by the native inhabitants of North America.

Through Brainerd, Edwards posits that "true religion" becomes vividly apparent when set in contrast to the dark, heathen savagery of the colonial wilderness. Both Brainerd and Edwards use the phrase "true religion" to define Protestant righteousness over and against the dark and pagan specter of Catholicism and its accompanying primitive and "savage" occultism. True religion comes to represent the almost unattainable ideal of authentic faith, the faith of a convert so assured of salvation as to escape the threat of hypocrisy—the self-misdiagnosed reception of saving grace that plagued Reformation Calvinism and distorted the intended symmetry between the Visible and Invisible Church. Alternating descriptions of the true light of Christ and the darkness of heathen savagery take on familiar allegorical proportions throughout *The Life of David Brainerd*. Yet Edwards does not entirely pit one against the other. Instead, Brainerd's description of the revivals that he so successfully enacts illuminate for Edwards how "true religion" may be discovered outside of monotheistic cultures. Brainerd models for Edwards that each local American Indian revival functions as evidence of God's historical and providential purpose across all global cultures. Each revival stands as a living test for the fulfillment of Edwards's opus, the *History of the Work of Redemption*.

The allegorical contrast between the light of Christ and darkness of "heathen savagery," the outward display of religion among Brainerd's converts and the inward transformation of the missionary's own soul, work in a dialectical pattern of mutual reinforcement and salvific self-making. The arduous conditions of the wilderness made true religion apparent through the light displayed as evidence of divinity on David Brainerd's soul. Within the hagiographic scheme in which Edwards scripts Brainerd's life, the missionary's death at such a young age affirms his status as one who has reached this spiritual ideal.[9] Figured as a type of the ultimate wilderness frontier through the frame of John 3:14–21, Brainerd's imminent death permitted Edwards to clearly see evidence of "true religion" on the missionary's soul. Edwards became deeply invested in what he saw as Brainerd's extraordinary piety and grace and became intent on studying and recording his life and religious experience through his own hagiographic account because Brainerd exemplified for him a new kind of conversion. On his deathbed, Brainerd extolled a mode of conversion that transcended the epistemological pitfalls of language. Edwards used Brainerd's *Life* as a template for putting forth a new model of conversion that would circumvent the dangers of hypocrisy that invariably resulted from trying to translate the inward experience of grace into any sort of external form. *The Life of Brainerd* also establishes itself as an allegory for a foundational relationship between Protestant religious experience and the sense of belonging to the continent of North America. Through his rendering of Brainerd, a portrait that might be described as the first American Christ, Edwards fashions a nativist Protestant religious identity, an inextricable link between American nature and American grace that would become intrinsic to his own nativist millennialism. As a New Light missionary, Brainerd converts without getting mired in the intricacies of the colonial language encounter as his predecessors had. From Brainerd's journey and encounters with indigenous people, Edwards begins to perceive a new vision of American nature and grace.

Brainerd's dying prayer is Christlike, reiterating the journey of Jesus told in the third chapter of the Book of John. It is also a type of national exile, reflecting the corporate identity of the New World Church fleeing to the wilderness on an errand of national redemption:

> Here I am, Lord, send me; send me to the ends of the earth; send me to the rough, the savage pagans of the wilderness; send me from all that is called comfort in earth, or earthly comfort; send me even to death itself, if it be but in thy service and to promote thy kingdom.[10]

On his deathbed, Brainerd pleas for a repetition of the journey that he has just lived and whose end is near. Like Jesus, he views his mission as one of bringing "light into the world" and the promise of salvation into the wilderness.[11] Narrating his dying moments, Edwards fashions him into a Christ type, and in this case a particularly American Christ. Brainerd's prayer poignantly reveals that the essence of true religion can only be encountered through one's sojourn through the depths of savage North America. Edwards attributes Brainerd's spiritual success to his capacity to "fors[ake] the world, with its possessions, delights, and common comforts, to dwell as it were with wild beasts in a howling wilderness."[12] Through this practice of missionizing under harsh conditions, *The Life of David*

Brainerd presents a new portrait of an Anglo-Protestant missionary, one that ironically resembles the journeys described in the century before his birth in the *Jesuit Relations.* Brainerd shares with the Jesuits the integral connection between the inward transformation of the missionary soul and wilderness conditions of extreme duress—a kind of wilderness penitentialism inherently available, in Edwards's and Brainerd's soteriology, to the Indian populations that Brainerd serves.

The shared language of suffering in the service of divine purpose derives from and circulates through a range of homiletic traditions, *Spiritual Exercises*, Psalters, Books of Hours, a tradition of American primers, the Book of Job, and John Bunyan's *Pilgrim's Progress.* Compare Brainerd's wilderness suffering with Gabriel Marest's in his letter to the Society, dated 1695:

> The cold of winter raged, bitter beyond conception. My way led through storms and snows, and over marshes scarcely frozen firm,— which everywhere afforded but treacherous footing, and cut my feet and legs. I had to sleep beneath the open sky; and meanwhile I was attacked by a fever and the general malady. Still I felt that I must not yield to these lest, above all, I should fail in my duty to the sick.[13]

In *The Life of David Brainerd,* the same pattern of suffering recurs throughout:

> Wednesday, June 19, 1745. Rode to the Indians at Crossweeksung: Found few at home: Discoursed to them however; and observed them very serious and attentive. At night I was extremely worn out and scarce able to walk or sit up. Oh, how tiresome is earth! How dull the body![14]

The suffering experienced by Marest and Brainerd is one that the land inscribes upon the material body. The compulsion to serve a divine call and a millennial design placed the human body in arduous conditions. Marest describes a pattern whereby the land literally writes itself onto his body: the frozen ground cuts his feet and legs; the open sky induces fever and malady. The land subjects the missionary's flesh to the service of transforming his soul, of bringing the missionary closer and closer to fulfilling the purpose of the call that brought him into the wilderness in the first place.

In *The Life of David Brainerd,* not only the land but also the native peoples that Brainerd encounters on his travels distress his body. This pattern typifies Brainerd's experience at Crossweeksung. He preaches so effectively that his "discourse" takes its physical toll. This oscillation between serving God and collapsing into fatigue and sickness persists through all of Brainerd's travels, culminating with his early death from consumption. Through its depiction of the land and indigenous inhabitants, *The Life of David Brainerd* gradually claims Native America as the core facet of Anglo-American Protestantism. Through a relation of proximity and mutual dependence, Native America becomes both the material and spiritual engine of an unfolding Protestant millennial history. The natural world, from its savage otherworldliness to its divine types is an indexical measure of the history of redemption. Brainerd's journal entries record how the wilderness' "savage Pagans" come to the divine light of Christ. Their physical presence within the world embodies for Brainerd, and thus, Edwards, both a site of the wilderness' darkness and the site of its transformation through the Holy Spirit. As such it mirrors the dissolution of darkness—the regeneration of the postlapsarian "wildness" or wilderness within Brainerd's own soul through saving grace.

The mark of true religion for Brainerd comes from the convert's ability to move beyond this real, external threat and away from the potential inward danger of delusion. His spiritual journey moves in dialectical fashion between his own secret piety and his encounters on the missionary frontier (and in turn between the secret piety revealed in the journal and the reader's own identifying encounter). The clarity of true religion comes from the contrast between darkness and light, literally figured through Brainerd's own dark moments of looming despair as he walks through the "dark thick grove" of a natural world filled with savage bodies and the "unspeakable glory" of Christ's salvific light that becomes available to him in brief moments of evangelical encounter.[15] His inward faith refracts back to him through his experience in nature and his observations of native conversion. This experience of edifying faith in the savage wilderness depends on Brainerd's capacity for self-isolation, his ability to let go of what he thinks he knows about divine signs. What propels him forward is a desire for an unmediated encounter with God that he witnesses in the spiritual transformation of the Indian convert.

The Life of David Brainerd not only records Brainerd's efficacy as a missionary: it would also become an exemplar for scores of missionaries around the world in the coming decades and in the nineteenth century because it models a new form of Protestant conversion, one that is specifically designed to resolve the theological conundrum of language's fallen status. Over the course of Anglo-colonial history, from the mid-1630s through Edwards's own Communion Controversy, ministers recognized language as an inherently inadequate but none-theless necessary means of conveying evidence of the spirit. In the testimonies of faith practiced in Puritan congregations and in mis-sionary communities, language was both the vehicle of religious communication and the very medium that could lead to enthusiastic delusion.[16] If religious experience could be expressed, it could also be fudged, faked, or mistakenly interpreted or misattributed.

Brainerd's conversion experience begins with the verbal aliena-tion that he experienced through life on the frontier. He writes that he "live[s] in the most lonesome wilderness" with "one single person" who could "speak English."[17] This probably requires qualification since he relied heavily on indigenous interpreters for the linguistic skills that he came to acquire. Nonetheless, the experience of linguis-tic alienation constitutes a major trope within *The Life of David Brainerd*, reflecting yet another point of connection to the *Jesuit Relations*. Unable to communicate the experience of his own inner journey, Brainerd spends most of his time in his study, where he regains his bodily strength before his work on the frontier. A profound dis-connection from the languages and voices that surround him cata-lyze Brainerd's movement between the solitude of his own soul and the North American wilderness. This is the quintessential American experience of several missionaries before Brainerd, including Eliot, Gravier, Hawley, Marest, Mayhew, Rale, Sergeant, and Williams, all of whom journey through a wilderness of unintelligible tongues. Brainerd's *Life* personalizes this history, describing a direct connection between linguistic alienation and spiritual experience.

While recognizing that linguistic isolation fostered his spiritual "walk" with god, Brainerd also understood the practical need to have some command of American Indian languages in order to perform the work of conversion. A 1745 letter to the "Honorable Society for Propagating Christian Knowledge," which was preserved as an ap-pendix to the 1765 edition of *The Life of David Brainerd* published in Edinburgh, explains that the "most successful *method*" that he has dis-covered is verbatim translation where he dictates an English discourse to indigenous interpreters who then translate. Based on this transla-tion, Brainerd claims to observe the native meaning and authority of specific words, how syntactical construction operates, and "the root from whence particular words proceed."[18] He claims that this process allows him to "gai[n] so much knowledge of their language," such that he could understand what they say, particularly as it relates to spiritual subjects.

Yet his linguistic studies also suggest that Delaware is not reducible to the bare Christian truths expressed in English. In this same letter, Brainerd explains that it is impossible to know through this verbatim transcription what parts of speech to use to convey the exact meaning in Delaware. His process of language acquisition is observational in mode, much as it is for his Jesuit counterparts. He does not attain nearly the linguistic proficiency of Rale, Gravier, or Picquet, but he does understand, like these Jesuits and like Josiah Cotton and Experience Mayhew before him, that Delaware conforms to a completely distinct syntactical structure with words formed to represent a cosmos quite different from that of Christianity. Part of Brainerd's particular difficulty is that his own knowledge of the language is insufficient. He must rely on interpreters who are themselves "unlearned, and unacquainted with the rules of language" and insufficiently trained in theology and religious discourse.[19] In order to translate Christian texts accurately, interpreters have to have a more sophisticated sense of the way that English syntax differs from Delaware and a more precise understanding of the complexity of religious vocabulary. The translation of ill-defined concepts and poorly understood spiritual truths only exacerbates the disparity inherent between the two languages. He expresses regret that he has little time for the "study of the Indian Languages" given all the time that he spends traveling. Although he confesses to have "taken considerable Pains to learn the Delaware Language," he is discouraged at the prospect of learning other Indian tongues given the sheer number.[20]

Brainerd tailors his efforts to achieve linguistic proficiency for practical concerns. Even though he is the eighteenth-century missionary who lives in closest proximity to his proselytes, his writings on the Delaware have none of the insightful observations into linguistic nuance that French Jesuits Maillard and Picquet captured in their writing. Moreover, Brainerd inhabits a theological perspective that is not the least bit elastic when it comes to accurately conveying spiritual truths through words. The Jesuits believed in the malleability of language and in their assurance that faith was the inevitable fruit of ritual practice. Brainerd must acquire his authority and success as a missionary through means other than linguistic expertise.

Thus, even though his process of linguistic acquisition through observation and the mirroring of his own spiritual experience with that
of his wilderness proselytes resembled the Jesuits in some key ways,
the outcome is quite different.

In his influential missionary tract, *Mirabilia* (1746), from which
parts of *The Life of David Brainerd* were compiled, Brainerd espouses
a form of evangelical conversion that is entirely independent of language.[21] Unlike the carefully transcribed and translated Massachusett
testimonies of the previous century, the measure of native piety is
nonverbal: "weeping," "crying out," "sweet Melting and bitter Mourning,"
and "bitter Groans." Such "affecting Evidence" breaks through language's semiotic barrier, revealing "the Reality and Depth of their
inward Anguish."[22] In this particularly poignant description, the
modern reader might well interpret the source of this anguish as a
collective cry against a long colonial history of tribal displacement,
aggressive colonial policies, and European diseases for which native
populations had little or no immunity. Yet for Brainerd and his readers,
this is the truest evidence of "the amazing divine Influence" of God
working "powerfully among them." The conclusion that he draws from
this extraordinary success is that God has gifted him with an extra-
linguistic capacity for communication: "And thus God manifested
that, without bestowing on me the *Gift of Tongues*, he could find a
Way wherein I might be as effectually enabled to convey the Truths
of his glorious Gospel to the Mind of these poor benighted *Pagans*."[23]

Brainerd's phrase "gift of tongues" refers to the divine gift that God
bestows upon the church and the Apostles (1 Corinthians 12:28) to
ameliorate this confusion of tongues brought about by God's curse at
the Tower of Babel. Since their earliest encounters, Protestant missionaries to the New World interpreted the varied and unfamiliar
indigenous languages that they encountered in the wilderness as a
sign of post–Tower-of-Babel Confusion. This biblical association led
inexorably to the philological association of American Indian languages with Hebrew. As John Eliot wrote in a series of letters included in the 1660 publication of Thomas Thorowgood's *Jews in
America*, the degenerated "strange speech of the Heathen" has long
obscured the biblical origins of the New World inhabitants as descendants of the ten lost tribes. According to Thorowgood, Eliot
learned to navigate the "exotick and difficult" Massachusett language,
and, in doing so, discovered its links to Hebrew.[24] While the language discovered upon Eliot's initial encounter, full of long words

and unpleasing sounds, was a clear indication of a barbarous population, Eliot's project of translating Christian texts into Massachusett was believed to redeem the language, to forge a connection between indigenous word and scriptural truth.[25] Caught up in the millennial fervor of England in the 1650s, Eliot's claim for philological continuity between Hebrew and Massachusett took on special resonance.

One can see Brainerd's indebtedness to this tradition in a 1645 edition of Buxtorf's *Hebrew Grammar*, which he carried with him on his arduous wilderness journeys and then left in the Edwards's possession when he died in 1747 (see Fig 5.2). The book is tattered and threadbare from use in the wilderness. Most interestingly, the book is bound in rudely made animal-hide velum, painted with an American Indian design. As a material object, the book tells a provocative, if somewhat speculative, story. It echoes the narrative of linguistic isolation recounted in *The Life of David Brainerd* and records Brainerd's own struggle to learn Hebrew as well as Delaware. The aspirations of his predecessors suggest that Brainerd also hoped to discover similarities between the scores of languages spoken along the New Jersey and Pennsylvania frontier and Hebrew as the ancient, sacred, and original scriptural tongue.[26] Yet as he relates at length the near impossibility of mastering the syntax of Delaware and translating his sermons from English, he seems a long way away from making an analogical connection with Hebrew. While the original binding has been worn away, the book itself is completely intact, in good condition, and lacking any notes or marginalia, as though it had been little read. The overlay of the indigenous cover seems symbolically suggestive of the significant obstructions Brainerd saw between his linguistic capacities and his desired object of ministering in the Delaware language.

By the mid–eighteenth century, conceptions of Hebrew were changing from understandings of Hebrew as the *ur* biblical language and therefore the most authentic representation of the Word of God to aesthetic ideas about Hebrew's poetic and expressive capacity. This transition is perhaps most vividly illustrated by Robert Lowth, the English grammarian, Oxford professor of poetry, and bishop. Lowth delivered a series titled *Lectures on the Sacred Poetry of Hebrew* in Oxford in 1753. His lectures set out new terms for understanding the psalms as poetry and for thinking about them in relation to the aesthetic and philosophical category of the sublime. Rather than the *ur* biblical language, Hebrew emerges as the *ur* language of poetry in these lectures:

FIGURE 5.2. Johann Buxtorf, *Lexicon Hebraicum* (1645), Princeton University, Department of Rare Books and Special Collections.

A principle which pervades all poetry, may easily be conceived to prevail even in a high degree in the poetry of the Hebrews. Indeed we have already seen how daring these writers are in the selection of their imagery, how forcible in the application of it; and what elegance, splendour, and sublimity they have by these means been enabled to infuse into their compositions. With respect to the diction also, we have had an opportunity of remarking the peculiar force and dignity of their poetic dialect.... It is impossible to conceive any thing more simple and unadorned than the common language of the Hebrews. It is plain, correct, chaste, and temperate; the words are uncommon neither in their meaning nor application; there is no appearance of study, nor even of the least attention to the harmony of the periods. The order of the words is generally regular and uniform.[27]

In his introduction to the *Psalterium Americanum*, Mather argues that the translation of the psalms from Hebrew should not follow any pretense to poetry but should rather stick as close to the original as possible. He writes that the psalms are "*Golden Keys*, to the Immense Treasures of *Truth*, which have not been commonly used."[28] Lowth's disquisition reflects the opposite conceptualization of Hebrew, that rather than a semiotically precise replication of the Word of God, Hebrew is artful and uniquely expressive of the most admirable features of poetry. What is particularly interesting and relevant about the Lowth passage is that missionaries and philologists would make similar claims about the indigenous languages of North America in the antebellum period. This is the stance that Peter Du Ponceau and John Heckewelder took on Lenni Lenape. It is also the aesthetic ideal that James Fenimore Cooper attempted to translate into his *Leatherstocking Tales*. The mid–eighteenth century reflects a shift both in the conceptualizations of Hebrew and in attitudes toward indigenous tongues. During this time period, American Indian languages outlived their usefulness for missionaries interested in capturing and recuperating original, sacred, biblical languages. However, theories of the aesthetic and archaeological potential of indigenous languages would soon appear, giving new purposes for missionaries such as Heckwelder who spent decades learning and collecting Lenni Lenape. His efforts aligned perfectly with emerging notions of the aesthetic capacity to be discovered in North American languages. This new perception is faintly visible in Edwards's Stockbridge sermons. Even though he himself did not know Mohican, he borrows from a rich storehouse of Mohican metaphors and nature imagery to artfully convey theological points.

Stockbridge

The Stockbridge mission began about a decade before Brainerd conducted his successful American Indian revivals in New Jersey and

Connecticut. The Scottish Society for the Propagation of Christian Knowledge (SSPCK), the same organization to which Brainerd made his reports, sponsored Stockbridge along with a few other missions merging the revival of Anglo-Protestant evangelizing efforts with imperial-political strategies. Of particular concern was the need to provide reinforcement, both spiritual and material, against French-Jesuit success and against the perceived Jesuit influence in enlisting Catholic Indians in the French military cause. Never losing sight of what they deemed their spiritual duty to proselytize American Indians, the SSPCK also believed that missionizing the Housatonic Mohicans in the Connecticut River Valley would ensure military allies and provide added protection to frontier settlements. Additionally, several Puritan ministers beginning with Solomon Stoddard, Jonathan Edwards's influential grandfather, emphasized the necessity of spreading the gospel among the American Indians to stave off God's anger, which was being made manifest through epidemics, Indian wars, and French and Indian alliances. John Stoddard, Edwards's maternal uncle, joined the chorus, advocating missionizing the Mohican since they were one tribe believed to be untouched by French influence. Yet this Anglo-Protestant fantasy of the Mohican tribe as *tabula rasa* proved to be untrue. John Sergeant, the first missionary of Stockbridge in 1710, recorded in his diary:

> January 26th.——The *Lieutenant* [Umpachenee] ask'd me what I thought of the Celibacy of the *Romish* Clergy, and of their severe Methods of doing Penance? I was a little surpriz'd to hear him ask such a Question; for I did not suppose our *Indians* knew any Thing of the Matter. However, I readily told him, that those Things were vain Inventions of Men; and unprofitable Services; that I did not judge any Man; but I was sure no Body was under Obligation to do them; that our Business was to mortify our Lusts and Passions, and to regulate our Lives by the reveal'd Will of God, and not to go beyond *that*.——[29]

Sergeant's surprise comes from his assumption that the Mohicans had not been exposed previously to Catholic doctrine. Pervasive fears of French and American Indian alliances were becoming paramount in the context of eighteenth-century imperial wars. Massachusetts Bay governor Jonathan Belcher expressed grave concern to the clergy over the specter of French-Catholic missionary success and strongly urged the Stockbridge mission as a kind of safeguard against the further encroachment of the French on the souls and political allegiances of Indian tribes.

By 1734, the Mohican also found themselves at a crossroads and increasingly in need of British protection. Prior to this date, the Housatonic Mohicans had existed in a state of relative autonomy, encountering Europeans only fleetingly through trade with the Dutch, and brief encounters, as Sergeant's diary suggests, with French Catholics. The Mohican had been archenemies with the Mohawk since 1609, and by the early eighteenth century, decades of near constant warfare had substantially depleted their numbers and property. Moreover, New Englanders, who were by and large more religiously minded than the Dutch, began to move into the Connecticut River Valley in greater numbers, encroaching on indigenous lands. By 1680, the Mohican had already been driven from their homeland on the Hudson River banks. This coincided with the formation of the River Indian Confederacy in 1675. Tribal leaders Konkapot and Umpachenee led the initiative to tolerate if not accept the Christian mission. Their reasons were strategic, in that the mission promised territory and protection. Yet fueled by his own sense of the declining power of traditional Mohican faith, Konkapot, in particular, evinced an interest in Christianity. In the face of depleted tribal strength and lost territory, the religion of Konkapot's forefathers seemed to him all but spent and politically untenable. Mohican powwows often conceded their lack of power over the perceived spiritual protections associated with Christianity.[30]

In August 1735, the pan-Indian alliance known as the River Indian Confederacy met in Deerfield to discuss the English presence. Governor Belcher attended and attempted to convince the Housatonic, Canagwa, and Saucatuck tribes of the benefits of accepting the Christian mission. In each exchange between tribal chief and governor, wampum was presented and exchanged out of deference to native customs. Governor Belcher then delivered an address that stressed that the British and native tribes were common subjects under King George, that the English looked upon the Indians as "Children" and promised to offer them the same protections accorded to English subjects. Additionally, he described the importance of Christianity as "a serious thing" that "ought to be always born on [their] Minds."[31] Significant in Belcher's address is the rhetorical pains that he takes to unite British subjecthood with Christianity. He emphasizes that the two are inextricably intertwined, one cannot be a praying Indian without also becoming an imperial subject of the Crown. Konkapot's response is one of gratitude for the Christian teachings offered through the mission: "Father, we can't but thank you for the Love and Care you have taken of us as to Our Knowledge of the Gospel."[32] The Deerfield meeting culminated with the ordination of John Sergeant to be the first minister at Stockbridge. During the 1735 convening, the decision over whether or not to accept the mission split. The Housatonic Mohicans, or Muh-he-ka-neew, meaning "the people of the ever-flowing waters," a reference to their original home on the banks of the Hudson River, aligned with the English while the Hudson River Indians refused this alliance. As was typically the case in such instances of missionary settlement, the British promised land in exchange for submission to the gospel.[33] Deferential though the tone of Konkapot's speech is, he does not acknowledge Belcher's desire for Mohican submission to the Crown. He responds to the spiritual benefits of the mission without acknowledging the political implications of British protection and colonial subjagation.

Within months of settling in Mohican territory, Sergeant had convinced the Mohicans to help him build a meetinghouse that also doubled as a schoolhouse, with their wigwams arranged around this central building. Sergeant found the language extremely difficult, and unlike any European languages. In the early phase of the mission, he confessed that he was "not able to converse much with them in their own Language" and had to rely on a Dutch interpreter.[34]

But Sergeant still committed to spending time each day teaching the children to read in their own language and to sing. He prayed with them in their own language, using interpreters when necessary. Sergeant soon gained the trust of tribal leaders Umpachenee and Konkapot and when he returned to Yale in the winter of 1734, they permitted their sons to accompany him. This enabled a reciprocal language exchange: Sergeant made good strides in learning the Mohican language and the sons of Umpachenee and Konkapot learned English.[35]

Despite Sergeant's efforts to become an effective preacher of Mohican and to teach young Mohican boys to read and write in their native tongue, the effort to inculcate Mohican-language Christianity in the mission shifted radically by the 1740s. Financial backers of the mission increasingly advocated English-language instruction. Benjamin Colman helped to enact a plan for sending Mohican females to English families to learn English. Samuel Hopkins records some resistance to this plan among the Mohican, particularly "the Lieutenant" (Umpachenee) who had initially been a strong supporter of the mission. This resistance suggests that the Mohican were willing to accept and even embrace Christianity as long as their new-found faith did not require them to sever traditional ties to their own culture. The loss of a Christian-Mohican culture in Stockbridge signaled the replacement of Mohican values with English ones. This was not a sacrifice that the Mohican had counted on nor that they were willing to embrace. Along with Coleman, Sergeant developed a vision for "civilizing" the Mohican that demanded English-language instruction. When he baptized his proselytes, he gave them Christian names. Konkapot and Umpachenee became John and Aaron.[36] Sergeant describes his plan for Indian education in a printed 1743 letter to Benjamin Coleman:

> What I propose therefore in general is to take such a *Method* in the Education of our *Indian Children*, as shall in the most effectual Manner change their whole Habit of thinking and acting; and raise them, as far as possible, into the Condition of a civil industrious and polish'd People; while at the same Time the Principles of Vertue and Piety shall be carefully instilled into their Minds in a Way, that will make the most lasting Impression; and withal to introduce the *English Language* among them instead of their own imperfect and barbarous *Dialect*.[37]

Anglo-Protestants had long been less permissive than the French Jesuits in terms of the continuance of indigenous cultures. Indeed, Catholicism's capacity to absorb cultural diversity is a main reason for the superior success of the Jesuits.

Still in his letter to Coleman, Sergeant describes arriving at a method of education that was entirely different and significantly more assimilationist than that of his predecessor John Eliot. Eliot also believed that inculcating civility was a necessary prerequisite for Christianization. This was the impetus behind the ordering of the Praying Towns, the meetinghouse construction, the reconfiguration of the wigwams, and the requirement of new grooming habits described in the Eliot Tracts.[38] Yet, Eliot also believed that the Massachusett language should be preserved. He believed that an integral component of Massachusett conversion was learning to speak in a redeemed Algonquian tongue. Eliot's advocacy for the language stemmed from a fundamental belief that Massachusett was a language was fallen, but not irreparably so. By retraining Indian children to read and speak a redeemed version of their mother tongue, he imagined that his praying Indians would ultimately generate a sacred space more nearly tailored to their own spiritual aptitude, testifying to the status of their souls in the vestige of a biblical language newly infused with divine light.

Even though Sergeant conceded to a connection between Mohican and Hebrew, he did not maintain Eliot's millennial aspirations for a redeemed version of what he often referred to as a "barbarous *Dialect*." For Sergeant, the Mohican language was not merely a sign of savagery but its cause. Effectively, missions had free native speakers from a language that chained them to the Fall in order to transform heathens into Christian subjects. Centuries of contact between the English tongue and Christianity had repaired the language. English translations of the Bible and a long tradition of English-crafted theologies, prayers, hymns, meditations, primers, and the like had built a spiritual vocabulary and syntax that had transformed or "redeemed" the once heathen tongue. It was this notion of a redeemed language—a language mutually constitutive with the theologies of the Reformation—that underwrote Sergeant's missionary pedagogy. All aspects of indigenous culture, from belief systems and cultural practices to labor habits, had to be suppressed in order for Christianity to thrive. As Sergeant states further on in the letter: "the *Indians*, in general, are a People *difficult* to be reformed from their own *foolish*, barbarous, and wicked Customs." He attributes the failures of the Anglo-Protestant mission to a neglect of the need to "*promot[e] Industry* among them." He would continue to try to raise money for his school throughout his missionary career. While the school never quite enjoyed the stability and fame of Wheelock's school at Dartmouth, Sergeant's vision fostered a significant shift in attitudes toward Indian education, particularly and devastatingly apparent in nineteenth-century federal education policies that advocated a network of boarding schools and other institutions that removed Indian children from their culture and people in order to sever them permanently from their native language and spiritual practices.

John Sergeant served as Stockbridge missionary from 1734 until his untimely death in 1749. During this time, he baptized 129 Mohicans and attempted but failed to implement a culture of

Christian worship in the Mohican language.[39] Samuel Hopkins memorialized Sergeant's experience in Stockbridge in his *Historical Memoirs* (1753), a history that draws largely on the missionary's journals. After Sergeant died, the mission fell into disarray. Sergeant failed to align the mission with Britain's imperial goals. The boarding school that Sergeant started lured nearly 100 Mohawks with the promise of education. But even the boarding school did not survive the incompetent hands of missionary Martin Kellog who refused to defer to his replacement, Gideon Hawley. After arriving in Stockbridge in 1751, Edwards did his best to apply himself to missionary tasks, but two years after his arrival the school burned down, most likely from arson. The departure of the Mohawks ended Sergeant's mission but not his religious influence on colonial and later national Indian educational policy that quickly found its way into more secular institutional practices. Edwards took up the task of attempting to unite Mohican language and conversion to an Anglo-Protestant purpose.[40]

Accidental Missionary

Edwards worked to inculcate New Light conversion theology and revivalist millennialism among the Mohican population residing at Stockbridge. In doing so, he struggled to situate the local context of the mission within the global-millennial framework of the *History of the Work of Redemption*. He wrote of his plan to teach scriptural history to his Stockbridge proselytes in a 1751 letter to one of the mission's benefactors, Sir William Pepperrell:

> I can see no good reason, why children can't, or mayn't, be taught something in general of ecclesiastical history, and be informed how things, with regard to the state of religion and the church of God, have gone on, as to some of the main events, from the time when the Scripture history ended to the present time, and how certain prophecies of Scripture have been fulfilled in some of those events; and they may also be told what may yet be expected to come to pass, according to Scripture prophecies, from this time to the end of the world.[41]

Even as he encountered the material realities of a mission struggling to attain its own identity and authority in light of the specter of Moravian and Catholic success, Edwards aspired to construct a grand narrative of Anglo-Protestant triumph. Moreover, he hoped to inculcate this narrative among his proselytes, so that Stockbridge would become both an incubator of ideas for and a laboratory of experience of his largely a priori theological system.

Before even arriving there, though quite possibly with Brainerd's missionary legacy in mind, Edwards included the professions of faith of two Mohican Indians, Cornelius and Mary Munnewaumummuh, in an unpublished draft to the preface of the "Farewell Sermon" that he preached upon leaving Northampton.[42] These declarations largely follow the conventional narrative arc of the genre: unwavering faith in God, recognition of the human debt to the Doctrine of Original Sin, evidence of inward regeneration, and the outward expression of a desire to lead a pious life. It seems surprising, given their conventionalism, that Edwards began his "Farewell Sermon" with these two professions. What was so exceptional about these two Indians' words—their professions of faith—that would induce Edwards to use them to begin one of the most important sermons of his career?

The sermons that Edwards preached to his Mohican audience almost immediately on his arrival in Stockbridge shed light on this question.[43] Through his interpretive narrative, Edwards configured Christian Mohicans as types within an unfolding biblical prophecy. He attempted to situate the Mohican people within a frame of religious, national, and global conflict, while simultaneously forecasting their own eschatological erasure out of the imminent historical present. In the very same letter in which Edwards speaks of teaching Housatonic children about the "prophecies of Scripture," he also explains that this instruction needs to take place in English.[44] Edwards repeats this disparaging assessment of Mohican in a letter to Stockbridge sponsor Isaac Hollis. In that letter, he explains that the "barbarous languages" of the American Indians are "exceeding barren and very unfit to express moral and divine things."[45] Within Edwards's eschatology native words are useful only as ancient artifacts of a long-forgotten past, decoupled from the living bodies of praying Mohicans who were increasingly required to assimilate by learning English as a prerequisite to their salvation.

This attitude toward indigenous words as primitive artifacts persisted well beyond Edwards's years at Stockbridge and well beyond the religious context of revivalism. Describing indigenous words as Old Testament types, artifacts of a long-forgotten past, migrated from the religious hermeneutic fashioned by Brainerd and Edwards to a philosophical and archaeological ideal that made a lasting impact on American letters. Beginning with Thomas Jefferson, statesmen, philologists, and philosophers of the late eighteenth and early nineteenth century began to prize indigenous tongues as an archive of America's primitive past. This was an ideology rooted specifically in the Anglo-Protestant missionary history of the First Great Awakening.

Within weeks of his arrival in Stockbridge, Edwards preached a sermon titled "The Things That Belong to True Religion." The sermon describes a form of belief free from the dangers of hypocrisy and delusion, a faith built upon the missionary precept of David Brainerd who espoused a model of conversion based on the inner light of grace made manifest independent of language. In this sermon, the conversion of individual Indian proselytes provided proof of the imminence of a New World millennial fulfillment. Embellishing the narrative from Acts 11:12–13, the sermon explains that Cornelius was one of the first "heathens" to come to Christ. The latter-day Cornelius who begins Edwards's "Farewell Sermon" with a profession of faith suddenly reveals his fulfillment in this older Christian type. The centrality of Edwards's placement of Cornelius's profession of faith is meant to initiate the logic of biblical figuration. His turn to typology is significant, because, according to Edwards, "true religion" begins in the moment of an individual's conversion then initiates the spread of faith from the ancient Hebrews to the great Western nations. The Indians at Stockbridge, and particularly the Mohican Cornelius himself, embody the fulfillment of sacred typology.

Typological fulfillment was at the core of Edwards's and Brainerd's particular millennialism and its context for the American Indian. Much of the Second Great Awakening's absorption with figuration drew on the New Light extension of typology meant to verify and extend sacred history to modern day. By creating a third stage of fulfillment, in which eighteenth- and nineteenth-century revivalists modeled themselves upon New Testament types, modern evangelical subjects, following Edwards and other New Lights, cast national history as part of the New Testament narrative and rendered both themselves and their lives part of the sacred current of biblical history. In doing so, they revivified sacred history and the Bible's relevance for the modern age. Edwards cast both the American Indians and New Light revivalists as spiritual counterparts, united both in their existence in a kind of postlapsarian exhile and in the special role they would play in the Fall's reparation through the coming of the millennial reign.

Cornelius's conversion at Stockbridge continued the process initiated by the apostle Peter to the warrior Cornelius recorded in the Book of Acts.[46] This 1751 sermon teaches that "true religion" is primitive Christian religion, scripturally recorded as fifteen hundred years old but becoming newly visible among the New World descendants of the original ancient heathens. Edwards writes of this scriptural history in his *History of the Work of Redemption*, a text designed to offer historical evidence for the second coming of Christ. He derives his sense of sacred chronology in part from Robert Millar's *History of the Propagation of Christianity, and the Overthrow of Paganism* (1723), one of the few books that he brought with him to Stockbridge.[47] And one of the key millennial texts of the growing revivalism in the early eighteenth century. Millar's *Propagation of Christianity* posits the veracity of scriptural history through world history, specifically the spread of Christianity around the globe. Millar systematically goes through every region where Christian missionaries have traveled in order to offer "a plain view, how vast a work it is to propagate the *Christian Religion* over so great a part of the world."[48] But for Edwards, it also suggests the extent to which world history is also sacred history. Edwards takes from Millar a model for understanding Christianity on a global scale. Each revival, each successful missionary enterprise, is proof of the global phenomenon of the second coming of Christ. True religion flourished on American soil, having taken root through the missionary success of Brainerd and then through the piety of the Mohicans in Stockbridge. True religion existed in Edwards's theological imaginary as a place where biblical time stood still, waiting for its continuance on the emergence of the Protestant Reformation. Edwards's aim was not so much to promote the ten lost tribes theory as his predecessors had, but rather to forge a literal typological connection between the Cornelius converted in Acts and the embodied version of this biblical type living and praying in Stockbridge, Massachusetts.

Edwards honed this sermon to accord with Protestant right to the continent of North America and the larger global apocalypse in which New England and America and indigenous people and Protestant revivalists were enfolded.[49] "True religion" emerges as the foil to hypocrisy and also to the larger enemy within the apocalyptic battle, visibly manifest through the ongoing conflict between the

French and their Native American allies. Edwards goes on to explain in his sermon that "true religion" was ancient, primitive, and the opposite of Catholicism:

> True religion don't consist in praying to the Virgin Mary and to saints and angels. It don't consist in crossing themselves, in confessing sins to the priest, and worshipping images of Christ and of the saints, and other things that the French do.[50]

While a mainstay of Protestant self-identification since the Reformation, this proclamation took on special resonance in the early 1750s, a time when the French and the English were not only competing for numbers of New World souls but also for dominion across the vast American continent from Virginia to Nova Scotia. True religion as Edwards presents it in this sermon and elsewhere inscribed divine righteousness into the imperial wars. And, crucially, it revitalized the connection between the American Indian and the Protestant revivalist. When spoken through the voice of the present-day Cornelius, true religion justified Protestant Britain's own imperial presence in the New World by making the claim to the land and conversion of the land's natural inhabitants sanctioned by God. For Edwards it was written into the typology that revealed both the Indian and the Protestant reformer to be linked through New Testament types to the fulfillment of Old Testament typology. Edwards positioned Cornelius as a spokesperson for the Anglo-Protestant cause through his spoken words as well as his oral performance of coming to the "true" faith. Cornelius's and Mary's professions of faith, offered at the beginning of Edwards's "Farewell Sermon," symbolize the incipient unleashing of the ancient and primitive essence of Christianity that Edwards would continue to foster during his time at Stockbridge and in his later theology. While real in and of itself, this unleashing encapsulated in the Mohican profession was also a parallel biblical typology for the ancient and primitive essence of Christianity embodied in revivalism. The two histories, which would become one through the millennial reign, were evidence of the spiritual truth of the other, for it was to this ancient and primitive essence of Christianity to which Protestantism lay claim through its restoration of true religion throughout the fallen world.

Combined with Edwards's act of bearing witness to the conversion experiences observed through Brainerd's missionary activity, the

embodied testimonies of Mary and Cornelius animated the new millennial history that Edwards preached about in his 1739 sermon
series on the *Work of Redemption*. In this sermon series, Edwards
created a typological link between American Indians and the "barbarous nations" found in the fifth-century "Roman empire," an association that Millar also makes.[51] The mark of the barbarian was the
sound of their words, which had a scriptural as well as onomatopoeic resonance. Indeed since ancient Greece, "Barbarians" was a
category used to identify non-Greeks who were thought to utter
meaningless "barbar." In his letter to the Corinthians, Paul defines
the barbarian as one whose speech is incomprehensible to anyone
not familiar with the voice of a particular nation.[52]

In *A History of the Work of Redemption*, Edwards retells this millennial history in order to place New England in an eschatological
frame. Within this frame, indigenous words represent an archaeological key that unlocks a broader ancient and primitive past, one to
which both America's indigenous people and Protestant revivalists
are heir. In the New World as in the Old Testament, numerous "barbarous nations" renounced "Heathenism and embraced Christianity,"
their meaningless barbar changed into a chorus of testimony about
the great expanse of Christendom.[53] The barbarian was thus central
to a historical understanding of the gospel's progress. The testimony
of newly Christianized Indians signals a transformation from darkness to light, from the meaningless linguistic chaos of the fallen
world to the purity of an original doctrine understood through the
universal signs of human comprehension.

A History of the Work of Redemption made New England representative of the Old Testament transition from Moses to David, beginning with the redemption out of Egypt. Starting with the renewal
of the covenant between God and the elect in the twenty-ninth chapter of the Book of Deuteronomy, the Bible foretells how God preserves his church and "wonderfully possessed his people of this
land." Through a classic typological hermeneutic of rendering present historical events as literal fulfillments of the narrative types recounted in the Old Testament, Edwards assigns New England the
geographical and spiritual position within this historical overview.
The witnessing of this work carries forth from one sermon to the
next over the time of several months; the breadth of the work spreads
like the dispersal of nations following the collapse of Babel from the
voice of God in the garden to "remote parts of the world."[54]

Edwards's Stockbridge sermons reveal his efforts to instigate this vision of a global millennial event through a local revival among the Mohican Housatonic Indians. The Stockbridge sermons were preached with simultaneous translation, which partly accounts for the truncated spiritual messages. Several of the Stockbridge sermons also show a convergence of Christian and Mohican cosmologies and epistemologies. Edwards frequently draws from biblical metaphors that have spiritual meaning for his own hermeneutics and a corresponding symbolic value in Mohican culture. In 1751, he preached "Christ Is to the Heart Like a River to a Tree Planted by It." The sermon begins with epigraphs from Psalm 1:3, Jeremiah 17:8, and Isaiah 33:21, followed by a doctrine that condenses these scriptural passages into the singular statement: "Christ is to the heart of a true saint like a river to the roots of a tree that is planted by it."[55] The scriptural symbolism of the river corresponds to the translation of Muh-he-ka-neew, the indigenous name from Mohican, which means "the people of the ever-flowing waters." This is an image Experience Mayhew used in preaching to the Wampanoag on Martha's Vineyard, a likely source for Edwards, given Mayhew had greater knowledge of indigenous language and cosmology. Whether from Mayhew or his own study, Edwards clearly expands and repositions the trope toward a typological end. The tree planted by the river is simultaneously a reference to the Mohican origins story, their ancestral homelands on the banks of the Hudson River, and its roots a metaphor of Christ's love. Edwards unites the indigenous cosmos with scriptural figuration and grounds both in the local landscape of Stockbridge, Massachusetts.

Elsewhere in his writing, Edwards derived spiritual meaning from tree and river imagery. In *Images and Shadows of Divine Things*, he writes, "There is a wonderful analogy between what is seen in RIVERS... [t]he innumerable streams, of which great rivers are constituted, running in such infinitely various and contrary courses, livelily represent the various dispensations of divine providence." This analogy goes on at some length. He sees in earthly rivers a type of divine interconnection. That rivers have one "common end and ultimate issue, and all at length discharging themselves at one mouth into the same ocean," showcases how everything tends toward one. The boundlessness of the ocean is a typological representation of God.[56] This use of natural imagery reflects Edwards's ongoing effort to expand the historically used biblical typology to include more elements discoverable in the natural world. Through the eyes of what "Divine and Supernatural Light" (1733) identifies as "the spiritual man," the natural world becomes newly apparent, not as the foreboding howling wilderness that previous generations looked on as evidence of nature subsequent to the Fall, but rather as a landscape of spiritual plentitude.

Edwards's cosmology, as it evolves in his writing on the natural world, resembles cosmologies more readily associated with an indigenous perspective on the permeability between the natural and the supernatural and on the animate qualities of nature. Another sermon, "God Is Infinitely Strong," reflects this convergence. On the one hand, the sermon describes a version of divine omnipotence that is deeply resonant with Edwards's Calvinist heritage:

> Man's knowledge is not large enough: it can't reach so far as the greatness of God. [A] nutshell can't contain all the waters of the sea: so the mind of man.... We are so far from knowing all of God, that we know but little of ourselves: but little of our bodies, little of our souls.[57]

This is a familiar Calvinist principle; God is omnipotent and omniscient. Human faculties have been irreparably damaged in the Fall such that neither God nor the soul's status can be known while on earth. The "nutshell" resonates with the famous line from *Hamlet*, "Oh God, I could be bounded in a nutshell and count myself kind of infinite space, were it not that I have bad dreams" (Act 2, Scene II). This line in *Hamlet* is an allusion to book 2 of Boethius's *De consolation*, which contrasts the limited wisdom that one can accumulate on earth to the vastness of the cosmos.[58] While Boethian and Calvinist impulses are both apparent in Edwards's sermon, he also develops a sense of God's ubiquity that is a decided departure from the bent of Reformed Calvinist doctrine that emphasized God's more distant withdrawal from the corruption of a fallen world. Not only has God "made all things,"

> He takes care of all things and orders all [the] stars. [He orders the] clouds [and the] winds, [and] makes the trees grow. [He] orders all the affairs of all mankind, [and determines] how they shall live. [He] gives 'em meat and drink, [but he also dispenses] all their trouble and afflictions, [and determines] when they shall die.[59]

Here Edwards describes a God that is much more involved in the daily occurrences of the natural world than in more traditional

Calvinist Puritan accounts. The world that Edwards describes is postlapsarian but not abandoned. Rather, this is a world with far more permeability between visible and invisible realms than ministers preaching in New England in the generations before Edwards would have accepted. Part of this conceptualization of the natural world has to do with Edwards's interest in nature—his recorded observations of the natural world epitomized by his study of spiders—but also his revivification of typology.

Beginning with *Images and Shadows*, perhaps even earlier in his personal notebooks, Edwards's thinking reflects a desire to extend typology to a hermeneutics of nature, a way of reading signs within the landscape as evidence of God. A hyperbolic version of this hermeneutic certainly seems to be at play in the passage quoted above, yet Edwards also takes his interpretation even further here. The idea of God as playing an explicit and omnipotent role in the governance of the natural world ascribes much more causal divine agency to natural events than revealed in Edwards's previous writings. On the one hand, this intensified vision of divine influence in nature might be read as a way of appealing to his audience. By describing God's direct and powerful influence on the cosmos, nature, humankind, and food sources, Edwards may have been trying to appeal to American Indians whose own traditional beliefs aligned with this sense of divine agency. Indeed, as illustrated by the Housatonics' rationale for accepting the Stockbridge mission, native populations had good reasons—including material ones—for currying favor with such a powerful God. Yet, Edwards's description of divine omnipotence does not seem exclusively geared toward strategic ends. This is a sermon that takes up a major Calvinist question about Christian cosmologies, about the extent to which the human faculties have the capacity to perceive God's infinite strength. The Boethian/Calvinist perspective with which Edwards begins is much more limiting than the view on God's place within nature with which the sermon concludes. In a faith defined by the paradox of unknowable knowledge and the limits of human understanding, this passage registers a certain kind of evolution in Edwards's thinking. The world described here partakes of the notions of animate and inanimate nature associated with traditional indigenous systems of belief.

Sergeant, Edwards's predecessor, observed and recorded several rituals and beliefs associated with Stockbridge Indian religion prior to the arrival of Christians. He did so in a disparaging manner, hoping to demonstrate the benighted state from which he hoped to rescue the Indians. Rituals included animal sacrifice, quartered deer offered up to Manitou, the Great Spirit, in acknowledgment of Manitou's status as the giver of all things. The Indians reported to Sergeant that they learned of this ritual from a prophet who had descended from heaven. The prophet had earned their respect by bringing all kinds of good fortune, from clearing the land of monsters to providing snowshoes to facilitate winter walking. Another ritual involved a bear chase in autumn, in which the wounded bear was believed to turn the leaves red. By winter, the Indians killed the bear, linking his fat with the falling snow. Finally, summer melted the fat and turned it into the sap that rose in the trees.[60] Even though Edwards learned of traditional Stockbridge Indian belief through Sergeant's disparaging observations, there is a great deal of resemblance between the Indian God depicted through these rituals and the Christian God described in Edwards's Stockbridge sermons. Both works discussed above draw from this Mohican cosmology in order to describe a God that Edwards's proselytes would perceive as more familiar than a more traditional Calvinist God.

Edwards's aim in describing Christianity's God as palpably interactive in the natural world was not simply an appeal to traditional systems of belief. Rather, he also exhibited a kind of anthropological interest in Mohican depictions of the supernatural, for the idea of a God that had not abandoned the natural world to a state of postlapsarian chaos was more theologically reassuring. Edwards's encounter with the Mohican belief system culminated a career devoted to making nature a more intelligible map of providential design and evidence of grace. The Mohican cosmos offered Edwards a way of elaborating the hermeneutics of nature that he began to flesh out in *Images and Shadows*.

Toward a Linguistics of National Nostalgia

During Edwards's time in Stockbridge in the 1750s, the young Yale-educated missionary Gideon Hawley made frequent appearances in Stockbridge. His journals describe periods of spiritual refreshment in the Edwardses' home after conditions of extreme duress while traveling and preaching among the Six Nations. Hawley exhibited a pattern similar to David Brainerd's, and one is led to imagine that his frequent visits and spiritual disposition reminded Edwards of his late protégé. Hawley's journals are replete with descriptions of Indian conversion that blend a kind of residue of traditional indigenous belief with Christianity. Hawley disparagingly describes remnants of beliefs that are still present in Mohawk culture, including the use of wizards or conjurers to treat the sick. His journal oscillates between disavowal of indigenous beliefs and a willingness to learn as well as partake in Indian culture. He describes following "Indian custom" in the use of the wampum but then also preaching that he "was a minister of Christ."[61]

In one conversion narrative about which Hawley writes extensively, a sick boy sees visions, including one of hell in which "people squirmed like worms in the fire."[62] The boy expands evocatively on hell's torments and concludes with his own recognition of Original Sin. There is no way of knowing from Hawley's journal which aspects of the conversion experience incorporate aspects of traditional belief. However, the boy's visions and affective response far exceed what would be typically narrated in an Anglo-Protestant congregation. Hawley provides another source for Edwards's exposure to ethnographic descriptions of indigenous religious experience. While filtered through the perspective of an evangelical Christian, these descriptions nonetheless reflect a blurring of cosmological worlds, the influence of native beliefs on Christianity as well as the reverse.

Contemporary with Edwards's time in Stockbridge, Hawley's mission was deeply bound up in the devastation and uncertainty of the Seven Years War. On December 20, 1755, Hawley writes in his journal of "alarming News from almost every Quarter and many False Stories which kept us in a perpetual Russle." He confesses his desire to "quit them [the Mohawk] immediately at least fly into the Woods for Shelter." During this same year, Edwards sent his ten-year-old son, Jonathan Jr., to accompany Hawley so that he could learn the Mohawk language. Edwards's desire that his son learn Mohawk is somewhat surprising given his own view on indigenous languages as irreparably fallen and therefore incapable of expressing spiritual truths. In the case of his son, Edwards apparently felt that it would make him a better missionary. As the war escalated, Hawley writes in his journal that he wished "Jonathan was at home with his Parents who must be concerned for him."[63] Still, the experience seemed to have made a deep impression on the young Edwards who grew up to be an astute student of indigenous languages. As a minister and advocate of his father's typology, he not only realized the theological implications encoded in them but also saw anthropological potential for the new nation.

In 1789, Thomas Jefferson thanked James Madison for sending him a "pamphlet" "on the Mohiccon language," written by Jonathan Edwards Jr.[64] By this time, Jefferson was already immersed in the business of studying indigenous tongues, which he viewed as an archive of national history and as scientific clues to the origins of this Native American population. The pamphlet *Observations on the Language of the Muhhekaneew Indians* (1789) sketches an unprecedented arc of comparative linguistics for North America. The younger Edwards introduces the concept of an "original language," from which contemporary variations of "Mohegan," Massachusett, Delaware, Penobscot, Shawnee, and Chippewa derive.[65] By describing something akin to "proto-Algonquian," the *Observations* reaches a level of historical linguistic advancement commensurate to Sir William Jones's Third Anniversary Discourse to the Asiatic Society of Calcutta in which he identified a relationship between various European languages and Sanskrit and Persian.[66] Yet for all of its scientific advancement, Edwards Jr.'s *Observations* makes an odd claim about this original language: the "structure of the language coincides with that of the Hebrew, in an instance in which the Hebrew differs from all the languages of Europe, antient or modern."[67] He represents an important historical juncture in the history of Anglo-Protestant linguistics, between the Hebraic and Asiatic thesis, between the evangelizing function of missionary linguists and the archaeological philosophy of early republic and antebellum statesmen and philosophers.

Ultimately, the similarities between Jefferson's Indian Vocabulary project and Edwards Jr.'s *Observations* are more striking than their differences. Edwards Jr. wrote more as a linguistic anthropologist than as theologian. Both projects participated in the historical process of linguistic preservation in the face of radical human erasure. Proposing neither revitalization nor preservation beyond mere recorded remnants of an otherwise soon to be forgotten past, he does not treat Mohican as a living language. By the end of the eighteenth century, missionary linguistics survived primarily as a means of easing communication during worship. The Indian School at Stockbridge implemented a program to teach the natives English. As Jedidiah Morse reports to the Secretary of War on Indian Affairs in 1822:

> Most of them understand English; numbers can read and write it, and several are able to instruct others. They are more advanced in the knowledge of our language, and in civilization, than any Indians in our country; and many of them are capable of rendering essential service in accomplishing the plan of the government in respect to other tribes.[68]

Morse's remarks reflect a colonial policy of assimilation or removal as the twinned forces defining white and Indian relations in the early years of the Republic. The purpose of assimilation was to elicit the help of native tribes in carrying out government plans. Though Morse describes the Mohicans as somewhat uniquely poised to do this, the first phase of their own displacement had already occurred in 1785 when they moved from Massachusetts to land given them by the Oneidas in upstate New York.[69]

The *Observations* does not mention conversion even though it was written at the same time that the younger Edwards was also leading the "New Divinity Movement" and participating, to a degree, in the Second Great Awakening. Through the task of collecting indigenous languages, both the younger Edwards and Jefferson effectively decoupled these languages from the living bodies that originally spoke them. Edwards Jr. must have apprehended a fate similar to Jefferson's narrative of natural extinction for the Mohican. The words that he learned while playing with native children on his father's reservation resounded in his adult mind as fading echoes of a past with an uncertain place in the nation's future. He published his *Observations* as a kind of eulogy to a past and a people from whom he had long since separated. Behind the scientific frame of each study was a lament for the nation's aboriginal past. In an era rife with warfare and the violent policies of removal, this lament took the form of national mourning. Vocabulary lists, Hebraic associations, and claims to the American continent as the original antiquity helped to construct a myth about the Indian as connected to the land but then relinquishing this connection in order to make way for the next great civilization. Whereas a long colonial history of missionaries saw Algonquian as the foundational language of the New Israel, Jefferson, Edwards Jr., and their contemporaries saw Indian grammar as a sacred script prophesying the rise of a civilized and enlightened nation in the early republic.

The *Observations* is a mournfully retrospective text: "Out of my father's house, I seldom heard any languages spoken, beside the

Indian"; these were my "school-mates" and "play-fellows"; I "thought"
with them; their words were richer and more familiar to me than my
own "mother tongue."[70] The publication of this text three years after
the first phase of Stockbridge migration was not coincidental. The
forty-year-old Edwards Jr. experienced contemporary US policy as his
own personal loss. The end of the Seven Years War brought with it a
dramatic decrease in native populations. As Hawley writes in a 1765
marginalia comment that reflects on the 1754 section of his journal:

> I was at the place where Scannaviss lived in the year 1765 & there was
> not an Indian lived there—In the year 1761 was there and Scannawiss's
> [widow] lived there and three or four with her. The Indians who used
> to dwell here are many of them dead ~~but most~~ the rest removed. The
> Indians decrease very fast.[71]

The preface to Edwards Jr.'s *Observations* registers this loss. His
schoolmates and play-fellows are the ghosts of a past still vividly
etched within the author's mind. Paying homage to these ghosts, the
Observations records for future generations an invaluable linguistic
record of a group of languages under constant threat of extinction.
Edwards Jr. compensated for this threat by ascribing a sacred etymology to the language through his own explanation of Mohican's
Hebraic origins. On the question of origins, he equivocates "North
American Indians" are of either "Hebrew" or "Asiatic extraction."[72]
This equivocation reflects an individual caught between competing
impulses: his skill as a linguist, his belief as a theologian, and his af-
fection for childhood friends. The text registers the historical trauma
of indigenous displacement and deracination through an inability to
chart the science of linguistics to human origins. The *Observations*
clings ardently to theological beliefs in the sacred, prophetic content
of indigenous words. These beliefs persisted alongside the rise of
comparative linguistics and alongside the concomitant displacement
of native populations.

Franco-Catholic Communication and Indian Alliance in the Seven Years War

War had no sooner been declared in 1754 than the new children of God, of the king, and of M. Picquet thought only of proving their fidelity and valour.

—J. J. LEFRANÇOIS DE LALANDE, *Mémoire sur la vie de M. Picquet, missionnaire au Canada*

By the 1750s, Britain had a sizable population of more than a million people in the American colonies needing room to grow. The population of New France was considerably less, somewhere around 55,000. Moreover, French settlements were less permanent and more scattered. Yet colonists within New France, primarily comprising Jesuit priests and fur traders, had established settlements that were carefully protected and controlled, thus thwarting Britain's efforts to advance into new territory.[1] These contests over land and sovereignty in North America escalated during the global conflict of the Seven Years War (1754–1763).[2] In a bloody imperial conflict that lasted almost a decade, each side felt the imminent threat of loss and had to recalibrate military strategy and colonial warfare. Due to France's significantly smaller colonial population and the interwoven nature of its trade and missionary settlements with native inhabitants, France relied heavily on American Indian allegiance in its effort to win the war. Maintaining these alliances required superior knowledge of indigenous languages.

The Seven Years War had a direct impact on the longer colonial history of missionary linguistics. Advanced missionary expertise in indigenous languages and colonial strategies of manipulation permitted French North Americans to shore up alliances at the same time as they sought to ingrain Catholic ritual in indigenous communities. Despite their overtures toward totalizing control, however, the hierarchy set in place by French Catholic government and ecclesiology permitted greater degrees of syncretism and interpretive fluidity in translated Christian texts. This had the unintended effect of producing a body of Catholic catechistical texts—including hymnals and prayer books—that contained signs with a multiplicity of meanings. French colonial efforts produced an indigenous Catholicism that would long outlast the imperial presence of the French in North America. While the French did maintain strong native alliances throughout the war, their attempt to impose indigenous Catholicism as a lasting mark of colonial domination in fact triggered the transformation and reinterpretation of religious ritual and practice.

The Anglo-American rhetorical conflation of "popery" and "savagery" to emerge during the Seven Years War was hardly surprising given the millennial understandings of imperial conflict leading up to 1754. This conflation was in fact a direct response to French military strategy. Customs official Archibald Kennedy observed the deteriorating state of Anglo-Indian relations in 1754 and suggested emulating the French as a means of ameliorating the situation: "If we intend to convince them [the Indians] that we are really in earnest, and that they should fight for us, we must fight along with them…the *French* seldom fail of this Method."[3] Kennedy describes proximity and interconnection as key facets of French military strategy. French nobleman and naval officer Roland-Michel Barrin de la Galissonniére affirms this perception. Explaining the reasons for the French "superiority over the English," he describes French Canadians "who are accustomed to live in the woods like the Indians, and become thereby not only qualified to lead them to fight the English, but to wage war even against these same Indians when necessity obliges."[4] This passage echoes numerous French Jesuit accounts of spending hours in the wigwams of American Indians to learn their language and culture. The intense ethnographic engagement that French colonials had exercised throughout their 150 years in North America paid off through strong military alliances during the war, permitting France to maintain a stronghold despite the disproportionate colonial populations.

French and American Indian military alliances created a climate in which Anglo-Protestants could readily identify the impetus behind the imperial war with the Protestant battle against the dual bulwark of the New World Anti-Christ.[5] An Anglican minister preached in Philadelphia in 1755:

The *British* Nation no sooner possessed this new World, than the Light of the Gospel shone forth with a pure, a reformed Lustre.... Protestantism seemed to be a Blessing designed for this Part of *America*. That corrupt Branch of Christianity, if it yet deserves the Name of Christian, called *Popery*, made its Appearance only to be loaded with its deserved Contempt...the Banners of *France* are now displayed, her Fleets have sailed, her Armies been transported, to establish at once the Thrones of Tyranny and Superstition in this Western World. Efforts black and horrid! Efforts destructive of every Thing sacred and good.[6]

The rhetoric of this sermon and other sources contained the raw material that James Fenimore Cooper had at his disposal as he depicted such scenes of the Seven Years War such as the Fort William Henry Massacre (1757) in his historical romance *The Last of the Mohicans* (1826). Cooper encapsulates the Anglo-American sentiment represented by Reading and others through the statement that the "Iroquois are thorough savages."[7] Divisions between redeemed and savage, noble and fallen, good and bad Indians that structure Cooper's early *Leatherstocking Tales* fall along the Franco-Catholic and Anglo-Protestant axis that crystalized during the Seven Years War. During this time, not only did Anglo efforts at constructing American Indian alliances prove less fruitful, but British-Americans practiced an entirely different model of colonialism that involved almost completely abandoning previous missionary efforts to learn native languages and to teach native proselytes in their own mother tongue. In keeping with the patterns established among missionaries such as David Brainerd and the plans for an Indian school at Stockbridge, Christian Indian schools and the Anglican Society for the Propagation of the Gospel increasingly imposed English as the lingua franca of Christianity and British nationalism. In doing so, the British sought to regulate worship in such a way as to make Christian, British, and ultimately American identities inseparable and unintelligible in languages other than English. Living native languages were increasingly received as savage sounds in the Anglo-American imaginary, even as records of these languages began to constellate a key archive of America's natural historical and archaeological past by the late eighteenth century. In contrast, the French successfully ingrained indigenous Catholicism as their lasting colonial mark in North America, using the extensive knowledge of Mohawk, Mi'kmaq, and other languages accrued by the Jesuits as their basis for doing so.

Mohawk Battle Hymns

In François Picquet's Mohawk mission of La Présentation (1749–1759, Oswegatchie, now Ogdensburg, N.Y.), linguistic knowledge was a source of authority and military intelligence. The manipulation of indigenous words and symbols was thought to secure native allegiance to France and to inscribe Catholicism as a lasting mark of France's imperial presence in the New World. However, indigenous Catholicism, a syncretic blend of Mohawk cosmology and Catholic doctrine, emerged. French missionaries had, for generations, honed their evangelizing skills through creative translations of Christian texts, translations that did not depend on a one-to-one correspondence between the Word and signified phenomenon but rather exhibited a looser connection between ritual worship and the expression of religious truths. Catholicisms indigenous to North America took shape within local communities where translated Christian texts circulated for generations. Indeed many of the documents created by French missionaries during the colonial period are still in circulation today. The codification of indigenous Catholicisms is associated with the missionary practices that occurred during the Seven Years War when the strategic value of indigenous worship to French military strategy heightened. The indigenous capacity to enact forms of Catholic worship in their own tongue became a crucial vehicle and marker of political and religious allegiance. Yet the translation of Christian texts into Mohawk permitted hymnals powerful modes of aural expression: the hymnal generated multiple meanings within the circumscribed framework of ritual worship. Imperial conflict augmented the missionaries' desire to hear the singing of Catholic hymns in native languages and to observe other forms of indigenous-Catholic worship. Religious ritual reflected colonial domination, even as the syncretic components of indigenous Catholicism also opened up avenues for the circumvention of French colonial control.

The scant archive narrating the history of Picquet's interactions with the Mohawk Indians living south of the Great Lakes does not leave much of a record of indigenous undermining of French colonial control. Most of the existing scholarship on Piquet is hyperbolic about his successes, emphasizing his service as a chaplain in France's army and his ability to enlist the Six Nations to the French cause. This scholarship, consisting primarily of French Jesuit biographies that are one hundred years old or more, elides Mohawk agency almost completely.[8] Picquet's interaction with the Mohawk has been largely narrated by Catholic historians invested in a specific religious and national memory of the French presence in North America. This skewed perspective amplifies the Euro-centrism of the archive. The exchanges that took place between Picquet and his Mohawk proselytes allows access to Mohawk modes of guarding their own cultural autonomy and integrity during this period of intensified French colonial efforts to shore up alliances and allegiances. Alongside the scant information on the life of Picquet, a hymnal that Picquet used in the mission, *La Présentation*, and presumably carried with him on his travels, offers clues to the complexity of the language encounter.

Following his training at the Séminaire de Saint-Sulpice in Paris, where he was ordained priest in 1734, Picquet, like many of his Jesuit brethren, became a skilled Franco-American linguist. At the beginning of his missionary sojourn in the New World, Picquet took up residency at the Lac des Deux Montagnes where he devoted a decade to learning Iroquois custom and language for the Sulpician mission. During this time, against the backdrop of the War of Austrian Succession (known in the North American context most commonly as the War of Jenkins' Ear, 1739, and as King George's War, 1744–1748), Picquet solidified his goal of winning the Iroquois nations over to the French before settling in his own missionary community on the banks of the St. Lawrence River in 1748. In his St. Lawrence mission, Picquet wrote hymns and catechetical texts in Mohawk, Huron, and Iroquois. His manuscript notebook, compiled during his years as a missionary, reveals the great care that he took in order to compose these hymns.[9]

Small and portable, designed to be carried with him on his journeys through Mohawk country, the pages toward the back of the hymnal contain practice sheets where Picquet carefully worked out how to set Mohawk words to music. The hymns honoring the saints and the Pater are carefully composed with the musical notes that are set as they would be in a traditional Catholic hymnal. Mohawk words accord with the musical score. Picquet used his own orthographical scheme to translate the primarily oral Mohawk language into a written language. His decisions for orthography accord with modern guides to Mohawk-language learning, suggesting that he at least attempted to accurately represent what he heard. Standard orthography for

Mohawk makes use of twelve letters from the roman alphabet and a glottal marker, the same letters and marker that we see in Picquet's hymnal. The vowel and consonant combinations also appear to be commensurate.[10] Through his system of transcription, Picquet was able to match each syllable to one note on the page of the hymnal. Musicality was important to Picquet, as he followed the French colonial precedent for aesthetically pleasing translations as established by Jean de Brébeuf in his Huron Christmas carol and by Le Clercq's translation of the Lord's Prayer into Mi'kmaq ideograms. In the sacred space of ritual worship, the integrity of the translation ceased to matter. The ordering of the hymns to begin each worship session took precedent over the precision of meaning. Picquet's success with baptisms, as evidenced through the log in the back of this notebook, reflects his effectiveness in creating this ritual space.

This written translation of the hymns into Mohawk clearly distorts Mohawk's syntactical structure, which comes with a specific set of conventions for elocution. To set Mohawk to music, Picquet had to force the words to accord with a Christian master-script. Meant to be sung, however, hymns comprised both words and music. These dimensions of the hymn might come together in the ritual space that Picquet created for worship, or they might not. In fashioning the words themselves, Picquet built on his in-depth knowledge of Mohawk, which allowed for a more dialectical interaction between music and word resulting in the Catholic hymn's transformation through its syncretic blend with Mohawk. In fashioning this translation, Picquet drew from the long medieval tradition of translating Latin hymns into the vernacular.[11] Middle English and French lyric frequently departed from the Latin original through alteration in syntax, vocabulary, rhythm, images, and allusions. This departure from the original was not a form of loss or deterioration. The vernacular took on its own "tone and atmosphere." Shifting imagistic emphasis brought about a "sweetening" tone that added a dimension of emotion and warmth to the music.[12]

Even a cursory glance at representative manuscripts from each time period reveals striking continuity of practice between medieval translation of Latin hymns into European vernaculars and Picquet's translation of hymns from French into Mohawk. Immediately, one sees commensurate patterns of textual variance, or *mouvance*, which occurs when the musical line extends beyond the written word.[13] Musicologist Emma Dillon identifies *mouvance* as a key facet of song in medieval France. The pairing of words with pitch is present in the translation, but other elements of song are not, namely indications of melody and also rhythm. Textual variance enables us to imagine transmission and transformation through performance. Songs are oral processes of creation and re-creation; what is absent from the written page, namely the indications of the key elements of rhythm and melody, are precisely the crucial ingredients of the song's aural qualities. Another common facet of medieval French song and Mohawk hymns was that both precede the era of sound recording. As such, each preserved script represents a history of sounds that cannot be captured.[14] The archive, as it pertains to medieval French song and eighteenth-century Mohawk hymnody is in this sense equally elusive. And yet, there is a crucial epistemology encoded in the song's sound that falls in between poetry and music. Sonic utterance cannot be scripted. Song, therefore, must be unscripted from the written record.[15]

In the case of the Mohawk hymns, we might ask how one does this and, if successful, what is left? Perhaps there is no record beyond this written fragment that might give us some sense as to how these hymns sounded when sung and performed by Picquet's proselytes. We begin to acknowledge the "song's sounding life" as it existed within this eighteenth-century community by emulating the approach practiced by many scholars of New France and by reading the *Jesuit Relations* for evidence of what this scene of aural/oral worship may have sounded like, while also examining the traditional role of song in Mohawk culture.

The *Relations* recount a history of French missionary surprise and admiration at the Mohawk capacity to effectively sing translated hymns. A 1735 Jesuit letter from Sault St. Louis reports on the importance of singing to the success of the mission: "For our savages singing is a necessary adjunct, as they are incapable of prolonged mental application." The letter goes on to report that the natives are exceptionally skilled at this mnemonic device. They sing with an "ear so correct that they do not miss a half-tone in all the church hymns."[16] This precision is particularly remarkable when one considers the textual variance recorded in Picquet's notebook, the complete absence of any written indication of how the song should be sung. Jesuit observations on Mohawk singing also indicate that sound was more important than meaning, or, at least that correct sound needed to precede accuracy of meaning. This focus on the sonic utterance speaks directly to the unscriptable aspects of the history of song, of the way in which the aural and oral performance of a hymn in a designated ritual space superseded the need for translational precision. Jesuits' missionary practice, in explicit contrast to the English, permitted the spirit to reside within this performative space of song.

The medieval history of translation from Latin hymn to vernacular lyric is instructive in imagining what happened when Mohawk was set to the music of a Catholic hymnal, particularly given that most of the hymns in Picquet's notebook date from the fourteenth century or earlier.[17] Rather than the integrity of meaning conveyed through the Latin hymn, meaning mutated through the translation, with new modes of emphasis and allusion guided by the structure of the vernacular language itself. This was the opposite of the theory of translation that Cotton Mather put forth in his *Psalterium Americanum* (1718), which explains that

> Our Poetry has attempted many Versions of the PSALMS... [but] they *leave out* a vast heap of those rich things, which the Holy SPIRIT of GOD speaks in the Original Hebrew; and that they *put in* as large an Heap of poor Things, which are intirely *their own.* All this has been merely for the sake of preserving the *Clink* of the *Rhime.*[18]

The principle guiding Mather's translation theory as presented in the *Psalterium* is that the authentic and original meaning of the psalms in Hebrew should be preserved as much as possible, over creating a poetically pleasing translation. Mather also discusses this in the *Magnalia*, explaining that "*detractions* from, *additions* to, and *variations* of" were "offen[sive]" to the psalmist.[19] Psalms differed from hymns generically, for they were more intently based on the authenticity of God's word, rather than devotional poems written by individuals. In the Protestant tradition, psalters rather than hymnals structured church singing in colonial America for much of the seventeenth and eighteenth centuries, with standard congregational hymnals not appearing until the mid-nineteenth century. Song as an integral facet of church ritual followed suit with this principle of authentic translation. Anglo colonists "lined out" their psalms, meaning that the clerk or elder read one or two lines so that those who could not sing joined in. In contrast to the Catholic hymnals, words mattered more than song. Gradually, over the course of the eighteenth century, the role of the singing master grew in prominence in church service, leading to more florid rendering of psalm tunes.

The emphasis that Mather places on maintaining the original meaning when translating from Hebrew to English structured Protestant missionary approaches to psalter and hymnal translations as well. Pedagogies of reading enacted through the *Indian Primer* persist in Puritan and Anglican translations of psalters and hymnals into indigenous languages in the eighteenth and early nineteenth centuries, beginning with Experience Mayhew's *Massachusett Psalter*, first published in 1709 (see Fig. 6.1). Mayhew's *Psalter* is organized much like Eliot's Bible, with the Massachusett text in one column, alongside the English. There is absolutely no musical notation, indicating a less structured and more improvisational singing culture, as opposed to the robust and ritualized communal experience of hymnal singing among the Jesuit missions.

From the 1710s through the early nineteenth century, psalter and hymnal translations became one way for the Mohawk to guard the integrity of their language and preserve part of their culture in the face of ongoing efforts of colonization, evangelization, and frontier violence. The Mohawk proved quite resistant to learning English under the religious instruction of Anglican missionaries working for the Society for the Propagation of the Gospel (SPG). The Book of Common Prayer was printed in Mohawk in 1715, 1769, and then in 1787 by Mohawk Joseph Brant, who received his religious instruction in Moor's Charity School. Brant's identity is significant here because for much of the eighteenth century, the Mohawk themselves insisted upon practicing the Christian faith in Mohawk, in resistance to British attempts to teach them English. The 1787 edition credits SPG's

FIGURE 6.1. Experience Mayhew, *Massachusetts Psalter* (1709).

efforts, executed by missionaries Henry Barclay and John Ogilvie, to translate "passages of Scripture, Occasional Prayers, and some singing Psalms" with the widespread circulation of bilingual Mohawk and English Christian texts. This preface gently elides the history of struggles between Mohawks and Anglican missionaries over whether or not the liturgy would be learned in English or Mohawk. Brant's edition also points out that the vast majority of Mohawk prayer books were destroyed in the American Revolution, indicating a thriving scribal culture of these texts, which have since been lost. Finally, the preface explains that the purpose of the bilingual Christian texts is to encourage missionaries to learn Mohawk and Mohawk to learn English, indicating a transparency of meaning between the English and Mohawk versions of Scripture and prayer.[20]

The assumption behind this description of the hymnal as a language-instruction text is precisely the opposite to the Jesuit production of syncretic missionary textual objects. Rather than blending the indigenous cosmology and religious culture into the ritual space of the Christian song, the Anglican psalter/hymnal assumes that both reading audiences—Mohawk and English—will derive the same meaning from the words. Embedded in this approach are vestiges of Mather's theory of a translation that cedes scriptural authority to the original even here. Meaning is fixed in Protestant practices of Christian translation. Even if instructing Mohawk in English was one intended function of the hymnal, it tended not to work out in practice, as evidenced through the long history of Mohawk chiefs translating Christian texts into Mohawk: Joseph Brant; William Johnson, a Mohawk preacher responsible for a 1763 printing of the Mohawk prayer book in Boston; and John Norton, who translated a Mohawk version of the Gospel of John.[21] These Mohawk translations became a way of preserving language and hence culture among the Mohawk, though they did not seem to foster a form of indigenous Anglicanism commensurate to the indigenous Catholicism discussed above. While it is perfectly possible that the bilingual text permitted a double vision of the gospel's meaning, depending on whether a Mohawk or English person read the text, the textual variance in Picquet's hymnal permitted the simultaneous performance of two distinct cosmologies through song in a way that was not present in the Protestant hymnal.

The Society for the Propagation of the Gospel persisted with this tactic of producing and circulating bilingual Christian texts. *Ne Karoron Ne Teyerihwahkwatha, A Collection of Psalms and Hymns* in 1839 shows a remarkable pattern of continuity across a hundred-year period of Protestant psalter and hymnal translations into North American languages. *Ne Karoron Ne Teyerihwahkwatha* shows the psalm or hymn in Mohawk alongside the English (see Fig. 6.2). There is little musical notation or suggestions for how the song should be performed. The intention behind this bilingual arrangement was to suggest a kind of fixity of meaning. Mohawk words are contorted loosely into rhyme schemes, either couplets or abba. The translator attended to the poetical dimensions of the text but left the singing ritual completely unregulated, suggesting a great deal of variation in live performances.

Picquet, by comparison, structures the sonic utterance much more precisely. He pairs each Mohawk syllable to a musical note, emphasizing the song rather than words. Each performance of the Mohawk Catholic hymn was thus bound by the form sketched in the hymnal yet it also opened a space where the actual meaning of the words was less fixed, more open to the interpretation of the performers. The difference between song and writing systems meant that song could escape some of the logocentric bias that Europeans brought to the New World.[22] While musical notations denote a certain process of transcription, they are written in the service of creating an aural/oral performance. The ritual of Catholic song as it was performed and enacted in New France generated a syncretic quality, heightened due to the primarily oral facets of the Mohawk language, where inflection determines meaning, much more so than in English, French, or other traditionally literate languages. Moreover, traditional Mohawk belief strongly associated singing and spirituality. Mohawk ceremonies and rituals employ song to maintain equilibrium between the individual

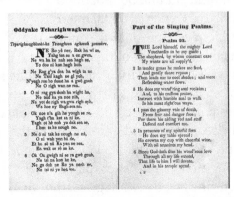

FIGURE 6.2. *Ne Karoron Ne Teyerihwahkwatha, A Collection of Psalms and Hymns* (1839).

and the spiritual worlds. Songs pertained to the change of seasons, healing rituals, and ceremonies of condolence and mourning. Given these traditions, we can reasonably assume that the Mohawk Picquet converted to Catholicism had a long history of song before his arrival, and that they understood song as spiritual practice. The pre-contact existence of a thriving song culture was what the Jesuits admired about the Mohawks' singing skills in the *Relations*. Quite possibly for this reason, the hymnals featured in Picquet's notebook are often musically challenging and sophisticated by nature.

The motet featured below, inherently polyphonic, worked well in vernacular translations. Since the thirteenth century, theorists of the motet have associated the genre with learned listeners who supposedly had the capacity to appreciate subtle art. It was not a choral form typically sung among the masses, who were thought to lack the capacity to understand the motet's richly aesthetic powers of symbol, number, and allusion. That alone makes the motet an interesting choice of genre for Picquet to include in his Catholic hymnal (see Fig. 6.3). Additionally, motets are homogeneously imitative, blending diverse textures and contrasting lines of both words and music.[23] Motets are also contrapuntal, consisting of varying melodies. Religious motets were written for a particular holy day and sung at Mass between the Credo and Vespers. The multilayered textuality of the song, the aesthetic power conveyed through highly developed images, and the dramatic role of the motet in Catholic religious ritual made this genre a logical choice for Picquet to employ in his Mohawk mission. The motet was conducive to the kind of syncretism that Picquet hoped to foster among his Mohawk converts. The motet generated a language of prayer that superseded linguistic and cultural boundaries but that could still be mobilized in the service of French national interests.

By creating a blended Catholicism among the Mohawk, Picquet gained the invaluable allegiance of this tribe to the French cause. Yet in doing so, he also fostered an indigenous Catholicism that far outlived France's colonial control in North America. Songs, particularly religious and ceremonial songs, could act as retainers for the preservation of Mohawk language and culture, from the mid-eighteenth century to the present day. The St. Regis Catholic Church on the Akwesasne Reservation is one such place where this is the case. Founded by Jesuits in 1755, the St. Regis Catholic Church is still fully operational and is one of the few places where Catholic hymns are sung in Mohawk during Mass every Sunday as a way of keeping the

FIGURE 6.3. François Picquet, *Prayer Book*, Newberry Library, Chicago, Ill.

native language alive.[24] The historical irony that could be drawn from this scenario is striking: the colonial forces that participated in the language's destruction are now acting in the service of its preservation. Indeed, some historians of Christian songs in native languages suggest that Christianity actually played a role in the retention of native languages through missionary translations of Scripture and

hymns. A compilation produced in the early twenty-first century includes Christian songs in fifteen different languages.[25] Yet this claim
for Christianity's participation in a complex act of preservation does
not take into account that traditional indigenous singing practices
and rituals were enfolded into these translations. The very act of
preservation through Christianity's influence depended on a porous
and malleable sense of a shared song culture. I believe that this is
why some practicing Christian Mohawk in the St. Regis Choir, for
example, observe that there is no contradiction between practicing
one's faith in Mohawk and practicing in French or English. Catholicism
has long stood alongside Mohawk traditions, offering an intercultural blend of prayer, language, and ritual worship.

Ethnographers observe that Mohawk rituals for grief and condolence remain consistent over time and place. The chants employed in
such rituals unleashed a spiritual force intended to both honor the
dead and renew the energy of individual mourners such that the
community could move forward.[26] In the eighteenth century, Anglican,
Jesuit, and indigenous missionaries alike attempted to enfold these
traditional Mohawk practices within a Christian framework. Mohawk
Joseph Brant's hymnal contains a chapter "The Order for the Burial
of the Dead," which begins by instructing priests and clerks to meet
at the entrance to the churchyard and then advance "towards the
Grave," saying or singing. Brant's instruction for what to say or sing
consists of words from Scripture. He offers no melody whatsoever,
continuing with the conventions of the Anglican hymnal of placing
the emphasis on words rather than sound.[27] Yet, this instruction to
advance "towards the Grave" echoes the movement that Deserontyon
records in his condolence ritual. Picquet also includes a "Graduel
pour la masse des morts" in his hymnal. The Gradual was a chant
sung in a traditional Catholic Mass. By including it here, Picquet integrates one of the older and most important aspects of Catholic Mass
into Mohawk Christian practice. In making song and ritual an integral part of Anglican and Catholic practices of honoring the dead,
both Picquet and Brant create a space for the syncretic inclusion of
more traditional Mohawk practices of ritual condolence.

Picquet drew the Mohawk to the Catholic religion and ultimately
to French national interest by focusing ritual worship on the singing
of traditional Catholic hymns and the recitation of homilies that
were rich in poetical images. He achieved a large number of baptisms by paying close attention to the indigenous traditions, includ-

ing origins stories that fostered distrust and even hatred of those from different clans. Picquet transformed this tradition into a rallying cry for alignment with French national interests and defiance of the English, carefully yoking religious worship to military action. A banner made of white silk and trimmed with gold is material evidence of symbolic union between religion and war. Sent to Picquet's mission, *La Présentation*, by the nuns of the congregation of *Oka*, the Lake of the Two Mountains, the banner contains the symbol of the cross and also the symbol of each clan composing the Five Nations of the Iroquois. This conflation of Christic and indigenous imagery is still present in many Mohawk Christian congregations today, such as the St. Regis Catholic Church. Picquet's banner was used primarily for church ceremonies, including processions on feast days, and for decoration in the church. But Picquet also used the banner to unite the Five Nations in their love for France and opposition to the English by carrying it through the battlefields, including the capture of Fort Necessity, Fort William Henry, Fort Lyddius (Fort Edward), Corlar (Schenectady), and finally Fort Oswego. By mobilizing this emblem in the dual service of Catholic worship and French military conquest, Picquet was able to align Iroquois fealty with French war efforts.

The function of the banner during the Seven Years War resembles the *Labarum*, or standard of the cross that sanctified Constantine's army in the fourth century. Edward Gibbon's description of the *Labarum* in his *History of the Decline and Fall of the Roman Empire* (1776–1788) bears a striking resemblance to descriptions of the form and function of Picquet's banner. The original *Labarum* was enormous, requiring fifty guards to carry it into battle. The symbols displayed on the banner consisted of the arms of Constantine and the cross. According to Gibbon:

In the second civil war Licinius felt and dreaded the power of this consecrated banner, the sight of which, in the distress of battle, animated the soldiers of Constantine with an invincible enthusiasm, and scattered terror and dismay through the ranks of the adverse legions. The Christian emperors, who respected the example of Constantine, displayed in all their military expeditions the standard of the cross.... The solemn epithets of, safety of the republic, glory of the army, restoration of public happiness, are equally applied to religious and military trophies; and there is still extant a medal of the emperor Constantius,

where the standard of the labarum is accompanied with these memorable words, BY THIS SIGN THOUGH SHALT CONQUER.[28]

Gibbon describes the power of a symbol that Picquet also aspired to
achieve through his use of the religious banner in New France. As
with the labarum, the French colonial banner melded symbols of
spiritual and secular power into a totem of Christian militancy.

King Louis XV recognized Picquet's comparable success in making
such a consecrated symbol as to "animate" "invincible enthusiasm"
among the Mohawk members of the French army by rewarding him
with a pension for winning the allegiance of the Six Nations.[29] In
fostering continuity across centuries, including hymns dating from
the third century and battle tactics aligned with the fall of Rome,
Picquet grafted an ancient imperial template onto North America,
enfolding the Mohawk Indians into a grand Christian design of imperial triumph. By 1755, Picquet had fully devoted himself to the
conflict between France and Britain in North America. He became a
military adviser in the army and actually took part in expeditions
against Fort Bull, east of Lake Oneida in New York, and in Oswego.
In 1758, François-Gaston Lévis, commander of the infantry battal-
ions dispatched to Canada, was charged with the task of leading
three thousand troops into Mohawk territory in order to try to force
the Mohawk to attack British settlements on the Mohawk and
Hudson Rivers.[30] Had Lévis been successful, this would have signaled a massive shift in the war's momentum, since the Mohawk
were the most pro-British of all of the Iroquois nations. At the time,
Picquet was both the most successful missionary to the Mohawks
and the most skilled in their language. Lévis immediately recognized
the potential of Picquet's power and knowledge for his military strategy. While attempting to defend Fort Niagara from British attack,
Lévis and his fellow officer, Pierre Pouchot, realized that Piquet's
mission could be used to defend the river passage leading to the
fort.[31] According to Lévis's 1758 letter to the Secretary of War, Picquet
accompanied the army officers in their endeavors to convey military
strategy to the natives. Not only Picquet's linguistic knowledge but
also his reputation among the Mohawk turned into an invaluable military asset.[32] This strategy of building alliances through insider knowledge of language and culture was a unique facet of mid-eighteenth
century French colonialism. In contrast to the Anglo-Protestant approach, which witnessed a revival through the implementation of

English-language instruction and more affective modes of conversion, the French shored up their ethnographic expertise to build a formidable defense.

Ideographs and Ideologies of War

Another massive point of conflict and torn indigenous allegiance during the war, Acadia provides an interesting comparison to the Great Lakes region where Piquet exhibited his military and diplomatic influence. Pierre Maillard studied theology at the Séminaire de Saint-Esprit in Paris before coming to North America and settling at the Malagawatch mission on Cape Breton as the missionary to the Mi'kmaq Indians in the spring of 1735. During the War of Austrian Succession, Maillard begin to use his influence on the Mi'kmaq to organize attacks on British troops. In 1749, Maillard relocated his missionary headquarters to the Isle de la Sainte-Famille (now Chapel Island) where he built permanent settlements.[33]

Like Picquet, Maillard kept a manuscript notebook of Catholic prayers in the language of the population that he sought to convert. In Maillard's case, the Lord's Prayer and the sign of the cross inscribed in Mi'kmaq ideograms had already been in circulation in Cape Breton for nearly a century. Where Picquet bridged the linguistic divide through music, Maillard used the ideographic symbols that he had inherited from his predecessor, Father Christian Le Clercq, who claimed to have developed these symbols from an indigenous system of writing.[34] As discussed in more depth in chapter 2, in the seventeenth century, Le Clercq used this system of ideographs in order to more effectively translate Catholic prayers into Mi'kmaq. Maillard thus entered a missionary community in Cape Breton, where an advanced mnemonic system for learning Catholic prayers and syncretic forms of worship had been in place for generations. The ideographs enabled Le Clercq to translate liturgies, hymns, and catechisms into Mi'kmaq. Maillard expanded the ideographic system developed by Le Clercq, devoting voluminous manuscript pages to recording and then translating the ideographs. From them, Maillard made an extensive prayer book for the Mi'kmaq community.[35]

Although this proliferation of Catholic-Mi'kmaq signs served primarily an evangelizing purpose, Maillard also developed a program for his own extensive study of the Mi'kmaq language. His notebooks

are replete with grammatical and syntactical observations. He created an orthography of Mi'kmaq based on the Roman alphabet for
his own purposes. Maillard did not believe that the Mi'kmaq people
should have access to this alphabetic version of their language. He
espoused the idea that teaching indigenous populations to read and
write would be dangerous. His *Account of the Customs and Manners
of the Micmakis and Maricheets Savage Nations*, published originally
in English in 1758 from a French manuscript, explains Maillard's
belief that the knowledge of sacred texts should remain with the
priests. Maillard's rationale is that Mi'kmaq literacy would be dangerous because their mind is too keen. They should be kept in ignorance lest they become convinced that they know a lot more than
their teachers.[36] Maillard's imposition of a knowledge hierarchy is
beset with a series of ironies. He arrives at a notion of the Mi'kmaq
mind as intelligent and therefore dangerous through a study of their
language: "the abundance of words in this language surprized, and
continues to surprize me every day the deeper I get into it. Every
thing is proper in it; nothing borrowed, as among us."[37] In conveying
his surprise, Maillard observes that Mi'kmaq is a much richer language than he imagined it to be when he first started to study it in
detail. He also elevates Mi'kmaq above French as a purer language,
less corrupted by the admixture of forms inevitable in the composition of complex languages.

Embedded in Maillard's assumptions are those of several Enlightenment philosophers of linguistic origins, from Giambattista Vico to
Jean-Jacques Rousseau. Both Vico and Rousseau recount a narrative
of loss as language transforms from its original primitive state to the
medium of communication in refined nations. According to Rousseau:

> By a natural progression all lettered languages must change character
> and lose force as they gain clarity, that the more one aims at perfect
> ing grammar and logic the more one accelerates this progress, and
> that in order to make a language cold and monotonous in no time,
> one has only to establish academies among the people that speaks it.[38]

Described here and elsewhere in eighteenth-century language philosophy is a trade-off. Language originated in the passions rather than
in reason; development of a reasoned discourse came at the cost of
figural linguistic plentitude. Yet this postlapsarian trajectory also presented a philosophical problem, particularly as it was implemented

in practice among first-hand observers of so-called primitive tongues. Missionaries such as Maillard heard sounds in present historical time, not as vestiges of an ancient world. This caused a problem of historical disjunction; it is difficult to hear embodied spoken sounds as historically distant. Consequently, first-hand observers often heard indigenous languages as at once primordially savage as well as capable of great refinement. As Maillard explains in a letter dated March 27, 1755:

> As nothing inchants those people more than a style of metaphors and allegories, in which even their common conversation abounds, I adapt myself to their taste, and never please them better than when I give what I say this turn, speaking to them in their own language.[39]

The colonial problem that Maillard faces is how to manage an indigenous language that in many ways seemed more pure and refined than French. This was particularly dangerous since refined tongues indicated the complexities of the "savage" mind. Maillard turned his attention to creative translations of the ideographs, designed to be parochial. He then expressed satisfaction that through these parochial translations, the Mi'kmaq quickly learned all that he wanted them to know. He retained the knowledge that he deemed too dangerous and therefore susceptible to abuse. The Mi'kmaq read the hieroglyphs from left to right and the form and meaning fix in their mind, Maillard reports.[40] Form and meaning are one in Maillard's description of his own pedagogical practice. But to teach the Mi'kmaq the Roman alphabet, to give them access to Scripture and other translated Christian texts, would sever this intimate connection between form and meaning. As a highly skilled linguist who wrote extensively on the comparative aspects of his linguistic work, Maillard well knew that words conveyed an uneasy relationship to their signified meaning. His objective as a missionary was to keep sign and referent linked in the mind of his Mi'kmaq proselytes, to fix the form rigidly such that there was no room for the autonomy that comes through interpretation.

Maillard inscribed his Mi'kmaq proselytes within an enclosed symbolic system that was exactly the opposite of the world opening to him through his ethnographic linguistic study. For the purposes of advancing his own knowledge, he matched each Mi'kmaq symbol to its correspondent indigenous word written in the Roman alphabet. He also wrote a *Grammaire de la Langue Mikmaque*, a text that developed a model for correctly learning the basics of Mi'kmaq grammar. Maillard explains the care he took in studying the language and imposing his own rules of orthography. For example, in spelling, he uses the character "8" to represent sounds without a corresponding equivalent in the Roman alphabet.[41] Enamored with the Mi'kmaq language, Maillard records his perpetual surprise at the language's richness. He claims for Mi'kmaq a purity that far exceeded French with its semblance of ancient historical roots. In his 1755 letter, he explains that he is at a loss to account for these apparent linguistic anomalies. He supposes that perhaps some light might be shed by investigating "whether there was any affinity or not between their language, and that of the Orientalists, as the Chinese or Tartars."[42] This speculation reveals something of the esteem to which Maillard held the Mi'kmaq language, for Chinese characters held a significant intellectual resonance in seventeenth- and early eighteenth-century Europe when the comparative study of oriental languages fueled biblical criticism as well as the rise in humanist philology.[43]

Despite his attempt to create an enclosed symbolic system for the purposes of evangelization, Maillard observed that the Mi'kmaq possessed a fecundity of expression containing "ease, fluency, and richness."[44] Their prose, Maillard explains, has a particularly literary quality, for it "naturally runs into poetry, from the frequency of their tropes and metaphors; and into rhime."[45] This makes the language naturally conducive to song. As Rousseau explains, song along with poetry were among the first discourses of early linguistic utterances. Recurring rhythm, melody, and speech inflection meant that poetry and music were born along with language. Rhythm and sound conveyed meaning.[46] Maillard both admired indigenous expressions of these forms and also presented the composition of hymns as an ideal vehicle for creating a sacred ritual space in which to witness the New World presence of a universal Catholic spirit. Yet while Maillard finds the language itself highly conducive to these instruments of evangelization, he guards his philosophical and linguistic knowledge by carefully controlling the circulation of Catholic texts. Only specific prayers, recorded in Mi'kmaq ideographs, are made available to his proselytes.

Maillard used his linguistic knowledge to moderate the distribution of sacred signs among the Mi'kmaq and thus carefully control the parameters of Franco-Catholic allegiance among this indigenous population. He makes an explicit link between Catholic conversion and the military potential of the Mi'kmaq nation for the French army: "All these savages go under the name of *Mickmakis*. Before the last war they could raise about six hundred fighting-men, according to an account given in to his most Christian majesty."[47] The indigenous name "Mickmakis" identifies a fierce army of six hundred "savages." In his writings on the military potential of the Mi'kmaq, Maillard begins with ethnographic descriptions of their rituals of thanksgiving and celebration following the hunting season in which the ancestral lineage is honored. He paints a vivid picture of the song and dance involved in these celebrations and the specific features of a performance that is bodily as well as sonic. The ritual leader's body "trembl[es]" at times, and then stands straight, erect, and measured at others. Clearly articulated syllables, "*Ywhannah, Owanna, Haywanna, yo! ha! yo! ha!*" elicit a particular response from the audience, which acts as the chorus. Such observations, Maillard informs his readers, not only give insight into Mi'kmaq thought and action, they also suggest the military potential if one could mobilize this population. Though dispersed throughout Cape Breton Island and St. John, Maillard's "savages," with their unison cries and ritual performances, were united under the sign of their instruction in the "Christian religion."[48]

Maillard's *Lettres* record his own success in implementing the signs of Franco-Catholicism so thoroughly as to not only ensure Mi'kmaq allegiance but also to enlist a population of "savages," guaranteed to police the boundaries of the empire, perhaps even more effectively than the French. He describes a scene of torture that the natives within his missionary community enacted upon a British soldier who could not make the sign of the cross. Maillard's language changes within this particular passage to fit the brutality of the scene that he is narrating. The "Mickmakis" become "les sauvages," a shift in name designation that signifies the eruption of an inner violent nature lurking just beneath the surface of an otherwise tranquil demeanor. With hatchets raised, "les sauvages" stand in sharp contrast to the Englishman, described as poor (in the sense of an object of pity) and young. The Englishman tries desperately to appease them, making a sign of the cross with his right hand and then with his left and even crying out at one point that he is a Christian. The response of the "savages" is telling of their commitment to the specificity of the sign, for the Englishman fails to make the sign of the cross to their satisfaction. Reaching their conclusion, the savages cry out: "il n'est

donc pas Priant, il est anglois, aglachiè8 8là" (He is not Christian, he
is English).[49] The natives tie the Englishman to a tree, slash his limbs,
burn them and then place them in a pot of boiling water. The detailed and exceptional brutality of the scene repulses the reader, suggesting that Maillard seeks to make a point about a form of savagery
that exceeds European norms and can thus be usefully employed in
war times. The verdict is telling. Were the soldier a true Christian, he
would know how to make the sign of the cross mechanically, without
thinking about which hand to use, without faltering. When he cannot,
he becomes immediately legible as the enemy, one identifiable across
national boundaries that accord seamlessly with the bifurcation of
religious identity into Christian and non-Christian. Because he is
English, he is non-Christian. Maillard's repetition of the word anglois in Mi'kmaq enforces Franco-Mi'kmaq alignment on this issue.

While acting as intermediaries between the Mi'kmaq and French
military officials, both Maillard and Picquet sought to leave indigenous Catholicism as a deep and permanent mark of the lasting
French presence in Acadia.[50] As if anticipating the outcome of the
war, which they certainly might have done by 1758 when Maillard
wrote his most extensive record of Mi'kmaq custom, religion, and
language, each missionary made sure that the French would win the
battle for souls if not the battle for land.[51] The Seven Years War intensified French colonial insistence on hearing indigenous words nar-
rate the presence of a Catholic spirit within missionary communities
as well as the application of Catholicism as a strategy of allegiance
against the British. While recognizing an intact ethnographic difference among the populations that they sought to convert, colonists
thrived off of incorporating disparate native peoples under the um-
brella of Franco-Catholic imperial dominance.

Imperialist Configurations of Indigenous Words

The fate of Anglo-Protestant missionary linguistics in the two decades preceding and then during the Seven Years War was precisely
the opposite of the liaisons between Picquet and Maillard and French
military officials. Less dependent on the American Indians for military strength, the British missionary enterprise was not utilized in
the same way that it was in the case of the French. Rather, Anglo-
Protestants recognized the threat that the French missionary and

military intelligence produced during the war. Writing from his congregation in Albany to the Society for the Propagation of the Gospel on July 7, 1750, John Ogilvie expressed his "fear (if some Measures are not taken to prevent it) that the French Priests by their craft & Policy will lead away most of the Indians [Mohawks] into the French Interest." One such measure that Ogilvie described to the SPG was the support of a "schoolmaster" to promote and encourage the spread of the "English Language" among Indian children. This, Ogilvie imagines, will serve the twofold goal of promoting civility and Englishness, for the Indians have "universally degenerated since the War." He describes them as "intensely given up to Drunkenness," having "lost all sense of Religion," and existing at best "in a State of Indifference." With the help a schoolmaster, religious instruction, and a fresh supply of Bibles and prayer books, Ogilvie proposes that they may put some hope in the rising generation.[52] English-language instruction accomplished the dual goal of facilitating both civility and conversion.

Missionary schools of the mid-eighteenth century codified this alignment of English-language instruction and Protestantism. Though they attended to the evangelization of indigenous souls with the renewed fervor due to the Great Awakening's millennial promise, this generation of British missionaries differed from their seventeenth-century predecessors in more readily dismissing the challenges of linguistic difference in favor of a model of assimilation. Eleazar Wheelock founded Moor's Charity School in 1754 with the view that indigenous language was wild and English civil. SPG letters describing the state of missionary affairs in the wake of violent imperial conflict mandate English language instruction for American Indian children. The letters contain numerous requests for more English prayer books as well as money to pay schoolmasters. Designed to create a buffer from the French and the Iroquois, these schools reified the relationship between English and Christianity in order to replicate values of civility and Protestant order among native proselytes in contrast to the perceived primitive savagery of French and Indian Catholicism.

Mid-eighteenth-century missionaries did not engage with the same nuanced attention to grammatical difference, nor did they pursue the enterprise of their predecessors in seeking a state of semiotic recuperation where redeemed Algonquian tongues would speak Christian truths in a new light. When native languages were preserved in Anglo-Protestant missionary communities, it was through the translated hymnals largely authored by indigenous preachers before the nineteenth century. Increasingly, the view of native languages as irreparably fallen and barbarous was the reigning motif and accepted paradigm for an almost complete reliance on interpreters as well as the rationale for requiring proselytes to learn English. As native converts were increasingly required to do so, indigenous words were decoupled from the living bodies that originally spoke them, though they continued to have an afterlife both in Protestant millennial history and in a new era of linguistic anthropology and American archaeology, inaugurated by Thomas Jefferson.

The convergence between mid-eighteenth-century French and British missions and imperial conflict produced an exceptionalist paradigm of Anglo-American Protestantism in contradistinction to a Franco-Catholic appropriation of the indigenous word as a lasting mark of a dying empire. Secular priests scattered in various posts throughout New France sought to formally brandish the Mi'kmaq and Mohawk with the embodied performance of Catholic ritual and prayer set to the tune of their own native tongue. In the Anglo-Protestant context, by contrast, indigenous words were theologically remapped as artifacts of a long-forgotten biblical past. This past forecasted the ascent of Anglo-Protestant Christendom. Mid-eighteenth-century French missionary linguistics narrated the empire's decline with the nostalgia of lost worlds, medieval melodies set to Mohawk works, banners as traces of ancient empires. By the time the British had taken over former French territory, political leaders as well as missionaries began to read indigenous words as evidence of their own natural and divine right to the North American continent.

Unruly Empiricisms and Linguistic Sovereignty in Thomas Jefferson's Indian Vocabulary Project

En route home to Monticello following the second term of his presidency in 1809, Thomas Jefferson's possessions were stolen. Upon finding a pile of handwritten papers in trunk number twenty-eight, the thief promptly threw the contents into the James River in a fit of frustration at not finding something more valuable. A few scattered sheets of paper were collected from the banks of the James River, dried, and preserved. Trunk number twenty-eight contained Indian Vocabularies, compiled from a standardized broadside that Jefferson sent to Indian agents on the United States frontier with instructions that they should compile word lists of Miami, Cherokee, Chickasaw, Nanticoke, Shawnee, and Creek and then send the broadside back to him.[1] Jefferson's goal was to "collect all the vocabularies I can of the American Indians." He wished to preserve an archive of a past population whom he believed to be on the brink of extinction and to offer scientific proof of "common parentage" between American Indians and Asian peoples (see Fig. 7.1).[2]

Having envisioned the Vocabulary project in his *Notes on the State of Virginia* (1783) and then amassing data for it from 1791–1809, Jefferson was devastated by this loss. It took him six years before he could write about it to Peter Du Ponceau, who was then secretary of the Philosophical Society's Historical and Literary Committee and who had written to Jefferson to request his archive of Indian Vocabularies. Jefferson's reply revealed his sadness, "Perhaps I may make another attempt to collect, altho' I am too old to expect to make much progress in it."[3] The scattered remains from the banks of the James River embody the irony of Jefferson's purported goal of linguistic preservation. Almost impossible to read, these records survive as material reminders that the written word can be as ephemeral as the spoken sound. Of the estimated four hundred vocabularies

FIGURE 7.1. Thomas Jefferson, "Comparative Vocabularies of Several Indian Languages, 1802–1808," American Indian Vocabulary Collection, American Philosophical Society.

that Jefferson collected, only twenty-three, representing nineteen languages, remain in the American Philosophical Society archives.

Literally splattered with mud from the riverbank, torn and blotted from immersion in water, the words recorded on the lists are elusive to the modern reader. What's left of the archive is difficult to place within the developing linguistic science of Jefferson's day. It takes an even greater leap of imagination to see how these faint archival traces accomplish Jefferson's purported goal of recording the "languages" that "so many of the Indian tribes" spoke before becoming "extinguished."[4] Jefferson's lament to Du Ponceau was for more than just the loss of a valuable archive. It was also a statement of defeat due to having spent twenty years on a project that he perceived to have failed long before the thief scattered the contents of trunk twenty-eight in the James River. The contrast between Jefferson's apprehension of his Indian Vocabulary project as a failure and the cultural and linguistic value of the vocabularies points to a conceptual crux in historical understanding. Interactions between indigenous speakers of Unkechaug, Nanticoke, and Cherokee and statesmen Benjamin Hawkins, David Campbell, William Vans Murray, and Jefferson himself did not conform to the format of knowledge to which Jefferson, and the broader Enlightenment network in which he participated, wished them to adhere. Although to some degree this is a universal facet of all languages in their capacity to resist translation, the specific linguistic information that indigenous informants conveyed to Indian agents refused to be collapsed into linear accounts of American Indian origins or indexical relations among nations, which Jefferson defined as the main purpose for gathering Indian tongues.

Jefferson intended indigenous speakers to be the objects of his scientific inquiry, serving two goals. He hoped to penetrate the vast terra incognita west of the Mississippi and throughout the southeastern regions of the United States by gathering linguistic and ethnographic data on the tribes who resided there.[5] Natural science as practiced in the Indian Vocabulary project and then most famously in the Lewis and Clark expeditions served as a guise for political and diplomatic access to American Indian nations.[6] Additionally, as part of the engine of Enlightenment progress that would serve to uphold governmental policies of removal and assimilation, Jefferson sought to use the vocabularies to trace Indian origins and to inscribe primitive American aboriginals within the savage state of linear stadial history.[7] Yet Indian speakers, including two elderly anonymous women from the Unkechaug tribe, the Nanticoke land proprietor Mrs. Mulberry, and a group of unidentified "old [Cherokee] Indians" that Hawkins claimed to know, controlled the process of knowledge accumulation. While the lists themselves appear as empirical artifacts of a failed early philological experiment, Jefferson's correspondence reveals the force of the center of calculation behind the lists. Writing to figures as various as Ezra Stiles, Benjamin Hawkins, James Madison, the Comte de Volney, and the Marquis de Lafayette, letters on the topic of Indian tongues record Jefferson's ideological aspirations for proving an *ur* American antiquity as well as his frustration and eventual despair over his own failure to do so.[8]

Through the ideological veil of his day and the ever-intensifying political mandate to acquire more land for the new nation, Jefferson saw neither the empirical value nor the scientific validity of his collected vocabularies. Yet the vocabularies contain useful knowledge of another measure and for another audience. Even amid the fragments of an archive lost to the accidents and tragedies of history, this knowledge persists for tribal descendants as well as scholars of indigenous history and literature today.

The first and only vocabulary recorded by Jefferson himself was on June 14, 1791. On the back of an envelope he scribbled a rudimentary list of words spoken by three elderly women of the Unkechaug tribe of Long Island. Tribal descendants today use the list as an aid in recuperating an otherwise inaccessible past: the language of the Long Island Indians, which no one has spoken since the early nineteenth century.[9] As sparse as the list appears, it is one of the few remaining records of an eastern Algonquian tongue identified as extinct. The list has consequently taken its place among a host of documents that have been repurposed from their original colonial use to one of language revitalization (see Fig. 7.2).[10]

Due to its meager archival remnants, the Indian Vocabulary project has not received as much scholarly attention as other facets of Jefferson's oeuvre. Scholars who have written on it have amply documented the practice of vocabulary collecting caught up in larger conflicts between ideology and empiricism, concluding that the accumulation of linguistic knowledge facilitated the acquisition of land. Scholars have also amply established the intricacies of the relationship between science and politics, empiricism and ideology, in Jeffersonian science, while missing what is recorded in plain sight: the complexity of the encounters that took place between Indian

FIGURE 7.2. Jefferson, "Vocabulary of the Unquachog Indians," 1791, American Indian Vocabulary Collection.

agents and indigenous peoples who were reducible neither to a political agenda nor to objects of inquiry.[11] If Jefferson's motivations had been more purely political, he would have been less devastated by the loss of his archive of Indian Vocabularies. By 1809, at the end of his second term as president, vast amounts of territory had been secured through the Louisiana Purchase, leaving Jefferson more sanguine about the nation's future. Rather, Jefferson regretted his inability to verify his hypothesis scientifically, to prove through comparative vocabularies the validity of the Asiatic theory of American Indian migration, which had long been a speculation among philosophers.

At least for the standards of the day, Jefferson's scientific methodology was sound. In the late eighteenth century, comparative vocabularies were deemed an effective means of studying languages and indexing historical relations among nations. Jefferson wished to contribute an account of American Indian origins to an international conversation on the relationship between language and human history. Yet interactions between indigenous speakers and Indian agents thwarted the possibility of arriving at convincing evidence through a stable and standardized record of primitive tongues. Instead, the lists display telling instances of cross-cultural mistranslation. Indigenous words spill beyond Jefferson's rules of orthography and beyond the word list itself in formal defiance of Jefferson's goal of recording the ancient and pure sounds of primitive America. Indian Vocabularies accomplished the task of preservation, not in the terms that Jefferson imagined as an archaeology of America's ancient past, but rather as a visible record of the lived cultural experience of Indian country, an experience that authors of the dominant natural and national histories of the time relegated to the margins.

Amerindian Languages and International Science

Jefferson's Vocabulary project followed on a long history of attempts to uncover Indian origins that are as old as the discovery of the Americas. Jefferson and his contemporaries American botanist Benjamin Smith Barton and the French philosopher Comte de Volney positioned their linguistic work on American Indian origins against the Hebraic theory, or the belief that American Indians descended from the lost tribes and that similarities existed between Hebrew and Natick, or Chickasaw, or Mahican. Yet Hebraic and Asian theories of descent had coexisted since the sixteenth century and were not as different as they may have then seemed.[12] Foundational and authoritative texts such as Spanish Jesuit José de Acosta's *Historia natural y moral de las Indias* (1590) and Dutch explorer Joannes de Laet's *Nieuwe Wereldt Ofte Beschrijvinghe van West-Indien* (1625) first proposed that American Indians were of Asian descent. The Hebraic argument emerged and stubbornly persisted on the margins of colonial discourse, surfacing in such texts as Thomas Thorowgood's *Jews in America* (1650), Joseph François Lafitau's *Moeurs des Sauvages Américains* (1724), James Adair's *History of American Indians* (1775), William Robertson's *History of America* (1777), Jonathan Edwards Jr.'s *Observations on the Language of the Muhhekaneew Indians* (1788), and Elias Boudinot's *Star in the West* (1816). Whether Hebraic or Asiatic, theories of American Indian origins sutured connections between the land and its natural inhabitants. Indian words thus occupied a place within American nature as repositories of ancient knowledge and symbols of the mythic structure underlying the rise of the new nation, for the explanation of where the American Indian came from also functioned as a means of explaining disappearance.

The Comte de Volney, a long-time friend and correspondent of Jefferson's, countered the Hebraic thesis most forcefully in his *View of the Climate and Soil of the United States of America* (1804). No stranger to religious controversy, Volney was also the author of *The Ruins, or a Survey of the Revolutions of Empires* (1795), a text so controversial for its anti-religious views that Jefferson entered into a secret agreement with

Volney to translate the text into English in 1796. With the specter of the ruins of the Ottoman Empire and the gloomy state of Europe in mind, Volney fled to America shortly after the publication of *The Ruins* to enjoy the "peaceful and smiling aspect of the United States." It was there that he interviewed the Miami chief, Little Turtle, collected a Miami vocabulary, and then made a study of the language. Volney prefaces his study with an attack on James Adair's "extravagant idea" that the "savages are descended from the Jews," which has led to gross "misrepresentations." Volney observed "a real analogy between the mythological ideas of the savages of North America and those of the Asiatic Tartars, as they have been described to us by the learned Russians."[13] While Volney's purpose was to pit science against religion, and reason against the distorting lens of providential design, this rhetoric masks an underlying homology between the two theories of Indian origins.

As strange as it may now seem, in the seventeenth century, the Hebraic thesis was perfectly in keeping with structures of reasoned discourse. Mosaic ethnology, the belief in one Old Testament patriarch for every nation, was the framework used by philosophers and missionaries alike to chart connections between languages and nations.[14] Yet by the late eighteenth century, the Hebraic thesis was more of a placeholder than a serious theological proposal, operating as a bulwark against the forces of rapid historical change, as its authors worked to reintegrate humans within some sense of a cosmic whole. Adair was a fur trader from the southeastern United States and a self-proclaimed "English-Chickasaw." Self-taught in Chickasaw, Hebrew, Christian theology, and Enlightenment philosophy, Adair published a *History of American Indians* in 1775. He found that Chickasaw "appears to have the very idiom and genius of Hebrew." The *History* presents forms of Chickasaw speech as vestiges of an ancient sacred meaning that survived intact through the very nature of their separation from historical time. Even though there is some sense of loss and depletion as these forms move away from an irrecoverable original, the meaning can nonetheless still be heard as a "completion of the manifestations of God's infinite wisdom and power." Nature exudes a sense of divine worship in Chickasaw, for the American Indian conception of God exists in smoke, fire, and clouds. According to Adair, "They often change the sense of words into a different signification from the natural, exactly after the manner of the Orientalists."[15] The *ur* sounds of an original divine language come through Chickasaw like music or poetry.

Adair's conceptualization of a sonic divine original, still faintly recognizable in Chickasaw words, partakes of the romantic philology that would emerge shortly after his *History*.[16] In natural histories of North America, this romantic philology of indigenous words flourished in the 1790s and 1800s. In his *View of the Climate*, Volney heard in Miami the same mythical and mystical wholeness that Adair heard in Chickasaw. Following Jefferson, Volney also felt that North America lacked all proof of the ancient arts through the absence of ruins but that indigenous words could act as monuments. Phrases containing a certain number of syllables, verses spoken or sung, and ideas fixed by words in a precise manner constitute the rustic simplicity from which the "divine art of poetry" comes. Volney compares Miami verse to the songs of the bards Ossian, Odin, and Homer. In keeping with Jefferson's interests, Volney struggled to establish links between the Tartar tribes of Siberia and the languages of North Americans. Although harshly critical of Adair, he also mapped sonic links between the Miami language and Greek, Arabic, and Hebrew.[17] Written with the goal of encoding a renewable Eden in the very structure and grammar of an indigenous tongue, the language section of *View of the Climate* describes Miami as regenerative; from it the divine art of poetry could be created for the present age.

Volney, Adair, and Jefferson each partook in an attempt to study human history through language on the North American continent. In the wake of the shattering of biblical linguistics and the consequent challenge to Mosaic ethnology where one Old Testament patriarch stood for one nation, language history emerged as the primary tool for ethnographic grouping over the eighteenth century. Language and nation were understood by Enlightenment philosophies to be parallel developments.[18] Giambattista Vico, Jean-Jacques Rousseau, Adam Smith, Johann Gottfried Herder, Wilhelm von Humboldt, and Lord Monboddo all wrote essays on the origins of language. Each essay took as its starting point a primal linguistic scene that was always, by necessity, speculative. Language philosophers built their analyses on conjectural beginnings. Yet, as Lord Monboddo explains in his preface to his essay *Of the Origins and Progress of Language*, "The history of man" would "be exceedingly imperfect without the knowledge of that original state."[19] In imagining each primal linguistic scene, language philosophers drew a line of demarcation between primitive and modern tongues.

To the extent that primitive languages were believed to still exist in the eighteenth century, philosophers felt that they could be found only among so-called barbarous populations in regions far from civil societies including India, Africa, and the extremities of America. Philosophers believed that the languages spoken among these populations were frozen in time. Jefferson envisioned his Indian Vocabulary Project as lending empirical validity to the construction of a primal linguistic scene in philosophical circles. While generating a valuable archive of the nation's past, the vocabularies were also designed to identify linguistic origins more precisely and thus advance knowledge of human history.

In his *Notes*, Jefferson declares the study of indigenous tongues an essential ingredient of the continent's natural and national history. Jefferson imagined that such languages would "construct the best evidence of the derivation of this part of the human race."[20] The *Notes* reorients the eighteenth-century quest to discover the origins of language and their relation to human history toward North America, not only as a site for collecting primitive tongues but also as a site for witnessing the replacement of these indigenous tongues with the pinnacle of civilized modernity in Anglo-America.[21] He presented the Indian as a unique and exceptional feature of the American landscape through which enlightened Europeans could begin to see American culture in embryonic form. The Indian is a "shade" or a pale and distant copy of "our own race," he wrote.[22]

When elected president of the American Philosophical Society in 1797, Jefferson institutionalized an effort to preserve Indian languages as part of an American antiquity. Wishing to archive the American Indian's organic relationship to the land, he formed a committee that saw to the "recovery of complete skeletons of mammoths and other poorly understood animals; detailed information about prehistoric earthworks and mounds; study of changes in the land's surface features; and research on the culture and languages of American Indians."[23] Jefferson placed his vision of North America's natural grandeur at the center of the committee's mission. The 1780 charter described literally pulling "unexplored treasures" from American soil.[24] As with the famed mastodon excavations, the committee viewed American Indian languages as national treasures and ancient natural artifacts, rather than the speech of living populations.[25] Establishing the prestige of science in the United States was necessary to counter George-Louis Leclerc Comte de Buffon, since part of the belief about American degeneracy was the assumption that America would not produce any great scientists.[26] This Indian Vocabulary project was at once part of Jefferson's nationalist agenda of disproving Buffon's theory of species degeneration and international in his hope that a definitive discovery of Indian origins would establish the prestige of U.S. science on a global scale.[27]

Jefferson began his study of the "American aboriginal" with a visit to an Unkechaug town on Long Island where he sat with two old women as well as James Madison and General William Floyd and jotted a vocabulary of their language on the back of an envelope (see Fig. 7.2).[28] By the late eighteenth century, the Unkechaug community provided Jefferson with what seemed to be visible evidence of his Indian extinction theory. The original colonial land grant had dwindled from 175 to 50 acres, and a century of disease and war had diminished the population to about a dozen families. Upon entering a scene of an impoverished people barely surviving due to European disease and a long history of encroachments on their native land base, Jefferson declared a site of rapid language loss where "there remain but three persons of this tribe now who can speak its language."[29] Knowing nothing of the language, Jefferson listened to two old women, producing a phonetic list of the sounds they spoke, the "orthography" of which, he tells us, "is English." True to his empirical mode, Jefferson tried to capture the knowledge offered by these Unkechaug informants as best he could.

The rudimentary phonetic sketch recorded on scrap paper leaves open to question whether Jefferson pointed at objects and recorded the spoken Unkechaug name, or the two women offered up their own vocabulary selections. While it is impossible to know the process of selection, the recorded words give some indication of this as a collaborative exchange. Some words are quotidian and universal in nature, such as *woman, child, boy, girl, eyes, nose, to walk, to lie, to sit*. Others emerge from the context of Unkechaug culture and land: *fish hawk, whippoorwill, musket, strawberries, mulberry tree, Indian corn, turkey, squash, tobacco, hominy, oyster, clam, arrow, tomahawk, watermelon, wampum, moccasins*. If we envision this scene as one of linguistic collaboration, whereby the two old Unkechaug women aspired to teach Jefferson something of their culture, the miniscule writing on the margin shows Jefferson's attempt to impose order on the Unkechaug lexicon. In the margins, Jefferson divides the list into taxonomies: quadrupeds, birds, insects, plants.[30] None of the categories describes cultural or ethnographic words. Each consists of things that one would find in nature, or universal concepts such as human body parts, celestial bodies, family members, colors, verbs, and numbers. Additionally, there are no abstract concepts, none of the theological words that Jefferson's missionary predecessors constantly struggled with such as God, good and evil, sin, and the afterlife.

The manuscript record of the Unkechaug vocabulary is the only surviving list compiled before the first known printing of Jefferson's broadside in 1792 (see Fig. 7.3). We can thus deduce that even if manuscript word lists preceded the broadside (none are extant), Jefferson viewed this Unkechaug encounter as a basis for finalizing his broadside before sending it to the printer. Many of the 282 words on the printed broadside replicate the Unkechaug list. Asking for translations of animals, plants, minerals, elements, body parts, numbers, and seasons, Jefferson created a lexicon that he intended to transcend alteration through space and time. In the twentieth century, this method of selecting a universal vocabulary has been dubbed "lexicostatistics." Scientists distinguish between a "cultural" vocabulary that "changes at a relatively constant rate" and "the fundamental everyday

FIGURE 7.3. Jefferson, "Vocabulary Form," American Indian Vocabulary Collection.

vocabulary" that retains elements across time but changes at a constant, calculable rate.[31] While a long way away from this kind of scientific knowledge, Jefferson spent the 1780s familiarizing himself with the Enlightenment version of lexicostatistics through "vocabularies" sent to him from Hawkins, the acquisition of a Bengali vocabulary published in London in 1788, Peter Simon Pallas's *Vocabularia Comparativam*, and a perusal of Jonathan Edwards Jr.'s *Observations on the Language of the Muhhekaneew Indians* (1788).[32] Jefferson's vocabulary broadside is thus a combination of homegrown words specific to local indigenous cultures and the more universal lists circulating at the time.

Deceptively simple in appearance, vocabulary lists shaped the birth of modern philology. Sir William Jones used vocabularies to develop his theory of an Indo-European language family; his Jesuit predecessor in India, Gaston-Laurent Coeurdoux, used similar lists in his assessment of linguistic roots in *Moeurs et Coutumes des Indiens* (1777).[33] The British orientalist and linguist William Marsden composed comparative vocabularies of Malayo-Polynesian languages and Chinese. A few years before Jefferson began his vocabulary project, Catherine the Great commissioned the Pallas to classify 200 Asian languages based on a list of 130 core words. From this study came a comparative dictionary of all the languages of Europe and Asia, first published in St. Petersburg from 1786–1789 as *Linguarum totius orbis vocabularia comparativam*.[34]

As Jefferson explained in an 1809 letter to Barton, his lists consisted of approximately 250 words to Pallas's 130, stating that "73 were common to both, and would have furnished materials for a comparison from which something might have resulted."[35] His broadside contains entities that Jefferson assumed would have been named early in the population's history in order to establish a basis for comparison with the Tartar languages collected by Pallas. Both Pallas and Jefferson intended their lists to consist of timeless entities and natural objects. As he explained in a 1798 letter to William Linn, his vocabulary captured "the names of natural objects chiefly."[36] Conjoining anthropology to natural history, the broadside was supposed to be true to form across time and place and in accordance with the harmony of natural law (see Fig. 7.4).

One aspiration for the broadside was to record the simplest, most primitive, and necessary conceptions that all languages name at their creation.[37] Yet, Jefferson also included words that reveal the peculiarities of indigenous languages as they evolved in relation to American

FIGURE 7.4. Benjamin Smith Barton, *New Views on the Origin of the Tribes and Nations of America* (1797). John Carter Brown Library, Providence, R.I.

nature. While retaining 73 of Pallas's words provided a basis for comparison, it left the majority of space for a deviant lexicography. The words in common with Pallas are also the words that Barton used in his *New Views of the Origins of the Tribes and Nations of America* (1797), a text that purports to accomplish what Jefferson failed to do, namely place the languages of North America into a comparative global frame to prove the Asiatic connection. These words accord with a universal schema: *fire, water, earth, sun, moon, star, cold, eye, nose, hair, mouth, blood, I*. These words appear on lists across time and place, from Pallas's *Vocabularia Comparativa* to Jefferson's vocabulary broadside to Barton's *New Views*, even to Morris Swadesh's list, finalized in 1971. While subtle variations occur across each of the lists, Jefferson's departures are more notable than the others. His list includes foods, plants, and animals unique to North America: *Indian corn, the mammoth (his discovery), buffalo, elk, moose, polecat, raccoon, possum, eagle, turkey, turkey buzzard, sycamore, poplar, ash, elm, beech, birch, maple, oak, chestnut, hickory, walnut, locust, mulberry, tobacco*. Several of these words come directly from the cultural aspects of the Unkechaug vocabulary discussed above, suggesting a tantalizing postulation. If it is the case that the two old Unkechaug women influenced Jefferson's choice of recorded words, then they also influenced the organization of national knowledge of indigenous tongues as codified through the 1792 broadside.

Verbs constitute another category of deviation between Jefferson's list and that of Pallas and of Barton. In contrast to the absence of verbs on Pallas's and Barton's lists, Jefferson has close to thirty, including "to smoke a pipe." Beyond the actual lexicon, Jefferson may have been aware of some of the unique aspects of indigenous verbs as observed by his contemporaries. According to Moravian missionary David Zeisberger, there were no "auxiliaries" in native tongues. Verb tenses were inflected through objects and persons rather than time; adjectives were understood as deriving from verbs.[38] Jefferson recorded the English verb on his broadside in the infinitive, thus ignoring—willfully or not—the contrast between Euro and Amerindian syntax. By focusing on verbs, Jefferson may have aspired to discover the exceptional facets of North American tongues, or he may have speculated that the syntactical expression peculiar to this part of speech could be traced comparatively to other such "barbarous" languages.

Through his vocabulary broadside, Jefferson issued a request for two conflicting goals. He wished to collect primitive words, unchanged across the Northwest Passage thousands of years prior to European settlement of North America, but he also wished to capture a lexicon of indigenous cultures and ways of relating to the land. The vocabulary lists extended the project that Jefferson began in his *Notes on the State of Virginia*, where the desire to secure the promise of a national future ultimately clouded empiricism. Imagined as standing outside of politics, philosophy, and history, nature was a powerful engine of social change in the eighteenth century. As Jefferson conceived of it in his *Notes*, American nature exhibited an important point of contrast to Europe's monuments of civilization with its raw, grand, and untouched form. From this raw material, elemental facts could be converted into national promise.[39]

The antiquity that Jefferson hoped to capture through his vocabulary lists functioned in a fashion similar to nature in the *Notes*. In a 1786 letter to Ezra Stiles, Jefferson wrote that "the settlement of our continent is of the most remote antiquity." The brickwork used among the "Indians along the waters of the Ohio" was proof of "a greater degree of industry than men in the hunter state usually possess," for this was the state that Jefferson deemed the American Indian to be in. Spilling past the contemporary norms of linguistic classification, Jefferson's Vocabulary Project repeats the assumption operative in the *Notes* that a sequence of natural facts could be converted into national promise. As effective as this method may have been in the *Notes*, in gleaning an extensive catalog of natural facts while maintaining a portrait of an elusive force that could not be comprehensively studied through Enlightenment taxonomies, it broke down in the Indian Vocabulary Project where Jefferson repeatedly failed to match the empirically gathered word to his broader thesis about American antiquity. He built his theory of American antiquity on a "single" erroneous "fact" mistakenly assumed to prove that the Asians descended from the Americans:

> Among the red inhabitants of Asia there are but a few languages radically different. But among our Indians the number of languages is infinite which are so radically different as to exhibit at present no appearance of their having been derived from a common source. The necessary time for the generation of so many languages must be immense.[40]

This idea of America as the cradle of civilization proved as sustainable an ideology for Jefferson as the Hebraic theory did for theologians and missionaries of generations past and present. The vision of genetic America positioned the Indian in an *ur* antiquity that naturalized displacement as part of a cycle of global *translatio imperii* from America to Asia to Europe and then back to America. Jefferson's vision of genetic America rested on a specious presumption even for the science of his day. Missionaries and philosophers all around him, including Edwards Jr. and the Moravians John Heckewelder and David Zeisberger, were discovering radical similarities in native words. Even Jefferson's friend and collaborator Barton had to point out the absurdity of this claim. In the lengthy "Preliminary Discourse" of *New Views*, a text dedicated to Thomas Jefferson, Barton quotes Jefferson's "opinion" that "the nations of America are 'of greater antiquity than those of Asia.'" He refutes this claim on the basis of insufficient data and cites extensive evidence to the contrary.[41]

Barton's refutation of Jefferson's origins thesis suggests his awareness that Jefferson's insistence on American antiquity superseded scientific objectivity. So intent was Jefferson to link America with the birth of human civilization, that the question of human origins as it related to comparative linguistics was fated to remain a late eighteenth-century mystery.[42] Jefferson's successor in the philological study of Indian languages, Peter Du Ponceau, recognized the futility of this quest for human linguistic origins only a decade later. Translating David Zeisberger's *Grammar of the Lenni Lenape* into English in 1816, Du Ponceau explains that "philology has taught us the impossibility" of discovering an original language. The accumulation of linguistic knowledge over the eighteenth century ironically defeated philologists' motivating purpose of synthesizing all of the world's languages into one cohesive whole.[43]

On Collecting and Resistant Structures

Orthographic adaptations of standardized American Indian speech followed from the impact of Noah Webster's 1783 speller on American English. American Indian boarding schools emerged in the mid-eighteenth century with John Sergeant's 1743 plan for the Stockbridge mission and Eleazar Wheelock's Moor's Charity School at Dartmouth in the 1760s. By 1817, the popular nineteenth-century editions of Jonathan Edwards's *Life of David Brainerd* (1746) inspired the creation of the Brainerd School in Tennessee and the Foreign Mission School in Cornwall, Connecticut. These schools were founded on the premise that all aspects of American Indian culture were to be eradicated and replaced with Protestant values of civility and work. Designed for young Indian children who were removed from their homes in order to receive such an education, the boarding schools required a uniform curriculum including reading, writing, spelling, arithmetic, history, geography, and grammar.[44] While the ultimate objective of the Brainerd mission was to teach Indian children English, the missionaries appointed by the American Board of Commissioners of Foreign Missions maintained that it would be easier to teach Choctaw and Cherokee children to read in their own native tongue before attempting English. John Pickering, the philologist from Boston who later became president of the American Academy of Arts and Sciences in 1839, took on the task of establishing a standard orthographic scheme for American Indian languages.[45] In 1820, the American Academy printed Pickering's *Essay on a Uniform Orthography for the Indian Languages of North America*. Pickering based his rationale on the work of Sir William Jones and the Comte de Volney, both of whom wrote pamphlets on how to adapt Asiatic languages to Roman letters. Following Jones and Volney, Pickering advises "ascertaining" "every elementary sound" and then arranging the letters "which we may choose to represent those sounds, in the order of our own alphabet." Pickering sets a standard for North American languages, consisting of an assemblage of sounds that, once ascertained by the Euro-American listener, could be arranged into alphabetical representation on the page. The assumption of a hierarchy between oral and written languages is implicit here, for Pickering goes on to state that "Indian tongues" are easier to translate phonetically because they are oral, "unlike the Asian languages."[46] Numerous spellers for native speakers followed, including the *Spellings for the Schools in the Chipeway Language* (1828) and James Edwin's *O-jib-ue Spelling Book Designed for the Use of Native Learners* (1835).

Influenced by the same international currents of applying the Roman alphabet as the orthographic standard of non-Western tongues, Jefferson wrote that "writing sounds for the expression of which our alphabet is not adapted" would always produce variation. Yet Jefferson also believed that North American languages could nonetheless be mapped into a literal phonetics of modern English.[47] Of the Unkechaug, he declared simply: "The orthography is English."[48] Jefferson attempted to standardize spelling across the lists. "It would be best to use the English orthography," he wrote to the Virginia statesman David Campbell for his vocabulary of the Cherokee. The spelling should be phonetic; "arbitrary characters" were only to be used when there were sounds "incapable of expression" in English letters. This method accords with one of the two outlined by Jones and "recommended by respectable authorities": basing the manner of written expression on aural pronunciation. Jones recognized the inherent limitations of this system: "new sounds are very inadequately presented to a sense not formed to receive them" and "grammatical analogy is destroyed" through this mode of representation.[49]

To compensate for variation, Jefferson urged his correspondents to provide "some explanation as to the orthography used."[50] On his "Vocabulary of the Chickasaw Indians of Tennessee," statesman and surveyor Daniel Smith writes directly on his broadside: "The oo is founded as in the English words moon noon. h at the end of words, is a mark of aspiration." Maryland congressman William Vans Murray does the same for his "Nanticoke Vocabulary" in 1792: "ah! in poetical exclamation or surprise."[51] As Smith and Van Murray's phonetic keys suggest, Jefferson's method followed from Jones's and consisted of recording a series of sounds through phonetic reproduction in standardized English. He wished to capture the empirical fragment of primitive tongues without acknowledging the precarious nature of pronunciation or the thematic content, grammar, syntax,

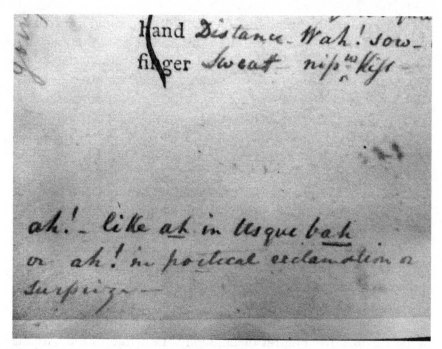

FIGURE 7.5A. William Vans Murray, "Nanticoke Vocabulary," American Indian Vocabulary Collection.

or changeable nature of that language. Assuming that American Indian phonemes existed within a natural and unchanging state, Jefferson constructed an archive of recorded sounds divorced from their signifying context. He emphasized that the vocabulary list was an "object of science," and that the "collection and comparative view of the Indian languages" was the "only means that we can have of coming at the descent and relations among them."[52] Orthographic uniformity was important; for following the example of Pallas's *Linguarum comparativam*, Jefferson hoped to discover a radical acquaintance with Asian languages. Recording a series of sounds through phonetic reproduction in standardized English letters, Jefferson sought in his lists to capture the empirical fragment of primitive tongues without acknowledging the changeable nature of that language. Erroneously presuming that American Indian phonemes existed within a natural and unchanging state, Jefferson constructed an archive of recorded sounds that could then be remapped into a new system of natural historical signification.

Simple though they may seem, Jefferson's instructions on orthography proved challenging, for the Indian agents collecting data for

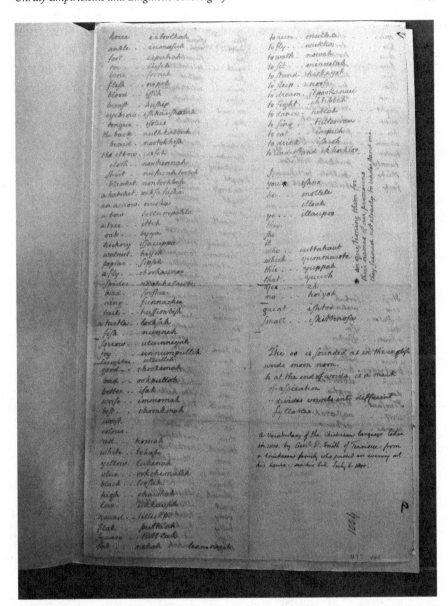

FIGURE 7.5B. Daniel Smith, "Chickasaw Vocabulary," American Indian Vocabulary Collection.

him often worked with limited linguistic skills and knowledge of the languages they were reporting. Additionally, the reality of the American frontier was a far cry from Jefferson's fantasy of linguistic purity where phonemes remained unchanged across time and place. Benjamin Hawkins, Indian agent to the Creeks, Cherokees, Choctaws, and Chickasaws who enjoyed a fair degree of diplomatic success during his nearly thirty-year career shuffling between Philadelphia, North Carolina, and the Creek settlement on the Ohio River, seemingly attempts to enlighten Jefferson as to these realities of frontier life in a letter written on July 12, 1800: "I am now in the woods like an Arab chief in tents...and at the moment I am writing I hear the languages of Scotch, French, Spanish, English, Africans, and Creeks."[53] Hawkins describes a world of Babylonian confusion. In equating the Creek agency nestled on the banks of the Ohio to a scene from Genesis, Hawkins offers Jefferson an analogy for imagining the primitive conditions in which he lives. Yet far from the primal linguistic scene invoked by eighteenth-century philosophers, where languages had been frozen in time and maintained a deep connection to the specificity of place, Hawkins's description depicts more recent histories of colonization and conquest. From this hodgepodge of European, African, and American Indian tongues, the purity of linguistic genealogy was difficult to discern. Hawkins's letter suggests that life on the southeastern frontier exposed the difficulty, if not impossibility, of fulfilling the empirical requirements at the heart of Jefferson's scientific goal. Nonetheless, Jefferson knew that Hawkins's access to southeastern languages was indispensable to his goals. By 1800, some of Jefferson's letters to Hawkins took on a tone of desperation in his plea for more word lists: "I know your relations are not very direct: but as I possess not means of getting at them, I am induced to pray your aid."[54] To ensure the success of his project, Jefferson needed records of the languages to which Hawkins and a select few had access.

After some coaxing, Jefferson received from Hawkins a comparative study of the southeastern languages: Creek, Chickasaw, Choctaw, and Cherokee (see Figs. 6a and 6b) in 1800. He also received a "Vocabulary of the Cherokee Language" in the same year from David Campbell, which reflects a great deal of variation in comparison to Benjamin Hawkins's Cherokee vocabulary. As shown in Figures 6a and 6b, Campbell lists the first words for fire, water, earth, air, and sky as "achelah, oumah, caught, caughtno lu hee, and cal la lit tee." Hawkins, by contrast, lists them as "àcheluh, ummuh, càtuk, catoose, canlalate." The discrepancies fly in the face of Jefferson's goal of orthographic uniformity, which must have been especially disappointing given that Jefferson had written to Campbell that year to explain that he needed information on Cherokee to "complete his object" of establishing "the descent and relations among the Indians."[55] In his letter to Jefferson that accompanies the comparative vocabulary,

Hawkins gave one possible explanation that might account for this variation. "The Creek," he writes, "is obtained from the purest source, one of my assistants, an interpreter, a chief of the nation, one of our greatest orators."[56] But "the Cherokee is at best doubtful."[57] Accuracy was contingent and depended on the expertise of the interpreter or chief available at the time of the recording, and in this case, Hawkins was not at all sure of the correctness of the Cherokee.

To be sure, any transcriber of an oral language or audio recording would struggle to achieve accuracy and consistency. And in Jefferson's day, orthography wasn't standardized yet, and the pronunciation received by untrained ears was precarious. Yet two lists of North Carolinian words recorded in the same year, as part of the same project, and producing dramatically different results reflects the problematic tenets underlying Jefferson's approach. To the right of the first column of Cherokee words on Hawkins's list is a second column titled "the dialect of the old Indians I know." In some cases, the words on Hawkins's second list resemble that on Campbell's more closely, suggesting the possibility that at least two versions of Cherokee existed within the same region at the same time. This variation flies in the face of one of Jefferson's central assumptions of the timeless purity of a linguistic core and thwarts his goal of comparing ancient roots to determine connections between American and Asian languages. By presenting substantial word variations within two generations of living Cherokee speakers, Hawkins's list reveals the rapidity of linguistic change even for words that were supposed to be universal.

The Cherokee Syllabary, developed by Sequoyah in the 1820s, only two decades after Campbell and Hawkins sent their vocabularies to Jefferson, reveals that the difficulties of orthography encountered by Campbell and Hawkins went well beyond reliability of their sources. Writing Cherokee sounds straightforwardly into the Roman alphabet so that the sound replicates the word spoken by a native speaker is essentially impossible. This was the motivation behind Sequoyah's writing system as well as the reason for its immediate success. Designed for a native speaker, the eighty-five characters composing Sequoyah's Syllabary bear no relation to English. The Syllabary takes into account the particular facets of Cherokee; characters are phonemically rather than phonetically different. The Syllabary ignores certain details of pronunciation such as aspiration, long and short vowels, and tone because these elements are a function of speech style in Cherokee.[58] But as reflected in the modern *Cherokee English*

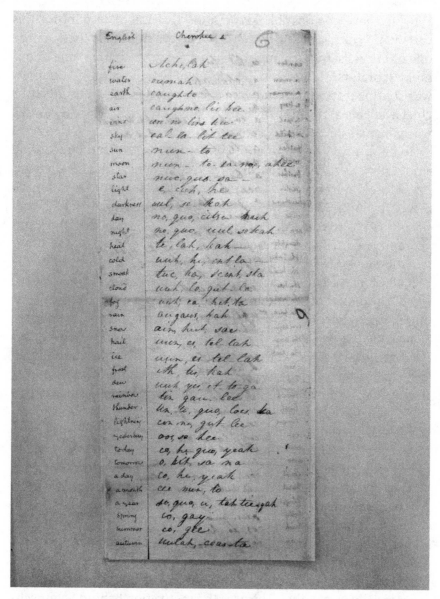

FIGURE 7.6A. David Campbell, "Vocabulary of the Cherokee Language," 1800, American Indian Vocabulary Collection.

Dictionary by Durbin Feeling and William Pulte, these aspects of pronunciation must be incorporated into the Standard English translation of Cherokee words for nonnative speakers. The translation of Cherokee into Standard English is no small task, for the representation of consonants varies considerably among contemporary experts.[59] To make matters even more complex for Jefferson and his

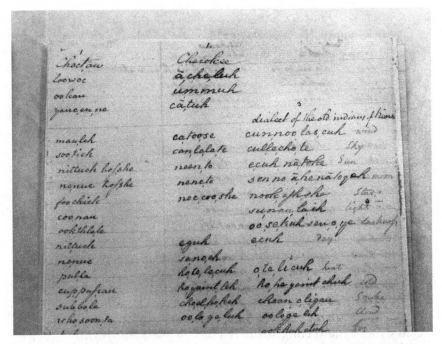

FIGURE 7.6B. Benjamin Hawkins, "A Comparative Vocabulary of the Creek, Chickasaw, Choctaw, and Cherokee Languages," American Indian Vocabulary Collection.

cohort, Cherokee has a unique system of classificatory verbs, consisting of free or bound morphemes that denote a characteristic of the entity to which they refer. The choice of a verb stem depends on inherent properties in the noun's referent such as shape and consistency as well as whether the noun is animate or inanimate.[60] While this classificatory system is unique to Cherokee, the phenomenon of verbs as syntactical markers of something other than time is common to many American Indian languages.[61]

Sequoyah possibly derived his sense of the power of the written Cherokee word in part from the fumbled attempts of Hawkins. According to Samuel Lorenzo Knapp in his first lecture on American literature, the Cherokees referred to Sequoyah's Syllabary as "the talking leaf" that permitted them the power to "speak by letters." The conflation of the oral and written is telling here, for the point of the Syllabary is that unlike Hawkins's and Campbell's unsuccessful attempts to record Cherokee words in English orthography, Sequoyah succeeded by "ascertaining all the sounds in the Cherokee language."[62] Elias Boudinot, the Cherokee founder of the first American Indian

newspaper, The *Phoenix Sun*, agreed with Knapp's take on the significance of Sequoyah's invention, using his syllabary to print the
Phoenix Sun as a bilingual American Indian newspaper, beginning in 1827.

Lexicons of Nostalgia

Just as Sequoyah was thought to bring the Cherokee word to life, the
words recorded on the Indian Vocabularies were collected from still-
living human beings whose world view seeped through the pages of
Jefferson's broadsides as a palimpsest refusing erasure. Defying the
terms of timeless universality, indigenous world views convey the flux
of rapid historical change and a deep attachment to place. Nowhere in
Jefferson's Indian Vocabulary archive does this palimpsest come
across more clearly than in the "Vocabulary of the Nanticoke" collected by Maryland congressman William Vans Murray in 1792.[63] In
1748, twelve Indians who self-identified as Choptank leased a six-
thousand-acre plantation in Locust Neck Town, which Murray identifies as "the ancient Indian settlement on Goose Creek." During the
Seven Years War, the Nanticokes in this region migrated up through
Pennsylvania and then to Lake Ontario, where they merged with the
Six Nations under protection of the French government. The few
Nanticokes who remained in Locust Neck merged with the Choptank.
The languages of the two tribes were mutually comprehensible and
became even more so through their shared existence in Maryland.
Mulberry was the name on the land deed. When Colonel Mulberry
died, the land went to his wife, Mrs. Mulberry, who was also Murray's
interviewee in 1792. When Mrs. Mulberry died, the land went to the
state.[64] As Murray enclosed his Nanticoke vocabulary along with a
letter to Thomas Jefferson, what he described in Locust Neck Town
easily fit with Jefferson's theory of "natural extinction":

> The tribe has dwindled almost into extinction. The little town where
> they live consists but of four genuine old wigwams, thatched over
> with the bark of the Cedar—very old—and two framed houses—in
> one of which lives the queen Mrs. Mulberry, relict of the Colonel who
> was the last Chief.
>   They are not more than nine in number.... They speak their language
> exclusively among themselves. A few years must totally extinguish

the remains of this Tribe and it will be owing to you Sir if a trace is left of their language.[65]

Murray learns the Nanticoke or Choptank words recorded on his broadside directly from Mrs. Mulberry. Mrs. Mulberry gave Murray the words that Jefferson required but she also created a vocabulary of

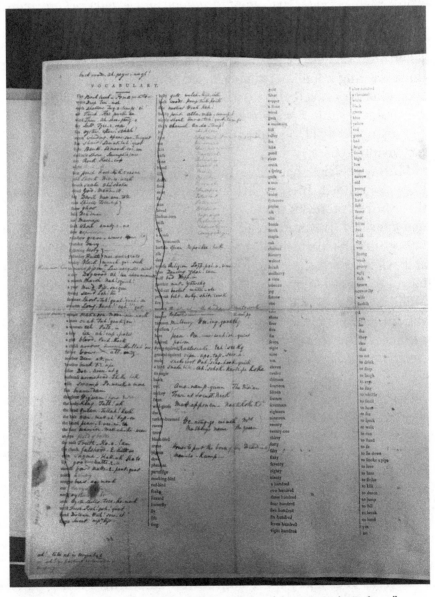

FIGURE 7.7. William Vans Murray, "Vocabulary of the Nanticoke Indians," 1792, American Indian Vocabulary Collection.

her own. Since the additional words exceeded the limits of Jefferson's list, Murray simply crossed out the original list and made up one of his own. Filled with the terms of recent history, the supplemental list implodes the theory of natural extinction. A discourse of warfare and military terms pervades the list with words such as *field of battle, peace, war, warrior, blood, arrows, bows, arrowhead, King, Queen.* Themes of disease, burial, and spirituality also pervade the list with words such as *God, Devil, ghost, deadman, grave, bury, whore, marriage, copulation, religion and dancing,* and *money.* Mrs. Mulberry's list expands the culturally specific terms that first appeared through Jefferson's exchange with the two Unkechaug women. Defying the universalizing impulse of standardized vocabulary lists of the time, Mrs. Mulberry's list flatly refuses to describe a Nanticoke world view constrained within a primitive past. Instead she brings history's legacies of displacement, disrupted migratory patterns, and colonial contact vividly to life.

Murray explains that just as the tribe had declined, language had likewise declined. There is such a paucity of words for abstract ideas that Murray expresses his surprise to find a word for *Truth, shame, and falsehood.* The presence of these words belies Jefferson's attempt to organize the broadside list according to concrete natural objects and primitive concepts, exposing the capacity for conceptual thinking and a refusal to be erased into antiquity and nature. As for Mrs. Mulberry's words for natural objects, there is nothing universal about them. Like Jefferson's *Notes on the State of Virginia,* they are specific to the countryside of Maryland: *back woods, oyster, back creek, banks, shore, perch, crab, eel, honeysuckle, oyster shells, rattlesnake, poison, dogwood,* and *marsh.* Each recorded word evokes the "place-word" of the indigenous landscape.[66] Native languages evolve through an intimate connection to their environment, which is also, in direct contrast to Jefferson's broadside, the landscape of history.

With the single exception of a 1785 word list by John Heckewelder, this vocabulary is all that remains of the Nanticoke and Choptank languages, although both were connected to Delaware of which there are ample Lenni Lenape records.[67] Zeisberger's *History* also has a few scattered words and provides an ethnographic account of the Nanticoke language and religious practice. He provides a possible reason for the extensive terminology for death and burial practices on Mrs. Mulberry's vocabulary list. Nanticoke burial practices consisted of opening the grave three or four months after the funeral, cleaning the flesh from the bones, drying them, wrapping them in linen, and then interring them again. Heckewelder gives a variation of this account that involves scraping putrid flesh from bones in order to remove them to "the country they dwell in."[68] The bones were then buried together in an ossuary, such as the Indian charnel house featured in John White's watercolors. This custom is of southeastern origin with similar practices occurring among Natchez, Choctaw, Chickasaw, Creek, and Seminole tribes. While not enough is known about the Nanticoke belief system to assess the significance of this burial practice, ethnographic data gathered from other tribes suggest that it may have been a way for the spirit of the deceased to travel to the spirit land. These words do not stand in microcosmic relation to American nature as a whole, but represent a population that has adapted to the particular conditions of time and place.

The Unkechaug, Nanticoke, and Cherokee vocabularies exemplify the difficulty of correctly ascertaining a linguistic core among disparate populations with interconnected pre- and post-contact migratory patterns. As Jefferson's project grew from the simple task of collecting to one of compiling, it proved increasingly difficult to manage. Writing to William Linn almost ten years after beginning his language project, Jefferson laments: "I do not permit myself to form as yet a decisive opinion, and therefore leave the slight one I had hazarded to the result of further enquiry."[69] The challenge of shifting through the layers of linguistic diversity in North America to find the "radical languages" proved a near-impossible task. Jefferson struggled with a growing doubt that his theory was correct so he preferred to leave it, without substantiation.

In the midst of his growing dismay over the shortcomings of the Indian Vocabulary project, Jefferson served as secretary of state (1790–1793) and president of the United States (1801–1809). Although codification of Indian removal policies would not occur until Andrew Jackson's administration, the presence of the American Indian within the nation's borders proved to be one of Jefferson's greatest political challenges. The acquisition of new land and expansion westward were core elements to the agenda of Jefferson's administration.[70] Federal pressures on American Indian nations to cede land and "civilize" mounted over these decades, eliciting varied responses from Indian nations and local settlers.[71] Scientific inquiry also aided political and diplomatic access to American Indians. Reappointed by President Jefferson as principal agent for Indian Affairs in 1801,

Benjamin Hawkins was a frequent correspondent with Jefferson on the Indian Vocabulary project. Jefferson's linguistic queries offered Hawkins a context for assuring the Creek elders that Jefferson was "the friend of all the red people and of humanity." Native replies came in the form of respectful pleas for the restoration of violated boundary lines. One elder, Tootehoomuh, complained of "white people and stock" on native land. Another, Elautaulau Hoomuh, stated that white people are building houses on native waterways. Despite Hawkins's claim for Jefferson's concern for his "red children," distrust appeared throughout these Indian speeches. The elders recommended that "red people and an interpreter" accompany the whites when they redraw the boundary line. They refused the liquor provided for them by the US government and insisted that "the chain of friendship, like an iron chain, should never be broken."[72] For nearly the next decade of Jefferson's presidency, the chain of friendship would be broken repeatedly as Congress made a priority the cessions of land claimed by Cherokee, Choctaw, and Chickasaw nations. The Indian Vocabularies were designed to serve as empirical proof that America's indigenous inhabitants were still in the savage state, thus justifying their displacement by white settlers.

On the one hand, the Indian Vocabularies can be read as a measure of national nostalgia. By preserving a fragment from the past as a remnant of national history, Jefferson attempted to assuage the trauma of US Indian policy through his Indian Vocabularies. We hear this sentiment in Jefferson's statement that "it is to be lamented... that we have suffered so many of the Indian tribes already to extinguish, without our having previously collected and deposited in the records of literature, the general rudiments at least of the languages they spoke."[73] When Edwards Jr. sent his *Observations on the Language of the Muhhekaneew Indians* (1788) to George Washington, Washington's reply echoed this national sentiment almost verbatim: "I have long regretted that so many Tribes of the American Aborigenes [*sic*] should have become almost or entirely extinct without leaving such vestiges, as that the genius & idiom of the Languages might be traced."[74] Both Jefferson and Washington treated Native Americans as vanishing populations, their words as artifacts of dead people such as the bones Jefferson excavated on his properties.

Not only did this sentiment ignore the living cultures of these peoples, the bare words of the languages were inadequate for drawing conclusions about the age and origins of the cultures. This lament was not only for the trauma of colonialism, the violence of frontier wars on the nation's borders and in Indian country, or the passage of stadial history from one civilization to the next, it was also a confrontation with the undead, a forced recognition of the contested nature of US sovereignty as long as Indian nations held competing claims to the land. Even though collected as part of an apparatus of state power, the vocabulary lists record a refusal on the part of the indigenous speaker to have his or her language condemned to the atavistic detritus of American antiquity.

Unruly Empiricism and the Science of Empire

The matrix of Jefferson's broadside included words that served a purpose other than his stated intention. Rather than reveal Asiatic origins, they tied the Indians to the very land from which they were being wrested. The intrinsic link between indigenous language and the land could not be severed, for as Barton writes: "from the Atlantic to the Mississippi," Lenni Lenape names identify "waters, mountains, and valleys of the country."[75] North America would remain an undiscovered country without these signposts dotting the landscape of the new nation as an indelible homage to the past. The vocabularies collected by Jefferson are coauthored documents produced out of a complex negotiation between agent and Indian. Whether intentionally or not, variant spoken sounds and alternative lexicons were produced by native speakers, altering the way that Nanticoke, Unkechaug, and Cherokee words were preserved for study by future generations. Indigenous speakers thwarted Jefferson's desire for uniformity as well as his and his contemporaries' insatiable quest for evidence of origins that would ensconce the indigenous word in a primitive past. Revealing patterns of unruly empiricism, of oral performance, transcription, and preservation that defy Jefferson's attempt to impose orthographic or taxonomic order, the vocabularies insist upon the embodied presence of the living speaker in the act of transmission.

Indigenous Metaphors and the Philosophy of History in Cooper's *Leatherstocking Tales*

The Last of the Mohicans (1826), James Fenimore Cooper's most commercially successful novel, stages a campfire discussion between Chingachgook, Uncas, and Hawkeye about the best route to take the following day. Watching the scene unfold, Major Duncan Heyward notes that even though he does not himself speak the Algonquian tongue, "the language of the Mohicans was accompanied by gestures so direct and natural" that he had "little difficulty in following the thread of their argument." By contrast, Hawkeye remains "obscure" and "unexcited" until the precise moment when the course of action was "about to be decided against him." At which point:

> he arose to his feet, and shaking off his apathy, he suddenly assumed the manner of an Indian, and adopted all the arts of native eloquence.... The Mohicans listened gravely, and with countenances that reflected the sentiments of the speaker. Conviction gradually wrought its influence, and towards the close of Hawkeye's speech, his sentences were accompanied by the customary exclamation of commendation. In short, Uncas and his father became converts to his way of thinking, abandoning their own previously expressed opinions, with a liberality and candour, that, had they been the representatives of some great and civilized people, would have infallibly worked their political ruin, by destroying, for ever, their reputation for consistency.[1]

Hawkeye, America's favorite wilderness hero and the Cooperian protagonist—also known by the appellations Natty Bumppo, Deerslayer, Pathfinder, the Trapper—masters this scene with the Franklinian ease of careful improvement through emulation. His upbringing among the Delaware gives him the exclusive right among all of Cooper's characters to "assume the manner of an Indian" and to display the "art of native eloquence." Yet his status as "the white man," as he himself so often remind us, also endows him with a superior capacity for reason. He captures the mythic power of the Indian tongue, but he does so without relinquishing reason.

Hawkeye's words flow effortlessly, mimicking the light and graceful movements of the canoe, to which he alludes by both tongue and sign, should the group chose the course that he favors. Conversely, he "delineates" the "long and painful path" that Uncas and his father had preferred, with words that mirror the frenzied dangers of rocks and watercourses. So powerful is Hawkeye's capacity to connect his body to nature, to use "signs" that are "too palpable to be mistaken," that Uncas and his father become "converts." Had they been "representatives of some great and civilized people," their reputation would have been ruined. But the point here is that they are not. On the one hand, this scene seems to reinforce a stagnant racial hierarchy, the inevitability of "the white man" to out-think and to out-rationalize the Indian. On the other hand, the scene exposes the limitations of a "great and civilized people," for whom political success comes at the expense of liberality, honest self-evaluation, and candor.[2]

As a literary trope, the "last Mohican" marks the passage of stadial history from one civilization to the next. Yet this passage also exhibits a certain kind of nostalgia for the traits of the "noble savage," believed to be lost to the next historical shift. Through Hawkeye's linguistic performance, Cooper both forecasts the death of the Mohican Indian in this scene and tries to inscribe a usable indigenous past into the nation's make-up. "The arts of native eloquence" function as a recursive force that reconnects civilized people to nature and to the savage state. Hawkeye's emotive expression reconnects word to nature, generating a mythic structure within the text that propels the narrative forward.

Cooper began *The Leatherstocking Tales* in the 1820s, a particularly precarious and transitional phase in US history. The War of 1812 solidified the contours of the nation-state, permitting the United States to emerge on an Atlantic and global scene with new economic and structural power. At the same time, the cultural separation from Britain was more acutely felt after the War of 1812, augmenting the urgency to forge a uniquely American literary idiom. Anticipating Ralph Waldo Emerson's roadmap for developing a distinctive national literary tradition, Cooper drew on the cyclical stadialism of eighteenth-century philosophical history to create a grand narrative frame in which to place the fledgling new country. In an effort to generate a myth for early nationalism, Cooper presented a narrative arc in the first three *Leatherstocking Tales* that swept across the first two hundred years of social change in America, from the hunting culture of the indigenous populations, through initial white settlement, through the establishment of ordered and stable civilization.[3] Cooper based this narrative structure on the works of such philosophical historians as Adam Ferguson, William Robertson, and Dugald Stewart. Following the formula established by his Scottish counterpart Sir Walter Scott, Cooper's historical romances take on the so-called primitive peoples and languages of North America as the infant mirrors self and society.[4] The historical romance functioned as a portable transatlantic genre, offering Cooper a way to interpret historical data, to enfold the literatures and languages of the "primitive" past into a new national historical consciousness. A cyclical model of stadial history provided Cooper with a dialectical momentum of dualities that he considered integral to the mythic structure of the new nation: civilization versus wilderness, order versus chaos, authority versus freedom, and collective republican virtue versus rugged individualism. He sought to integrate these dualities into a coherent and meaningful whole.[5] Yet the dilemma of the early *Leatherstocking Tales*—indeed the very condition that the iconic character Hawkeye, or, more commonly, Natty Bumppo, represents—is a fundamental inability to make the successful transition from the second settlement phase to the third vision for a stable ordered society, which is always imminent but never fully realized in Cooper's *Tales*.

Part of this forestallment was an American design, namely the belief of such prominent early republic voices as Benjamin Rush and Thomas Jefferson who saw settlement and agriculture as the American ideal. As Rush states in his "Enquiry into the Natural History of Medicine Among the Indians in North-America" (1774), "Civilians have divided nations into savage, barbarous, and civilized. The savage, live by fishing and hunting. The barbarous, by pasturage or cattle; and the civilized, by agriculture."[6] Cooper's novels are more troubled by this vision than the works of his early-republic counterparts. The civilized ideal of US society remains blurred and ambiguous throughout the novels. Due, in part, to his own experience as a literary author, landowner, and son of a pioneer, settler, and land speculator, Cooper's ambivalence toward the civilizing impulse in contemporary US society was more deeply felt. The first novel in

The Leatherstocking series to appear—though the penultimate novel in the narrative's chronology, *The Pioneers* (1823), fashions Cooper's father, the wealthy land speculator of Otsego County, into the fictional character Judge Temple. The rise and fall of William Cooper can be tracked through the son's attempt to reconcile his father's life in fiction.[7] Judge Temple's daughter, Elizabeth, often represents the novel's moral center and compass:

> "The enterprise of Judge Temple is taming the very forests!" exclaimed Elizabeth, throwing off the covering, and partly rising in the bed. "How rapidly is civilization treading on the footsteps of nature!"[8]
>
> "But, my dear father," cried the wondering Elizabeth, "was there actual suffering? where were the beautiful and fertile vales of the Mohawk? could they not furnish food for your wants?"[9]

The Pioneers is a novel about the disequilibrium between nature and the civilizing impulse of the 1790s, when William Cooper accumulated thousands of acres in Otsego County. This disequilibrium involved an ongoing tension between agriculture and nature, between greed, economic interest, and Lockean ideas of "natural" social equity and parity—key ingredients in the social contract. Natty and Chingachgook are the novel's twin voices of lament, each seeking to restore some sense of balance, and in doing so, exerting a critique of the destructive force of irrational slaughter and the unchecked exploitation of nature.

Language, is at the heart of Cooper's ambivalence over the nation's future. His *Leatherstocking Tales* showcase how language in performance may translate one culture into another and transform colonial violence, war, and genocide into an epic history of national grandeur. Yet the *Tales* also register language's limitations. As a student of indigenous Americana, who read widely about American Indian tongues, even if he did not speak them, Cooper was aware how language could register loss and death. He saw this loss not only as an index of culture—the dying traits of the noble savage—but also as an index of lost knowledge. In particular, Cooper understood indigenous tongues—specifically Lenni Lenape, which, following the Moravian missionary John Heckewelder, he identified as an *ur* American language—as conveying particular forms of knowledge about American nature integral to the nation's success and future. In the broader context of *The Leatherstocking Tales*, Natty Bumppo

exhibits the qualities that most approximate those of the American
Indian and is the sole white character fluent in several Indian languages. Cooper positions Natty throughout the *Tales* as the conduit
for the transmission of the knowledge encoded within Delaware
words. Yet Natty ultimately fails in this task, or rather is stuck in the
transitional state that is at once savage and civil. He cannot figure
out how to transform the natural landscape—without destroying
it—into the ingredients required for a national future.

Cooper's novels both register the knowledge encoded in indigenous tongues and resist the translation of this knowledge into a
usable past. In doing so, Cooper forestalls the development of a literary device that might ameliorate the underlying tension between the
project of preserving indigenous languages practiced by his contemporaries and what amounted to a US policy of genocide. Natty's si-
lences, his peculiar speech, and his unsuccessful attempts to reflect
upon his own existence abstractly reflect the nation's fumbled linguistic transition to a new American idiom.[10] The novels reflect
Cooper's effort to secure a place for the indigenous lexicon and the
natural world in the nation's future. Yet this effort ultimately falls
short as Cooper cannot reconcile the preservationist linguistic project with the US policy toward its native inhabitants. Lenni Lenape
was a living language for Cooper in a way that it was not for authors
writing about Native Americans from a European perspective. In
search of a uniquely American literary voice, Cooper could not resist
the allure of Lenni Lenape, even as this allure destabilized the arc of
progress designed for the *Leatherstocking Tales*.

Mark Twain felt the frustration. If the rules of art demanded that
"a tale shall accomplish something and arrive somewhere," *The
Leatherstocking Tales* "accomplis[h] nothing and arriv[e] in the air."[11]
This set the durable critical puzzle. Some attributed this to aesthetics,
others to history.[12] Whatever the cause, critics noted the novels'
stunted narrative progression. Cooper's inability to imagine a satis-
fying future for the nation, the object at the center of each of the five
novels, comes, in part, from his ambition to assimilate indigenous
customs of speaking into his novels. In *The Leatherstocking Tales*,
Cooper sets up a fantasy of *translatio imperii* whereby native arts of
eloquence would become American ones and the vast knowledge of
American nature encoded in indigenous tongues could be translated
into popular historical romances. Yet repeatedly, this structure of
translation is curtailed. Indian speech remains an enclosed and

impenetrable system. Far from being a conduit, Natty Bumppo becomes a historic anomaly—an anachronism to national change and, increasingly, a figure too eccentric and pathetic to sustain bi-cultural heroism. He alone of the white characters is fluent in Indian languages, and even when he speaks in Mohican or Lenape, it serves instrumental purposes. One has the sense that Natty's native eloquence is partial, its limitation both the cause and function of its instrumentality. He is a proficient mimic and ably reads the land, but the natural "gifts" that distinguish Indians from whites—to which he repeatedly alludes—thwart full assimilation. Because such gifts are natural—endowed, he professes by the Maker—they cannot be learned or transmitted in any way, except through bloodlines. Although raised among the Delaware and later adopted by Chingachgook, Natty is not of native blood.

This is Cooper's own dilemma. Like the rest of his white characters, Cooper did not speak Lenape or Mohican. He knew about Lenni Lenape through his primary historical source on the topic, Heckewelder's 1820 *Narrative of the Mission of the United Brethren Among the Delaware and Mohegan Indians*, and other works.[13] Heckewelder attuned Cooper to one aspect of indigenous tongues that he tried to translate using metaphor. Hawkeye's speech mimics dangerous rocks and watercourses. Yet metaphor is also where the fantasy of translation ends. Ultimately, the novels become fixed on the limits rather than the possibilities of translation, and in consequence fracture the arc of stadial history and halt before a realized civil society.

In Heckewelder, Cooper heard the powerful capacity of Lenape metaphors to emulate the contours of American nature. While the power of Lenape metaphors was not without precedent in the English literature of New World exploration, the analogical imagination of Lenape speakers captivated Cooper by its authenticity. As an aspiring author determined to forge something that might resemble a uniquely American literary voice a decade before Emerson's call for it and Emerson's own literary experiments, indigenous tongues seem to offer a unique perspective, possibly even a way to capture and concretize epistemic slippage between the respective world views. Cooper adopted the Lenni Lenape use of metaphor as a basis for the Anglo-American idiom of his novels. This is what gives the novels their enduring significance—the thing we recognize as the sometimes-fumbled beginnings of an American literary tradition—as well as the forms that repeatedly lack closure. Ultimately, Cooper had to map his fictive stadialist model onto a landscape still inhabited by living speakers of the very languages he hoped to absorb as part of America's usable past, a past that was an impediment to its future.

Language and Land

Cooper's incorporation of indigenous speech reflects the romanticized portraits of American Indians and their languages in early republic and antebellum literature.[14] This romance of primitive *ur* language rose in the late eighteenth-century in the linguistic philosophy of Lord Monboddo and Wilhelm von Humboldt and joined with Heckewelder's ethnographic and historical source texts.[15] Given to romance himself, Heckewelder, along with his colleague David Zeisberger, had deep knowledge of the Lenape or the Delaware tongue that they recorded through extensive writings on the subject. Cooper's aestheticized vision of indigenous America found in these source texts a way to present indigenous tongues as eloquent and metaphorical.

Cooper's preoccupation with Lenape stemmed from one of the major philosophical preoccupations of the eighteenth century: a desire to identify the origins of language. The 1826 preface to *The Last of the Mohicans* contains an origins story in miniature. Cooper explains that the name "Lenni Lenape" "signifies, an 'unmixed people,'" the ancestors of the tribes populating "that immense region which lies between the Penobscot and the Potomac, the Atlantic and the Mississippi." The Mohican are one such descendant. The British, Cooper explains, changed their name to "Delaware." To the north and adjacent to the Lenape were the "Mengwe," "another people" according to Cooper, registering the distinction between Algonquin and Iroquoian language groups. The "Mengwe" divided into Six Nations (Mohawks, the Oneidas, the Senecas, the Cayugas, and the Onondagas). The "Mengwe" were given the name of "Iroquois" by the French. In Cooper's classic fashion, he sets the stage for this novel by dividing American Indians into two groups, the good and the bad. The former aligns with English Protestantism while the latter aligns with French Catholicism. Though less powerful than the Lenape, the "Mengwe" aligned with the Dutch and then the French, forcing the Delaware to become weaker militarily. In

Cooper's history, this arrangement emasculated the Delaware, causing them to become "in the figurative language of the natives,
'women'."[16]

This short origins story sets the stage for the primary historical
actors in Cooper's romance, dividing native populations into mythic
good and evil. The evil force of the "Mengwe" pervades the novel
with a blend of Christian cosmogony (in Miltonic tones) and eighteenth-century gothic horror:

> It seemed, for near a minute, as if the demons of hell had possessed
> themselves of the air about them, and were venting their savage hu-
> mours in barbarous sounds. The cries came from no particular direc-
> tion, though it was evident they filled the woods, and, as the appalled
> listeners easily imagined, the caverns of the falls, the rocks, the bed of
> the river, and the upper air.[17]

With this identification as demonic power Cooper may transfer
blame for the Mohican's inevitable death from US genocide to a
fierce and militaristic band of "bad" Indians whose destructive force
has been both strengthened and further corrupted by French
Catholicism. The dying Mohicans speak a dying language. Descending
from an original tongue, Mohican codes as primordial, as connected
to nature, to a sense of place, and to human bodies and their sensory
capacity. This perception of primitive tongues was also the motivating force behind an eighteenth- and early nineteenth-century
philosophical and Romantic quest for the origins of words and
human history.

Over the eighteenth century, numerous philosophers tried their
hand at resolving the philosophical problem of recapturing this original moment of linguistic creation. Jean-Jacques Rousseau, Adam
Smith, Johann Gottfried Herder, Wilhelm von Humboldt, and Lord
Monboddo all wrote essays on the origins of language.[18] Each essay
takes a primal linguistic scene as its starting place, analogous to and
replacing biblical origins.[19] The possibility of language as comprising
roots that evolved from a deep sense of attachment to place in an organic relationship to the natural world had important ramifications
for uniting otherwise disparate populations under the sign of the
nation.[20] Whereas English had no claim to an original connection to
the continent of North America, Lenape did and even a claim to the
status of an *ur* language of American antiquity.

Part of Cooper's aspiration was that Lenape might function as a key to the vast terra incognita of the American West. Cooper's key was Edwin James's *Account of an Expedition from Pittsburgh to the Rocky Mountains* (1823), which envisioned the prairies as impenetrable inland deserts, thwarting agrarian fantasies. On his travels across the desert plains of Nebraska, James describes a sentient landscape, pulsing with a continuously changing atmospheric presence:

> For several days the sky had been clear, and in the morning we had observed an unusual degree of transparency in every part of the atmosphere. As the day advanced, and the heat of the sun began to be felt, such quantities of vapour were seen to ascend, from every part of the plain, that all objects, at a little distance, appeared magnified, and variously distorted. An undulating or tremulous motion in ascending lines was manifest over every part of the surface. Commencing soon after sunrise it continued to increase in quantity until the afternoon, when it diminished gradually, keeping an even pace with the intensity of the sun's heat. The density of the vapour was often such as to produce the perfect image of a pool of water in every valley upon which we could look down at an angle of about ten degrees. This effect was several times seen as so perfect and beautiful as to deceive almost every one of our party. A herd of bison, at the distance of a mile, seemed to be standing in a pool of water; and what appeared to us the reflected image was as distinctly seen as the animal itself. Illusions of this kind are common in the African and Asiatic deserts, as we learn from travellers, and from the language of poets. They are called by the Persians *sirraub*, "water of the desert;" and in the Sanscrit language, Mriga trichna "the desire or thirst of the antelope."[21]

James, who would himself become an astute student of Ojibwe, calls on ancient languages to describe desert phenomenon for which there is no word in English. Unlike the more common effect of refraction, for which there is an English word as we learn in the next paragraphs, the distortions produced by "vapour" in the afternoon heat create an effect that is visually and linguistically unintelligible. Such illusions require the language of poets and novels, or the metaphors encoded in the very syntax of what was then believed to be two of the most ancient languages, Persian and Sanscrit, and impress Cooper as a genealogy of the Mohican language.

A manuscript pamphlet, rescued from a "junk shop" in Albany and now held in the Watkinson Library archives reveals that James made a study of comparative vocabularies of "Menomini, Ojibway, and Sioux-Dakota," around 1825–1826. Comprising fairly standard lists of words and expressions, James's vocabulary record goes well beyond the simple word lists represented by Jefferson's project. At 110 pages in length, the pamphlet contains simple expressions such as "I will bring eggs" and "I will make a fire" at the same time that it includes words for objects found in nature: *maple, river, oak, pine, black walnut*. The pamphlet is small, bound together with string, such that it could be carried through a wilderness expedition.[22] In light of the passage quoted above, it seems James likely imagined that a study of these comparative vocabularies might give him some insight into the otherwise elusive nature of the landscape he was writing about.

Cooper, in his writings about the prairies of the American West, aspired to find a language adequately descriptive of the vast and impenetrable landscape west of the Mississippi. According to the aging and wise Natty Bumppo, often referred to in *The Prairie* (1827) as "the trapper," knowing the prairie requires full sensory immersion: apart from sight, "there are both scents and sounds in the air." These are no ordinary scents and sounds. The trapper tells Middleton that one could pass "a year on these Prairies" and still "mistak[e] a turkey for a horse, or conceiting fifty times that the roar of a buffaloe bull was the thunder of the Lord." The prairie deceives. "There is a deception of natur' in these naked plains, in which the air throws up the image like water, and then is it hard to tell the Prairies from a sea."[23] The prairie disrupts and distorts the organic relationship between the sign and the thing being signified in the natural world. The unknowing observer, after all, might mistake the prairie for a sea. It is a world that renders the senses unreliable. Here nature has the effect of disorienting one's visual capacity, sense of smell, and hearing, undermining the empirical basis of Enlightenment epistemology. The novel sets itself to the task of restoring some kind of rational order, so that the reader begins to see as the trapper does:

> The river was to be traced far through the endless meadows by its serpentine and smoking bed, and the little silvery clouds of vapour which hung above the pools and springs were beginning to melt in air, as they felt the quickening warmth, which, pouring from the glowing sky, shed its bland and subtle influence on every object of the vast and unshadowed region. The Prairie was, like the heavens after the passage of the gust, soft, calm and soothing.[24]

Echoes of James's passage are evident. This is an animate natural world, one malleable at its molecular level, as pools and springs melt into vaporous clouds. While James turns to Persian and Sanscrit to make sense of these natural phenomena, Cooper renders the prairie legible through a kind of lexical transparency in English. From the dialogue between the trapper and Middleton about the prairie's illegibility, to the omniscient narrative voice that begins chapter 31, the prairie's descriptive transformation is dramatic. The landscape is described exactly as it is perceived, rather than being transcoded into literary conventions and poetic tropes. "Serpentine and smoking bed" and "silvery clouds of vapour" create images in the reader's mind of the movement of the river across the "endless meadow" that blends in its infinity with the "glowing sky." The description is onomatopoeic and alliterative as the omniscient narrator matches his verbal cues to the movement of the landscape. "Natur's deception"—the distortions that beguile the senses—has transformed the prairie into an "unshadowed region." Thus marks the typological transformation from darkness into light—restoring the Western empirical basis of knowledge formation—as the prairie directs the nation westward through its "calm" and "soothing" "vastness." On the one hand, this is a transformation with clear antecedents in the Christian and—more specifically—Puritan tradition. Reading nature for dispensatory signs had a hermeneutics rooted in the theology of Jonathan Edwards and popularized in subsequent sermons and novels.[25] Yet, this passage also reveals Cooper's attempt to marry the indigenous methods of reading the land that he learned from Heckewelder to this Puritan tradition.

By chapter 32 of *The Prairie*, we have learned that the Bush caravan carrying the patriarch Ishmael, his wife, Esther, and their children must reverse their course in search of more fertile ground to the east:

> For the first time, in many a day, the squatter turned his back towards the setting sun. The route he held was in the direction of the settled country, and the manner in which he moved, sufficed to tell his children, who had learned to read their father's determinations in his mien, that their journey on the Prairie was shortly to have an end.[26]

The reversal of the squatter's course at this climactic moment in the novel reaffirms the cryptic symbolism of the prairie through an unintelligible supernaturalism. The repeated appearance of Esther's fragmented Bible gestures toward a defunct and irrelevant semiology. Nonetheless, the Bible is the only "article in the nature of a book" that could be found among the squatter's possessions. We are told that the "fragment" had been thumbed and "smoke-dried till the print was nearly illegible." Both its fragmentation and its gradual erasure due to climate symbolize, at once, its outdated knowledge and arcane form, ill-suited to the task of serving as an adequate guide to life on the prairie. For Esther, this is "a melancholy relick of more prosperous and possibly more innocent days." On the prairie, "the word of God" meets with the limits of intelligibility and is ultimately left behind as the detritus of an unsuccessful venture.[27] It is at this moment in the journey of Ishmael and Esther—the point at which they retreat east—that the prairie again becomes illegible: "The regular formation of the country, such as it has been described in the earlier pages of our book, had long been interrupted by a more unequal and broken surface." The landscape resumes its ominous foreboding, becoming "an ancient country, incomprehensibly stripped of its people and their dwellings." The vast emptiness of the land, introduced by the narrator as an "unshadowed region" and a type of heaven only the chapter before, here becomes a sign of eerie genocidal erasure.[28] "Incomprehensibly stripped" suggests a violent and inexplicable absence, a far cry from the organic disappearance of previous populations and their dwellings in an ideal version of the cycles of stadialist history. What is left of life in this region is scant and infertile, mixing more readily with the inanimate rocks than creating a generative support system for more life.

A "solitary willow" occupies the spot that Ishmael chose for his herds. It stands not as promise of the land's plentitude but of its parsimony, a symbol of prairie life as ancient and inaccessible: "As if in mockery of the meagre show of verdure that the spot exhibited, it remained a noble and solemn monument of former fertility." The reader wonders at this diminished fertility and thwarted legibility of the landscape, for the narrator merely hints at this prelapsarian state, as much an invocation of exile or banishment ("incomprehensively stripped") as it is of substantive loss. Either way, the narrator qualifies the ephemerality with an allusion to providential stability: "In all things it proclaimed the frailty of existence" and "the fulfilment of time."[29] A frail existence does not regenerate but rather dies out, much like the previous populations and dwellings of the prairie, whose lives seem commensurate to the willow's former fertility. The "fulfillment of time" offers a counterpoint to existence's frailty.

Within this sentence's coordinating conjunction, the willow's temporality shifts from the profane to the sacred, from death to prophetic consummation. "The fulfillment of time," denotes a millennial arc that supports a cyclical view of history, the notion that the peoples "incomprehensibly stripped" of their dwellings were part of a larger dispensational plan. Except that life has also ceased through time's fulfillment. The willow now stands on hallowed and hollowed ground, unyielding and unreceptive to its new inhabitants; hostile, in fact, to the point that they are forced to reverse their journey from the west, back to the east, itself a millennial marker of the Christian dispensation.

The scene that concludes this chapter brings this sense of dark foreboding to a gothic climax by dramatizing Abiram's death. Abiram kills the firstborn son of Esther and Ishmael; his death is punishment for this sin:

> The moon broke from behind a mass of clouds, and the eye of the woman was enabled to follow the finger of Ishmael. It pointed to a human form swinging, in the wind, beneath the ragged and shining arm of the willow... The leaves of the sacred book were scattered on the ground, and even a fragment of the shelf had been displaced by the kidnapper in his agony. But all was now in the stillness of death. The grim and convulsed countenance of the victim was at times brought full into the light of the moon, and again as the wind lulled, the fatal rope drew a dark line across its bright disk. The squatter raised his rifle, with extreme care, and fired. The cord was cut, and the body came lumbering to the earth, a heavy and insensible mass.[30]

The contorted corpse of Abiram, the scattering of the leaves from the Bible on the ground, and the use of the willow tree to perform the hanging bespeak a biblical hermeneutics out of joint, an unsuccessful effort to impose a typological reading on this westward land. Abiram's role within the novel itself is a warped version the punishment of Abiram, a participant in Korah's Rebellion, in Numbers 16. Abiram challenges Moses's authority in the biblical version of the story. Specifically, Abiram and Dathan, sons of Eliab, question why Moses did not lead his followers to the Promised Land but rather to the wilderness to die.[31]   Abiram, a fragment of an Old Testament type, has an unresolved presence within this chapter, like the "leaves of the sacred book" that fail to provide a narrative arc for the plot. Their defacement seems to refuse any attempt at reconstructing the narrative. As readers, we have difficulty placing these Old Testament types within a narrative frame not only because they not only remain unmoored from their proper location within the "fulfillment of time" referred to in the description of the willow tree, but also because their identities are as misaligned in their approximation of the true biblical figures as the narrative's plot is in its transmogrification of the holy text. The killing of Abiram has the sense of both inevitability and purposelessness. It is the occasion for the reversal of Ishmael's westward course, but not the cause.

The references to unknowing and incomprehensibility that punctuate this scene—the "insensible mass" that falls to the earth following an inchoate sacrificial death, the unhallowed land symbolizing the frailty of existence, Ishmael's turn back east, and Natty's refusal to die anywhere in "civilized" America—can all be attributed to the untranslatability of knowledge embedded within indigenous tongues. This is a knowledge that cannot be transmitted. As a consequence, in Cooper's *Tales*, the story of a rising US civilization remains incomplete.

If the reversal of the Bush caravan to the East's more familiar terrain symbolizes one deferral of westward promise, Natty's refusal to die in a state of civility represents another. The "dweller of the forests" who lived "in the wilderness for threescore and ten years" insists on being left on the riverbank where he makes his way to the Pawnee village, his chosen site of death.[32] Upon arrival, Natty "perform[s] the office of an interpreter" for the last time, as Hard-Heart addresses his people. He begins by speaking of "the antiquity and renown of his own nation," of their successes in "hunts and on the war path." Addressing not only the Pawnee but also the "Pale Face" members of the audience (Middleton, Natty, Inez, the naturalist, and Paul), Hard-Heart restores a sense of intelligibility to the great prairie, using "the metaphorical language of an Indian." He compares the "countless numbers" of whites to "the flights of migratory birds in the season of blossoms, or in the fall of the year." His speech exemplifies delicacy and grace, as he makes no mention of the violence inflicted on the "red-men" by the whites. And he "soothe[s]" the "resentment" that members of his tribe might feel through "indirect excuses and apologies." The moment of diplomacy and peace in the final pages of *The Prairie*, chronologically the last in the *Leatherstocking* sequence, comes from the eloquence of a Pawnee chief, with the dying Natty performing his last act as interpreter. Hard-Heart places the "Wahcondah" on equal footing with the "Great Spirit of the Pale Faces." Both have "veiled...countenances" and often "look darkly on [their] children."[33] The worlds of nature and of the spirit are thus restored through this final speech of the Pawnee chief.

The prairies reanimate with legibility and vitality in the final moments of Natty's life. Beyond his work of interpretation, his words are scarce in these final pages. "Anan!" is as close as he comes to an explanation. Goodbyes from the bee-hunting naturalist and Middleton are met with an "extraordinary, silent, laugh."[34] The scene of his death takes several days, as Natty sits poised in the Pawnee village with the "light of the setting sun" falling "upon the solemn features." The symbol of westward expansion itself hovers around Natty's bare head with his "thin, locks of gray, fluttering lightly in the evening breeze." To the Pawnees, Natty's death represents the loss of a "sage and counsellor," and in his dying hours, Natty continues to utter "wholesome maxims." To Hard-Heart Natty proclaims that "I die, as I have lived, a christian man...horses and arms are not needed to stand in the Presence of the Great Spirit of my people!"[35] Here we have the familiar reiteration of Natty's Christianity, though as elsewhere, the reader wonders what exactly this means. Who are Natty's people and who is their "Great Spirit"? It is a question, we finally realize, embodied in the constant shifting of The Leatherstocking Tales' most vital signifier, which persistently refuses to make the tales' protagonist legible by reducing his identity to a series of enigmatic synecdoches: Deerslayer, Hawkeye, Pathfinder, Trapper, Leatherstocking, and even, oddly, Natty (as the abbreviation of a proper name and a sartorial joke that references the literary and national fashion of such backwoods names). The Tales end with this question in mind, as Natty's dead body is supported equally by Middleton and Hard-Heart. In his death announcement to the tribe, Le Balafre's voice "seemed a sort of echo from that invisible world to which the spirit of the honest trapper had just departed."[36] What was this invisible world? One to whom both La Balafre's voice and the voice of the Wahcondah belong. Middleton has the last say in this scene, though we are told "only" via one small liberty: to place a stone on Natty's grave with a simple inscription requested by Natty himself.

The Prairie distorts the metaphor of the setting sun of westward expansion. In the end, things do in fact arrive in the air as Twain lamented. Natty's death resolves nothing. We are no closer to knowing the fate of the potentially five hundred thousand Indian souls living in the Great Plains. We do know that for the "Pale Faces," life on the prairies as they currently exist is largely unsustainable, owing entirely to the illegibility of the region's natural world. For the Pale Faces in the novel, the prairies resume their sense of "illimitable and dreary wastes...the rushing wind sound[s] like the whisperings of the dead."[37] This natural landscape makes sense only when animated by an indigenous cosmos, the force of the Wahcondah. Creator of metaphors that enliven the meaning of the prairie, the Wahcondah "pours the rain from his clouds...shakes the hills...[and] scorches the trees [with] the anger of his eye."[38] Without the force of this integrated system of nature and spirit, the prairies become "another Babel."[39] Language, the sole vehicle for transferring the knowledge contained within the prairies, is what dies with Natty. As Tachechana says when she places her infant son at the feet of Inez, in another allusion to the sacrifice of Isaac, "strange tongue[s]" are replacing the "forgot[ten] voice of the mother."[40]

Cooper accords a specific epistemological power to indigenous languages, a power that he both hopes to extract from them for his own authorial purposes and that also prevents him from seeing a clear path through Natty's wilderness vision toward the nation's future. The *Tales* are an attempt to use the indigenous tongues in pursuit of a national literary tradition, in part, as a way to reconcile the dueling realities of US genocidal policy toward the natives with the still-living presence of indigenous populations.

Among his literary milieu, Cooper was not unique in attempting to harness the aesthetic potential he found in indigenous languages. The attempt had many adherents and animated a larger conversation among philosophers, statesmen, and authors of the 1810s and 1820s. The sentiment of the *Archaeologia Americana*, a journal of the American Antiquarian Society, stated that "oral language is the chief object which can, in any degree, supply literary data from a people who are wholly destitute of books. It enables us, in a measure, to speak with by-gone generations, by supplying facts for analogy and comparison."[41] Thus Cooper was not alone in his confidence that the syntax, grammar, and sounds of native languages offered the most enduring monuments of American antiquity and a history on which Anglo-America could build.

Just a few years on in 1845, in "Literature and Art Among the American Aborigines," the so-called Southern version of Cooper,

William Gilmore Simms presents a vision of national artistic production that maps directly onto stadial history via American Indian
languages:

> —so, the nature of the savage, sterile while traversing the wide prai-
> ries of Alabama, or ranging the desert slopes of Texas, subdued and
> fettered by the hand of civilization among the hills of the Apalachy,
> becomes a Cadmus, and gives a written language to his hitherto
> unlettered people.* The most certain sources of a national literature,
> are to be found in the denseness of its population, in its readiness to
> encounter its own necessities.[42]

The starred reference is to the Cherokee alphabet, a recent historical
invention that was believed by Simms and others to have given
a previously "unlettered people" a national literary history. C. C.
Trowbridge and Henry Rowe Schoolcraft were also collecting information on the mnemonic symbols of the North American Indians
at about this time.[43] Throughout the 1810s and 1820s, efforts to dismiss American Indian languages as primitive or savage repeatedly
failed. Indian agents, statesmen, and fiction writers admired the elegance of the Cherokee Syllabary such as with Simms.

Yet even as Henry Schoolcraft and his coterie of like-minded geographers and ethnographers recognized indigenous systems of writing, American Indian agents encountered linguistic complexity.
Despite the training materials comprising simplistic taxonomies, vocabulary lists, phonetic worksheets, and questionnaires with which
they were sent to the frontier, Enlightenment linguistic taxonomies
did not hold up in practice. When Schoolcraft presents us with the
Missouri Indians' "symbolic record" of their interaction with US
troops, "the Indians themselves were depicted without hats, this
being, as we noticed, the general symbol for a white man or
European."[44] Schoolcraft noted that this representation is drawn "according to their conventional rules," indicating the post-contact adaptation of indigenous systems of writing that would counter theories
of static, linguistic primitivism.

Yet, even while acknowledging the intricacies of indigenous writing systems and their adaptations to the historical present, early
nineteenth-century philosophers, missionaries, and statesmen sought
to inscribe American Indians within a primitive past. As Eleazer
Williams, the Mohawk Episcopalian clergyman and missionary, said
in a sermon to his Iroquois brethren in 1819:

> We see that you cannot, many years longer, live in any part of the United States in the hunter-state. The white people will push their settlements in every direction & destroy your game, and take away your best lands. You have not strength to defend yourselves, were you disposed to make war with the white people. They have become too powerful to be resisted or restrained in their course.[45]

Williams had himself become an accomplished missionary linguist at this point, publishing *The Book of Common Prayer* in Iroquois as well as several spelling books. His papers contain sheet music and several sermons in Iroquois. As the passage from the sermon above illustrates, Williams represents a transitional phase between the functional use of missionary linguistics and a philosophical impetus to collect and preserve indigenous tongues as part of a forgotten past. This sermon illustrates just how deeply the ideology of stadialist history penetrated the missionary frontier, serving as a justification for removal. The lengthy correspondence between Heckewelder and Du Ponceau epitomizes the concerted efforts to redirect a long history of missionary linguistics toward a new era of building an archive of American antiquity. The pattern incipient in Anglo-American religious and philosophical culture since David Brainerd's Indian missions in the New Jersey and Pennsylvania wilderness in the 1730s and 1740s and Jonathan Edwards's seven-year Stockbridge mission to the Housatonic people beginning in 1751 coalesced around an emergent national literary culture. Languages of North America were seen as integral to the US past but irrelevant to its present and future.

Cooper's romantically inflected, nationalist longing for an authentic linguistic and indigenous literary tradition took up a particular set of contradictions. The historical dislocation of the early United States, deracinated from Great Britain's ancient history, intensified the need for an *ur* antiquity. Yet the sources for constructing an *Archeologia Americana* were the same indigenous populations that early republic and antebellum governmental policy focused on removing to make way for westward expansion. This created a temporal contradiction highlighted in Cooper's novels: American antiquity lived within the present, a population whose language and customs could be relegated to the past, but this was a past that would not easily release its grasp on the land that Anglo-America wished to adopt and inhabit. Land was a space, in other words, where the past was preserved. For this reason, Cooper begins *The Prairie*—chronologically the last of *The Leatherstocking Tales*—with the Louisiana Purchase of 1803, a subject, we are told in the first sentence of chapter 1, about which "much was said and written, at the time." A symbol of great national promise, the Louisiana Purchase "gave us the sole command of the great thoroughfare of the interior, and placed the countless tribes of savages, who lay along our borders, entirely within our controul." The "us" within this opening statement is the Anglo-American readership that Cooper clearly sees himself addressing: a collective group of people who share in the national ideals of "political justice," the economic promise of "inland trade," and the hope for a common "language [and] religion."[46]

National promise contains, however, the relentless undercurrent of violence, injustice, tyranny of the majority, and anxiety of devolution. A preface, introduction, and epigraph precede the first chapter of *The Prairie*, each containing its own meditation on the forces that might derail the American story of national promise. In an ostensible convention of apology for the artistic license that will permit him to veer from historical accuracy, Cooper's preface explains that "sound" supersedes literal truth. For instance, "the Great Spirit" has been "uniformly" titled "Wahcondah," a name that elides the linguistic distinctions in the two American Indian nations introduced in the story.[47] The reader wonders what the Great Spirit has to do with the telling of American history, particularly this moment of the acquisition of the vast American "desert," the "final gathering place of the red men."[48] What role does this "Great Spirit" play in the narrative of national promise, where early on in the narrative the travelers have the distinct impression of "a supernatural agency" among them?[49] Cooper contrasts this sense of the nation's future, the "luxuriant fertility" of the United States, with the unsettling still-living presence of "one and five hundred thousand Indian souls." If the great prairies became the symbol of the nation's future in 1803, it also became the haunted graveyard and gathering place for the "remnants of the Mohicans, and the Delawares, of the Creeks, Choctaws, and Cherokees." Constructing a competing claim to Manifest Destiny, Cooper tells us that these tribes "are destined to fulfil their time on these vast plains."[50] As such, the introduction frames the novel in terms of two competing temporalities of providential design: on the one hand, the English who have succeeded the French and established their dominion; and, on the other hand, the "red men" who still very much belong to a present-tense historical frame. United

States sovereignty fractures not only over competing claims over who lives within the present. Early American antiquity had to be borrowed from sources more diverse and remote than the Celtic traditions that the English wished to claim as their own and then condensed into a "truth" that was not "literal" but rather evocative of the "sound" of the "Great Spirit." "In the endless confusion of names, customs, opinions, and languages which exist among the tribes of the West," Cooper attempts to make the North American past somewhat consonant with the present.[51]

Romantic philology, archaeology, and antebellum literature were mutually informing enterprises in the antebellum United States. Fact and fiction interplayed in all attempts to construct an integrative and coherent account of American antiquity. William Cullen Bryant's "The Prairies" (1832) goes back to the legend of the "moundbuilder" race that "vanished from the earth" at the moment that "the red man came."[52] This deep story makes contemporary American Indians just one more colonizing race, analogous to, rather than victimized by the new Americans. This historiography corresponds to Cooper's sense of the "time of the red man" in *The Last of the Mohicans*.[53] Yet neither Bryant's nor Cooper's "red man's time" fit a justification for Indian removal or defense of US sovereignty and westward expansion. These works stir with palpable nostalgia for native traditions and aesthetic forms. This aesthetic desire was not merely about the collection of curiosities or objects from a primitive past. It was about preserving indigenous forms of communication and communion with the natural world, lest American letters lose the key ingredient for making the landscape of the continent legible.

Indigenous Metaphor

Some paragraphs in to his introduction to *The Last of the Mohicans*, Cooper makes a striking statement about the aesthetic potential of Indian languages:

> The imagery of the Indian, both in his poetry and his oratory, is Oriental,—chastened, and perhaps improved, by the limited range of his practical knowledge. He draws his metaphors from the clouds, the seasons, the birds, the beasts, and the vegetable world.

In this, perhaps, he does no more than any other energetic and imaginative race would do, being compelled to set bounds to fancy by
experience; but the North American Indian clothes his ideas in a
dress that is so different from that of the African, and is Oriental in
itself. His language has the richness and sententious fulness of the
Chinese. He will express a phrase in a word, and he will qualify the
meaning of an entire sentence by a syllable; he will even convey different significations by the simplest inflexions of the voice.[54]

The passage almost replicates Herder's claim about the fundamental
similitude that spans so-called primitive languages, ancient and
modern, by drawing a parallel between Indian and Oriental poetry
and oratory.[55] Yet Cooper also emphasizes the exceptional status of
Indian speech by comparing it favorably to that of the African. There
are clear echoes here of Thomas Jefferson's *Notes on the State of
Virginia*, which lauded the oratorical skills of Logan while denigrating
the capacity for civilization to be found among Africans. Significantly,
Jefferson uses poetry as the benchmark of refined civilization, describing the poetry of Phillis Wheatley, the acclaimed black Boston
poet, as evidence of the inability of people of African descent to produce component verse.[56] The same hierarchy operates in this passage
from Cooper, lauding the sententious speech of American Indians in
contrast to "that of the African."

Throughout *The Last of the Mohicans*, Cooper's narrator strives to
emulate the cadence of Indian speech in the hope of conveying some
of this aesthetic potential. The landscape has a lyrical quality, consisting of sounds that must be heard to be known and a music that needs
a language to be understood.

> The vast canopy of woods spread itself to the margin of the river,
> overhanging the water, and shadowing its dark current with a deeper
> hue. The rays of the sun were beginning to grow less fierce, and the
> intense heat of the day was lessened, as the cooler vapours of the springs
> and fountains rose above their leafy beds, and rested in the atmos-
> phere. Still that breathing silence, which marks the drowsy sultriness
> of an American landscape in July, pervaded that secluded spot, inter-
> rupted, only, by the low voices of men, the occasional and lazy tap of
> a wood-pecker, the discordant cry of some gaudy jay, or a swelling on
> the ear, from the dull roar of a distant water-fall.[57]

Nature is animate. The wooded canopy "shadows" the dark river current; solar rays are "fierce"; water vapours "rest" in the atmosphere.

The silence "breathes," all in the drowsy, sultry scene of an American landscape in July. On the surface, this is a very Cooper-esque passage: a Romanticism applied to the American landscape as if it is staging the Hudson River School, with its hallmark blend of proto-realism and supernaturalism-the wild luminosity of Thomas Cole.

Yet, in *The Last of the Mohicans* and elsewhere, Cooper's style draws not only from Romanticism and the painterly aesthetics of American landscape artists; he also strives to capture his fantasy of the sonic utterance of Indian words and to translate this into the voice of his novels.

The passage above appears toward the beginning of chapter 3, just after an account of the wooden tunes of the New England psalmist, David Gamut. Like the Bible featured in *The Prairie*, Gamut's psalms are comically inadequate to their landscape. The psalms, long famous for their spiritual purity, clear transmission of Hebrew, and association with primitive Christianity, come across in this novel as wooden and out of place, fine for spiritual edification in New England but unfit as the "native poet[ry]" of the forest.[58] In the colonial period theologians in the New England tradition believed in the commensurability between ancient tongues represented by the psalms and the Massachusett language, which they also believed to be an ancient though fallen language. The translation of the psalter into Massachusett was meant to marry an otherwise fallen indigenous history with this biblical past.

By the time Cooper was writing his novels, over a hundred years later, indigenous history could no longer be sutured this way. The psalms appear in *The Last of the Mohicans* as an awkward and out-of-date tradition, peculiar to New England yet inadequate for an American wilderness in July.

The sounds of this landscape require a new native poetry. Chapter 3 begins with a stanza from Bryant's "Indian at the Burial Place of His Fathers":

> Before these fields were shorn and tilled,
>   Full to the brim our rivers flowed;
> The melody of waters filled
>   The fresh and boundless wood;
> And torrents dashed, and rivulets played,
> And fountains spouted in the shade.[59]

Cooper's historical novels make a refrain of this pre-civilization harmony—all energy and music. Cooper's chapter at once evokes and declares the historical distance of this world. Now only "feeble and broken sounds" interrupt this landscape: the woodpecker's "lazy tap," the jay's "discordant cry," and the dull roar of the waterfall.[60] The melody is a thing of the past, unrecognizable to sojourners in the woods today.

As Chingachgook and his son, Uncas converse, they seem figures from this lost world:

> It is impossible to describe the music of their language, while thus engaged in laughter and endearments, in such a way as to render it intelligible to those whose ears have never listened to its melody. The compass of their voices, particularly that of the youth, was wonderful; extending from the deepest bass, to tones that were even feminine in softness. The eyes of the father followed the plastic and ingenious movements of the son with open delight, and he never failed to smile in reply to the other's contagious, but low laughter.[61]

Pure, natural, and prelapsarian, the Mohicans' voices fuses with the speakers' bodies and their surroundings. One has to hear it otherwise the musical quality supersedes what can be conveyed in written English.

Mohican is at once untranslatable yet diffused everywhere in Cooper's text. Its untranslatability is a consequence of its status as a language that predates the Fall, whose ancient music has been frozen in time. Cooper stages multiple scenes in which the reader bears witness to but cannot understand the lyrical nature of the exchange between Uncas and Chingachgook. At the same time, Cooper channels this into a new American prose style. Natty Bumpo describes an exchange between Uncas and Chingachgook as the "sounds of the woods." He understands this music, for he has "listened" to it in Delaware "for thirty years" and can convey its sense and sensation to the reader. The myth Cooper links to the indigenous tongues preserves centuries-old debates about the prelapsarian world, in which many theologians, following a particular rabbinical tradition, believed that all of creation shared in the elements of a universal language. Through his acquaintance with the Delaware tongue, his own ear has become accustomed to "the whine of the panther" and the "whistle of the cat-bird." In a novel set during the Seven Years War, he can recognize the "devilish" sounds of the "Mingoes," the mortal enemies of the Delaware, whose ominous war cries come in "savage humours in barbarous sounds" throughout the novel.[62]

On the one hand, depictions of Indian speech recognize radical differences from modern English. On the other hand, these depictions evoke real knowledge. Both Hawkeye and the narrator, for example, describe the Hudson River in terms a reader might imagine and participate in:

> If you had daylight, it would be worth the trouble to step up on the height of this rock, and look at the perversity of the water! It falls by no rule at all; sometimes it leaps, sometimes it tumbles; there, it skips; here, it shoots; in one place 'tis white as snow, and in another 'tis green as grass; hereabouts, it pitches into deep hollows, that rumble and quake the 'arth; and thereaway, ripples and sings like a brook, fashioning whirlpools and gullies in the old stone, as if 'twas no harder than trodden clay. The whole design of the river seems disconcerted. First it runs smoothly, as if meaning to go down the descent as things were ordered; then it angles about and faces the shores; nor are there places wanting, where it looks backward, as if unwilling to leave the wilderness, to mingle with the salt! Ay, lady, the fine cobweb-looking cloth you wear at your throat, is coarse, and like a fish net, to little spots I can show you, where the river fabricates all sorts of images, as if, having broke loose from order, it would try its hand at every thing. And yet what does it amount to! After the water has been suffered to have its will for a time, like a headstrong man, it is gathered together by the hand that made it, and a few rods below you may see it all, flowing steadily towards the sea, as was foreordained from the first foundation of the 'arth![63]

This passage is what makes Cooper's novels notoriously difficult to read, calling into question their success as American literary experiments. Sentences run at excessive length; metaphors and similes pile up, making it difficult for the reader to parse the difference between the image being described and the images summoned to facilitate that description (such as the awkward description of the cobweb-looking cloth); the narrative length is often overwhelmingly disproportionate to the work that the passage does to convey relevant information, and, at times, the status of the information conveyed is, at best, negligible to character development or to the plot's advancement. Occasionally over-written and stylistically clumsy, such passages are often dismissed as the fumbled attempts of an early author to craft American-style prose in the decades before the giants of the American Renaissance.

Yet here as elsewhere, something else is at stake in Cooper's often unsatisfying attempts at descriptive prose. Cooper fashions Hawkeye's speech to emulate some of the key features of Indian speech, at least as represented in the text. The passage itself contains an onomatopoetic relation to the river, for it also leaps and tumbles with little heed to rule. The flow of the paragraph, like the flow of the river, is "disconcerted." Cooper's prose style stages an aspect of the natural world in order to make speech imitative of the natural landscape, much in the way he had observed and tried to recapitulate the harmonious melody of Mohican and Delaware words. In this attempt at a representational translation Cooper's aesthetic success falls short. Metaphors appear forced rather than natural and organically connected to the land. And in bending and parsing his syntax in imitation of the natural language he sees in the Mohican and Delaware tongues, he chops up the natural rhythms of the language he seeks to transform. In so doing, his style becomes the opposite of melodious; the sharp edges of broken syntax and fragments of metaphor fracture the linguistic consonance of the scenes he seeks to create.

The rationale behind Cooper's attempt to absorb the cadence of the Delaware and their use of metaphor into Hawkeye's voice is more than a desire for aesthetic success. This mode of adopting strategies of Indian speech into English is at the heart of Cooper's historical novel, his attempt to create a link between America's indigenous past and its progressively evolving Anglo-American future as an organic transition that elides the violence of contemporary US Indian policies. Ultimately, the literary endeavor is troubled because, as with the clumsiness of the passage above, his experimental style evolves into the structure of *The Leatherstocking Tales* as a whole: the attempt to thwart a history of American discovery, settlement, civilization, and ultimate devolution required in its stead a mythic cycle of sacrifice, death, generation, and regeneration.

Throughout *The Leatherstocking Tales* and particularly in *The Last of the Mohicans*, Cooper describes Indian languages much in the terms that we have seen throughout eighteenth- and early nineteenth-century language philosophy. The imaginative quality of the words, particularly in oratory and poetry, derives from their proximity to the natural world. Metaphors are emulative of nature. Indian speech also exudes a natural connection to the body. The relationship between speech and the body's sensory experience of the world is so aligned that ideas appear as clothes. Yet the cost of such a heightened proximity to nature, along with the richness of the imagery to come with it, is rationality. Following philosophical historians from Vico to Adam Smith, Cooper came to view the loss of a certain poetic quality of words as the cost of a rational logic. Passages in which Indian speech is represented but not translated—such as the dialogue between Chingachgook and Uncas quoted above—introduce the reader to an indigenous linguistic world that is at once replete with imagination and imagery and relegated to a less developed phase of human history. Cooper both elevates the quality of Delaware words in contrast to the fallen status of modern languages and presents these words as frozen in time, and, therefore, unavailable for recuperation as living languages. What he proposes is the absorption of these patterns of Indian speech into new national language. *The Last of the Mohicans* is Cooper's testing ground of the American novel.

Cooper was fascinated with the metaphoric capacity of indigenous tongues. This interest, developed in the United States from 1810 to 1830, was in effect a nostalgia of the Puritan typological system for the mystical wholeness of American Indian languages. This typology depended on a closed hermeneutic system in which the metaphorical—or, more properly, the figural—was also literal at the level of the whole of human history. This was European interest in primitive languages transplanted to America. The doctrine that begins Ralph Waldo Emerson's chapter on "Language" in his essay *Nature* (1836) makes the lingering vestiges of the Puritan hermeneutic abundantly clear: "words are signs of natural facts...nature is the symbol of spirit." Whereas Hugh Blair's concept of the poetic use of metaphor depends on the capacity of the writer to create an association within the mind of the reader, Emerson's system leaves less to chance. "If traced to its root," Emerson goes on to tell us, "every word" borrows from a "material appearance." All words are borrowed from "sensible things" much like the Romantic concept of savage language posited that expression was the consequence of emotions elicited by sensible objects.[64]

The Emersonian poet is also an etymologist, archaeologist, and "Language-maker." His job is to hear how the "deadest word" was once "a brilliant picture." In this way, "Language is fossil poetry." And then Emerson evokes a metaphor from nature to explain what he means:

As the limestone of the continent consists of infinite masses of the shells of animalcules, so language is made up of images, or tropes, which now, in their secondary use, have long ceased to remind us of their poetic origin.

Language is a repository for knowledge of nature and the supernatural. This knowledge is hidden, buried, and "forgotten" by the "archives of history." The task of the poet, for Emerson, is to resuscitate this meaning, to reinvigorate the sense of "expression" as a "second nature."[65] Emerson's philosophy of language evolves in part out of a system of Puritan typology where the gradual loosening of seventeenth-century doctrinal precepts increasingly made objects in North American nature available for prophecy. In Emerson's case, a *telos* directed toward unfolding the truth of the Over-Soul replaces biblical history, but his system of reading nature's types as the avenue through which one arrives there is no less precise. Emerson envisions a world in which meaning-making is not a condition of associative thought but rather a method of excavating the original meaning of the word. Less subtly refined versions of Puritan types proliferate in aesthetic representations of American nature in the early nineteenth century, perhaps most famously in landscape paintings such as Thomas Cole's *St. John in the Wilderness* (1827), which links a scene from *The Last of the Mohicans* (1826) to a biblical type. The American landscape was a template to be read and understood, both for the archaeological wisdom of its past and what that past might indicate about things to come.

American Indian languages were believed by Du Ponceau, Heckewelder, and Cooper to be uniquely expressive and therefore an apt canvas for philological discoveries that would both establish the international presence of American science and a national literary tradition. This was not a new insight. Missionaries to North America had long observed the poetic logic of indigenous tongues. They observed in particular a propensity toward the formulation of metaphors, which stemmed from indigenous beliefs in the nonmaterial power of objects. In the early seventeenth century, French Jesuit Jean de Brébeuf noted of the Huron that their language consisted of "an infinity of Metaphors" through which they "dignif[ied] their style of language" as "born orators."[66] Out of this infinity of metaphors arose various forms of misunderstanding Indians' meanings.[67] The "metaphoric sensibility" that Europeans associated with "Indian talk" enabled colonists and Euro-Americans to take on Indian identity at key points in the War for Independence, such as the Boston Tea Party. Metaphors allowed for a certain form of fluid identity, enabling Whigs to take on or "play" Indian, or Natty Bumppo to become Hawkeye, Deer-slayer, Leather-stocking, and Path Finder. A few decades later, in antebellum fraternal societies, the integration of metaphor into society practices enabled forms of commemoration, the ritualized collective preservation of the nation's past, which was also a means of eliding the genocidal policies of nation-building.[68]

Metaphors proliferate in Lenni Lenape, though not for any of the explanations offered by European colonists and Enlightenment philosophers. Metaphor is intrinsic to human thought and therefore present in abundance in all languages.[69] In Lenape the difference from that of European perspectives is the mode of thought. Language reflects a culture's cosmology. In many indigenous languages, plants and animals take animate and inanimate forms. Verbs are conjugated or nouns are gendered to reflect the animacy or inanimacy of the object.[70] As Heckewelder explains in an 1816 letter to Du Ponceau, "Indians" are "particular" in "distinguishing words between living things & such as are without life." The root changes when the sensible object named is infused with the spirit of the "Creator," such that "any thing lying on the Earth, floor or any where…have proper words to express the living from what has no life."[71] The practice of naming sensible objects in Lenape, in other words, accords with Aristotle's classic definition of metaphor as "giving the thing a name that belongs to something else."[72] But in Lenape cosmology, there is no bifurcation between the sensible object named and the spirit to which it refers, whether or not the object is animate.

Some European writers interpreted this linguistic economy as a paucity of thought or a mental limitation. Metaphors merely supplemented what could not be described, so the addition of the prefix "Lenni" to objects in nature changed a literal meaning to a metaphorical one. Compound words that often express complex thoughts in a single phrase were not infrequently mis-recognized as the language's representational limitations. Some linguists simply assumed that specific names had to be attributed to a variety of objects due, at least in part, to the impoverished vocabulary of New World languages. In a text cited multiple times in Heckewelder's correspondence with Du Ponceau, Cadwallader Colden went further than most. He proposed that the use of "many metaphors in their discourse" was a direct result of "having but few words, and few complex Ideas."[73] Though more severe in its assessment, Colden's observation accords with Blair's estimation that "the barrenness of language, and the want of words, be doubtless one cause of the invention of tropes." Further on in the same lecture, Blair describes the "character of the American and Indian Languages" as "bold, picturesque, and metaphorical" due to the "savage"—inflected here with its French connotation, "wild"— state of men at the "beginnings of society."[74]

Heckewelder works to correct this perspective for Du Ponceau. First, he explains how compound words work: "Nadhotawall" means "come with the Canoe & take us across the River or Stream." "Wulama- lefsohalian" means "thou who maketh me happy."[75] Compound words not only "name the thing," Heckewelder explains, they also describe function, giving two assignations to one object. Heckewelder acknowledges that this is a primary reason for the disparaging com- ments made about indigenous languages:

> I know very well that many People are under the Idea that the Indian Languages contain but few words, or at least not a sufficiency, so as to express themselves without making signs with their hands while speaking. Now this is erroneous, & I am satisfied that they do not labor under any difficulty on this score—they have sufficient words to convey their Ideas to one another, the same as we have, & in many instances, they with few words will say more to the purpose then we can do in our Language with double that number.[76]

Heckewelder both universalizes Lenape—they have just as many words as we do—and elevates the language above European tongues (English, German, and French as the most presently on the minds of Heckewelder and Du Ponceau in their correspondence). Compound words, with their ability to describe essence or relation as well as name, are more expressive as well as more precise.

In his *Account of the History, Manners, and Customs of the Indian Nations* (1819), a text that was in process and much discussed during these years of correspondence, Heckewelder publishes some of his insights. He develops a theory of "metaphorical expression" in Lenape that begins with a disclaimer: "The Indians are fond of meta- phors. They are to their discourse what feathers and beads are to their persons, a gawdy but tasteless ornament." He then explains that for this, they should not be judged too harshly and lists several examples. The list is entirely in English. Heckewelder does not include the original Lenape. He does, however, translate the metaphor itself. *"The sky is overcast with dark blustering clouds,"* he tells us, means "We shall have troublesome times; we shall have war." "*A black cloud has arisen yonder,"* means "War is threatened from that quarter, or from that nation." Most of the metaphors are observations of nature that name the phenomenon but are used to describe imminent war. Heckewelder also describes proper names, all of which derive from nature: "*Beaver, Otter, Sun-fish, Black-fish, Rattle-snake, Black-snake, & c.*"[77] Through this pairing of two translated phrases, the literal transcription of the metaphor, and then of the metaphor's meaning, Heckewelder emphasizes that metaphorical expression is literal for the Lenape speaker, not symbolic. There is no distinction between the animate natural world and the unfolding of historical events.

In Lenape, as Heckewelder understood the language and cosmology, human bodies link nature to history, just as philosophers from Vico onward believed that primitive languages derived their expressive capacity from the body's interactions with the natural world. Indian names are descriptive, Heckewelder tells us, reflective of "personal qualities or appearances" immediately associable with animals or phenomena in nature.[78] Consider Heckewelder's explanation to Peter Du Ponceau of the meaning of Lenni Lenape as "the original people." "Lenni" means "Original" as well as "common, plain, pure, simple," Heckewelder explains, while "Lenape" is a gender-neutral term for people. "Lenni" is a word used for a great many things in the Lenape landscape. "Lenni haiki" means "common, plain, Earth, Soil or Land" and plants that have always grown on the land, such as linden trees, are identified through the prefix "Lenni" to differentiate them from other trees not indigenous to the region. Consequently, "Lenni" refers to any aspect of nature—people, land, trees, and vegetables—that have been there since the time of Creation. As gifts of the "great Spirit," Heckewelder explains, these animate forms are considered as "original," as "not having deviated or changed from their original designation by the Creator."[79] This is the same connection that can account for Western philosophy's fascination with indigenous oral cultures, and indeed the same connection that attracted Cooper to the expressive potential of Delaware. An example is the shaman's capacity to enter into a rapport with plants, animals, forests, and winds. Shamanistic ritual reflects a sensual connection to nature believed to have been lost to "literate" and "civilized"

Europeans who view these aspects of nature as merely the pleasant backdrop of more pressing human concerns.[80] Imbricated in the observer is a desire to "return to things themselves," to a phenomenal field that precedes scientific schematization and its "derivative sign-language" through which one comes to know a countryside in relation to prior knowledge of "forest[s], prairie[s], [and] river[s]."[81] The more ancient the language the more palpable the residue of this mythic structure can be. Heckewelder's account of Lenape, upon which Du Ponceau began to build his philosophical accounts of American Indian linguistic origins and upon which Cooper crafted expressive forms in his novels, exhibited this phenomenological desire for a lost primordial language that conveyed a more integral relationship to the natural world.

Heckewelder recognized the facility of translation from metaphor to literal meaning as essential to the portability of Lenape expression into European languages. He notes that many of the listed names cited in his *History, Manners, and Customs* are "not real Indian names" but rather names "given [the Indians] by the whites." Unlike mastering Lenape grammar or syntax, the system of metaphorical expression is relatively easy to work out and copy, providing a user-friendly way through which "whites" could adopt certain forms of Indian speech.[82] Lenape metaphors wield compelling possibilities for emulation, not only for the purposes of assuming—perhaps subsuming—cultural identities but also because of their symbolic resonance, the ways in which they constitute a direct connection to American nature and possibilities for integrating a connection between the literal and the metaphorical into English. Literal metaphors translate meaning from symbol to type or prophecy. They can be anticipatory of future events and often bespeak a recasting of the Puritan system of typology, where a historical event adumbrated its fulfillment in a more complex future event, all of which had been set into motion by the Messianic plan. In the case of the Lenape, the landscape, rather than history, predicts the sequence of human events as inevitable and as culminating in a predetermined future. Cooper hoped to capture this ontology of Lenape language and cosmos in his fiction. His novels integrate the Lenape forms of metaphorical expression that he learned from Heckewelder as means of translating indigenous knowledge of American nature into a literary form and then as a mechanism for literalizing the metaphorical. By absorbing the symbolic dimensions of Lenape into American English,

Cooper sought to infuse his fiction with the same kind of prophetic certainty.

A text with which Cooper certainly would have been familiar, from which he derived some of his theories of language, was Adam Smith's *Theory of Moral Sentiments* (1759), first printed in the United States in 1817. It later contained an essay, "Considerations Concerning the First Formation of Languages." Smith explains that "in the beginnings of Language," one "particular word" could describe an entire event, whereas now language gets divided into the metaphysical and compositional elements of a given referent. Consequently, the expression of each event has become "more intricate and complex" while the whole system of language has become "more coherent, more connected, more easily retained and comprehended."[83] Smith's essay encapsulates the trade-off within each eighteenth-century narrative of linguistic decline: the progress of civil society made language more pliable and expressive while relinquishing the primordial connection between nature and the word found in the "savage state." Smith's theories on the metaphoricity of primitive tongues may very well have served as a context for Cooper's reading of Heckewelder.[84] Smith also made the point that modern languages emerged through histories of contact and that this was another contrast to primitive languages, which evolved through a fundamental relationship between place and nature. Cooper shares Smith's perspective on both points of language development. He made the metaphoric language an attribute in his American Indian characters. They speak with a natural ease. Words often blend with body, such as this description of the Mohegan (Chingachgook) in *The Pioneers*:

> Mohegan was uttering dull, monotonous tones, keeping time by a gentle motion of his head and body. He made use of but few words, and such as he did utter were in his native language, and consequently, only understood by himself and Natty.[85]

The Mohegan's language and other instances of Indian speech are represented as continuous with nature but also as irreconcilable with the configuration of a new national language. Cooper understood national language to comprise multiple tongues, thus marking a departure from this primal linguistic scene. In this respect, Cooper rendered in novelistic terms the central premise of language philosophers who saw population migration and histories of conquest as central to a process of linguistic decline. Composite modern languages exposed a further and further decoupling of the word from its relation to the human body, to nature, and to a mythic relation to the natural world. For Cooper, only metaphors could be captured, translated, and salvaged for modern times. Central to his novelistic project was the aim of recapturing what he believed to be an original Delaware mythopoesis as the foundational structure of the nation in the novel form.

SHADOWS BEFORE

Throughout the *Tales*, Natty embodies America in a transitional state. Raised in the wilderness among the Delaware, he is both acutely aware of racial bloodlines yet unable to leave the wilderness behind for the stable confines of civilization. He is a mixture of "the civilized and savage states," or of white and Indian society, inured with restlessness.[86] He reminds us that his bloodlines are pure white and, repeatedly in *The Deerslayer*—chronologically the first novel in the *Tales* but the last published—that "[his] gifts are white."[87] When in *The Prairie*, settler/squatter patriarch Ishmael Bush's challenges him to declare, "to which people do you belong?" Natty replies that while he sees "little difference in Nations," he is a "man, without the cross of Indian blood."[88] Cross is the curse of interbreeding, one as Natty explains, "half-and-halfs" are "altogether more barbarous than the real savage."[89] Natty Bumppo is an echo of Sir Walter Scott's "middle-of-the-road hero."[90] "Without a cross," Natty shuns his baptismal name and is buried under a mere initial. He exhibits some of the Protestant qualities of piety and chastity while his worship partakes of nature and the woods.[91]

In the hero who passes from youth, to maturity in the fullness of his powers, to old age, and finally into death across the novels, *The Leatherstocking Tales* stage the process of America's discovery, settlement, and rise of civilization as a cycle of stadial history. As the narrator frames the action of *The Prairie*, "The march of civilization with us, has a strong analogy to that of all coming events, which are known 'to cast their shadows before.'" The reader has the distinct sense that the ascendance of the "Anglo-American," as we bear witness to the "citizen['s]" advancement along the "endless wastes of the prairie," repeats a script that has come before.[92] It is a biblical cant of human sacrifice, death, generation, and regeneration. Indigenous languages are the sublimated heart of Cooper's epic cycle. *The Prairie* opens with the promise of the Louisiana Purchase of 1803, an event that ensures the "peaceful division of this vast empire" into a sequence of "neighbor[s]" sharing the same "language,... religion, and... institutions."[93] The work of the *Tales* is the undoing of the certainty of this outcome through remembrance of the past, not the past of the nation but rather the past of the land upon which the fledgling nation finds itself uneasily perched. It is, as the sage old Natty tells the bumbling and naive beekeeper in *The Prairie*, important to know the "natur'" and "language" of the "Indian."[94] Yet he is, himself, already an anachronistic artifact. He alone of the new civilization he counsels is fluent in those cultural forms, representing Sioux and Delaware as the dispensable artifacts of past civilizations, repositories that stand in for the lost forms of natural knowledge foretelling things to come.

As all dialogue in Indian is translated for the reader and only one non-Indian speaks indigenous tongues, Indian words are represented as both on the brink of extinction and as wielding the power to forecast, with prophetic certainty, a grand narrative of national rebirth. Yet like Natty Bumppo's sole capacity to speak the languages, the Indian tongues come to stand in for the thing they also exemplify, the impossibility of authentic knowledge transmission between the transitioning civilizations. Ultimately, the knowledge of American nature encoded within the Delaware tongue could not be transferred or absorbed into the fabric of American nationalism. Natty's journey toward the setting sun is a journey whose end is deferred, for its conclusion—like the closure of the *Tales* themselves—must await the judgment of the unrestrained nation.[95]

The civilizing process represented in the *Tales* is postlapsarian as well as post-Babylonian. Ultimately, the knowledge of American nature encoded within the Delaware tongue could not be so easily transferred or absorbed into the fabric of American English. Natty's westward flight from one settlement to the next reveals the fatal flaw of deep-seated contradictions in the civilizing process. Like his protagonist, Cooper is neither able to abandon the legacies of the Delaware nor establish the possibilities for indigenous speech and peoples within his national vision. A powerful counter-voice to antebellum optimism, discontent, restlessness, and dark foreboding pervades the final stages of Natty's life. By the third novel in the series and the final in historical chronology, Natty is "driven... from his beloved forests to seek a refuge, by a species of desperate resignation, on the denuded plains that stretch to the Rocky Mountains."[96] Natty's fate is a mirror for Cooper's own dissatisfaction with the boundaries of the "civilized" young nation, where the inevitability of Indian removal, the forced migration of indigenous populations west, was a tragic inversion of Natty's own restlessness. Ultimately, the language of the Delaware could not be heard above the din of an epic tale of Edenic expulsion.

REMEMBERED FORMS OF A LITERARY NATION

The final chapter of this book explores Cooper's transformations of colonial approaches to indigenous languages as repositories of knowledge into fiction. In his *Leatherstocking Tales*, Lenni Lenape appears as the ancient *ur* language of America, forecasting grand narratives of national rebirth with prophetic certainty. The Lenni Lenape word, unintelligible to characters other than those of Lenape descent and the singular Natty Bumppo, is the sign that makes the world of nature flesh for future generations of Anglo-Americans. Cast at once as prophetic and primitive, the rhetorical rendering of the Indian in Cooper's novels also strives to efface a Native American present. Cooper was not unique in his effort to fictionalize the Anglo-American language encounter, or in his attempt to reconcile the expansionist ethos of the new nation-state with an indelible indigenous past. For other antebellum writers, the American Indian presence haunts or lingers more emphatically, refusing to leave a landscape that is itself infused with Indian words. As Lydia Sigourney asks at the beginning of her poem "Indian Names" (1838), "How can the red men be forgotten, while so many of our states and territories, bays, lakes, and rivers, are indelibly stamped by names of their giving?" The question is, of course, rhetorical. As Sigourney goes on to explain:

> their memory liveth on your hills,
> Their baptism on your shore,
> Your everlasting rivers speak
> Their dialect of yore.[1]

A landscape of the forgotten ghosts of the past also haunts William Cullen Bryant's poem "The Prairies."

> And the mound-builders vanished from the earth.
> The solitude of centuries untold
> Has settled where they dwelt.

The mounds overwhelm this poem. They give form to an eerie empty stillness, a topography that obscures even the prairie's horizon. Listening to his steed's gallop, the speaker notes the "hollow beating of his footstep seems a sacrilegious sound." The mounds recall the "race that long has passed away" and the speaker reflects self-reproachfully, yet nostalgically, on "those upon whose rest he tramples." What once was is now nothing more than "a forgotten language, and old tunes, from instruments of unremembered form." Yet the wind remembers the forgotten language. The "prairie-wolf" hunting in the fields, the gopher mining in the ground, the vultures on top of the uncovered sepulchers, insects, and birds that "scarce have learned the fear of man," all remember the form of the race that long has passed. Amid this remembrance of forms, on a prairie "quick with life," the speaker finds that he is "in the wilderness alone."

In the final line of "The Prairies," the speaker finds himself without a map, without the Indian guide and Abenaki dictionary that led Thoreau in *The Maine Woods*, without the transparent eyeball that would magically descend onto the vacated landscape of Emerson's bare common. The speaker of "The Prairies" finds himself only faintly aware of the forms and ghosts emanating from the palimpsestic layers of civilization to come before. The past is an ambiguous temporal marker in the poem. It is as ancient as "the Greek" but also inexact: a series of unremembered forms. The solitude of centuries untold are cyclical: "thus change the forms of being," the speaker tells us. From the indelible "Indian Names" in Sigourney's poem to the "forgotten language" of Bryant's, indigenous words linked America's present to its indigenous past in the antebellum literary imaginary.

American authors were by no means the first to deploy this construct of the Romantic Indian. Beginning in the 1790s, Romantic Indians proliferated in poems by Robert Southey, François-René Chateaubriand, and Thomas Moore. They appear as primitive, inspired orators, children of nature, and above all, as figures of pathos, a people passed over by the triumphant rise of European civilization in the midst of constructing a new empire.[2]

Central to the strict line of demarcation between primitive and modern tongues in literature was a philosophical supposition that primitive languages conveyed a poetic logic that was then supplanted by a rational logic over time. In North America, seventeenth-century millennial-inspired missionary attempts at discerning an original pre-Babel language in native dialects were gradually supplanted by an enlightened universalism. Narratives of linguistic decline, integral to this enlightened universalism, made the idea that primitive languages were discoverable in their natural and untouched state especially compelling. Yet, this declension theory of linguistic modernity was not simply one of loss. Reason-based civility was believed to have gained a greater degree of discernment in recognizing the representational errors inherent in so-called primitive tongues. Poetic languages of the ancient nations evolved into what Giambattista Vico calls the "vulgar languages" of the present day.[3]

So-called civilized societies purportedly accepted the limitations of language as a medium of human communication and as a means of expressing universal or metaphysical truths. For example, Vico explains that the poetic tropes governing the "first words of nations" are now classified as synecdoche.[4] The term exists to classify a mode of representation, necessitated by the foundational rational logic that signs do not cohere precisely to their referent. Deriving his theory from Lucretius's *De rerum natura*, Vico revived for the eighteenth century the notion that language emerged from the spontaneous expression of feeling. Citing classical sources as well as travel narratives, Vico proposed that in the first age after the Flood, humanity spoke in a tongue that was imaginative, animistic, and therefore more poetic than the reason-infused logic that would come to dominate thought and communication centuries later. Like the eighteenth-century language philosophers to follow him, Vico cited the prevalence of song among American Indians as a still-living remnant of this ancient form of natural and emotive expression.[5]

In the latter half of the eighteenth century, Hugh Blair contrasted the transition from primitive to modern tongues as follows: "Language is become, in modern times, more correct, indeed, and accurate; but however, less striking and animated: In its ancient state, more favorable to poetry and oratory; in its present, to reason and philosophy."[6] One of the main reasons for the loss of this poetic potential over time was that more modern tongues confronted language's partial representational capacity.

Philosophers and missionaries alike believed that metaphor was the most basic and common element of the first languages. Vico explains that metaphor has the power to convey "sense and emotion on insensate objects." Early "pagan" poets used metaphor to animate physical bodies. Vico likewise explains that metaphor and myth were the twinned features of primitive languages. The poetic logic of ancient languages prefigured all human action and therefore functioned as the key to philosophical history. Each metaphor is a "miniature myth," meaning that it wields an imaginative capacity deriving from the human body as well as from "human senses and emotions."[7] Central to Vico's new science, myth prefigured all human action, thus forecasting the historical transition from poetic to rational logic. Metaphor stood at the origin of language as the foundational myth. Vico attributed the proleptic quality of historical forecasting to this foundational myth and therefore to language itself. More rationally based modern tongues presented a greater range of rhetorical possibility while also decoupling metaphor from the literal and thus foreclosing some of the metaphor's mythic or prophetic power.

In his lecture titled "Metaphor," Blair explains that a metaphor is a comparison between the literal and another object. The comparison is made in the mind and expressed without words to denote the comparison. Yet, he is careful to warn that the literal and the metaphorical should not be conflated in good poetry and prose. To do so would be to invite confusion. The fascination with literal metaphors, believed by many eighteenth-century language philosophers to be pervasive in primitive languages, might thus be understood as a form of longing, a desire to recuperate the capacity of metaphors to connote a sense of mystical wholeness. For enlightened language philosophers, metaphor represented the postlapsarian loss of poetic logic and the dawn of an age of reason that made language more straightforward while also accepting the condition of linguistic fragmentation and partial representation.

The propensity for metaphor that many eighteenth-century Euro-Americans found in indigenous tongues reflected a European philosophical value and romanticized commemoration of the noble savage. As Blair writes:

> We find, that this is the character of the American and Indian Languages; bold, picturesque, and metaphorical; full of strong allusions to sensible qualities, and to such objects as struck them most in their wild and solitary life. An Indian chief makes a harangue to his tribe, in a style full of stronger metaphors than a European would use in an epic poem.[8]

Similarly, in his *Defense of Poetry* (1821), Percy Shelley explains that the "savage," meaning in a state of nature, uses "plastic or pictorial imitation" to "express the emotions produced in him by surrounding objects." Romantics located the "conjectured origin" of poetry in the "naturally rhythmical and figurative, outcries of primitive men."⁹ This form of commemoration preserves the linguistic value of indigenous culture in American consciousness while eliding Indian existence.

But because of the liminal political condition of indigenous people in the antebellum United States and the aesthetic need of imperial insitutions to justify this condition by constructing narratives of inevitable cultural death and demise, Romantic Indians sit somewhat uneasily alongside Romantic celebrations of primitive language and poetry. For one, it was neither possible nor desirable to imagine a direct line of descent from primitive Indian tongues to modern English. John Heckewelder's *Account of the History, Manners, and Customs of the Indian Nations* (1819) promises "the true history of those people, who, for centuries, have been in full possession of the country we now inhabit." In so doing, he relied on the oral history of the Lenape, which had been passed down through generations: "we know," he writes, "that all Indians have the custom of transmitting to posterity, by a regular chain of tradition."¹⁰ Staunchly committed to an accurate portrayal of historical truth, on the one hand, yet willing to incorporate indigenous myth, on the other, Heckewelder's *Account* invites a question: what function did the study of Indian words serve antebellum Americans? Moreover, if not an empirical index of population origins, what purpose did Indian words serve? For Heckewelder, Indian words conveyed bold, aesthetic potential. He viewed his goal as one of recuperating the beauty of Indian languages from centuries of writers who mistakenly perceived them as barbarous.¹¹ His aspirations toward truth were twofold. He wished to convey with historical accuracy the recent movements of American Indian tribes, and he hoped to convince his reader of the beauty of the Indian tongue.

Peter Du Ponceau led efforts on the part of the American Philosophical Society to draw from this highly specialized missionary knowledge new insights into the philological riches of North America. As the report from the Historical Literary Committee states, Heckewelder's conveyance of certain knowledge of the Indian nations, "among whom he resided more than forty years...gave us clear insight into that wonderful organization which distinguishes the languages of the aborigines of this country from all the other idioms of the known world."¹² He provided the A.P.S. with an extensive manuscript containing the grammar of the Lenape or Delaware Indians that was published in the *Transactions* in 1819.¹³ Along with

Heckewelder's Lenape Dictionary and Zeisberger's *Grammar*, the Committee used missionary knowledge to establish the uniqueness and familial consistency of indigenous American tongues, "from Greenland to Cape Horn."[14] The goal of the committee was to prove grammatical consistency across all the indigenous languages spoken in North America, to demonstrate the fundamental difference between these language groups and those of the "old hemisphere," both ancient and modern, and to exhibit the richness of the American tongue in terms of "order, method, and regularity."[15] Understanding the Lenni Lenape language, Du Ponceau explained, was key to understanding the foundation of metaphysics as well as some of the more profound human mysteries. He wished to assuage the ongoing trauma of erasure threatened by contemporary removal debates and frontier wars while simultaneously leveraging the value of America's natural resources on an international scale, as the Philosophical Society entered debates with France, Germany, and other European countries.

An accomplished philologist, Du Ponceau was preoccupied with the study of American Indian languages throughout his career. His *Memoire sur le systeme grammatical des langues de quelques nations indiennes de l'Amerique du nord* (1838) won the Comte de Volney language prize, securing a place for American linguistics in the international scene. This publication reveals what Du Ponceau found so compelling in his study of Indian tongues. "L'esprit humain" can be studied through language, he tells us. This sentiment conveys the vestiges of romantic philology that clearly persist in his work. Yet, the inability to pronounce Indian tongues as dead, like the persistent effort to collect, compare, and study their grammatical forms speaks to an ongoing national nostalgia. Du Ponceau expresses his fascination with primitive languages, which, he believes, are more closely aligned with nature and therefore approach a higher degree of semiotic perfection.[16]

Du Ponceau's purpose was to establish the place of American linguistic study on an international scale. Yet he also viewed American Indian languages as more connected to the natural landscape than the tongues of the "old hemisphere" and thus wielding unique aesthetic potential. For philologists such as Du Ponceau and aesthetic theorists such as Samuel L. Knapp, American Indian languages thus constituted a substantial resource for the project of developing a national literary heritage. Lecturing on *The Means of Making Our National Literature Independent of That of Great Britain* in Philadelphia in 1834, Du Ponceau chastises Americans for their "mental depend-ence" on Great Britain due to the "congeniality of manners, habits and literary opinions with the nation whose language we speak." While it is natural for "nations who speak the same language...to imitate the literary productions of each other," Du Ponceau con-cedes, he nonetheless warns that imitation leads to sterility and de-generation. He advocates incorporating other models from other nations into the US literary production in order to "work" the English language "up into delicious honey." Diversifying linguistic origins could counteract the degeneracy that takes place when American authors simply mimic what is taking place on the other side of the Atlantic.

Because they stemmed from a bounded space that nonetheless contained an entire cosmology, indigenous words resisted fictions of effacement in American literary history in a way that also distin-guishes the American literary fascination with native languages from its broader European context. When Henry Schoolcraft arrived at Sault Ste. Marie as a federal Indian agent in 1822, he had been com-missioned by Lewis Cass to disprove the theories percolating in the Philosophical Society's Historical and Literary Committee about the intrinsic beauty of Indian languages. It was in Sault Ste. Marie that Schoolcraft met and married his wife, Jane Johnston, or Bamewa-wagezhikaquay, an Ojibwe woman who grew up in a bilingual house-hold. She received an education from her Scotch-Irish father's English library and she wrote poetry in English and in Ojibwe.

She raised her children, John and Jane, in Ojibwe until her husband mandated that the children be sent to a boarding school in the East. In a particularly poignant poem, "On Leaving My Children John and Jane at School in the Atlantic States, and Preparing to Return to the Interior," she chooses to express the tension between mourning the separation from her children and connection to her ancestral land in Ojibwe:

> She gwau go sha ween
> Ba show waud e we
> Nin zhe ka we yea
> Ishe ez hau jau yaun
> Ain dah nuk ke yaun
> Ain dah nuk ke yaun
> Nin zhe ke we yea
> Ishe ke way aun e

Nyau ne gush kain dum

But soon
It is close however
To my home I shall return
That is the way I am, my being
My land
My land
To my home I shall return
I begin to make my way home
Ahh but I am sad[17]

Jane Schoolcraft protested but ultimately deferred to her husband's wishes. Yet she writes her poem of mourning in her mother tongue, the language that her own mother, Ozhaguscodaywayquay, spoke, the language that bound her to her home in Sault Ste. Marie. The pain expressed is palpable and tangible. It is not at all the romanticized mourning of Bryant's poem, though Henry Wadsworth Longfellow would use Jane Johnston Schoolcraft's story and her literary production as a source for his *Song of Hiawatha* (1855).

Jane's poetry was not published in her lifetime, but Henry circulated manuscript copies among friends. What did he make of this poem in light of the contemporary ideologies of American Indian languages? The expression of the inextricable link between language, land, and cosmos, and the acute feeling of loss accompanying a mother's separation from her children reveals a powerful mode of resistance through language. The poem defies contemporary understandings of indigenous languages as either poetic or savage. The Ojibwe humanizes the conditions of the still-living populations who read, spoke, and wrote in their own mother tongue. Here I mean mother tongue literally, the language passed down by the generations of mothers who, like Jane, transmitted this knowledge to their children as the only way of preserving the traditional native notion of ancestral home. So, the storytelling grandmother in N. Scott Momaday's *House Made of Dawn* (1968) who "could have whole and consummate being" in words and language only. Or, more bluntly, a stanza from the Mojave American poet and language activist, Natalie Diaz's "Cloud Watching":

A tongue will wrestle its mouth to death and lose—
language is a cemetery.

Tribal dentists light lab-coat pyres in memoriam of lost molars—
Our cavities are larger than HUD houses.
Some Indians' wisdom teeth never stop growing back in—
we were made to bite back—
until we learn to bite first.[18]

Diaz's stanza speaks to the value of language stripped of centuries of romantizication, language death, Christianization, and erasure. Resurfacing in American literary history time and again, indigenous words show that myths of Indian origin and extinction were not only ineffective but also flawed from their inception. After all, the complex and multifarious civilizations that preceded the rise of US nationalism continuously reappear as inextricably bound to the land and therefore as integral to the meaning of America.

{ NOTES }

Introduction

1. Louis Nicolas, "Grammaire Algonquine, ou des sauvages de l'Amérique septentrionnale," *Manuscrits Américains 1, Bibliothéque National*, Paris, France. Diane Daviault has edited a modern edition of this manuscript: *L'algonquin au XVIIe siècle: Une édition critique, analysée et commentée de la grammaire algonquine du Père Louis Nicolas* (Quebec: Press of the University of Quebec, 1994), 19.

2. Daviault postulates that the language is most likely Ojibwe based on the geographic information provided in Nicolas's *Histoire Naturelle*, though it is difficult to tell precisely and Nicolas worked with nearly fifteen distinct tribes during his time in New France. Quotes are from ibid., 24.

3. Volney, *View of the Climate and Soil of the United States of America... Translated from the French* (London, 1804), 469–470.

4. William Gilmore Simms, *Views and Reviews in American Literature, History and Fiction* (New York: Wiley and Putnam, 1845), 104–105.

5. Sabine MacCormack, *On the Wings of Time: Rome, the Incas, Spain, and Peru* (Princeton, N.J.: Princeton University Press, 2007), 174–175.

6. Chrestien Le Clercq, *Nouvelle Relation de la Gaspesie* (Paris: Chez Amable Auroy, rue Saint Jacques, 1691) in the John Locke Library Collection, Bodleian Library, Oxford University, United Kingdom. See John Harrison and Peter Laslett, *The Library of John Locke* (Oxford: The Oxford Bibliographical Society by the Oxford University Press, 1965), no. 778. On early modern Protestant efforts to translate the Bible, see Noel Malcolm, "Comenius, Boyle, Oldenburg, and the Translation of the Bible into Turkish," *Church History and Religious Culture* 87, no. 3 (July 2007): 327–362.

7. Henry D. Thoreau, *The Maine Woods*, ed. Jeffrey S. Cramer (New Haven, Conn.: Yale University Press, 2009), 4.

8. My comparative analysis of French and Anglo missionary literature has been influenced by Gordon Sayre's *Les Sauvages Américains: Representations of Native Americans in French and English Colonial Literature* (Chapel Hill: University of North Carolina Press, 1997), 1–49.

9. The implementation of English as a uniform standard among indigenous proselytes was always partial and incomplete. Chapters 3, 4, and 5 explore indigenous resistance to this missionary formula, which came from the SPG (Society for the Propagation of the Gospel) but also from Jonathan Edwards and the advent of Indian Schools at Stockbridge and Dartmouth. See William B. Hart, "Mohawk Schoolmasters and Catechists in Mid-Eighteenth-Century Iroquoia: An Experiment in Fostering Literacy and Religious Change," in *The Language Encounter in the Americas, 1492–1800*, edited by Edward G. Gray and Norman Fiering (New York: Berghahn Books, 2000), 230–257. See also Hilary E. Wyss, *English Letters and Indian Literacies: Reading, Writing, and New England Missionary Schools, 1750–1830* (Philadelphia: University of Pennsylvania Press, 2012).

10. Linguist Edward Vajda is the first to present linguistic proof of a connection between the Yeniseian languages of Siberia and Na-Dene, spoken in North America. "A Siberian Link with the Na-Dene," *Anthropological Papers of the University of Alaska*, New Series, 5 (2010): 31–99.

11. On the relationship between text, oral tradition, memory, and origins stories, see Andrew Newman, *On Records: Delaware Indians, Colonists, and the Media of History and Memory* (Lincoln: University of Nebraska Press, 2012), especially 190–194.

12. James Adair, *The History of the American Indians* (London, 1775), 12, 35.

13. Deloria writes that the Bering Strait serves as an "ecclesiastical" and then a "scientific trail from Jerusalem to North America." *Red Earth, White Lies: Native Americans and the Myth of Scientific Fact* (New York: Scribner, 1995), 18.

14. Euro-Americans consistently believe in their sovereignty over the land of North America from the mid-seventeenth century through the present day. The reason for this belief essentially comes down to feelings of superiority, whether rooted in Christianity or ideas about the proper cultivation of the land. Acquiring knowledge of indigenous populations was a key component of conquest. For British imperial notions of sovereignty over indigenous populations, see Kent McNeil, *Common Law Aboriginal Title* (Oxford: Clarendon, 1989). For notions of sovereignty from the colonial period to the United States present day, see Kevin Bruyneel, *Third Space of Sovereignty: The Postcolonial Politics of U.S.–Indigenous Relations* (Minneapolis: University of Minnesota Press, 2007).

15. Stuart Chase, Foreward to *Language, Thought, and Reality: Selected Writings of Benjamin Lee Whorf* (Cambridge, Mass.: MIT Press, 1956), vi, 78. While I realize that the Sapir-Whorf thesis has been contested by linguists, his insight into linguistic relativity is nonetheless useful in this context for this is what the missionaries confronted in their efforts to translate indigenous concepts into purportedly universal Christian truths.

16. Lawrence Venuti, *The Scandals of Translation: Towards an Ethics of Difference* (New York: Routledge, 1998), 9.

17. Emily Apter has written about untranslatability in relation to world literature. See Apter, *Against World Literature: On the Politics of Untranslatability* (New York: Verso, 2013), 31–44.

18. Jean de Brébeuf, "Relation of What Occurred in the Country of the Hurons in 1636," *The Jesuit Relations and Allied Documents: Travels and Explorations of the Jesuit Missionaries in New France, 1610–1791*, ed. Reuben Gold Thwaites (Cleveland: The Burrows Brothers Company, 1898), 10:119–121.

19. Jonathan Edwards, *Letters and Personal Writings*, The Words of Jonathan Edwards, vol. 16, ed. George S. Claghorn (New Haven, Conn.: Yale University Press, 1998), 413.

20. See chapter 7.

21. Oxford English Dictionary Online, s.v. "scripture, n." and "scripture, v.," accessed December 2015, http://www.oed.com/view/Entry/173593.

22. Vivian Salmon, "Thomas Harriot (1560–1621) and the English Origins of Algonkian Linguistics," *Historiographia Linguistica* 19, no. 1 (1992): 25–56.

23. Interestingly, this commentary comes not from travelers, missionaries, or colonists to the New World, but rather from mathematicians, philosophers, and linguists. In the seventeenth century, linguist and mathematician John Pell reportedly told John Aubrey Hariot that Hariot's alphabet looked like devils. See John Aubrey, *Brief Lives, Chiefly of Contemporaries*, ed. Andrew Clark (Oxford: Clarendon, 1898), 285.

24. Cordova, *How It Is*, 76–79. Cordova's insight here is much like John Locke's "conduit metaphor," or the notion that words are containers for thought. Eighteenth-century language philosophers and twentieth- and twenty-first- century linguistics have used the conduit metaphor as a way of understanding language change. Jean Aitchison, "Metaphors, Models, and Language Change," *Motives for Language Change*, ed. Raymond Hickey, 39–54.

25. Jan Assmann, "Translating Gods: Religion as a Factor of Cultural (Un)Translatability," in *The Translatability of Cultures: Figurations of the Space Between*, ed. Sanford Budick and Wolfgang Iser (Stanford, Calif.: Stanford University Press, 1996), 25–36.

26. Reuben Gold Thwaites, ed., The Jesuit Relations and Allied Documents: Travels and Explorations of the Jesuit Missionaries in New France, 1610–1791 (Cleveland: Burrows Brothers, 1897), 68:271–275.

27. This phrase belongs to Emma Dillon, "Unwriting Medieval Song," *New Literary History* 46, no. 4 (Autumn 2015): 618.

28. "Meet the Masters: Mohawk Choir of the St. Regis," February 28, 2000, North Country Public Radio.

29. Glenda Goodman, "'But they differ from us in sound'": Indian Pslamody and the Soundscape of Colonialism, 1651–75," *William and Mary Quarterly* 69 no. 4 (2012): 793–822.

30. Stephen Greenblatt, *Learning to Curse: Essays in Early Modern Culture* (New York: Routledge, 1990); Walter D. Mignolo, *Darker Side of the Renaissance: Literacy, Territoriality, and Colonization* (Ann Arbor: University of Michigan Press, 1995); and Jill Lepore, *The Name of War: King Philip's War and the Origins of American Identity* (New York: Knopf, 1998).

31. Quoted in Anna Ash, Jessie Little Doe Fermino, Ken Hale, and Leanne Hinton, eds., "Diversity in Local Language Maintenance and Restoration: A Reason for Optimism," in *The Green Book of Language Revitalization in Practice*, ed. Leanne Hinton and Ken Hale (San Diego: Academic Press, 2001), 19–20.

32. Ives Goddard, "The Classification of the Native Languages of North America," in *Languages*, ed. Goddard. Vol. 17 of *Handbook of North American Indians*, ed. William C. Sturtevant (Washington, D.C.: Smithsonian Institute, 1996), 290–323.

33. Bernard C. Perley, "Aboriginality at Large: Varieties of Resistance in Maliseet Language Instruction," *Identities: Global Studies in Culture and Power* 13 (2006): 187–208.

34. Laura J. Murray, "Joining Signs with Words: Missionaries, Metaphors, and the Massachusett Language," *New England Quarterly* 74, no. 1 (2001): 89.

35. Myra Jehlen, "History Before the Fact; Or, Captain John Smith's Unfinished Symphony," *Critical Inquiry* 19, no. 4 (1993): 677–692.

36. Scott Richards Lyons, "There's No Translation for It: The Rhetorical Sovereignty of Indigenous Languages," in *Cross-Language Relations in Composition*, ed. Bruce Horner, Min-Zhan Lu, and Paul Kei Matsuda (Carbondale: Southern Illinois University Press, 2010), 139.

37. David Murray, *Matter, Magic, and Spirit: Representing Indian and African American Belief* (Philadelphia: University of Pennsylvania Press, 2007).

38. See Kenneth M. Morrison, "The Cosmos as Intersubjective: Native American Other-than-human Persons," in *Indigenous Religions: A Companion*, ed. Graham Harvey (New York: Cassell, 2000), 23–36; Mary B. Black, "Ojibwa Power Belief System," in *The Anthropology of Power: Ethnographic Studies from Asia, Oceania, and the New World*, ed. Raymond D. Fogelson and Richard N. Adams (New York: Academic Press, 1977), 141–151; A. Irving Hallowell, "Ojibwa Ontology, Behavior, and World View," in *Culture in History: Essays in Honor of Paul Radin*, ed. Stanley Diamond (New York: Columbia University Press, 1960), 19–52.

39. The letter was printed as an appendix to Edward Winslow, *The Glorious Progress of the Gospel, Amongst the Indians in New England*...(London, 1649), 23. I am indebted to Cristobal Silva for bringing this reference to my attention, also discussed in chapter 2.

40. Thomas Shepard, *The Clear Sun-shine of the Gospel Breaking Forth upon the Indians in New-England* (London, 1648), 33. The Jesuits developed the practice of using the figure 8 to indicate sounds in indigenous languages that could not be represented through the Roman alphabet. Mohawk scholar Scott Stevens suggested to me that this may have been to resemble the sound for "huit" in French.

41. The passage can be translated as "language was always the companion of empire." Antonio de Nebrija, *Gramática castellana: Texto establecido sobre la ed. "princeps" de 1492*, ed. Pascual Galindo Romeo and Luis Ortiz Muñoz, with introduction, notes, and facsimiles. Prologue by D. José Ibáñez Martín (Madrid, 1946). The statement appears at the beginning of the *Prologo*, "siempre la lengua fue companera del imperio" (5). For an analysis of Nebrija's grammar as establishing a key relationship between Renaissance theories of writing and the colonization of Amerindian languages, see Walter D. Mignolo, "Nebrija in the New World: The Question of the Letter, the Colonization of Amerindian Languages, and the Discontinuity of the Classical Tradition," *L'Homme* 32, nos. 122/124 (1992): 185–207.

42. Ian K. Steele, "Exploding Colonial American History: Amerindian, Atlantic, and Global Perspectives," *Reviews in American History* 26, no. 1 (1998): 70–95. For a retrospective account on the success of this idea a decade later, see Paul Cohen, "Was There an Amerindian Atlantic? Reflections on the Limits of a Historiographical Concept," *History of European Ideas* 34, no. 4 (2008): 388–410.

43. Matt Cohen, *The Networked Wilderness: Communicating in Early New England* (Minneapolis: University of Minnesota Press, 2010); Kristina Bross and Hilary E. Wyss, *Early Native Literacies in New England: A Documentary and Critical Anthology* (Amherst: University of Massachusetts Press, 2008); Brett Rushforth, *Bonds of Alliance: Indigenous and Atlantic Slaveries in New France* (Chapel Hill: University of North Carolina Press, 2012), 15–71, 383–391; Germaine Warkentin, "Dead Metaphor or Working Model? The 'Book' in Native America," in *Colonial Mediascapes: Sensory Worlds of Early America*, ed. Matt Cohen and Jeffrey Glover (Lincoln: University of Nebraska Press, 2014), 47–75; Drew Lopenzina, *Red Ink: Native Americans Picking up the Pen in the Colonial Period* (Albany: SUNY Press, 2012); Birgit Brander Rasmussen, *Queequeg's Coffin: Indigenous Literacies and Early American Literature* (Durham, N.C.: Duke University Press, 2012).

44. David J. Silverman, "Indians, Missionaries, and Religious Translation: Creating Wampanoag Christianity on Seventeenth-Century Martha's Vineyard," *William and Mary Quarterly* 52, no. 2 (April 2005): 141–174; Tracy Neale Leavelle, "'Bad Things' and 'Good Hearts': Mediation, Meaning, and the Language of Illinois Christianity," *Church History* 76, no. 2 (2007): 363–394; Linford D. Fisher, *The Indian Great Awakening: Religion and the Shaping of Native Cultures in Early America* (New York: Oxford University Press, 2012); Glenda Goodman, "'But They Differ from Us in Sound': Indian Psalmody and the Soundscape of Colonialism, 1651–75," *William and Mary Quarterly* 69, no. 4 (2012): 793–822; Margaret J. Leahy, "'*Comment peut un muet prescher l'évangile?*': Jesuit Missionaries and the Native Languages of New France," *French Historical Studies* 19, no. 1 (Spring 1995): 105–131; Philip H. Round, *Removable Type: Histories of the Book in Indian Country, 1663–1880* (Chapel Hill: University of North Carolina Press, 2010); Patrick M. Erben, *A Harmony of the Spirits: Translation and the Language of Community in Early Pennsylvania* (Chapel Hill: University of North Carolina Press, 2012).

45. Anthony F. C. Wallace, *Jefferson and the Indians: The Tragic Fate of the First Americans* (Cambridge, Mass.: The Belknap Press of Harvard University Press, 1999); Bernard W. Sheehan, *Seeds of Extinction: Jeffersonian Philanthropy and the American Indian* (Chapel Hill: University of North Carolina Press, 1973); Edward C. Gray, *New World Babel: Languages and Nations in Early America* (Princeton, N.J.: Princeton University Press, 1999); Sean P. Harvey, *Native Tongues: Colonialism and Race from Encounter to the Reservation* (Cambridge, Mass.: Harvard University Press, 2015).

46. For recent discussions of the state of the field along these lines, see Sandra M. Gustafson and Gordon Hutner's special issue of *American Literary History*, "Projecting Early American Literary Studies" 22, no. 2 (2010). See also the forum on the 2012 reissue of Sacvan Bercovitch's *Puritan Origins of the American Self* in *Early American Literature* 47, no. 2 (2012): 377–442.

Chapter 1

1. Reuben Gold Thwaites, ed., *The Jesuit Relations and Allied Documents: Travels and Explorations of the Jesuit Missionaries in New France, 1610–1791* (Cleveland: Burrows Brothers, 1897), 5:27.

2. Bruce G. Trigger, *The Children of Aataentsic: A History of the Huron People to 1660* (Montreal: McGill-Queen's University Press, 1976), 2:665–724.

3. For an account of Brébeuf's life among the Huron-Wendat, see Erik R. Seeman, *The Huron-Wendat Feast of the Dead: Indian-European Encounters in Early North America* (Baltimore, Md.: Johns Hopkins University Press, 2011).

4. Edwin S. Gaustad, *Liberty of Conscience: Roger Williams in America* (Grand Rapids, Mich.: W. B. Eerdmans, 1991), 25.

5. Martha Nussbaum, *Liberty of Conscience: In Defense of America's Tradition of Religious Equality* (New York: Basic Books, 2008); James Calvin Davis, *The Moral Theology of Roger Williams: Christian Conviction and Public Ethics* (Louisville, Ky.: Westminster John Knox Press, 2004); and Teresa M. Bejan, "'The Bond of Civility': Roger Williams on Toleration and Its Limits," *History of European Ideas* 37, no. 4 (2011): 409–420.

6. This perspective began with Perry Miller who claimed that *The Key* was the nearest approach to objective anthropology that "anyone" [meaning any Anglo-American author] would achieve in a century. *Roger Williams: His Contribution to the American Tradition* (1953; repr., New York: Atheneum, 1962), 53. Since Miller's book, a strand of Williams criticism has persistently commented on his ethnographical perspective, weighing it, variably, against his religious commitments, criticism of his English reading audience, and in relation to John Eliot, who is often seen as a less skilled ethnographer. See John J. Teunissen and Evelyn J. Hinz, "Roger Williams, Thomas More, and the Narragansett Utopia," *Early American Literature* 11, no. 3 (1976/1977): 281–295; Anne G. Myles, "Dissent and the Frontier of Translation: Roger Williams's *A Key into the Language of America*," in *Possible Pasts: Becoming Colonial in Early America*, ed. Robert Blair St. George (Ithaca, N.Y.: Cornell University Press, 2000), 88–108.

7. Much of the scholarship on Williams's millennialism focuses on the warring theological tracts penned in dialogue with John Cotton and thus misses a full consideration of how this biblical and historical perspective relates to the *Key*. See Hans R. Guggisberg, "Religious Freedom and the History of the Christian World in Roger Williams' Thought," *Early American Literature* 12, no. 1 (1977): 36–48; and, especially, Jesper Rosenmeier, "The

Teacher and the Witness: John Cotton and Roger Williams," *William and Mary Quarterly* 25, no. 3 (1968): 408–431.

8. For a useful discussion of alien texts in comparative philology, particularly from a religious and postcolonial perspective, see Sharada Sugirtharajah, "Max Muller and Textual Management: A Postcolonial Perspective," in *Hermeneutics and Hindu Thought: Toward a Fusion of Horizons*, ed. Rita Sherma and Arvind Sharma (New York: Springer, 2008), 33–45.

9. James F. Keenan, SJ, makes this claim in "Jesuit Casuistry or Jesuit Spirituality? The Roots of Seventeenth-Century British Puritan Practical Divinity," in *The Jesuits: Cultures, Sciences, and the Arts, 1540-1773*, ed. John W. O'Malley, SJ, Gauvin Alexander Bailey, Steven J. Harris, and T. Frank Kennedy, SJ (Toronto: University of Toronto Press, 1999), 627–640. That Jesuitical practice was about inward striving rather than institutional critique is also the central argument of O' Malley's *The First Jesuits* (Cambridge, Mass.: Harvard University Press, 1993), esp. 243–284.

10. Martin Luther, *Lectures on Romans*, ed. and trans. Wilhelm Pauck (Philadelphia: Westminster Press, 1961), 3–37.

11. John Cotton, *Christ the Fountaine of Life* (London, 1651), 98–99.

12. On Cotton's and Williams's different perspectives on language and theology, see Rosenmeier, "The Teacher and the Witness," 408–431.

13. Roger Williams, *Christenings Make Not Christians: Or A Briefe Discourse Concerning That Name Heathen, Commonly Given to the Indians*. Vol. 7 of *The Complete Writings of Roger Williams*, ed. Perry Miller (New York: Russell and Russell, 1963), 31–33.

14. Ibid., 40.

15. Ibid.

16. Ibid., 36–37.

17. Ibid., 35–37.

18. Ibid., 33, 39.

19. Ibid., 40.

20. Roger Williams, *A Key into the Language of America*. Vol. 1 of *The Complete Writings of Roger Williams*, ed. J. Hammond Trumball (New York: Russell and Russell, 1963), 79.

21. Williams, *A Key*, 79.

22. This idea is much older than Christianity. The ancient Greeks thought that alien—that is, non-Greek speaking—peoples' languages sounded like "barbarbar," and so called them (onomatopoeically) *barbaros*. Williams thus intentionally places the Narragansett subjects of his memoir, history, and language key within a classical frame, observing both their linguistic "*Affinity*" with the "*Greek* Tongue" and their status as New World barbarian. As such, *The Key* partakes in a long tradition in Western history and ethnographic writing where the encounter with the non-English other is a mirror through which Williams sees himself and his "*Country-men*" (ibid., 84–86). For an account of this dynamic in the writing of Herodotus, see François Hartog, *The Mirror of Herodotus: The Representation of the Other in the Writing of History*, trans. Janet Lloyd (Berkeley: University of California Press, 1988), 3–11. In *Linguistics in a Colonial World: A Story of Language, Meaning, and Power*, Joseph Errington explains the colonial use of the word *barbarian* in New Spain, especially, as connoting sounds that "fall beyond the pale of language" (Malden, Mass.: Blackwell, 2008), 24–29.

23. Williams, *A Key*, 137.

24. Ibid., 98–99.

25. Ibid., 222.

26. Ibid., 142.

27. Ibid., 216, 143, 144.

28. Ibid., 230.

29. Saint Augustine, *Earlier Writings*, ed. and trans. John H. S. Burleigh (Philadelphia: Westminster, 1953), 62–101.

30. Williams, *A Key*, 230–231.

31. Ibid., 232.

32. Ibid., 276.

33. Ibid., 278–279.

34. Ibid., 216–217.

35. Ibid., 219–220.

36. Ibid., 222.

37. On the value of linguistic expertise in the early Jesuit missions, see O'Malley, *The First Jesuits*, 257; and Peter Burke, "The Jesuits and the Art of Translation in Early Modern Europe," in *The Jesuits II: Cultures, Sciences, and the Arts*, ed. John W. O'Malley, SJ, Gauvin Alexander Bailey, Steven J. Harris, and Frank T. Kennedy, SJ (Toronto: University of Toronto Press, 2006), 24–32.

38. Micah True argues that the Jesuits advertised their linguistic expertise as a way of positioning themselves politically. See *Masters and Students: Jesuit Mission Ethnography in Seventeenth-Century New France* (Montreal: McGill-Queens University Press, 2015), 27–54.

39. Thwaites, *Jesuit Relations*, 5:189.

40. Laurent DuBois, "The Jesuit Relations," in *A New Literary History of America*, ed. Greil Marcus and Werner Sollors (Cambridge, Mass.: The Belknap Press of Harvard University Press, 2009), 50–54.

41. Thwaites, *Jesuits Relations*, 5:35.

42. Micah True makes this claim about Amerindian linguistic expertise as a strategy to legitimize the Jesuit mission in *Masters and Students*, 42, 55–82.

43. On the function of the *Jesuit Relations* as an extension of the French Atlantic empire, see Bronwen Catherine McShea, "Cultivating Empire through Print: The Jesuit Strategy for New France and the Parisian *Relations* of 1632–1673" (PhD diss., Yale University, 2011). McShea's dissertation is part of a scholarly understanding of the Jesuits as part of a broader Atlantic network of cultural, scientific, and political interrelationships. See O'Malley, Bailey, Harris, and Kennedy, eds., *The Jesuits: Cultures, Sciences, and the Arts, 1540–1773*; Thomas Worcester, ed., *The Cambridge Companion to the Jesuits* (New York: Cambridge University Press, 2008); and Joseph A. Gagliano and Charles E. Ronan, eds., *Jesuit Encounters in the New World: Jesuit Chroniclers, Geographers, Educators and Missionaries in the Americas, 1549–1767* (Rome: Institutum Historicum Societatis Jesu, 1997).

44. See Paul Cohen, "L'Imaginaire d'une langue nationale: L'État, les langues et l'invention du mythe de l'ordonnance de Villers-Cotterêts à l'époque moderne en France," *Histoire Épistémologie Langage* 25, no. 1 (2003): 19–69. See also Donald R. Kelley, *Foundations of Modern Historical Scholarship: Language, Law, and History in the French Renaissance* (New York: Columbia University Press, 1970).

45. Frederick J. McGinness, "Preaching Ideals and Practice in Counter-Reformation Rome," *The Sixteenth Century Journal* 11, no. 2 (1980): 109–127.

46. Williams, *Christenings Make Not Christians*, 37.

47. O'Malley, *First Jesuits*, 264–272.

48. Williams, *Christenings Make Not Christians*, 36.

49. Thwaites, *Jesuits Relations*, 5:187.

50. Serge Gruzinski explains that the European use of imagery increased as a result of the "shock of conquest" as an attempt to compensate for the fragmentation of meaning that occurred as a result of the collision of disparate world views and representational systems, such as the replacement of ancient codices by alphabetic writing or the Spanish invention of Nahuatl words. *The Mestizo Mind: The Intellectual Dynamics of Colonization and Globalization*, trans. Deke Dusinberre (New York: Routledge, 2002), 33–51, 58.

51. Fernando Bouza, *Communication, Knowledge, and Memory in Early Modern Spain*, trans. Sonia López and Michael Agnew (Philadelphia: University of Pennsylvania Press, 2004), 2–29.

52. Thwaites, *Jesuit Relations*, 10:117–121.

53. John Steckley, *A Huron-English/English-Huron Dictionary (Listing both Words and Noun and Verb Roots)* (Lewiston, N.Y.: Edwin Mellen, 2007), 4.

54. Thwaites, *Jesuit Relations*, 10:119.

55. Ibid., 121.

56. Ibid., 125.

57. Ibid., 127.

58. Trigger, *Children of Aataentsic*, 1:77–78.

59. Steckley, *A Huron-English/English-Huron Dictionary*, 23.

60. Trigger, *Children of Aataentsic*, 1:75–76.

61. This was the translation of Father Diego Ledesma's *Doctrina Christiana*, which by the end of the sixteenth century had been translated from Latin into Spanish, Polish, and Lithuanian. John L. Steckley, "Brébeuf's Presentation of Catholicism in the Huron Language: A Descriptive Overview," *Revue de l'Universite d'Ottawa/University of Ottawa Quarterly* 48, nos. 1/2 (1978): 93–115.

62. Thwaites, *Jesuits Relations*, 10:125.

63. In Brébeuf's account, there is no clear explanation of why Aataentsic fell from the sky, but one account says that when her husband was very sick, he dreamed that he might be cured by eating a piece of fruit from a tree and that Aataentsic slipped while attempting to cut the fruit tree with an ax. Ibid., 127–129.

64. Ibid., 129.

65. David Tracy, *The Analogical Imagination: Christian Theology and the Culture of Pluralism* (New York: Crossroad, 1981).

66. Thwaites, *Jesuit Relations*, 10:127.

67. Ibid., 137.

68. Ibid., 139.

69. Ibid., 127.

70. The *Dictionnaire de la langue huronne*, collected and recorded by Recollect missionary Gabriel Sagard, may have preceded Brébeuf's slightly. Brébeuf penned his manuscript dictionary between the years 1625 and 1629. Jesuit priests were aided by preexisting work of the Recollect. Brébeuf's dictionary did not make it into print and has been lost. Sagard's *Dictionnaire* was printed as part of an effort to establish that the Recollect mission had not been a failure. See Gabriel Sagard, *Le Grand Voyage du Pays des Hurons* (Paris, 1632); Christian Le Clercq, *First Establishment of the Faith in New France*, ed. John G. Shea (New York, 1881), 1:248–249; and Thwaites, *Jesuit Relations*, 5:280–281n24.

71. Thwaites, *Jesuit Relations*, 5:87.

72. Ibid., 5:97.

73. Ibid., 10:91.

74. Ibid., 5:35.

75. John Steckley, "Huron Carol: A Canadian Cultural Chameleon," *British Journal of Canadian Studies* 27, no. 1 (2014): 55–74.

76. Edward Peters, *Heresy and Authority in Medieval Europe* (Philadelphia: University of Pennsylvania Press, 1980), 194–195.

77. Quoted in Seeman, *The Huron-Wendat Feast of the Dead*, 118.

78. For an analysis of Jesuit and indigenous perspectives on Brébeuf's martyrdom, see Emma Anderson, "Blood, Fire, and 'Baptism': Three Perspectives on the Death of Jean de Brébeuf, Seventeenth-Century Jesuit 'Martyr,'" in *Native Americans, Christianity, and the Reshaping of the American Religious Landscape*, ed. Joel W. Martin and Mark A. Nicholas (Chapel Hill: University of North Carolina Press, 2010), 125–158.

Chapter 2

1. Chrestien Le Clercq, *Nouvelle Relation de la Gaspesie, qui contient Les Mœurs & la Religion des Sauvages Gaspesiens Porte-Croix, adorateurs du Soleil, & d'autres Peuples de l'Amerique Septentrionale, dite le Canada* (Paris, 1691), Bodleian Library Locke 7.80c. John Harrison and Peter Laslett remark that Locke quoted from sixteen travel narratives in book 1 of the *Essay Concerning Human Understanding*. See Harrison and Laslett, *The Library of John Locke* (Oxford: Clarendon, 1965), 27–28. On Locke and travel narratives, see Daniel Carey, *Locke, Shaftesbury, and Hutcheson: Contesting Diversity in the Enlightenment and Beyond* (Cambridge: Cambridge University Press, 2006), chap. 3; Daniel Carey, "Travel, Geography, and the Problem of Belief: Locke as a Reader of Travel Literature," in *History and Nation*, ed. Julia Rudolph (Lewisburg, Pa.: Bucknell University Press, 2006), 97–136. Throughout this chapter, I will use the spelling "Mi'kmaq," as preferred by today's tribal members.

2. Chrestien Le Clercq, *New Relation of Gaspesia with the Customs and Religion of the Gaspesian Indians*, ed. William F. Ganong (Toronto: Champlain Society, 1910), 82.

3. The page list on the inside back cover is in Locke's hand; see "Appendix II C: Books with Notes and/or Page Lists by Locke," in Harrison and Laslett, *Library of John Locke*, 280–284. A substantial number of books with Locke's page lists are travel narratives. Based on a book list sent to him from J.-B. Du Bos, Locke acquired Le Clercq's *Nouvelle Relation* in 1698. Du Bos to Locke, Dec. 31, [1698]/Jan. 10, [1699], in *The Correspondence of John Locke*, ed. E. S. De Beer (Oxford: Clarendon, 1981), 6:534 (letter 2527).

4. Le Clercq, *New Relation of Gaspesia*, 80–81 ("Gaspesian," "trouble and labor," 81), 140 ("nothing").

5. In the mid-1640s John Eliot spent two winters in the wigwams of Natick Indians in an attempt to learn Massachusett. By 1646 he claimed to have begun preaching to the Wampanoag in their own language with the aid of his native interpreter, Cockenoe, to facilitate the question-and-answer period following the sermon. William Wallace Tooker, "John Eliot's First Indian Teacher and Interpreter Cockenoe-De-Long Island and the Story of His Career from the Early Records," in *Languages and Lore of the Long Island Indians*, ed. Gaynell Stone Levine and Nancy Bonvillain (Lexington, Mass.: Ginn, 1980), 176–189; Cotton Mather, "The Triumphs of the Reformed Religion in America; or, The Life of the

Renowned John Eliot," in *Magnalia Christi Americana; or, The Ecclesiastical History of New-England...*, [ed.] Thomas Robbins (Hartford, 1853), 1:526–583. Eliot's correspondence with Robert Boyle and Richard Baxter, as well as the publication dates of the texts in his Indian library, reveals that he continued with his translation project at least until 1688, only two years before his death. See F. J. Powicke, ed., "Some Unpublished Correspondence of the Rev. Richard Baxter and the Rev. John Eliot, 'The Apostle to the American Indians,' 1656–1682," *Bulletin of the John Rylands Library* 15, no. 1 (January 1931): 138–176; Michael Hunter, Antonio Clericuzio, and Lawrence M. Principe, eds., *The Correspondence of Robert Boyle*, 6 vols. (London: Pickering and Chatto, 2001).

6. The language of the southeastern Algonquians that Eliot worked with is "properly termed" Wampanoag, according to Jessie Little Doe Fermino, though it has also been called Natick and Massachusett. The "geographic provenance of the majority of the native written source material," Fermino writes, is in the present-day Mashpee, Aquinnah, Assonet, and Herring Pond Wampanoag communities. Anna Ash, Fermino, and Ken Hale, "Diversity in Local Language Maintenance and Restoration: A Reason for Optimism," in *The Green Book of Language Revitalization in Practice*, ed. Leanne Hinton and Ken Hale (San Diego: Academic Press, 2001), 19–35 (quotations, 28). Throughout this chapter I primarily use Wampanoag to refer to the language and people that Eliot worked with, though I maintain Massachusett in explicit historical contexts, such as my discussion on the texts in Eliot's Indian library since this is the term that he used to describe the language.

7. Initially, Eliot shared Cotton Mather's perspective that the length of the Indian words was a good indication that "they had been growing ever since Babel." Mather, "Triumphs of the Reformed Religion," 561. Eliot set himself the life task of ameliorating this fallen linguistic condition. He printed his *Indian Grammar Begun* in 1666, a text that specifies on the first page: "There be two parts of *Grammar*: 1. The *Art of making words*. 2. The *Art* of *ordering words* for speech." John Eliot, *The Indian Grammar Begun; or, An Essay to Bring the Indian Language into Rules, for the Help of Such as Desire to Learn the Same, for the Furtherance of the Gospel Among Them* (Cambridge, Mass., 1666), 1. Once he reduced Massachusett to order and rule, his aim was to enfold the language into "the universal language," which, according to Mather, was the same one that Jesus used to speak to Paul from heaven (Mather, "Triumphs of the Reformed Religion," **546**). *The Indian Dialogues* of 1671, a late Eliot tract, reflects discrepancies between English and Wampanoag understanding of doctrine and faith. Eliot's later letters to both Richard Baxter and Robert Boyle try to present the mission in a positive light, but they are peppered with disappointment in the depleted state of the mission, which contracted greatly following King Philip's War. In the decades following Eliot's death, Mather refused to print the Indian Bible on the grounds that it was too costly and that he wanted to teach the Indians English. See Mather, "probably to William Ashurst," Dec. 10, 1712, in *Selected Letters of Cotton Mather*, ed. Kenneth Silverman (Baton Rouge: Louisiana State University Press, 1971), 126–128. Natick is also described here as "one of our most languishing and withered Indian villages." Ibid., 126.

8. Harrison and Laslett identify 195 titles in the "Voyages and Travels" section of Locke's library. Harrison and Laslett, *Library of John Locke*. In addition to the Boyle correspondence and the Eliot and Baxter correspondence, see M. Greengrass, M. Leslie, and M. Hannon, eds., *The Hartlib Papers*, electronic edition. (Sheffield, UK, 2013), http://www.hrionline.ac.uk/hartlib/context. On mystical and Adamic theories of language, see Hans Aarsleff, "Language, Man, and Knowledge in the Sixteenth and Seventeenth Centuries"

(unpublished manuscript, 1971); James J. Bono, *Ficino to Descartes*. Vol. 1 of *The Word of God and the Languages of Man: Interpreting Nature in Early Modern Science and Medicine* (Madison: University of Wisconsin Press, 1995); Alison Coudert, "Some Theories of a Natural Language from the Renaissance to the Seventeenth Century," in *Magia Naturalis und die Entstehung der modernen Naturwissenschaften: Symposion der Leibniz-Gesellschaft Hannover, 14. Und 15. November 1975*, ed. Kurt Müller, Heinrich Schepers, and Wilhelm Totok (Wiesbaden: Steiner, 1978), 56–114. Eliot had biographical connections to this culture of linguistic millennialism. He was educated at Jesus College of the University of Cambridge, which had one of the premier language programs of the time. He overlapped at Cambridge with John Worthington, who later became master of Jesus College and served as a close correspondent of Samuel Hartlib as well as cataloger of Hartlib's papers. Henry More, Joseph Mede, and others with linguistic-millennial commitments were also in this circle of correspondents. Arthur Gray, Jesus College (London: F. E. Robinson, 1902). Finally, Eliot's connection to Boyle linked him to the early Royal Society; see Sarah Rivett, "Empirical Desire: Conversion, Ethnography, and the New Science of the Praying Indian," *Early American Studies* 4, no. 1 (Spring 2006): 16–45.

9. Several scholars have moved away from the previously accepted account that the seventeenth century was a period when philosophers universally believed in language's scriptural origins. See William Poole, "The Divine and the Grammarian: Theological Disputes in the Seventeenth-Century Universal Language Movement," *Historiographia Linguistica* 30, no. 3 (2003): 273–300; Rhodri Lewis, *Language, Mind and Nature: Artificial Languages in England from Bacon to Locke* (Cambridge: Cambridge University Press, 2007), 110–145; David Cram, "Linguistic Eschatology: Babel and Pentecost in Seventeenth-Century Linguistic Thought," *Language and History* 56, no. 1 (May 2013): 44–56.

10. On the significance and impact of the *Essay Concerning Human Understanding*, see Maurice Cranston, *John Locke: A Biography* (London: Longmans, 1957); Robert L. Armstrong, *Metaphysics and British Empiricism* (Lincoln: University of Nebraska Press, 1970), 80–90; Hans Aarsleff, *From Locke to Saussure: Essays on the Study of Language and Intellectual History* (Minneapolis: University of Minnesota Press, 1982); Jules David Law, *The Rhetoric of Empiricism: Language and Perception from Locke to I. A. Richards* (Ithaca, N.Y.: Cornell University Press, 1993); Michael Losonsky, *Linguistic Turns in Modern Philosophy* (Cambridge: Cambridge University Press, 2006), 1–52; Hannah Dawson, *Locke, Language and Early-Modern Philosophy* (Cambridge: Cambridge University Press, 2007); Matthew Lauzon, *Signs of Light: French and British Theories of Linguistic Communication, 1648–1789* (Ithaca, N.Y.: Cornell University Press, 2010).

11. For a 1999 study of the use of Mi'kmaq from the Nova Scotia Mi'kmaw Language Center, see Stephanie Inglis, "400 Years of Linguistic Contact between the Mi'kmaq and the English and the Interchange of Two World Views," *Canadian Journal of Native Studies* 24, no. 2 (2004): 389–402. For the rates of depletion among northeastern American languages, see Ives Goddard, "Eastern Algonquian Languages," in *Northeast*, ed. Bruce G. Trigger. Vol. 15 of *Handbook of North American Indians*, ed. William C. Sturtevant (Washington, D.C.: Smithsonian Institution, 1978), 70–77. Of particular note is the Wôpanâak Language Reclamation Project, founded and directed by Jessie Little Doe Fermino in collaboration with the Mashpee, Aquinnah, Assonet, and Herring Pond communities ("Wôpanâak Language Reclamation Project," Mashpee, Mass., 2013, http://www.wlrp.org). See also Sam Libby, "Tribes to Revive Language," *New York Times*, October 18, 1998 (for information on the Mashantucket Pequot Museum and Research Center); John L. Steckley, *Words of the*

Huron (Waterloo, Ont.: Wilfrid Laurier University Press, 2007); Patricia Cohen, "Indian Tribes Go in Search of Their Lost Languages," *New York Times*, April 5, 2010 (for a discussion of the Shinnecock and Unkechaug tribes' use of Thomas Jefferson's Indian Vocabularies). Though David L. Schmidt and Murdena Marshall are not directly using the Mi'kmaq hieroglyphs for purposes of language revival, they do see the textual history of the documents operating as an agent of cultural preservation in much the same way. See Schmidt and Marshall, ed. and trans., *Mi'kmaq Hieroglyphic Prayers: Readings in North America's First Indigenous Script* (Halifax: Nimbus, 1995).

12. On language death, see Goddard, "Eastern Algonquian Languages," 70–77. There were originally eighteen eastern Algonquian languages. At the time that Goddard conducted this study, only four of these languages were shown to have survived, with Mi'kmaq having the largest number of speakers by far. The study found a few hundred Maliseet and Passamaquoddy speakers and only a handful of Delaware speakers. For studies of the destructive impact of colonialism on the languages of the Americas, see David Murray, *Forked Tongues: Speech, Writing, and Representation in North American Indian Texts* (Bloomington: Indiana University Press, 1991); Stephen J. Greenblatt, "Learning to Curse: Aspects of Linguistic Colonialism in the Sixteenth Century," in *Learning to Curse: Essays in Early Modern Culture* (New York: Routledge, 1992), 16–39; Jill Lepore, *The Name of War: King Philip's War and the Origins of American Identity* (New York: Knopf, 1998); Walter D. Mignolo, *The Darker Side of the Renaissance: Literacy, Territoriality, and Colonization* (Ann Arbor: University of Michigan Press, 2003); Joseph Errington, *Linguistics in a Colonial World: A Story of Language, Meaning, and Power* (Malden, Mass.: Blackwell, 2008).

13. Genesis 2:19–20. For an account of seventeenth- and eighteenth-century philosophical and literary attempts to grapple with the "corruptions of speech" that ensued from the dissolution of Adam's power to name, see Tho[mas] Sprat, *The History of the Royal-Society...*(London, 1667), 39, quoted in Robert N. Essick, *William Blake and the Language of Adam* (Oxford: Clarendon, 1989), 1–45 (quotation, 42). Also see Robert Markley, *Fallen Languages: Crises of Representation in Newtonian England, 1660–1740* (Ithaca, N.Y.: Cornell University Press, 1993), esp. 63–95.

14. 1 Corinthians 14:11.

15. According to Böhme, "The Signature or Form Is not Spirit, but the Receptacle, Container, or Cabinet of the Spirit." When the spirit animates the form, the connection between form and spirit becomes comprehensible. Jacob Behmen [Böhme], *Signatura Rerum; or, The Signature of All Things...*(London, 1651), 2. As G. Lloyd Jones explains, knowledge of Hebrew became highly important to the Reformed biblical exegete because the translation of Scripture into the vernacular depended on knowledge of the original text. Aarsleff, "Language, Man and Knowledge"; G. Lloyd Jones, *The Discovery of Hebrew in Tudor England: A Third Language* (Manchester: Manchester University Press, 1983), 56–66; Frank E. Manuel, *The Broken Staff: Judaism through Christian Eyes* (Cambridge, Mass.: Harvard University Press, 1992), 8–39; Shalom Goldman, *Hebrew and the Bible in America: The First Two Centuries* (Hanover, N.H.: University Press of New England, 1993). On the Hartlib circle and mystical language theories in the 1640s, see C. A. Patrides, ed., *The Cambridge Platonists* (Cambridge, Mass.: Harvard University Press, 1970); Jim Bennett and Scott Mandelbrote, *The Garden, the Ark, the Tower, the Temple: Biblical Metaphors of Knowledge in Early Modern Europe* (Oxford: Museum of the History of Science, 1998); Lewis, *Language, Mind and Nature*.

16. Laura J. Murray, "Joining Signs with Words: Missionaries, Metaphors, and the Massachusett Language," *New England Quarterly* 74, no. 1 (March 2001): 62–93 (quotation, 74). Eliot made this observation when he first preached in Nonantum in 1646.

17. Thomas Hobbes, *Leviathan*, ed. Noel Malcolm (Oxford: Clarendon, 2012), 2:48 ("Names or Appellations," "mutuall utility"), 50 ("transferre," "Adam"), 62 ("When we conceive").

18. Henry More developed his philosophy of the Platonic potential of words in "A Platonick Song of the Soul," in *Philosophicall Poems* (Cambridge, 1647), where he describes a collection of his poetry as the representation of the inward sense of the soul's immortality. On the universal character, see More, *An Antidote Against Atheisme* (London, 1653); More, *The Immortality of the Soul* (London, 1659); John Wilkins, "To the Right Honourable William Lord Viscount Brouncker...," in *An Essay Towards a Real Character and a Philosophical Language* (London, 1668).

19. John Dury to Samuel Hartlib, May 30, 1645, in Greengrass, Leslie, and Hannon, Hartlib Papers, 3/2/127A–128A ("motion," 127A, "Law," 127B, "America," 128A).

20. Wilkins, *Essay Towards a Real Character*, 5. An entertaining anecdote suggests that Wilkins had been aware of missionary work in the Americas for some time. While Warden of Wadham College in the 1650s, he created a formal garden, the center of which featured a statue of Atlas containing a concealed pipe through which it was possible to project one's voice from a distance. Seeing one of his radical Puritan critics walking past the statue, Wilkins whispered instructions that he should "goe preach the Gospel in Virginia." See Barbara J. Shapiro, *John Wilkins, 1614–1672: An Intellectual Biography* (Berkeley: University of California Press, 1969), 120.

21. Eliot to Baxter, July 6, 1663, in Matthew Sylvester, [ed.,] *Reliquiæ Baxterianæ; or, Mr. Richard Baxters Narrative of the Most Memorable Passages of His Life and Times* (London, 1696), 293–295 (quotations, 294). See also Lewis, *Language, Mind and Nature*, 84.

22. Michael A. Mullet explains that the 1562 Council of Trent sought uniformity in the question of the Missal. Prayers and liturgies were to be performed according to Latin Rite, believed to be the ritual language of the one true church. Michael A. Mullet, *The Catholic Reformation* (New York: Routledge, 1999), 114. For a thorough analysis of confessional theologies, see Jean-Louis Quantin, *The Church of England and Christian Antiquity: The Construction of a Confessional Identity in the 17th Century* (Oxford: Oxford University Press, 2009).

23. Pierre Maillard, "Lettre de M. l'abbé Maillard, sur les Missions de l'Acadie et particulièrement sur les missions micmaques," *Les soirées canadiennes; recueil de littérature nationale* 3 (1863): 291–426, esp. 355–357. Maillard explained that the knowledge of sacred texts should remain with the priests and that the Mi'kmaq should be kept in ignorance lest they should become convinced that they knew a lot more than their teachers. Bruce Greenfield argues that Maillard's use of the hieroglyphs was hierarchical and conservative. Maillard wanted to control the flow of information by keeping his linguistic knowledge separate from this evangelization tool. Bruce Greenfield, "The Mi'kmaq Hieroglyphic Prayer Book: Writing and Christianity in Maritime Canada, 1675–1921," in *The Language Encounter in the Americas, 1492–1800*, ed. Edward G. Gray and Norman Fiering (2000; repr., New York: Berghahn, 2003), 189–211.

24. Importing a London printer for the specific purpose of printing an Indian library in New England is discussed at length in the correspondence between John Eliot and Robert

Boyle and other commissioners of the New England Company for the Propagation of the Gospel. "Accounts Accompanying Preceding Letter," Sept. 10, 1662, in Hunter, Clericuzio, and Principe, *Correspondence of Robert Boyle*, 2:49; "Boyle to Commissioners of the United Colonies in New England," Apr. 9, 1663, ibid., 2:75; "Commissioners of the United Colonies in New England to Boyle," Sept. 18, 1663, ibid., 2:121.

25. Mullet, *Catholic Reformation*, 167.

26. Reuben Gold Thwaites, ed., *The Jesuit Relations and Allied Documents: Travels and Explorations of the Jesuit Missionaries in New France, 1610–1791* (Cleveland: Burrows Brothers, 1897), 5:22–23 (quotations, 5:23).

27. From James Axtell and James P. Ronda's foundational work on Jesuits in New France forward, missionaries have been seen as upholding a utopian vision of spiritual renewal, cut off from the politics of the Old World. James P. Ronda, "The European Indian: Jesuit Civilization Planning in New France," *Church History* 41, no. 3 (September 1972): 385–395; James Axtell, *The Invasion Within: The Contest of Cultures in Colonial North America* (New York: Oxford University Press, 1985). See also Allan Greer, introduction to *The Jesuit Relations: Natives and Missionaries in Seventeenth-Century North America*, ed. Allan Greer (Boston: Bedford/St. Martin's, 2000), 1–19; Peter A. Goddard, "Canada in Seventeenth-Century Jesuit Thought: Backwater or Opportunity?" in *Decentring the Renaissance: Canada and Europe in Multidisciplinary Perspective, 1500–1700*, ed. Germaine Warkentin and Carolyn Podruchny (Toronto: University of Toronto Press, 2001), 186–199. In her dissertation Bronwen Catherine McShea challenges this notion of the French Jesuits as detached from the interests of the French Empire. Bronwen Catherine McShea, "Cultivating Empire Through Print: The Jesuit Strategy for New France and the Parisian *Relations* of 1632 to 1673" (PhD diss., Yale University, 2011).

28. Gallicanism was the ideology of resistance to Rome. While papal authority gained global control over missions through the Congregatio de Propaganda Fide of 1622, France, under the reigns of Louis XIII and Louis XIV, tightened national control, such that it became the "second front of the Catholic Reformation" (Mullet, *Catholic Reformation*, 154). As Mullet notes, Gallican Catholicism involved renewing the medieval system of coventual life, bringing a fuller Catholicism to the masses while also shoring up ecclesiastical authority and purging entrenched Calvinist Protestantism from France. Meanwhile, the Congregatio de Propaganda Fide was issued by Rome in 1622 in an attempt to bring coherence and uniformity to Catholic missions throughout the world. Luca Codignola, *Guide to Documents Relating to French and British North America in the Archives of the Sacred Congregation "de Propaganda Fide" in Rome, 1622–1799* (Ottawa: National Archives of Canada, 1991).

29. Mireille Pastoureau, Annie Chassagne, and Pierre Gasnault, *Le Dictionnaire de l'Académie française: 1694–1994, sa naissance et son actualité* (Paris: Institut de France, 1994), 16, 19–24, 31–36.

30. Le Clercq, *New Relation of Gaspesia*, 80–81 (quotations, 81).

31. Ruth Holmes Whitehead, *Nova Scotia: The Protohistoric Period, 1500–1630* (Halifax: Nova Scotia Museum, 1993), 5, 7.

32. Constance A. Crosby, "From Myth to History; or, Why King Philip's Ghost Walks Abroad," in *The Recovery of Meaning: Historical Archaeology in the Eastern United States*, ed. Mark P. Leone and Parker B. Potter (Washington, D.C.: Smithsonian Institution, 1988), 183–210 (quotations, 193).

33. Silverman, "Indians, Missionaries, and Religious Translation," 149.

34. Crosby, "From Myth to History," 194.

35. Le Clercq, *New Relation of Gaspesia*, 213, quoted in Wilson D. Wallis and Ruth Sawtell Wallis, *The Micmac Indians of Eastern Canada* (Minneapolis: University of Minnesota Press, 1955), 149.

36. This notion that Indian words were growing further and further away from a spiritual ideal was succinctly expressed by Cotton Mather when he attributed the length of Massachusett words to the fact that "they had been growing ever since Babel." Mather, "Triumphs of the Reformed Religion," 561–562 (quotation, 561).

37. According to Noel Malcolm, Johann Amos Comenius began the project of translating the Bible into Turkish in Holland in 1658. Robert Boyle funded William Seaman's translation of the Bible into Turkish in London, where the New Testament was published in 1666 as well as the Indian School at the College of William and Mary. Malcolm, "Comenius, Boyle, Oldenburg, and the Translation of the Bible into Turkish," *Church History and Religious Culture* 87, no. 3 (July 2007): 327–362. Boyle also funded the translation of the Bible into Irish Gaelic in 1681. The preface to the Irish New Testament states two reasons for the translation. The first is *sola scriptura*. Drawing on Hebrews 4:22, the preface states that "the very Word of God...is quick and powerful, and sharper than any two-edged sword, Heb. 4.22. For the same Reason Pious Fathers of Families should cause it to be read on fit Seasons to their Household." Second, the Irish Bible would allow "foreigners" to more easily learn the language. Quoted from Robert Boyle, copy of the preface to the Irish Testament, 1681, Boyle Papers, 1/4/16, Royal Society, London. Printed version: Huilliam O'Domhnuill, *Tiomna Nuadh ar dTighearna agus ar Slanuigheora Iósa Criosd* (London, 1681). See also R. E. W. Maddison, "Robert Boyle and the Irish Bible," *Bulletin of the John Rylands Library* 41, no. 1 (September 1958): 81–101.

38. The primer arose out of the catechistical context in the 1680s prompted by Benjamin Harris's arrival in Boston from England. The impetus behind the proliferation of primers from the late seventeenth through the eighteenth century was to break down the practice of faith into bare syllabic, syntactic, and metrically regulated rules. Paul Leicester Ford, ed., *The New-England Primer: A History of Its Origin and Development with a Reprint of the Unique Copy of the Earliest Known Edition...*(New York, 1897), 4–23. According to Patricia Crain, "Millions [of primers] were printed between 1690 and 1850" but "only a few hundred have been found." Patricia Crain, *The Story of A: The Alphabetization of America from the New England Primer to the Scarlet Letter* (Stanford, Calif.: Stanford University Press, 2000), 16.

39. John Eliot, *Communion of Churches; or, The Divine Management of Gospel Churches by the Ordinance of Councils...*(Cambridge, [Mass.,] 1665), 17.

40. Ives Goddard and Kathleen J. Bragdon, eds., *Native Writings in Massachusett* (Philadelphia: American Philosophical Society, 1988), 2:692 ("peahtammooonk"); "Letter from Zachary Hossueit, Indian preacher at Gay Head, to Solomon Briant (Priant), the Indian preacher at Mashpee," doc. 140, ibid., 1:358–361 ("Lord," 1:358, 359, 361). According to James Hammond Trumbull's *Natick Dictionary*, first published in 1903, "peantamóonk" means "prayer," but Trumbull relied on Eliot's translations. Hammond Trumbull, *Natick Dictionary: A New England Indian Lexicon* (Lincoln: University of Nebraska Press, 2009), 120. "Lordooe" does not appear in the *Natick Dictionary* at all.

41. James Hammond Trumbull, *Natick Dictionary* (Washington, D.C., 1903), 48–49; Goddard and Bragdon, *Native Writings in Massachusett*, 2:641.

42. Trumbull, *Natick Dictionary* (1903), 30.

43. Silverman, "Indians, Missionaries, and Religious Translation," 146. Later on in the article, Silverman notes some variation as "[Eliot] preferred to leave God and Jesus Christ untranslated for fear of corrupting them, but occasionally followed Mayhew's lead by using 'Manitoo' for God" (ibid., 159).

44. John Eliot, The Indian Primer; or, The First Book by Which Children May Know Truely to Read the Indian Language. And Milk for Babes (Boston, 1720), 18 (quotations).

45. On Aristotelian modes of perception, see Leen Spruit, *Species Intelligibilis: From Perception to Knowledge* (Leiden: Brill, 1994), vol. 1.

46. J[ohn] E[liot], *The Logick Primer: Some Logical Notions to Initiate the INDIANS in the Knowledge of the Rule of Reason; and to Know How to Make Use Thereof*...([Cambridge, Mass.], 1672), title page ("Iron Key"), n.p. ("rich Treasury").

47. Thomas Shepard Jr. letter, Sept. 9, 1673, Wod. Qu. CV, fols. 105–112, Woodrow Collection, National Library of Scotland, Edinburgh. The addressee of this letter is not known.

48. The letter was printed as an appendix to Edward Winslow, *The Glorious Progress of the Gospel, Amongst the Indians in New England*...(London, 1649), 23. I am indebted to Cristobal Silva for bringing this reference to my attention.

49. [John Eliot], *Indian Dialogues, for Their Instruction in That Great Service of Christ, in Calling Home Their Country-men to the Knowledge of God*...(Cambridge, [Mass.,] 1671), 37 (quotation). For readings of the Waban, see Jean M. O'Brien, *Dispossession by Degrees: Indian Land and Identity in Natick, Massachusetts, 1650–1790* (New York: Cambridge University Press, 1997), 31–65; Kristina Bross, *Dry Bones and Indian Sermons: Praying Indians in Colonial America* (Ithaca, N.Y.: Cornell University Press, 2004).

50. [Eliot], *Indian Dialogues*, 1 ("Instructive," "Learned"), 4 ("your praying"), 8 ("Book of God").

51. Ibid., 23.

52. Ibid., 12.

53. "President and Fellows of Harvard College to Boyle," Oct. 27, 1669, in Hunter, Clericuzio, and Principe, *Correspondence of Robert Boyle*, 4:151–152 (quotations, 4:151).

54. Tho[mas] Thorowgood conveys Eliot's linguistic ideal when he announces that "these naked Americans are Hebrewes" and that their language approximates Hebrew. "The learned Conjectures of Reverend Mr. John Eliot touching the Americans, of new and notable consideration, written to Mr. Thorowgood," in Thorowgood, *Jews in America; or, Probabilities, That Those Indians Are Judaical, Made More Probable by Some Additionals to the Former Conjectures* (London, 1660), 17–19 (quotation, 17). In Communion of Churches, Eliot extends this lost tribes argument into a vision for a unity of faith among all "Christian nations" where the church will speak a "Universal Language" modeled on Hebrew. Eliot, *Communion of Churches*, 20 ("Christian"), 17 ("Universal"). Mather summarizes Eliot's linguistic vision as a consolidation of "all languages" into a "universal language" that approximates the voice of Jesus (Mather, *Magnalia*, 546). Compare this idealism to the material history of the Indian library recounted in correspondence between Boyle and Eliot. In 1662 £500 was donated to defray the charge of printing the Bible. "Accounts Accompanying Preceding Letter," Sept. 10, 1662, in Hunter, Clericuzio, and Principe, *Correspondence of Robert Boyle*, 2:49; "Boyle to Commissioners of the United Colonies in New England," Apr. 9, 1663, ibid., 2:74–75. The report from Boston on Mar. 1, 1683/1684,

assures the commissioners of the New England Company that Eliot has been "frugall" in the expenses of the Old Testament. "Commissioners of the United Colonies in New England to Boyle," Mar. 1, 1684, ibid., 6:9 (quotation); "John Eliot to Boyle," Apr. 22, 1684, ibid., 6:14.

55. *Tears of Repentance* is Eliot's most thorough effort to produce the evidence of grace typically recorded in testimonies of faith in Anglo congregations. However, the success of this inward quest was always contested. The despair that I am attributing to Eliot in the 1660s through 1680s is in fact an extension of a state intrinsic to Puritanism. For a discussion of the impact of Eliot's missionary endeavors on Puritan epistemologies of conversion, see my third chapter, "Praying Towns: Conversion, Empirical Desire, and the Indian Soul," in Sarah Rivett, *The Science of the Soul in Colonial New England* (Chapel Hill: University of North Carolina Press, 2011), 125–172.

56. "John Eliot to Boyle," Apr. 22, 1684, in Hunter, Clericuzio, and Principe, *Correspondence of Robert Boyle*, 6:15–16 (quotations, 6:15).

57. The specter of King Philip's War is woven throughout Eliot's late letters. Eliot's 1684 letter to Boyle explained Daniel Gookin's plan to teach the Indians "the English tongue" as a "poynt of wisdom in civilizing them." The letter also reported the displacement and contraction of populations following the war. Ibid., 6:16. As for the transformation of Puritan theology toward more externalized forms of worship, see E. Brooks Holifield, *The Covenant Sealed: The Development of Puritan Sacramental Theology in Old and New England, 1570–1720* (New Haven, Conn.: Yale University Press, 1974).

58. "Commissioners of the United Colonies in New England to Boyle," Sept. 8, 1670, in Hunter, Clericuzio, and Principe, *Correspondence of Robert Boyle*, 4:182.

59. Le Clercq, *New Relation of Gaspesia*, 81 (quotations). In his *First Establishment of the Faith in New France*, Le Clercq positions his mission to the Mi'kmaq as an extension of Sagard's work among the Hurons. He explains that while the Recollects were among the Huron, Montagnais, and Algonquian nations in the 1630s, they "perfected dictionaries" and that he himself has "seen several fragments." Christian [Chrestien] Le Clercq, *First Establishment of the Faith in New France*, ed. and trans. John G. Shea (New York, 1881), 1:248–249 ("perfected," 1:248, "fragments," 1:249). The Establishment of the Faith is the second text attributed to Le Clercq in the late seventeenth century, but there is some debate as to whether he was in fact the author. Raphael N. Hamilton, "Who Wrote Premier Éstablissement de la Foy dans la Nouvelle France?" *Canadian Historical Review* 57, no. 3 (September 1976): 265–288. Regardless, Le Clercq clearly viewed Sagard's linguistic and missionary work as an important precedent for his own.

60. Carey, "Travel, Geography, and the Problem of Belief," 113.

61. Le Clercq, *First Establishment*, 141–142.

62. On Mi'kmaq cosmologies, see Whitehead, *Nova Scotia*, 5–7; Inglis, "400 Years of Linguistic Contact Between the Mi'kmaq and the English and the Interchange of Two World Views," 389–402; Anne-Christine Hornborg, *Mi'kmaq Landscapes: From Animism to Sacred Ecology* (Burlington, Vt.: Ashgate, 2008), 32–34.

63. V. F. Cordova, *How It Is: The Native American Philosophy of V. F. Cordova*, ed. Kathleen Dean Moore et al. (Tucson: University of Arizona Press, 2007), 76.

64. Schmidt and Marshall, *Mi'kmaq Hieroglyphic Prayers*, 6.

65. Le Clercq, *New Relation of Gaspesia*, 131. See also Schmidt and Marshall, *Mi'kmaq Hieroglyphic Prayers*, 6.

66. A few scholars of Mi'kmaq have posited that the ideograms developed by Le Clercq did indeed come from an indigenous system of writing. See Schmidt and Marshall, *Mi'kmaq Hieroglyphic Prayers*. Information on the petroglyphs comes from Ruth Holmes Whitehead, "A New Micmac Petroglyph Site," *Nova Scotia Museum* 13, no. 1 (1992): 7–12.

67. José de Acosta, *Natural and Moral History of the Indies*, ed. Jane E. Mangan, trans. Frances M. López-Morillas (Durham, N.C.: Duke University Press, 2002), 335 ("no nation"), 334 ("letters"). On Renaissance hierarchies of alphabetic writing, see Walter D. Mignolo, "Nebrija in the New World: The Question of the Letter, the Colonization of Amerindian Languages, and the Discontinuity of the Classical Tradition," *L'Homee* 32, nos. 122–124 (1992): 185–207; Arthur B. Ferguson, *Utter Antiquity: Perception of Prehistory in Renaissance England* (Durham, N.C.: Duke University Press, 1993), 56–57; Paolo Rossi, "La religion dei geroglifici e le origini della scrittura," in *Le sterminate antichità e nuovi saggi vichiani* (Scandicci: La Nuova Italia, 1999), 80–131; Francis Bacon, *The Instauratio Magna, Part II: Novum Organum and Associated Texts*, ed. Graham Rees and Maria Wakely. Vol. 11 of *The Oxford Francis Bacon*, ed. Graham Rees and Lisa Jardine (Oxford: Clarendon, 2004), 134–135.

68. *History of the New World* was first published in Dutch in 1625 by Bonaventure and Abraham Elseviers in Leiden. A Latin edition came out in 1633, followed by a French edition in 1640. See Rolf H. Bremmer Jr. and P. G. Hoftijzer, "Johannes de Laet (1581–1649): A Leiden Polymath [introduction]," *Lias: Special Issue* 25, no. 2 (1998): 135–136.

69. Giambattista Vico, *New Science: Principles of the New Science Concerning the Common Nature of Nations*, 3rd ed., trans. David Marsh (New York: Penguin, 2013), 172, 175.

70. Thomas Browne, *Pseudodoxia Epidemica* (London, 1646). On common writing, see Francis Lodwick, *A Common Writing* (1647). Both Lodwick and Thomas Browne are discussed in Lewis, *Language, Mind and Nature*, 49, 121.

71. Le Clercq, *New Relation of Gaspesia*, 84 (quotations).

72. Wallis and Wallis, *The Micmac Indians*, 151–171; Ruth Holmes Whitehead, *Elitekey: Micmac Material Culture from 1600 AD to the Present* (Halifax: Nova Scotia Museum, 1980).

73. Wallis and Wallis, *The Micmac Indians*, 151–171.

74. While the manuscript records originally created by Le Clercq have been lost, manuscript copies, such as the one featured in Figure 2.4, were made by his successor, Abbé Pierre Maillard, who lived and worked among the Mi'kmaq from 1735 to 1762. Catholic Church, Selections from the Catholic Prayer Book, MS 1627, Ayer Collection, Newberry Library, Chicago.

75. Le Clercq, *New Relation of Gaspesia*, 126. See also Schmidt and Marshall, *Mi'kmaq Hieroglyphic Prayers*, 7.

76. Le Clercq, *First Establishment*, 16 ("readily grasp," "who wishes"), 17 ("making marks").

77. On Mi'kmaq pictographs, see Whitehead, *Elitekey*; Joan M. Vastokas, "History Without Writing: Pictorial Narratives in Native North America," in *Gin Das Winan: Documenting Aboriginal History in Ontario: A Symposium at Bkejwanong, Walpole Island First Nation, September 23, 1994*, ed. Dale Standen and David McNab (Toronto: Champlain Society, 1996), 48–64; Greenfield, "The Mi'kmaq Hieroglyphic Prayer Book," 196.

78. Bruce M. White argues that the Ojibwa and Dakota valued French technology for its many applications to their lives, including religious applications, and argues that it is impossible to categorize objects as either utilitarian or non-utilitarian. Bruce M. White, "Encounters with Spirits: Ojibwa and Dakota Theories about the French and Their Merchandise," *Ethnohistory* 41, no. 3 (Summer 1994): 369–405; Pierre Déléage, *La croix et les*

hiéroglyphes: Écritures et objects rituels chez les Amérindiens de Nouvelle-France, XVIIe-XVIIIe siècles (Paris: Rue d'Ulm, 2009), 1–20. On early settlers to the Gaspé peninsula, see also Whitehead, *Nova Scotia*, 5–7.

79. Le Clercq, *New Relation of Gaspesia*, 50–51 (quotations, 50).

80. Le Clercq's postulation that the Gaspesian ideographs contained an incipient form of Christianity partook of the seventeenth-century French Jesuit tradition of Figurism, a controversial exegetical method of reading ideographs and hieroglyphs as embodying Christian tenets. See Kenneth Scott Latourette, *A History of Christian Missions in China* (New York: Macmillan, 1932); Ines G. Zupanov, "Aristocratic Analogies and Demotic Descriptions in the Seventeenth-Century Madurai Mission," *Representations* 41 (Winter 1993): 123–148; Peter A. Dorsey, "Going to School with Savages: Authorship and Authority Among the Jesuits of New France," *William and Mary Quarterly* 55, no. 3 (July 1998): 399–420.

81. Le Clercq, *New Relation of Gaspesia*, 50–51 ("presided," 50, "rendering," 50–51), 157 ("melt[ing]").

82. Locke, *Essay Concerning Human Understanding*, 469.

83. Etienne Bonnot de Condillac, *Essay on the Origin of Human Knowledge*, trans. and ed. Hans Aarsleff (Cambridge: Cambridge University Press, 2001).

84. On Boyle's influence on Locke, see Peter Alexander, *Ideas, Qualities and Corpuscles: Locke and Boyle on the External World* (Cambridge: Cambridge University Press, 1985). For Locke's belief in the tenuous nature of words, see his *Essay Concerning Human Understanding*, 251–252.

85. According to Anishinaabe scholar Gerald Vizenor, "native survivance is an active sense of presence over absence, deracination, and oblivion; survivance is the continuance of stories, not a mere reaction, however pertinent." Gerald Vizenor, ed., *Survivance: Narratives of Native Presence* (Lincoln: University of Nebraska Press, 2008), 1.

Chapter 3

1. Description based on my own examination of the manuscript. Jacques Gravier, *Dictionary of the Algonquian-Illinois Language*, Watkinson Library, Trinity College, Hartford, Conn. The dictionary is now also available online through the Watkinson Library Internet Archive. Information on the circumstances of the dictionary's production comes from "John F. Swenson to Mr. Jeffrey H. Kaimowitz, 13 March 1989," in Swenson, *John F. Swenson Letters re Gravier Dictionary*, American Indian Vocabulary Collection, Watkinson Library, Trinity College. According to Swenson, the corrections to Gravier's hand were most likely made by Julien Binneteau and Gabriel Marest.

2. Reuben Gold Thwaites, ed., *Jesuit Relations and Allied Documents: Travels and Explorations of the Jesuit Missionaries in New France* (Cleveland: Burrows Brothers, 1901), 5:87.

3. Other scholars have noted this increase in linguistic expertise by the third generation of French Jesuits. See Robert Michael Morrissey, "'I Speak It Well': Language, Cultural Understanding, and the End of a Missionary Middle Ground in Illinois Country, 1673–1712," *Early American Studies* 9, no. 3 (2011): 617–648; Tracy Neal Leavelle, *The Catholic Calumet: Colonial Conversions in French and Indian North America* (Philadelphia: University of Pennsylvania Press, 2012), 97–125; and Brett Rushforth, *Bonds of Alliance: Indigenous and Atlantic Slaveries in New France* (Chapel Hill: University of North Carolina

Press, 2012), 15–73. Similar expertise has also been attributed to third- and fourth-generation Puritan missionaries, most notably in Douglas L. Winiarski's excellent work on Josiah Cotton. "A Question of Plain Dealing: Josiah Cotton, Native Christians, and the Quest for Security in Eighteenth-Century Plymouth County," *New England Quarterly* 77, no. 3 (2004): 368–413.

4. Experience Mayhew, *Observations on the Indian Language*, ed. John S. H. Fogg (1722; repr., Boston: D. Clapp & Son, 1884), 8.

5. Gravier, *Dictionary*; Sebastian Rasles [Rale], *A Dictionary of the Abnaki Language, in North America*, in *Memoirs of the American Academy of Arts and Sciences* I, New Series, ed. John Pickering (Cambridge: Printer to the University, 1833), 370–575; Antoine-Robert Le Boullenger, *French and Miami-Illinois Dictionary*, John Carter Brown Library, Providence, R.I.; Josiah Cotton, *Vocabulary of the Massachusetts (or Natick) Indian Language*, in *Collections of the Massachusetts Historical Society*, 3rd ser., 2 (Cambridge, Mass.: Printed by E. W. Metcalf and Company, 1830), 147–257; Mayhew, *Observations on the Indian Language*.

6. The print archive is fairly substantial, including the seventeenth-century texts in John Eliot's "Indian library," for which he imported a specific printer by the name of Marmaduke Johnson. Of relevance to this time period, see also *The Massachusetts Psalter: Or, Psalms of David* (Boston: Printed by B. Green and J. Printer, 1709). Several sermons and catechisms exist in manuscript. See Josiah Cotton, Sermon. Massachusetts, 1710, Ayer Collection, Newberry Library, Chicago; Experience Mayhew, Sermons, Papers of Experience Mayhew, Massachusetts Historical Society, Boston; Prayer Book, Abnaki, American Indian Vocabulary Collection, Watkinson Library, Hartford, Conn.

7. Cultural myths of disappearing American Indians permitted the persistence of outmoded anthropological perspectives in the field of American studies. Ian K. Steele, "Exploding Colonial American History: Amerindian, Atlantic, and Global Perspectives," *Reviews in American History* 26, no. 1 (1998): 70–95. For a retrospective account on the success of this idea a decade later, see Paul Cohen, "Was There an Amerindian Atlantic? Reflections on the Limits of a Historiographical Concept," *History of European Ideas* 34, no. 4 (2008): 388–410. Books that explore intersections between indigenous and Atlantic studies include Jace Weaver, *The Red Atlantic: American Indigenes and the Making of the Modern World, 1000–1927* (Chapel Hill: University of North Carolina Press, 2014); Jodi A. Byrd, *The Transit of Empire: Indigenous Critiques of Colonialism* (Minneapolis: University of Minnesota Press, 2011); and Coll Thrush, *Indigenous London: Native Travellers at the Heart of Empire* (New Haven, Conn.: Yale University Press, 2016).

8. On natural philosophy and scriptural history from 1680–1720, see William Poole, *The World Makers: Scientists of the Restoration and the Search for the Origins of the Earth* (Oxford: Peter Lang, 2010), especially 75–84. On the breakdown of biblical linguistics, see Thomas R. Trautman, *Languages and Nations: The Dravidian Proof in Colonial Madras* (Berkeley: University of California Press, 2006), 1–41.

9. Quote is from Joseph François Lafitau, *Customs of the American Indians Compared with the Customs of Primitive Times*, ed. and trans. by William N. Fenton and Elizabeth L. Moore (Toronto: Champlain Society, 1977), 2:261.

10. For a theorization of this process during the Enlightenment, see Johannes Fabian, *Time and the Other: How Anthropology Makes Its Object* (New York: Columbia University Press, 1983).

11. As if anticipating the challenges of the doctrine of the permutation of letters, Matthew Hale writes: "Considering therefore the great instability of Languages, the great variations and changes to which they are subject, the great alterations that they have had, the great difficulty of finding any Language which (upon grounds barely of Reason, without Divine Revelation) we can safely call Original, and the great difficulty of deducing other Languages entirely from it: It is hard for us singly to lay any weight upon this Instance, to prove the Origination of Man upon a meer Moral Account or Topical Ratiocination thereof." *The Primitive Origination of Mankind, Considered and Examined According to the Light of Nature* (London: Printed by William Godbid, 1677), 165.

12. Ibid., 138.

13. Thomas Burnet, *The Theory of the Earth* (London: Printed by R. Norton, 1684), 193.

14. Robert Hooke, *The Posthumous Works of Robert Hooke…, Containing His Cutlerian Lectures, and Other Discourses, Read at the Meeting of the Illustrious Royal Society* (London: Sam Smith and Benj. Walford, 1705), 320. See also Poole, *The World Makers*, 95–113.

15. John Woodward, *An Essay Toward a Natural History of the Earth* (London: Printed for Ric. Wilkin at the Kings Head in St. Paul's Church-yard, 1695), 71–114.

16. Cotton Mather, *Magnalia Christi Americana: Or, the Ecclesiastical History of New England*, vol. 1 (Hartford: Silas Andrus & Son, 1855), 561–562.

17. David Boyd Haycock, *William Stukeley: Science, Religion and Archeology in Eighteenth-Century England* (Woodbridge, UK: Boydell Press, 2002).

18. Cotton Mather, *Genesis.* Vol. 1 of *Biblia Americana*, vol. 1, ed. Reiner Smolinski (Grand Rapids, Mich.: Baker Academic, 2010), 812.

19. For a discussion of the relationship between historical linguistics, natural history, and antiquarianism, see Brynley F. Roberts, "The Discovery of Old Welsh," *Historiographia Linguistica* 26, nos. 1/2 (1999): 1–21.

20. Edward Lhwyd, *Archaeologia Britannica: Texts and Translations*, ed. Dewi W. Evans and Brynley F. Roberts (Aberystwyth, UK: Celtic Studies Publications, 2009), 6–7.

21. For connections between John Eliot and the Royal Society, see Sarah Rivett, "Empirical Desire: Conversion, Ethnography, and the New Science of the Praying Indian," *Early American Studies* 4, no. 1 (2006): 16–45.

22. Paul-Yves Pezron, *The Antiquities of Nations, More Particularly of the Celtæ or Gauls, Taken to Be Originally the Same People as Our Ancient Britains…Englished by Mr. Jones* (London, 1706), title page.

23. Quoted from David Malcolm, *An Essay on the Antiquities of Great Britain and Ireland* (Edinburgh: Printed by T. and W. Ruddimans, 1738), 46. On the reception of Pezron, see Edward Lhwyd, "Part of a Letter from Mr. Edward Lhwyd to Dr. Martin Lister," *Philosophical Transactions* 20, no. 243 (1698): 279–280. Lhwyd reveals his opinion of Pezron in a letter to the Rev. John Morton, May 8, 1699: "I am affrayd all writers are a little byass'd to their native countrey, as well as this Abbot of Chambray, and that all that can be sayd in their favour is, that they are the best who have tincture of partiality. 'Tis certain that neither ye Saxons nor Danes ever subdued Wales, nor ye Normans totaly 'til near three hundred years after the conquest," in Edward Owen, ed., *A Catalogue of Manuscripts Relating to Wales in the British Museum*, part 4 (London: Issued by the Honorable Society of Cymmrodorion, 1922), 877–878. Original in Sloane Collection 4062 f. 301, British Library, London.

24. Nancy Edwards, "Edward Lhuyd and the Origins of Early Medieval Celtic Archaeology," *Antiquaries Journal* 87 (2007): 165–196.

25. For an account of the Druidical fascination, see Ronald Hutton, *Blood and Mistletoe: The History of the Druids in Britain* (New Haven, Conn.: Yale University Press, 2009), 49–124.

26. IMAGINES seu Figurae variorum Inscriptionum praecipue Sepulchralium, Stowe MS 1023, British Library, London, 3–6.

27. For an account of practices of rereading the land from the perspective of Christian history, see Alexandra Walsham, *Reformation of the Landscape: Religion, Identity, and Memory in Early Modern Britain and Ireland* (Oxford: Oxford University Press, 2011).

28. [David Malcolm and Edward Lhwyd], "A Letter to Archimedes," in *A Collection of Letters, in Which the Imperfection of Learning, Even Among Christians, and a Remedy for It, Are Hinted* (Edinburgh, 1739), Sections 6, 14, and 41. John Carter Brown Library, Brown University.

29. Ibid., 36, 44–45.

30. My analysis here builds on insights in Anglo-Saxon studies. See Allen J. Frantzen, *Desire for Origins: New Language, Old English, and Teaching the Tradition* (New Brunswick, N.J.: Rutgers University Press, 1990); Christopher Cannon, *The Grounds of English Literature* (Oxford: Oxford University Press, 2004); Michael Modarelli, "The Struggle for Origins: Old English in Nineteenth-Century America," *Modern Language Quarterly* 73, no. 4 (2012): 527–543.

31. Quoted poems include J. Keill *Scoto-Britannus*, "Ad Edvardum Luidium in Primum Archaeologiae Britannicae Volumen," Andreas Frazier *Eccl. Scot. Presb.*, "In *Edv. Luidi* Glossographiam," R. Jones *Maridunensis*, "In Amicissimi Viri *E.L.* Glossographiam," Collinus Campbell *Ardchattanus Pastor*, Lornensis, "In amici singularis *E. Luidii* Archaeologiam Britan," all included and translated in Lhwyd, *Archaeologia Britannica*, 68–75.

32. Daniel Droixhe, "Adam ou Babel? Théorie du signe et linguistique biblique de Descartes à Leibniz," in *Language Philosophies and the Language of Sciences: A Historical Perspective in Honor of Lia Formigari*, ed. Daniele Gambarara, Stefano Gensini, and Antonino Pennisi, 115–128. (Münster: Nodus Publikationen, 1996).

33. Giambattista Vico, *New Science: Principles of the New Science Concerning the Common Nature of Nations*, 3rd ed., trans. David Marsh (New York: Penguin, 2013), 182–183.

34. David Abram, *The Spell of the Sensuous: Perception and Language in a More-than-Human World* (New York: Pantheon, 1996), 40.

35. Vico, *New Science*, 489.

36. Ibid., 183.

37. Ibid., 402.

38. Ibid., 461.

39. On this concept of inventing tradition in the British Isles, see Hugh Trevor-Roper, "The Invention of Tradition: The Highland Tradition of Scotland," and Pyrs Morgan, "From a Death to a View: The Hunt for the Welsh Past in the Romantic Period," in *The Invention of Tradition*, ed. Eric Hobsbawm and Terence Ranger (Cambridge: Cambridge University Press, 1992), 15–43 and 43–101; R. G. Collingwood, *The Idea of History: With Lectures, 1926–1928*, ed. and with an introduction by Jan van der Dussen (New York: Oxford University Press, 1994), 1–10. See also Allen J. Frantzen's assessment of the relationship between the philosophy of history and textual criticism of Anglo-Saxon in *Desire for Origins*, 1–26, and J. G. A. Pocock, *The Ancient Constitution and the Feudal Law: A study of English Historical Thought in the Seventeenth Century* (New York: Cambridge University Press, 1987).

40. Much has been written about Jesuit linguistic skill, beginning with Victor Egon Hanzeli, *Missionary Linguistics in New France: A Study of Seventeenth- and Eighteenth-*

Century Descriptions of American Indian Languages (The Hague: Mouton, 1969). See also Peter A. Dorsey, "Going to School with the Savages: Authorship and Authority Among the Jesuits of New France," *William and Mary Quarterly* 55, no. 3 (July 1998): 399–420; Tracy Neale Leavelle, " 'Bad Things' and 'Good Hearts': Mediation, Meaning, and the Language of Illinois Christianity," *Church History: Studies in Christianity and Culture* 76, no. 2 (2007): 363–394; Peter Burke, "The Jesuits and the Art of Translation in Early Modern Europe," in *The Jesuits II: Cultures, Sciences, and the Arts*, ed. John W. O'Malley, SJ, Gauvin Alexander Bailey, Steven J. Harris, and T. Frank Kennedy, SJ (Toronto: University of Toronto Press, 2006), 24–32; and Marc Fumaroli, "The Fertility and Shortcomings of Renaissance Rhetoric: The Jesuit Case," in *The Jesuits: Cultures, Sciences, and the Arts, 1540–1773* (Toronto: University of Toronto Press, 1999), 90–106. Recently, Micah True has written about Jesuit linguistic expertise as an ideal expressed throughout the *Relations* in order to emphasize both the efficacy of the Jesuit mission in New France and also the "bi-directional" flow of knowledge between priests and indigenous populations. *Masters and Students: Jesuit Ethnography in Seventeenth-Century New France* (Montreal: McGill-Queens University Press, 2015), 51.

41. Julien Binneteau, "Letter of Father Julien Binneteau, of the Society of Jesus, to a Father of the Same Society," in Thwaites, *Jesuit Relations*, 65:69–71.

42. John W. O'Malley explains that the *Exercises* functioned as a basic course of movement that the Jesuits strove to make operative in whatever they did. The structure of the *Exercises* can thus be discerned in the course of their quotidian activities and in the annual reports. The year 1548 is the publication date with official papal approval. *The First Jesuits* (Cambridge, Mass.: Harvard University Press, 1993), 37–50, 87–90.

43. These letters of October 30, 1689, and August 26, 1690, are printed as the appendix to Mary R. Calvert's *Black Robe on the Kennebec* (Monmouth, Me.: Monmouth Press, 1991). Quotes are from 229, 231, and 238–239.

44. Scott Stevens, a native speaker of Mohawk, explained to me that the figure 8 is meant to designate a sound that approximates the pronunciation of the French word "huit."

45. Sebastian Rasles [Rale], quoted in "Supplementary Notes and Observations," in *A Dictionary of the Abnaki Language*, 566–567.

46. Thwaite, *Jesuit Relations*, 65:131; 64:193–195, 215, 225–229.

47. David J. Costa, *The Miami-Illinois Language* (Lincoln: University of Nebraska Press, 2003), 14.

48. Two recent studies of Jesuit dictionaries from this time period are Morrissey, " 'I Speak It Well,' " 617–648; and Leavelle, *The Catholic Calumet*, 97.

49. Lafitau, *Customs of the American Indians*, 1:26; 2:268.

50. Ibid., 1:53.

51. Ibid., 2:268.

52. Ibid.

53. Ibid.

54. Ibid., 2:260. "It was only towards the end of the fifteenth century that these immense regions [North and South America] were discovered" (ibid., 1:42). "When two peoples who speak languages so far apart as Iroquois and French meet for the needs of trade or for their common defence, they are forced, equally on both sides, to approach each other in their own language" (ibid., 2:261).

55. Ibid., 2:261.

56. Ibid., 1:45.

57. Ibid., 1:81–82.

58. Ibid., 86.

59. For an analysis of this shift, see E. Jennifer Monaghan, *Learning to Read and Write in Colonial America* (Amherst: University of Massachusetts Press, 2005), 169–188.

60. "Proposals for Propagating the Gospel in All Pagan Countries," Society for the Propagation of the Gospel Papers, vol. 7, 4–7. Lambeth Palace, London, United Kingdom.

61. Society for the Propagation of Christian Knowledge, Cambridge University Library, SPCK.MS.CN3/5.

62. Randall Palmer, *American National Biography Online*, s.v. "Freeman, Bernardus," accessed August 7, 2016, http://www.anb.org/articles/08/08-00504.html; Monaghan, *Learning to Read and Write in Colonial America*, 171.

63. "Society of the Propagation of the Gospels Papers," Series A:7, 203–204, Rhodes House, Oxford, United Kingdom.

64. Monaghan, *Learning to Read and Write in Colonial America*, 176.

65. In a letter probably addressed to Sir William Ashurst, dated December 10, 1712, Mather clearly recognizes the SPG's goal of instructing the proselytes in English but with the following caveat: "The grand concern of reprinting the Indian Bible often comes under our consideration. The most of your commissioners are averse to doing it at all, and rather hope to bring the rising generation by schools and other ways, to a full acquaintance with the English tongue, in which they will have a key to all the treasures of knowledge which we ourselves are owners of. My own poor opinion is that the projection of anglicising our Indians is much more easy to be talked of than to be accomplished. It will take more time than the commissioners who talk of it can imagine." *Selected Letters of Cotton Mather*, ed. Kenneth Silverman (Baton Rouge: Louisiana State University Press, 1971), 127.

66. Quoted in Mayhew, *Observations on the Indian Language*, 8.

67. Ibid., 9–11.

68. See Silverman, "Indians, Missionaries, and Religious Translation," 141–174.

69. Mayhew, *Observations on the Indian Language*, 6. Emphasis added.

70. Ibid., 12.

71. Josiah Cotton, *Vocabulary of the Massachusett (or Natick) Indian Language, Collections of the Massachusetts Historical Society*, 3rd ser., 2 (Cambridge, Mass.: Printed by E. W. Metcalf and Company, 1830), 147–257. The appendix to this printed edition of Cotton's Vocabulary explains that Cotton used the *Indian Primer* and the Eliot Bible to study the orthography of Massachusett (148).

72. Ibid., 242–243.

73. See Ives Goddard, "The Description of the Native Languages of North America Before Boas," in *Handbook of North American Indians*, vol. 17, ed. by Goddard (Washington: Smithsonian Institution, 1996), 17–42; Hilary E. Wyss and Kristina Bross, eds., *Early Native Literacies in New England: A Documentary and Critical Anthology* (Amherst: University of Massachusetts Press, 2008), 1–11; and Anna Ash, Jessie Little Doe Fermino, and Ken Hale, "Diversity in Local Language Maintenance and Restoration: A Reason for Optimism," in *The Green Book of Language Revitalization in Practice*, ed. Leanne Hinton and Ken Hale (San Diego: Academic Press, 2001), 19–35.

74. See Silverman, "Indians, Missionaries, and Religious Translation," 141–142.

75. Josiah Cotton, "Vocabulary of the Massachusett," 155, 157.

76. James Hammond Trumbull, *Natick Dictionary: A New England Indian Lexicon* (Lincoln: University of Nebraska Press, 2009), 35.

77. Ibid., 22.

78. Ibid., 19.

79. Josiah Cotton's phrase is "Negönne kuhquttumooonk," with "negönne" meaning "old, ancient, and so first in the order of time," and "kuhquttumoonk" meaning "he thirsts." *Vocabulary of the Massachusett (or Natick) Indian Language*, 155. Trumbull, *Natick Dictionary*, 42, 82.

Chapter 4

1. Thomas Charland, *Dictionary of Canadian Biography*, vol. 2, s.v. "Rale, Sébastien," accessed December 2, 2013, http://www.biographi.ca/en/bio/rale_sebastien_2E.html.

2. Sébastien Rasles, 1657–1724. Dictionary of the Abenaki Indian Language: Manuscript, 1691–1724. MS Fr 13. Houghton Library, Harvard University, Cambridge, Mass. There are several variations on the spelling of Rale's name. I use "Rale" throughout, except when quoting from another source.

3. Edward G. Andrew, *Imperial Republics: Revolution, War, and Territorial Expansion from the English Civil War to the French Revolution* (Toronto: University of Toronto Press, 2011), 49–52.

4. Thomas Kidd notes that the Treaty of Utrecht was a tenuous peace that left uncertain borders, particularly around the eastern settlements north of Salem. *The Protestant Interest: New England after Puritanism* (New Haven, Conn.: Yale University Press, 2004), 92; see also Kenneth M. Morrison, *The Embattled Northeast: The Elusive Ideal of Alliance in Abenaki-Euramerican Relations* (Berkeley: University of California Press, 1984).

5. David A. Bell, *The Cult of the Nation in France: Inventing Nationalism, 1680–1800* (Cambridge, Mass.: Harvard University Press, 2001), 3.

6. Robert M. Morrissey notices a marked increase in linguistic knowledge around the turn of the eighteenth century when Jesuits such as Jacques Gravier, Gabriel Marest, Jean Baptiste Le Boullenger, and Sébastien Rale developed exceptional linguistic skills. " 'I Speak It Well': Language, Cultural Understanding, and the End of a Missionary Middle Ground in Illinois Country, 1673–1712," *Early American Studies* 9, no. 3 (2011): 617–648.

7. There is no single unified attempt to implement English instruction in missionary schools in the late seventeenth/early eighteenth centuries. Rather, the process is gradual and contested by missionaries and native populations alike. By and large, however, at an institutional level, missionary organizations began to advocate for English instruction as both a simpler method of conversion and a means of "civilizing" "heathens" through the conventions of British culture. For example, in 1709, the author of the "Proposals for Propagating the Gospel in All Pagan Countries" writes, "Could we therefore remove that Barr by extirpating the various Dialects of the Indian Jargon, and establish in its room the knowledge of the English Tongue: That one Stept, I humbly suppose, would much facilitate the great design of civilizing and converting that part of the Heathen world." Society for the Propagation of the Gospel, vol. 7, 4–7ff. Lambeth Palace, London. While working for this organization, however, William Andrews conducted his mission in Mohawk because he felt that teaching the Indians English or Dutch would corrupt them. Additionally, the Mohawks were resolutely opposed to learning English, so the Ten Commandments, Lord's Prayer, and the gospel had to be translated into Mohawk. E. Jennifer Monaghan, *Learning to Read and Write in Colonial America* (Amherst: University of Massachusetts Press, 2005), 173–176; David Humphreys, *An Historical Account of the Incorporated Society for the Propagation of*

the Gospel in Foreign Parts (London: Printed by Joseph Downing in Bartholomew-Close near West-Smithfield, 1730), 276–312.

8. On the roots of British nationalism, linguistic and otherwise, see Linda Colley, *Britons: Forging the Nation, 1707–1837* (New Haven, Conn.: Yale University Press, 1992).

9. "Letter from Father Sébastien Rasles," in *Jesuit Relations and Allied Documents: Travels and Explorations of the Jesuit Missionaries in New France*, ed. Reuben Gold Thwaites (Cleveland: Burrows Brothers, 1901), 67:175.

10. Howard H. Peckham, *The Colonial Wars, 1689–1762* (Chicago: University of Chicago Press, 1964), 23.

11. New France had just three thousand inhabitants in 1663. A century later, the population had grown to sixty thousand. Morrison, *Embattled Northeast*, 8.

12. David Ogg, "The Emergence of Great Britain as a World Power"; and Philip S. Haffenden, "France and England in North America, 1689–1713," in *The Rise of Great Britain and Russia, 1688–1715/25*. Vol. 6 of *The New Cambridge Modern History*, ed. J. S. Bromley (Cambridge: Cambridge University Press, 1970), 254–283, 480–508.

13. Kidd, *Protestant Interest*, 91–114. As Dummer wrote to Vaudreuil as justification for Rale's death: "Fomenter & Incendiary to the Indians to kill, burn, & destroy, as flagrantly appears by many originall Letters & Manuscripts I have of his by me," Traske, ed., *Letters of Colonel Thomas Westbrook and Others*, 89. The letters and manuscripts to which he refers are, of course, those that the troops found in Rale's strongbox.

14. Pierre-Joseph de La Chasse, "Une Relation Inédite de la mort du P. Sébastien Racle, 1724," *Nova Francia* 4 (1929): 342–350.

15. Traske, ed., *Letters to Colonel Thomas Westbrook and Others*, 89.

16. Richard L. Haan, "Covenant and Consensus: Iroquois and English, 1676–1760," in *Beyond the Covenant Chain: The Iroquois and Their Neighbors in Indian North America, 1600–1800*, ed. Daniel K. Richter and James H. Merrell (Philadelphia: Pennsylvania State University Press, 2003), 41–57.

17. Cotton Mather, *Another Tongue Brought in, to Confess the Great Saviour of the World* (Boston: B. Green, 1707), 1–3. This text reflects the intense anxieties surrounding French and English competition for American Indian alliance. It is exemplary of what Richard L. Haan describes as the "diplomatic history of colonial North America." "Covenant and Consensus: Iroquois and English, 1676–1760," 41.

18. Evan Haefeli and Kevin Sweeney, *Captors and Captives: The 1704 French and Indian Raid on Deerfield* (Amherst: University of Massachusetts Press, 2003), 99.

19. Solomon Stoddard, *Question Whether God Is Not Angry with the Country for Doing So Little Towards the Conversion of the Indians?* (Boston: Printed by B. Green…and Sold by Samuel Gerrish, 1723), 6–7.

20. Ibid., 8–10.

21. "To the Rev'd Mr. Sam Johnson at Stratford in N. England," London 7 September 1737, Society for the Propagation of Christian Knowledge, Cambridge University Library, SPCK.MS.CN3/5.

22. Society for the Propagation of Christian Knowledge, Cambridge University Library, SPCK.MS. A.33 and CN1/1–2.

23. On the peripheral status of Anglo-American colonies from the turn of the eighteenth century on, see Charles L. Cohen, "The Colonization of British North America as an Episode in the History of Christianity," *Church History* 72, no. 3 (2003): 553–568. Jonathan

Eacott, *Selling Empire: India in the Making of Britain and America, 1600–1830* (Chapel Hill: University of North Carolina Press, 2016).

24. Stoddard, *Question Whether God Is Not Angry*, 10–12.

25. For an account of royal intervention in New France, see W. J. Eccles, *Canada Under Louis XIV, 1633–1701* (Toronto: McClelland and Steward, 1964).

26. Nicholas Dew, *Orientalism in Louis XIV's France* (Oxford: Oxford University Press, 2009), 1–27.

27. Raphael N. Hamilton calls Le Clercq's authorship into question, proposing that the text may have been written by Eusebe Renaudot, a member of the French Academy, and governor of New France Louis de Baude due to the text's appearance at a particularly strategic moment in French international affairs. "Who Wrote *Premier Établissement de la Foy dans la Nouvelle France?*" *Canadian Historical Review* 57, no. 3 (1976): 265–288.

28. Chrestien Le Clercq, *First Establishment of the Faith in New France*, ed. and trans. John G. Shea (New York: John G. Shea, 1881), 15.

29. Ruth Holmes Whitehead, "A New Micmac Petroglyph Site," *Occasional: An Occasional Journal for Nova Scotian Museums* 13, no. 1 (1992): 7–12.

30. Chrestien Le Clercq, *New Relation of Gaspesia with the Customs and Religion of the Gaspesian Indians*, ed. and trans. William F. Ganong (Toronto: Champlain Society, 1910), 144–156.

31. C. J. Jaenen, *Dictionary of Canadian Biography*, vol. 2, s.v. "Germain, Joseph-Louis, accessed Februrary 12, 2014, http://www.biographi.ca/en/bio/germain_joseph_louis_2E.html.

32. Thwaites, *Jesuit Relations*, 66:199–201.

33. Kenneth M. Morrison, *The Solidarity of Kin: Ethnohistory, Religious Studies, and the Algonkian-French Religious Encounter* (Albany: State University of New York Press, 2002), 81.

34. Henry Lorne Masta, *Abenaki Indian Legends, Grammar and Place Names* (Victoriaville, Q.C.: La Voix des Bois-Frances, 1932), 70.

35. In both Masta and Dr. Gordon M. Day's *Western Abenaki Dictionary*, weak verbs take an "i" as the vowel in their ending while strong verbs take an "e." According to Masta, "all Strong and Neuter Verbs end in 'mek' and the Weak Verbs in 'zik'" (74). For Day, the strong or animate ending is "meg," while the weak or inanimate ending is "zig." *The Western Abenaki Dictionary*, vol. 1 (Q.C.: Canadian Museum of Civilization, 1994), xxii. Differences in orthography are a product of how different writers, Abenaki and non-Abenaki, have undertaken the task of recording the sounds of spoken Abenaki. For Day, the "g" in the International phonetic alphabet is recorded as "g." For Masta, "g" and "k" are interchangeable. Both Masta and Day are writing about the Western Abenaki language, which, Day notes, is different from Eastern Abenaki. However, according to Hallowell's introduction to Masta's *Abenaki Indian Legends*, Masta's St. Francis Abenaki is closely related to dialects of New England peoples including "the Pigwacket, Sakoki, Aroosaguntacook, Norridgewock and Pennacook," all of which "belong to a single linguistic sub-group of the Algonkian stock. Collectively, these peoples have long been known as the Wabanaki" (Masta, *Abenaki Indian Legends*, 10). It can thus be reasonably inferred that despite the variations of orthography, region, and time, Rale's use of the "i" to designate inanimate verbs is comparable to Day and Masta's use of the same vowel. By the same token, Rale's use of "a" is comparable to Day and Masta's use of "e."

36. Tracy Neale Leavelle, "'Bad Things' and 'Good Hearts': Meditation, Meaning, and the Language of Illinois Christianity," *Church History: Studies in Christianity and Culture* 76, no. 2 (2007): 363–394.

37. Claude Allouez, *Facsimile of Pere Marquette's Illinois Prayer Book*, ed. J. L. Hubert Neilson (Quebec: Quebec Literary and Historical Society, 1908).

38. Charles E. O'Neill, *Dictionary of Canadian Biography*, vol. 2, s,v, "Gravier, Jacques," by Charles E. O'Neill, accessed February 20, 2014, http://www.biographi.ca/en/bio/gravier_jacques_2E.html.

39. Thwaites, *Jesuit Relations*, 64:233. Missionary reports in the early years of Gravier's mission are filled with lines such as this: "On the 18th of September, a child died without baptism through the obstinacy of the parents, who continually repelled me when I presented myself to administer the sacrament" (ibid., 183). Another report describes a "juggler's" embarrassment when his prediction that a child would die due to smelling a toad that carried death did not come true (ibid., 175).

40. See report on February 15, 1694, for Illinois continuing prayer during Gravier's absence (Thwaites, *Jesuit Relations*, 64:159). Also, Jesuit priest Gabriel Marest's letter to the Society of Jesus on November 9, 1712, claims that the "Illinois are much less barbarous than other Savages; Christianity and intercourse with the French have by degrees civilized them" (Thwaites, *Jesuit Relations*, 66:231).

41. Thwaites, *Jesuit Relations*, 64:163, 187.

42. Ibid., 64:195–215.

43. Ibid., 65:33–39.

44. Black, "Ojibwa Power Belief System," 142–144.

45. Thwaites, *Jesuit Relations*, 64:173, 187; Ibid., 66:233.

46. Morrissey, "'I Speak It Well,'" 617–648.

47. Claude Favre de Vaugelas, preface to *Remarques sur la langue françoise* (Paris, 1647).

48. For a useful overview of the dictionary project to come out of *l'Académie françoise*, see Mireille Pastoureau, Annie Chassagne, and Pierre Gasnault, *Le Dictionnaire de l'Académie françoise, 1694–1994: Sa naissance et son actualité* (Paris: Institut de France, 1994), especially 32–52. For a more detailed account, see Isabelle Leroy-Turcan, *Introduction à l'étude du "Dictionnaire étymologique ou origines de la langue françoise"* (Lyon: Centre d'études linguistiques Jacques Goudet, 1991); and R. L. Wagner, *Les Vocabulaires français* (Paris: Didier, 1967).

49. Jonathan Swift, *A Proposal for Correcting, Improving and Ascertaining the English Tongue* (London, 1712), 14.

50. Michael Silverstein, "Old Wine, New Ethnographic Lexicography," *Annual Review of Anthropology* 35 (2006): 481–496. Margaret C. Field shows that the multiple lexical entries for Navajo classificatory verbs is based on metaphor and conventionalized cultural knowledge (mythology and cosmology). Based on this, she proposes that as native languages become lexicalized over time they cease to be productive. An understanding of the role of metaphor is highly useful to linguists and students of Navajo as well as other native languages. "Metaphor, Mythology, and a Navajo Verb: The Role of Cultural Constructs in Lexicography of Endangered Languages," *Anthropological Linguistics* 51, nos. 3/4 (Fall and Winter 2009): 296–302.

51. "From John F. Swenson to Mr. Jeffrey H. Kaimowitz, 13 March, 1989," *Letters Re Gravier Dictionary*, American Indian Vocabulary Collection, Watkinson Library, Hartford, Conn.

52. Ibid., 27 March, 1989. In addition to Goddard, the letter notes several scholars at "a conference on Algonkian linguistics" who were dismissive of Gravier's work. Swenson attributes this to "an anti-Jesuit or anti-Christian bias" and concludes that "these people are still fighting the French and Indian war on the British side." Fortunately, to the extent that such prejudice existed, it seems to have fallen by the wayside. Carl Masthay transcribed nearly 50 percent of the dictionary, and currently the National Endowment for the Humanities has funded a program at the Myaamia Center for the translation of the rest of Gravier's *Dictionary* along with Le Boullenger's *Dictionary* (1720–1725), http://myaamiacenter.org/.

53. Thwaites, *Jesuit Relations*, 65:101–179.

54. Ibid., 65:123.

55. "Medecine" is a variation on the Old French, from Latin word *medicīna*, coming from the art of healing.

56. Thwaites, *Jesuit Relations*, 64:173.

57. Ultimately, Gravier's purpose in recording this exchange was to show how the dialogue "pleased" a "libertine" healer named Antoine, but that ultimately the indigenous power was undermined as the population began to ask Gravier to baptize them. Ibid., 64:173–177.

58. Abenaki refers to the tribes that inhabited the river basins of New Hampshire, Maine, and New Brunswick, including Pennacook, Saco, Androscoggin, Kennebec, Wawenock, Penobscot, Passamaquoddy, and Maliseet. Morrison, *The Embattled Northeast*, 5.

59. Olive Patricia Dickason, "Amerindians Between French and English in Nova Scotia, 1713–1763," *American Indian Culture and Research Journal* 10, no. 4 (1986): 31–56. In terms of aboriginal land rights, Stuart Banner makes a distinction between property and sovereignty, arguing that Anglo-Americans "consistently asserted sovereignty over American Indians," and then the question became, who owned the land? *How the Indians Lost Their Land: Law and Power on the Frontier* (Cambridge, Mass.: The Belknap Press of Harvard University Press, 2005), 7.

60. Traske, ed., *Letters of Colonel Thomas Westbrook and Others*, 90.

61. "Journal of the Rev. Joseph Baxter, of Medfield, Missionary to the Eastern Indians in 1717," *New England Historical and Genealogical Register* 21 (1867): 45–60.

62. Humphreys, *An Historical Account*, 285.

63. Society for the Propagation of the Gospel Papers, A7. 130–131, Rhodes House, Oxford, United Kingdom.

64. Humphreys, *An Historical Account*, 208.

65. Ibid., 285.

66. As Humphreys explains in his history of the SPG, "There is here no manner of Conveniency of Life for a Missionary. For four or five Months in the Year, there is scarce any stirring abroad, by Reason of the extream Coldness of the Weather, and the deep Snows that fall...there was nothing desirable to be seen, the Face of the Earth rude and uncultivated, like the wild Inhabitants" (ibid., 298).

67. John Wolfe Lydekker, *The Faithful Mohawks* (Cambridge: Cambridge University Press, 1938), 28–42.

68. Ibid., 38.

69. "He had taken great Pains to instruct some of the *Indians* who came to *Schenectady*, and had gained a good Knowledge of their Language, and with the Help of some Interpreters, had translated several Psalms, the Ten Commandments, the Creed, some Chapters of the Bible, into the *Indian* Language." Humphreys, *An Historical Account*, 286–287.

70. Monaghan, *Learning to Read*, 169–173. Freeman reported to the SPG: "I gathered several words but afterwards out of their Language I found 16 Alphabetical Letters (for they have no labial) by this Alphabet." SPG Papers, A.8:203–204.

71. Freeman, "Letter from Mr. Freeman to the Secretary, 10 October 1712," SPG Papers, Rhodes House, Oxford. A.7:203–204.

72. SPG Papers, A10:185, Rhodes House, Oxford.

73. Ibid., A9:219 and A9:355.

74. Ibid., A10:186.

75. Ibid., A9:123.

76. Ibid., A9:123–125.

77. "A Catalogue of the Bookes Sent by Mr. Barclay to Braintree in New England, August 25th 1703" contains a large folio Bible, Prayer Books, and catechistical lectures. Society of the Propagation of the Gospel Papers, B1.117, Rhodes House, Oxford.

78. SPG Papers, A11.317, Rhodes House, Oxford.

79. Humphreys, *An Historical Account*, 301–302.

80. Ibid., 215–216.

81. Ibid. See also "Clause Concerning the Negros," SPG Papers, Rhodes House, Oxford. A.9:68.

82. Humphreys, *An Historical Account*, 278.

83. Ibid., 305–311.

84. Thomas Mayhew's biography notes "they drew a *Writing* in their own Language, wherein they declared, *That as they had submitted freely to the Crown of* England, *so they resolved to assist the* English *on these* Islands *against their Enemies*" ("Some Account of Those English Ministers Who Have Successively Presided over the Work of Gospelizing the Indians on the Vineyard, and Adjacent Islands," in Mayhew, *Indian Converts*, ed. Leibman, 370).

85. Ibid., 379.

86. Mayhew, "Brief Account," 384.

87. "An Attestation by the United Ministers of Boston," in Mayhew, *Indian Converts*, ed. Leibman, 86.

88. Ibid., 90.

89. Laura Arnold Leibman, introduction to Mayhew, *Indian Converts*, 3.

90. Mayhew, *Indian Converts*, 83, 91.

91. Ibid., 323.

92. Ibid., 324.

93. This is David J. Silverman's assessment of "Cheepi," also known as "Hobbomock" or "Abbomocho." It is very interesting that Elizabeth's spectral appearance is seen as permissible evidence in *Indian Converts*, for, as Silverman points out, the English often associated Wampanoag Cheepi with the devil. "Indians, Missionaries, and Religious Translation: Creating Wampanoag Christianity in Seventeenth-Century Martha's Vineyard," *William and Mary Quarterly* 62, no. 2 (2005): 150.

94. Mayhew, *Indian Converts*, 343–344.

95. James Hammond Trumbull, *Natick Dictionary* (Washington D.C.: US Government Printing Office, 1903), 42, 49.

96. Mayhew, *Indian Converts*, 344.

97. Ibid.

98. Ibid., 91.

99. Cotton Mather, *Psalterium Americanum* (Boston: S. Kneeland, 1718), vii, xix.

100. Ibid., vi, xxiii.

101. The curious verb "enkindling" appears on p. xxiii; "Original Hebrew" and "Holy Spirit" appear on p. vii; and "blank verse" and "hidden treasures" are on the title page, which announces the aesthetic goal of the translation. Ibid.

102. Experience Mayhew, *Observations on the Indian Language*, ed. John S. H. Fogg (1722; repr., Boston: D. Clapp & Son, 1884), 10.

103. Authorized Version.

104. Sarah Cabot Sedgwick and Christina Sedgwick Marquand, *Stockbridge, 1739–1974* (Stockbridge, Mass.: The Berkshire Traveller Press, 1974).

105. Mayhew, *Observations*, 12.

106. As he writes in *Observations on the Indian Language*, "I learnt the Indian language by Rote, as I did my mother Tongue, and not Studying the Rules of it as the Lattin tongue is comonly learned" (ibid., 8).

107. Ibid., 12.

108. For a more in-depth discussion, see my chapter, "Evangelical Enlightenment," in *The Science of the Soul in Colonial New England* (Chapel Hill: University of North Carolina Press, 2011), 271–335. See also Kenneth P. Minkema, "East Windsor Conversion Relations, 1700–1725," *Connecticut Historical Society Bulletin* 51 (1986): 9–63; and "The Lynn End 'Earthquake' Relations of 1727," *New England Quarterly* 69, no. 3 (1996): 473–499.

109. Again, see "Evangelical Enlightenment,'" in Rivett, *Science of the Soul*, 271–335.

110. Carl Bridenbaugh, *Cities in the Wilderness: The First Century of Urban Life in America, 1625–1742* (New York: Capricorn, 1964), 303–363.

Chapter 5

1. Michael J. McClymond and Gerald R. McDermott, *The Theology of Jonathan Edwards* (New York: Oxford University Press, 2012), 560–561.

2. Jonathan Edwards, *Letters and Personal Writings*. Vol. 16 of *The Works of Jonathan Edwards*, ed. George S. Claghorn (New Haven, Conn.: Yale University Press, 1998), 413.

3. Samuel Hopkins, *Historical Memoirs, Relating to the Housataunnuk Indians* (Boston: Printed and Sold by S. Kneeland, 1753), 66–67.

4. Ibid., 16.

5. For a long time, the consensus was that Edwards's experience in Stockbridge was accidental, more of a writing retreat than a missionary sojourn. Scholars who take this perspective include Arthur Cushman McGiffert Jr., *Jonathan Edwards* (New York: Harper & Brothers, 1932), and Patricia J. Tracey, *Jonathan Edwards at Home and Abroad, Historical Memories, Cultural Movements, Global Horizons*, ed. David W. Kling and Douglas A. Sweeney (Columbia: University of South Carolina Press, 2003). Subsequently, scholars have examined Edwards's role as a missionary in more detail: Gerald R. McDermott, "Missions and Native Americans," in *The Princeton Companion to Jonathan Edwards*, ed. Sang Hyun Lee (Princeton, N.J.: Princeton University Press, 2005), 258–273; Rachel M. Wheeler, "Edwards as Missionary," in *The Cambridge Companion to Jonathan Edwards*, ed. Stephen J. Stein (Cambridge: Cambridge University Press, 2007), 196–214; and Wheeler, "'Friends to Your Souls': Jonathan Edwards' Indian Pastorate and the Doctrine of Original Sin," *Church History* 72, no. 4 (2003): 736–765.

6. Henry Warner Bowden, *The American Indians and Christian Missions* (Chicago: University of Chicago Press, 1981); Rachel Wheeler, *To Live upon Hope: Mohicans and Missionaries in the Eighteenth-Century Northeast* (Ithaca, N.Y.: Cornell University Press, 2008); E. Jennifer Monaghan, *Learning to Read and Write in Colonial America* (Amherst: University of Massachusetts Press, 2005), 143–191.

7. Jonathan Edwards, *The Life of David Brainerd*. Vol. 7 in *The Works of Jonathan Edwards*, ed. Norman Pettit (New Haven, Conn.: Yale University Press, 1985), 517.

8. Ibid., 518.

9. This passage from John typologically links Moses to Jesus, and the journey into the wilderness to the journey of eternal life: "And as Moses lifted up the serpent in the wilderness, even so must the Son of man be lifted up" (John 3:14, Authorized Version).

10. Edwards, *Life of David Brainerd*, 401.

11. John 3:19: "And this is the condemnation, that light is come into the world, and men loved darkness rather than light, because their deeds were evil" (Authorized Version).

12. Edwards, *Life of David Brainerd*, 512.

13. Gabriel Marest, "Journey and Mission of Father Gabriel Marest to Hudson's Bay, on the Coast of Northern Canada, in the Year 1694," in *Jesuit Relations and Allied Documents: Travels and Explorations of the Jesuit Missionaries in New France, 1610–1791*, ed. Reuben Gold Thwaites (Cleveland: Burrows Brothers, 1900), 64:263–269.

14. Edwards, *Life of David Brainerd*, 299.

15. Ibid., 138.

16. For a full examination of the Puritan theological crisis of knowledge and the testimony of faith, see Sarah Rivett, *The Science of the Soul in Colonial New England* (Chapel Hill: University of North Carolina Press, 2011).

17. Edwards, *Life of David Brainerd*, 71.

18. Appendix to [Jonathan Edwards,] *Account of the Life of the Late Reverend Mr David Brainerd* (Edinburgh, 1765), 439.

19. Ibid.

20. Ibid., 370.

21. David Brainerd, *Mirabilia Dei Inter Indicos, or the Rise and Progress of a Remarkable Work of Grace Amongst a Number of the Indians in the Provinces of New-Jersey and Pennsylvania* (Philadelphia: Printed and Sold by William Bradford in Second-Street, 1746).

22. Ibid., 33, 61, 90; Edwards, *Life of David Brainerd*, 317.

23. Brainerd, *Mirabilia*, 72.

24. Thomas Thorowgood, *Jews in America, or Probabilities That Those Indians Are Judaical* (London: Henry Brome at the Gun in Ivie-lane, 1660), 2.

25. In his hagiography of John Eliot, Cotton Mather suggests that the sheer length of Indian words is a clear indication that they "had been growing ever since Babel unto the dimensions to which they are now extended" (1:561–62). "The Triumphs of the Reformed Religion in America: Or, the Life of the Renowned John Eliot," in *Magnalia Christi Americana: Or, The Ecclesiastical History of New-England...*, ed. Thomas Robbins (Hartford, 1853).

26. Eliot and Thorowgood's text was part of a larger Christian-Hebraic movement in the seventeenth century. For an overview, see Frank E. Manuel, *The Broken Staff: Judaism Through Christian Eyes* (Cambridge, Mass.: Harvard University Press, 1992). Manuel argues that Hebraism is an under-examined humanist culture in the Renaissance and the

Reformation. He claims that the younger Buxtorf, who is the author of the lexicon that Brainerd carried with him on his travels, "initiated a new trend in the Protestant estimate of Judaism, discovering a rational philosophical Judaism" (88).

27. Robert Lowth, "Lecture 14: On the Sublime in General, and of Sublimity of Expression in Particular," in *Lectures on the Sacred Poetry of the Hebrews*, trans. G. Gregory (Boston, 1815), 191.

28. Cotton Mather, *Psalterium Americanum* (Boston: S. Kneeland, 1718), xix.

29. Hopkins, *Historical Memoirs*, 43.

30. Patrick Frazier, *The Mohicans of Stockbridge* (Lincoln: University of Nebraska Press, 1992), 1–16.

31. *At a Conference Held at Deerfield in the County of Hampshire* (Boston, 1735), 4, 5, 19.

32. Ibid., 16.

33. Hopkins, *Historical Memoirs*, 143.

34. For a history of the Stockbridge mission and how it compared to Moravian missions, see Wheeler, *To Live upon Hope*, 32–43; Sarah Cabot Sedgwick and Christina Sedgwick Marquand, *Stockbridge, 1739–1974* (Stockbridge, Mass.: Berkshire Traveller, 1974). Sedgwick and Marquand explain the meaning of Muhekaneew on p. 5.

35. Hopkins, *Historical Memoirs*, 16, 52, 58.

36. Ibid., 54.

37. Many of these rules of civility are spelled out in the list of "Conclusions and Orders made and agreed upon by divers Sachims and other principall men amongst the Indians at Concord, in the end of the eleventh moneth, Au. 1646," in Thomas Shepard, *The Clear Sun-Shine of the Gospel Breaking Forth upon the Indians in New-England* (London: R. Cotes, 1648), reprinted in *The Eliot Tracts: With Letters from John Eliot to Thomas Thorowgood and Richard Baxter*, ed. Michael P. Clark (Westport, Conn.: Praeger, 2003), 115–116.

38. John Sergeant, *A Letter from the Reverend Mr Sergeant of Stockbridge, to Dr Coleman of Boston* (Boston: Printed by Rogers and Fowle, for D. Henchman in Cornhill, 1743), 3.

39. Sedgwick and Marquand, *Stockbridge*, 1–24.

40. McClymond and McDermott, *The Theology of Jonathan Edwards*, 560.

41. Edwards, "To Sir William Pepperrell," in Claghorn, *Letters and Personal Writings*, 410.

42. "Drafts of Professions of Faith," The Jonathan Edwards Collection, Beinecke Rare Books Library, Yale University, f. 1245. I am indebted to Kenneth Minkema for sharing his transcription with me.

43. Wheeler examines how the move to Stockbridge impacted Edwards's doctrine of Original Sin. Wheeler, "Friends to Your Souls," 736–765. Her article on "Edwards as missionary" examines the effects of Edwards's life of frontier violence on his authoring of the *Life of Brainerd* and on the early Stockbridge sermons. "Edwards as Missionary," in Stein, *Cambridge Companion to Jonathan Edwards*, 196–214.

44. Edwards, "To Sir William Pepperrell," in Claghorn, *Letters and Personal Writings*, 413.

45. Edwards, "To the Reverand Isaac Hollis," in Claghorn, *Letters and Personal Writings*, 389.

46. Jonathan Edwards, "The Things that Belong to True Religion," in *Sermons and Discourses, 1743–1758*. Vol. 25 of *The Works of Jonathan Edwards*, ed. Wilson H. Kimnach (New Haven, Conn.: Yale University Press, 2006), 570–572.

47. Edwards's signed copy is preserved in the Jonathan Edwards Library at Princeton University. Rare Books, Edwards Collection, Princeton University Library.

48. Robert Millar, *History of the Propagation of Christianity, and the Overthrow of Paganism* (London: Printed for A. Millar, 1731), 2:224.

49. Gerald Robert McDermott parses these distinctions between New England, America, and the world in *One Holy and Happy Society: The Public Theology of Jonathan Edwards* (University Park: Pennsylvania University Press, 1992). Essentially, McDermott proposes that these entities are best thought of relationally, with the global apocalypse of course first and foremost in Edwards's mind. Stockbridge, Northampton, New England, and America are understood by Edwards as microcosms within this larger millennial whole.

50. Jonathan Edwards, "The Things that Belong to True Religion," in Kimnach, *Sermons and Discourses, 1743–1758*, 571.

51. Jonathan Edwards, *A History of the Work of Redemption*. Vol. 9 of *The Works of Jonathan Edwards*, ed. John F. Wilson (New Haven, Conn.: Yale University Press, 1989), 408.

52. For explanation and background, see note 21 in chapter 1.

53. Edwards, *History of the Work of Redemption*, 409.

54. Ibid., 193, 155.

55. Edwards, "Christ Is to the Heart Like a River to a Tree Planted by It," in Kimnach, *Sermons and Discourses, 1743–1758*, 602.

56. Jonathan Edwards, *Images and Shadows of Divine Things*, in *Typological Writings*, ed. Wallace E. Anderson (New Haven, Conn.: Yale University Press, 1993), 77.

57. Edwards, "God Is Infinitely Strong," in Kimnach, *Sermons and Discourses, 1743–1758*, 643.

58. This is Rhodri Lewis's argument in *Hamlet and the Vision of Darkness* (Princeton University Press, 246–248).

59. Edwards, "God Is Infinitely Strong," in Kimnach, *Sermons and Discourses, 1743–1758*, 644.

60. Frazier, *Mohicans of Stockbridge*, 21–22.

61. Gideon Hawley, Gideon Hawley Journal and Letterbook, Congregational Library, Boston, 111–114.

62. Ibid.

63. Ibid.

64. Thomas Jefferson, "'To James Madison,' Paris Jan. 12, 1789," in *8 October 1788 to 26 March 1789*. Vol. 14 of *The Papers of Thomas Jefferson*, ed. Julian P. Boyd (Princeton, N.J.: Princeton University Press), 436.

65. Edwards begins his *Observations* by saying that the Muhhekaneew Indians are called the Mohegans by the Anglo-Americans, which is a corruption of their name. The tribe that Edwards Jr. is in fact referring to here is the Mohican or Mahican tribe that lived in Stockbridge, Massachusetts. The Mohicans and Mohegans were conflated throughout the period, but Muhhekaneew is in fact the tribal name for the Mohican, meaning "people of the waters that are never still," referring to their original tribal territory in the Hudson River Valley. T. J. Brasser, "Mahican," in *Northeast*. Vol. 15 of *Handbook of North American Indian*, ed. Bruce G. Trigger (Washington, D.C.: Smithsonian Institute, 1978), 198–212; Oxford English Dictionary Online, s.v. "Mohican, n. and adj.," accessed September 15, 2013, http://www.oed.com/view/Entry/120736; Jonathan Edwards Jr., *Observations on the Language of the Muhhekaneew Indians* (London, 1788), 5, 8.

66. Lyle Campbell describes Edwards Jr.'s contribution to historical linguistics as commensurate with the work of British philologist Sir William Jones. *American Indian Languages: The Historical Linguistics of Native America* (Oxford: Oxford University Press,

1997), 29–30. Julie Tetel Andresen makes a similar connection in *Linguistics in America, 1769–1924* (New York: Routledge, 1990), 44–45. On Sir William Jones and the creation of a "new philology," see Hans Aarsleff, *The Study of Language in England, 1780–1860* (Princeton, N.J.: Princeton University Press, 1967), 115–161.

67. Edwards Jr., *Observations*, 11.

68. Jedidiah Morse, appendix to *Report to the Secretary of War…on Indian Affairs* (New Haven, Conn., 1822), 86.

69. Marion Johnson Mochon, "Stockbridge-Munsee Cultural Adaptations: 'Assimilated Indians,'" *Proceedings of the American Philosophical Society* 112, no. 3 (1968): 182–219.

70. Edwards Jr., preface to *Observations*.

71. Hawley, Journal, 79.

72. Edwards Jr., *Observations*, 16.

Chapter 6

1. Guy Frégault, *Canada: The War of the Conquest*, trans. Margaret M. Cameron (Toronto: Oxford University Press, 1969), 26–30. Frégault estimates that there were just over a million British colonists on the eve of the war and just over fifty thousand French colonists. Linda Colley explains that the mid-eighteenth-century population in British North America was the consequence of unprecedented growth as the numbers "quintupled between 1675 and 1740," in *Britons: Forging the Nation, 1707–1837* (New Haven, Conn.: Yale University Press, 1992), 70.

2. Nomenclature varies with regard to this war, as it is often called the "Seven Years War" in reference to the global conflict of which North America played only a part. Historians of Canada often refer to it as the War of Conquest.

3. Archibald Kennedy, *Serious Considerations on the Present State of the Affairs of the Northern Colonies* (New York, 1754), 11–14.

4. M. De La Galissonnière, "Memoir on the French Colonies in North America," in *Documents Relative to the Colonial History of the State of New York*, vol. 10, ed. E. B. O'Callaghan (Albany, N.Y.: Weed, Parsons, 1858), 223–224.

5. According to Frégault, "French barbarity and Canadian savagery provided inexhaustible themes for the propaganda that soon crossed the ocean and spread throughout Europe." *Canada*, 13. Linda Colley also explains that "apocalyptic interpretations of history" were pervasive during the Seven Years War, as "Britain stood in for Israel and its opponents were represented as Satan's accomplices." *Britons*, 31.

6. Philip Reading, *The Protestant's Danger and the Protestant's Duty* (Philadelphia: B. Franklin and D. Hall, 1755), 10–11.

7. James Fenimore Cooper, *The Last of the Mohicans* (Oxford: Oxford University Press, 2008), 137.

8. P. S. Garland, *The History of the City of Ogdensburg* (Ogdensburg, N.Y.: M. J. Belleville, 1927), 54.

9. Ibid., 41.

10. David Kanatawakhon Maracle, *One Thousand Useful Mohawk Words* (Guilford, Conn.: Audio-Forum, 1992), i–xxii.

11. My thanks to Julie Kim for suggesting this connection.

12. Siegfried Wenzel, *Preachers, Poets, and the Early English Lyric* (Princeton, N.J.: Princeton University Press, 1986), 41.

13. Emma Dillon, "Unwriting Medieval Song," *New Literary History* 46, no. 4 (Autumn 2015): 600.

14. Ibid., 618.

15. Ibid., 604.

16. Reuben Gold Thwaites, ed., *Jesuit Relations and Allied Documents*, vol. 68 (Cleveland: Burrows Brothers, 1901), 271–275.

17. The oldest hymn recorded in Picquet's notebook is the *Sub tuum praesidium*, which dates to approximately 250. François Picquet, "Prayer Book," Ruggles Collection, Newberry Library, Chicago, Ill.

18. Cotton Mather, *Psalterium Americanum* (Boston: S. Kneeland, 1718), vii.

19. Cotton Mather, *Magnalia Christi Americana: Or, the Ecclesiastical History of New-England...*, ed. Thomas Robbins (Hartford, 1853), 1:407.

20. Preface to *The Book of Common Prayer...Translated into the Mohawk Language*, trans. Joseph Brant (London, 1787), i–ii.

21. On William Johnson's prayer book, see E. Jennifer Monaghan, *Learning to Read and Write in Colonial America* (Amherst: University of Massachusetts Press, 2005), 184–185. John Norton's translation of the Gospel of John is in the Cambridge University Library.

22. Gary Tomlinson, *The Singing of the New World: Indigenous Voice in the Era of European Contact* (Cambridge: Cambridge University Press, 2007), 11–18.

23. Margaret Bent, "The Late-Medieval Motet," in *Companion to Medieval and Renaissance Music*, ed. Tess Knighton and David Fallows (New York: Schirmer, 1992), 114–119.

24. "Meet the Masters: Mohawk Choir of St. Regis," Feb. 28, 2000, North Country Public Radio, http://www.northcountrypublicradio.org/news/story/3581/20000228/meet-the-masters-mohawk-choir-of-st-regis.

25. Cherokee, Choctaw, Comanche, Creek, Hawaiian, Hopi, Kiowa, Mohawk, Navajo, Oneida, Ojibwe, Seminole, Sioux, Tewa (Tano), and Yup'ik. See *Beautiful Beyond: Christian Songs in Native Languages*, produced by Howard Bass, National Museum of the American Indian, Smithsonian Folkways Recordings, 2004, compact disc.

26. Horatio Hale, *The Iroquois Book of Rites* (Philadelphia: D.G. Brinton, 1883).

27. *The Book of Common Prayer...Translated into the Mohawk Language*, trans. Brant, 476.

28. Edward Gibbon, *The History of the Decline and Fall of the Roman Empire*, vol. 1, ed. David Womersley (New York: Penguin, 2005), 737–738.

29. Robert Lahise, *Dictionary of Canadian Biography*, vol. 4, s.v. "Picquet, Francois," accessed March 3, 2016, http://www.biographi.ca/en/bio/picquet_francois_4E.html.

30. Frégault notes that Lévis was third in a succession of commanders appointed by the French ministry of war, preceded by Dieskau and Montcalm. Frégault, *Canada*, 61.

31. Chevalier De Lévis, *Journal Des Campagnes Du Chevalier De Lévis en Canada de 1756 a 1760* (Montreal: C. O. Beuchemin & Fils), 1:189–198.

32. Ibid., 2:186–187.

33. For an overview and analysis of Maillard's missionary role as a secular priest, see Maxime Morin, "L'abbé Pierre Maillard: Une figure missionaire emblématique du XVII siècle acadien," *Études d'histoire religieuse* 75 (2009): 39–54.

34. There is not a huge amount of evidence to support this claim for an indigenous system of writing. However, a few scholars of Mi'kmaq have posited that the ideograms developed by Le Clercq do indeed come from an indigenous system of writing. See David

L. Schmidt and Murdena Marshall, eds., *Mi'Kmaq Hieroglyphic Prayers: Readings in North America's First Indigenous Script* (Halifax: Nimbus, 1995); and, for information on some pre-Columbian petroglyphs that support an indigenous origin of the hieroglyphs, see Ruth Holmes Whitehead, "A New Micmac Petroglyph Site," *Occasional: An Occasional Journal for Nova Scotia Museum* 13, no. 1 (1992): 7–12.

35. Most of this material is housed at the Archives de l'archidiocèse de Québec. A microfilm copy can be found at the American Philosophical Society in Philadelphia.

36. Bruce Greenfield argues that Maillard's use of the hieroglyphics was hierarchical and conservative. Maillard wanted to control the flow of information by keeping his linguistic knowledge separate from this evangelization tool. "The Mi'kmaq Hieroglyphic Prayer Book: Writing and Christianity in Maritime Canada, 1675–1921," in *The Language Encounter in the Americas, 1492–1800*, ed. Edward G. Gray and Norman Fiering (New York: Berghahn, 2003), 189–211.

37. [Pierre Maillard,] *An Account of the Customs and Manners of the Micmakis and Maricheets Savage Nations, Now Dependent on the Government of Cape-Breton, from an Original French Manuscript-Letter; Never Published* (London: Printed for S. Hooper and A. Morley, 1758), 33–34.

38. Jean-Jacques Rousseau, "Essay on the Origin of Languages," 1781, in *Collected Writings of Rousseau*, vol. 7, trans. and ed. John T. Scott (Hanover, N.H.: University Press of New England, 1998), 303–304.

39. [Maillard,] *Account*, 2–3.

40. "A l'aide de ces différens caractères, ils apprennent en très-peu de temps tout ce qu'ils veulent apprendre; et quand ils ont une fois bien mis dans leur tête la figure et la valeur de chaque caractère, ils nomment avec une facilité étonnante tout ce qui se trouve écrit de même dans leurs cahiers." Pierre Maillard, "Lettre de M. l'abbé Maillard sur les missions de l'Acadie et particulièrement sur les missions micmaques," in *Les Soirees Canadiennes*, vol. 3 (Quebec: Brousseau, 1863), 355–366.

41. "Le caracter grec 8 se prononce ou, ainsi m8 pronnoncez mou," in *Instruction sur la langue Mickmaque*, ed. Joseph Bellenger (Philadelphia, 1814). Publication comes from a manuscript prepared by Maillard on the structure of the language, orthography, nouns, pronouns, and numerals, with more extensive commentary on verb conjugation.

42. [Maillard,] *Account*, 33–34.

43. Nicolas Dew, *Orientalism in Louis XIV's France* (Oxford: Oxford University Press, 2009); D. E. Mungello, "European Philosophical Responses to Non-European Culture: China," in *The Cambridge History of Seventeenth-Century Philosophy*, vol. 1, ed. Daniel Garber and Michael Ayers (Cambridge: Cambridge University Press, 1998), 87–100; David Porter, *Ideographia: The Chinese Cipher in Early Modern Europe* (Stanford, Calif.: Stanford University Press, 2001).

44. [Maillard,] *Account*, 33–34.

45. Ibid., 34–35.

46. Rousseau, "Essay on the Origin of Languages," 318.

47. Preface to [Maillard,] *Account*, ii–iii.

48. [Maillard,] *Account*, 13–14, 2–3.

49. Maillard, "Lettre de M. l'abbé Maillard," 319.

50. On the lasting impact of Maillard's hieroglyphic system among the Eskonsi community in Cape Breton, see Schmidt and Marshall, *Mi'Kmaq Hieroglyphic Prayers*.

51. This record is Maillard's *Lettre de M. L'Abbé Maillard Sur Les Missions De L'Acadie et Particulièrement sur Les Missions Micmacques*. The letter existed only in manuscript in the eighteenth century but it has been reprinted in *Soirées Canadiennes* 3 (1863): 289–426.

52. "Rev. John Ogilvie, Albany NY, July 27, 1750," Society for the Propagation of the Gospel Papers, Rhodes House, Oxford, England, 102.3.

Chapter 7

1. Lewis and Clark amassed what was by far the largest collection of western Indian languages west of the Mississippi. Unfortunately, this portion of Jefferson's collection was a casualty of the 1809 robbery. Anthony J. C. Wallace, *Jefferson and the Indians: The Tragic Fate of the First Americans* (Cambridge: The Belknap Press of Harvard University Press, 1999), 151. Vocabulary lists discussed in the chapter come from the American Indian Vocabulary Collection, American Philosophical Society, Philadelphia, Pa.

2. Thomas Jefferson, " 'To James Madison,' Paris Jan. 12, 1789," in *Papers of Thomas Jefferson*, electronic edition, ed. Barbara Oberg and Jefferson J. Looney (Charlottesville, Va.: University of Virginia Press, 2009), 14.436 hereafter cited as Jefferson Papers.

3. Wallace, *Jefferson and the Indians*, 152.

4. Thomas Jefferson, *Notes on the State of Virginia*, ed. William Peden (Chapel Hill: University of North Carolina Press, 1955), 101.

5. Even Albert Gallatin, in creating the first ethnographic map of North America from word lists compiled by traders, agents, naturalists, and missionaries, considered the southern regions of the United States "as to language terra incognita." Quoted in " 'Must not their languages be savage and barbarous like them?': Philology, Indian Removal, and Race Science," *Journal of the Early Republic* 30 no.4 (Winter 2010): 506–532. Jefferson was one of the first to begin to compile linguistic data from these regions, writing to Benjamin Hawkins in 1800 with a request for information on "the great Southern languages, Cherokee, Creek, Choctaw, and Chickasaw" (*Jefferson Papers*, 31.435).

6. Diane Pearson, "Medical Diplomacy and the American Indian," *Wicazo Sa Review* 19, no. 1 (2004): 105–130.

7. Jefferson expresses this view throughout his letters, as in his letter to Hawkins, which states, "I have long believed we can never get any information of the antient [*sic*] history of the Indians, of their descent & filiation, but from a knowledge & comparative view of their languages" (ibid.). Eighteenth-century stadial history emerged from the writings of Giambattista Vico, Adam Ferguson, William Robertson, and Dugald Stewart who proposed four main stages in the rise of civil society: savage, barbarian, civil (agricultural), and over-civilized (commerce driven). For an explanation of the impact of stadial history on American literature, see George Dekker, *The American Historical Romance* (Cambridge: Cambridge University Press, 1987).

8. *Jefferson Papers*, 10.316, 31.435, 14.436, 29.224.

9. Patricia Cohen, "Indian Tribes Go in Search of Their Lost Languages," *New York Times*, April 6, 2010.

10. Ives Goddard, "Eastern Algonquian Languages," *Handbook of American Indians*, ed. Bruce Trigger (Washington D.C., Smithsonian Institute, 1978), 15:70–77.

11. Anthony J. C. Wallace, *Jefferson and the Indians: The Tragic Fate of the First Americans* (Cambridge, Mass.: The Belknap Press of Harvard University Press, 1999), 146, 161.

12. Daniel Droixhe, *La linguistique et l'appel de l'histoire, 1600–1800* (Geneva: Droz, 1978).

13. Constantin François Volney, *View of the Climate and Soil of the United States of America* (London: Printed for J. Johnson, 1804), A3, 403, 480.

14. Thomas R. Trautmann, *Language and Nations* (Berkeley: University of California Press, 2006), 1–12.

15. James Adair, *The History of American Indians*, ed. Kathryn E. Holland Braund (Tuscaloosa: University of Alabama Press, 2005), 295, 284, 283.

16. Marcus Tomalin, *Romanticism and Linguistic Theory* (New York: Palgrave Macmillan, 2009); Matthew Lauzon, *Signs of Light* (Ithaca, N.Y.: Cornell University Press, 2010).

17. Volney, *View of the Climate and Soil*, 484, 477.

18. Trautman, *Language and Nations*, 1–13.

19. Lord James Monboddo, *Of the Origin and Progress of Language* (Edinburgh: Printed for J. Balfour, 1809), v.

20. Jefferson, *Notes*, 101.

21. Keith Thomson, *Jefferson's Shadow* (New Haven, Conn.: Yale University Press, 2012); Peter Thompson, "'Judicious Neology': The Imperative Paternalism in Thomas Jefferson's Linguistic Studies," *Early American Studies* 1, no. 2 (2003): 187–224.

22. According to Brian Steele, this assertion of the American Indian as an embryo of the modern American character was in and of itself a refutation of Buffon. Jefferson argues that American Indians were less advanced than Europeans but that they simply had not evolved. This was not an intrinsic deficiency as European scientists claimed (58–63). *Thomas Jefferson and American Nationhood* (New York: Cambridge University Press, 2012). See also Thomson, "Judicious Neology," 71–72.

23. "Hugh Williamson to Thomas Jefferson, 3 March, 1798," *Jefferson Papers*, 30.158.

24. Wallace, *Jefferson and the Indians*, 156.

25. John Bayard, *Charter of the American Philosophical Society* (granted in 1780), in *Laws and Rules of the Administration and Order* (Philadelphia: Printed for the American Philosophical Society, 1910), 3–4; Julie Tetel Andresen, *Linguistics in America, 1769–1924* (New York: Routledge, 1990), 52.

26. Christopher P. Iannini, *Fatal Revolutions* (Chapel Hill: Published for the Omohundro Institute of Early American History and Culture, 2012).

27. Christopher P. Ianini, "*Notes on the State of Virginia* and the Natural History of the Haitian Revolution," *Clio: A Journal of Literature, History, and the Philosophy of History* 40, no. 1 (2010): 63–85; and Sandra Rebok, "Enlightened Correspondents," *Virginia Magazine of History and Biography* 116, no. 4 (2008): 328–369.

28. *Jefferson Papers*, 20.467; American Indian Vocabulary Collection, fol. 14.

29. *Jefferson Papers*, 20.467.

30. Ibid.; American Indian Vocabulary Collection, fol. 14.

31. Campbell, *American Indian Languages*, 1997; Swadesh 1952, 452.

32. *Jefferson Papers*, 13.651, 11.683, 14.436, 1.555–557.

33. Sylvia Murr, *L'Inde Philosophique entre Boussuet et Voltaire* (Paris: École française d'Extrême-Orient, 1987).

34. Trautmann, *Language and Nations*, 21–41.

35. *Jefferson Papers*, 1.555–557.

36. *Jefferson Papers*, 30.81.

37. Trautmann, *Language and Nations*, 1–35.

38. David Zeisberger, *A Grammar of the Language of the Lenni Lenape or Delaware Indians*, American Philosophical Society, Philadelphia, 1816, 10, 20. Although this manuscript was not printed by the APS until 1816, Zeisberger's manuscripts were in circulation long before. Quite possibly, Jefferson encountered such theories of the linguistic exceptionalism of indigenous tongues. Herman Wellenreuther and Carola Wessel, *The Moravian Mission Diaries of David Zeisberger, 1772–1781* (University Park: Pennsylvania State University Press, 2005).

39. Charles Miller, *Jefferson and Nature* (Baltimore, Md.: Johns Hopkins University Press, 1988), 1–20.

40. *Jefferson Papers*, 10.316.

41. Benjamin Smith Barton, *New Views of the Origin of the Tribes and Nations of America* (Philadelphia: Printed for the Author by John Bioren, 1797), xlv–lxiv; lxxxix.

42. Ibid., 81.

43. Zeisberger 1816, 7, 8.

44. Hilary E. Wyss, *English Letters and Indian Literacies* (Philadelphia: University of Pennsylvania Press, 2012), 33–37, 112, 116.

45. Althea Bass, *Cherokee Messenger* (Norman: University of Oklahoma Press, 1936), 34.

46. Pickering cites Jones's "Dissertation on the Orthography of Asiatick Words in Roman Letters" and Volney's "L'alphabet européen appliqué aux langues asiatiques." John Pickering, *An Essay on a Uniform Orthography for the Indian Languages of North America* (Cambridge: Hilliard and Metcalf, 1820), 2, 9.

47. "To David Campbell, Philadelphia, March 14, 1800," *Jefferson Papers*, 31.433.

48. *Jefferson Papers*, 20.467.

49. Sir William Jones, "A Dissertation on the Orthography of Asiatick Words in Roman Letters," *The Works of Sir William Jones*, vol. 3 (London: John Stockdale, 1807), 258.

50. "To William Dunbar, Monticello in Virginia, June 24, 1799," *Jefferson Papers*, 31.137.

51. American Indian Vocabulary Collection, fols. 7, 8, 15, 16; see figs. 5a and b.

52. *Jefferson Papers*, 31.433.

53. "Creek agency, July 12, 1800," *Jefferson Papers*, 32.50.

54. "Philadelphia, March 14, 1800," Jefferson Papers, 31.43.

55. *Jefferson Papers*, 31.433.

56. American Indian Vocabulary Collection, fol. 5.

57. "November 6, 1800," *Jefferson Papers*, 32.243.

58. Willard Walker and James Sarbaugh, "The Early History of the Cherokee Syllabary," *Ethnohistory* 40, no. 1 (1993): 70–94.

59. Janine Scancarelli, "Cherokee," in *Native Languages of the Southeastern United States*, ed. Heather K. Hardy and Janine Scancarelli (Lincoln: University of Nebraska Press, 2005), 351–384.

60. Marcin Kilarski, "Cherokee Classificatory Verbs," *Historiographia Linguistica* 36, no. 1 (2009): 39–73.

61. Benjamin Lee Whorf, "An American Indian Model of the Universe," in *Language, Thought, and Reality*, ed. John B. Carroll (Cambridge, Mass.: MIT Press, 1956); and Stephanie Inglis, "400 Years of Linguistic Contact Between the Mi'kmaq and the English and the Interchange of Two World Views," *Canadian Journal of Native Studies* 24, no. 2 (2004): 389–402.

62. Samuel L. Knapp, *Lectures on American Literature* (New York: Elam Bliss, 1827), 26.

63. American Indian Vocabulary Collection, fol. 16; see Fig. 7a.

64. C. A. Weslager, *The Nanticoke Indians* (Newark: University of Delaware Press, 1983), 148–164, 194–202.

65. *Jefferson Papers*, 24.389.

66. Lisa Brooks, *The Common Pot* (Minneapolis: University of Minnesota Press, 2008), 3–4.

67. Weslager, *The Nanticoke Indians*, 13–20.

68. James H. Howard, "The Nanticoke-Delaware Skeleton Dance," *American Indian Quarterly* 2, no. 1 (1975): 3.

69. *Jefferson Papers*, 30.238.

70. Blackhawk, 145–175; Wallace, *Jefferson and the Indians*, 161–189.

71. Many historians have written about the evolution from the early national US treaty system to the removal policy of the nineteenth century. Jennings dubbed this "the deed game" (128–145). Blackhawk argues that this focus on the US history of deeds and treaties has papered over a long history of colonial violence. See also Banner, *How the Indians Lost Their Land*; and Leonard J. Sadosky, *Revolutionary Negotiations: Indians, Empires, and Diplomats in the Founding of America* (Charlottesville: University of Virginia Press, 2009).

72. "Minutes of a Conference Between Brigadier General James Wilkinson, Benjamin Hawkins & Andrew Pickins," Foster 2003, 397–407.

73. Thomas Jefferson, *Notes on the State of Virginia*, ed. William Peden (Chapel Hill: University of North Carolina Press, 1955), 101.

74. George Washington 1788.

75. Benjamin Smith Barton, *New Views of the Origin of the Tribes and Nations of America* (Philadelphia: Printed for the Author by John Bioren, 1797), lix.

Chapter 8

1. James Fenimore Cooper, *The Last of the Mohicans*, in *The Leatherstocking Tales*, vol. 1 (New York: Literary Classics of the United States, 1985), 700–701.

2. Ibid.

3. Thomas Philbrick, "Cooper's *The Pioneers*: Origins and Structure," in *James Fenimore Cooper: A Collection of Critical Essays*, ed. Wayne Fields (Englewood Cliffs, N.J.: Prentice-Hall, 1979), 58–79.

4. George Dekker, *The American Historical Romance* (New York: Cambridge University Press, 1987), 74.

5. Philbrick, "Cooper's The Pioneers," 45–48.

6. Dagobert D. Runes, ed., *The Selected Writings of Benjamin Rush* (New York: Philosophical Library, 1947), 254. I wish to thank Julie Kim for pointing out this reference to me.

7. Alan Taylor, *William Cooper's Town: Power and Persuasion on the Frontier of the Early American Republic* (New York: Alfred A. Knopf, 1995), 54–56.

8. James Fenimore Cooper, *The Pioneers*, in *The Leatherstocking Tales*, vol. 1 (New York: Literary Classics of the United States, 1985), 212.

9. Ibid., 234.

10. Much has been made of Natty Bumppo's silence. David Simpson reads it as an image of a "state of pre-linguistic innocence," making both Natty and the Indians a "vanishing breed." I read Natty's silence quite differently, as a mark of post contact linguistic trauma where the inadequacy of words and, the profound erasure of indigenous tongues, thwart

efforts toward coherent articulation. *The Politics of American English, 1776–1850* (New York: Oxford University Press, 1986): 197.

11. Mark Twain, "Fenimore Cooper's Literary Offenses," *North American Literary Review* 161, no. 464 (July 1895), 1–12.

12. Jerome McGann, "Fenimore Cooper's Anti-aesthetic and the Representation of Conflicted History," *Modern Language Quartery* 73, no. 2 (2012): 123–155.

13. Cooper draws from Heckewelder's definition of the Lenni Lenape as an "unmixed people" and goes on to explain that several communities descended from this original people, including "the tribe that possessed the country which now composes the southwestern parts of New-England, and that portion of New-York that lies east of the Hudson, and the country even much farther to the south, was a mighty people, called the 'Mahicanni,' or, more commonly, the 'Mohicans.' The latter word has since been corrupted by the English, into 'Mohegan.'" Cooper, preface to *Last of the Mohicans*, 470.

14. On romantic Indians, see Kate Flint, *The Transatlantic Indian, 1776–1930* (Princeton, N.J.: Princeton University Press, 2009).

15. On Heckewelder's influence on Cooper, see Simpson, *Politics of American English*, 216–226; and Steven Blakemore, "Strange Tongues: Cooper's Fiction of Language in *The Last of the Mohicans*," *Early American Literature* 19, no. 1 (1984): 21–41.

16. Cooper, preface to *Last of the Mohicans*, 470–471.

17. Cooper, *Last of the Mohicans*, 544–545.

18. Jean-Jacques Rousseau, *Essay on the Origin of Languages*; and Johann Gottfried Herder, *Essay on the Origin of Language*, in *On the Origin of Language*, trans. John H. Moran and Alexander Gode (New York: Frederick Ungar, 1966); Adam Smith, *Theory of Moral Sentiments. To Which Is Added a Dissertation on the Origin of Languages* (London: Printed for A. Millar, A. Kincaid and J. Bell in Edinburgh, 1767); James Monboddo, *Of the Origin and Progress of Language* (Edinburgh: Printed for J. Balfour, 1773–1792); Wilhelm Von Humboldt, *On Language: The Diversity of Human Language-Structure and Its Influence on the Mental Development of Mankind*, trans. Peter Heath with an intro. by Hans Aarsleff (New York: Cambridge University Press, 1988).

19. Eighteenth-century language origin theory not only replaced biblical linguistics but also served as the foundation for new philosophical notions of human nature, culture, and society. See Catherine L. Hobbs, *Rhetoric on the Margins of Modernity: Vico, Condillac, Monboddo* (Carbondale: Southern Illinois University Press, 2002), 10–13; Thomas R. Trautmann, *Language and Nations: The Dravidian Proof in Colonial Madras* (Berkeley: University of California Press, 2006), 12–35; Michael Losonksy, *Linguistic Turns in Modern Philosophy* (Cambridge: Cambridge University Press, 2006), 17–21.

20. See Kenneth Cmiel's article, "'A Broad Fluid Language of Democracy': Discovering the American Idiom," *Journal of American History* 79, no. 3 (1992): 913–936.

21. Edwin James, *Account of an Expedition from Pittsburgh to the Rocky Mountains*, vol. 1 (Philadelphia, 1822), 490–491.

22. James Edwin, "Part of a Manuscript Note Book of Dr. Edwin James, Comprising a Comparative Vocabulary & Phrases, Menomini & Ojibway, and a Sioux-Dakota Vocabulary Tr(anslated). Written About 1825–6," American Indian Collection, Watkinson Library, Hartford, Conn.

23. James Fenimore Cooper, *The Prairie*, in *The Leatherstocking Tales*, vol. 1 (New York: Literary Classics of the United States, 1985), 1266.

24. Ibid.

25. See Gregory S. Jackson, "A Game Theory of Evangelical Fiction," *Critical Inquiry* 39, no. 3 (Spring 2013): 451–485.

26. Cooper, *The Prairie*, 1282.

27. Ibid., 1285.

28. Ibid., 1283.

29. Ibid.

30. Ibid., 1292.

31. Ibid., 1142.

32. Is it a small thing that thou hast brought us up out of a land that floweth with milke and hony, to kill us in the wildernesse, except thou make they selfe altogether a prince ouer us?" Numbers 16.13, *King James Version.* I am indebted to my colleague, Donald Vance Smith, for alerting me to this reading.

33. Ibid., 1296.

34. Ibid., 1302–1303.

35. Ibid., 1310.

36. Ibid., 1317.

37. Ibid., 1291.

38. Ibid., 1095.

39. Ibid., 1241.

40. Ibid., 1213.

41. Review of *Archaeologia Americana: Transactions and Collections of the American Antiquarian Society*, vol. 2, *North American Review* 45, no. 96 (July 1837): 34–35.

42. William Gilmore Simms, *Views and Reviews in American Literature, History and Fiction* (New York: Wiley and Putnam, 1845), 106.

43. Both Trowbridge and Schoolcraft were commissioned by Lewis Cass to collect information on American Indian languages in order to disprove Peter Du Ponceau's theory of the intrinsic beauty and aesthetics of indigenous languages. Sean P. Harvey, *Native Tongues: Colonialism and Race from Encounter to the Reservation* (Cambridge, Mass.: Harvard University Press, 2015), 148–152. Both Trowbridge and Schoolcraft instead ended up being fascinated by the complexities of the languages that they encountered. Schoolcraft, for example, describes the "art of picture writing" in "Considerations on the Art of Picture Writing, and the System of Mnemonic Symbols of the North American Indians," in *Oneóta, or Characteristics of the Red Race of America* (New York: Wiley & Putnam, 1845), 27–35.

44. Schoolcraft, "Picture Writing" 30.

45. Eleazer Williams, *Papers, 1758–1858*, Box 2, fol. 15, Ayer Collection, Newberry Library, Chicago.

46. D. H. Lawrence, *Studies in Classic American Literature*, ed. Ezra Greenspan, Lindeth Vasey, and John Worthen (Cambridge: Cambridge University Press, 2003), 52–54.

47. Cooper, *The Prairie*, 887.

48. Ibid., 881.

49. Ibid., 884.

50. Ibid., 894.

51. Ibid., 884.

52. William Cullen Bryant, "The Prairies," in *Nineteenth-Century American Poetry*, ed. William C. Spengemnn and Jessica F. Roberts (New York: Penguin, 1996), 22.

53. Cooper, *Last of the Mohicans*, 877. Ives Goddard argues that Cooper was the first author to popularize the terms "red man" or "redskin." " 'I Am a Red-Skin': The Adoption of

a Native American Expression (1769–1826)," *European Review of Native American Studies* 19, no. 2 (2005): 15–16. The "red man's time" refers to a prevailing early to mid-nineteenth-century theory following the discovery of the mounds in the Midwest that a lost race of Mound Builders occupied the North American continent prior to the "red man's" arrival. Bryant equates the disappearance of the Mound Builders with the arrival of the "red man" in his poem "The Prairies." Robert Silverberg, *Mound Builders of Ancient America: The Archaeology of a Myth* (Greenwich, Conn.: New York Graphic Society, 1968), 6, 86–88.

54. Cooper, *Last of the Mohicans*, 473.

55. Herder, *On the Origin of Language*, 135–165.

56. Jefferson's Logan remained an integral feature of early nineteenth-century ideas about Indian speech, as the mention of both Jefferson's work on Indian Vocabularies and Logan's speech in the *Transactions of the Historical Literary Committee of the American Philosophical Society* indicates. Wm. Tilghman, "Report of the Historical and Literary Committee to the American Philosophical Society," in *Transactions of the Historical Literary Committee of the American Philosophical Society*, vol. 1 (Philadelphia, 1819), xiii–xiv.

57. Cooper, *Last of the Mohicans*, 499.

58. The line reads, "During this eulogium on the rare production of his native poets, the stranger had drawn the book from his pocket." Cooper, *Last of the Mohicans*, 496–497. On the theory of the psalms in the New England tradition, see Cotton Mather's introduction to the *Psalterium Americanum* (Boston: Samuel Kneeland, 1718). The psalms are referred to as a miniature Bible, bespeaking the "*Tongue of Angels*," which more than anything "upon Earth…bring down the inextinguishable *Fire of* GOD from Heaven" (*Psalterium Americanum*, ii, xix). The importance of this book for encapsulating the purity of the spiritual word leads to the translation of the psalms into Massachusett at a time when the Massachusett language was believed to carry spiritual resonance with Hebrew. See *The Massachusett Psalter: Or, Psalms of David…in Columns of Indian and English* (Boston: Printed by B. Green and J. Printer, 1709). For a discussion of Protestant psalters in the American tradition and how they relate to missionary linguistics, see chapters 2 and 6.

59. William Cullen Bryant, "An Indian at the Burial-Place of His Fathers," quoted in Cooper, *Last of the Mohicans*, 499.

60. Cooper, *Last of the Mohicans*, 499.

61. Ibid., 701–702.

62. Ibid., 540, 544.

63. Ibid., 531–532.

64. Ralph Waldo Emerson, *Nature*, in *Emerson: Essays and Lectures* (New York: Literary Classics of the United States, 1983), 20.

65. Ralph Waldo Emerson, "The Poet," in *Emerson: Essays and Lectures* (New York: Literary Classics of the United States, 1983), 456–457.

66. Jean de Brébeuf, *Jesuit Relations and Allied Documents*, vol. 10, ed. Reuben Gold Thwaites (Cleveland: Burrows Brothers, 1901), 257–259.

67. Laura J. Murray, "Joining Signs with Words: Missionaries, Metaphors, and the Massachusett Language," *New England Quarterly* 74, no. 1 (2001): 62–93; and Jane T. Merritt, "Metaphor, Meaning, and Misunderstanding: Language and Power on the Pennsylvania Frontier," in *Contact Points: American Frontiers from the Mohawk Valley to the Mississippi, 1750–1830*, ed. Andrew R. L. Cayton and Fredrika J. Teute (Chapel Hill: University of North Carolina Press, 1998), 60–87.

68. Philip J. Deloria, *Playing Indian* (New Haven, Conn.: Yale University Press, 1998), 32–35, 65–66.

69. James Geary, *I Is an Other: The Secret Life of Metaphor and How It Shapes the Way We See the World* (New York: HarperCollins, 2011), 5–16.

70. There is an extensive literature on this, but for a succinct redaction of indigenous cosmologies in North America, see Kenneth M. Morrison, "The Cosmos as Intersubjective: The Native American Other-than-human Persons," in *Indigenous Religions: A Companion*, ed. Graham Harvey (New York: Cassell, 2000), 23–36. See also Joan M. Vastokas, "History Without Writing: Pictorial Narratives in Native North America," in *Gin Das Winan: Documenting Aboriginal History in Ontario*, ed. Dale Standen and David McNab (Toronto: Champlain Society, 1994), 48–65; and Bruce White, "Encounters with Spirits: Ojibwa and Dakota Theories about the French and Their Merchandise," *Ethnohistory* 41, no. 3 (1994): 369–405.

71. John Gottlieb Ernestus Heckewelder Letters, 1816–1822, to Peter Stephen Du Ponceau, American Philosophical Society, Philadelphia, Pa., 58.

72. Aristotle, *The Rhetoric and Poetics of Aristotle*, trans. Ingram Bywater (New York: Modern Library, 1954), 251. Quoted in Geary, *I Is an Other*, 8.

73. Cadwallader Colden, *The History of the Five Indian Nations* (Ithaca, N.Y.: Cornell University Press, 1958), xi. Quoted in Deloria, *Playing Indian*, 206n54.

74. Hugh Blair, *Lectures on Rhetoric and Belles Lettres* (Philadelphia, 1784), 122–123.

75. Heckewelder to Du Ponceau, 41.

76. Ibid., 24.

77. John Gottlieb Heckewelder, *An Account of the History, Manners and Customs of the Indian Nations Who Once Inhabited Pennsylvania and the Neighbouring States*, Transactions of the Historical and Literary Committee of the American Philosophical Society, vol. 1 (Philadelphia, 1819), 125, 129.

78. Ibid., 129.

79. John Gottlieb Ernestus Heckewelder Letters, 1816–1822, to Peter Stephen Du Ponceau, American Philosophical Society, Philadelphia, Pa., 19–34.

80. David Abram, *The Spell of the Sensuous: Perception and Language in a More-Than-Human World* (New York: Pantheon, 1996), 21–31.

81. Maurice Merleau-Ponty, *Phenomenology of Perception*, trans. Colin Smith (London: Routledge and Kegan Paul, 1962), ix–x, quoted in Abram, *Spell of the Sensuous*, 36. The phenomenological tradition that Abram identifies begins with Vico and ends with Merleau-Ponty. See especially, Merleau-Ponty, "The Body as Expression, and Speech," in *Phenomenology of Perception*, 202–233.

82. Heckewelder, *History, Manner, and Customs*, 129.

83. Adam Smith, *Theory of Moral Sentiments. To Which Is Added a Dissertation on the Origin of Languages* (London: Printed for A. Millar, A. Kincaid and J. Bell in Edinburgh, 1767), 463.

84. Colleen Glenney Boggs makes this observation in her chapter on Cooper in *Transnationalism and American Literature: Literary Translation, 1773–1892* (New York: Routledge, 2007), 61–89.

85. Cooper, *The Pioneers*, 165.

86. Ibid., 84.

87. James Fenimore Cooper, *The Deerslayer*, in *The Leatherstocking Tales*, vol. 2 (New York: Literary Classics of the United States, 1985), 600.

88. Cooper, *The Prairie*, 963–964. Richard Slotkin uses this expression of the "Man Without a Cross" as the title to his chapter on Cooper in *Regeneration Through Violence*, using it as a metaphor for the conflict of cultures that Cooper confronted through his *Leatherstocking Tales*. Richard Slotkin, *Regeneration Through Violence: The Mythology of the American Frontier, 1600–1860* (Middletown, Conn.: Wesleyan University Press), 466–516.

89. Cooper, *The Prairie*, 909.

90. Georg Lukacs, *The Historical Novel*, trans. Hannah Mitchell and Stanley Mitchell (Boston: Beacon, 1963), 72.

91. Leslie A. Fiedler, *Love and Death in the American Novel* (Champaign, Ill.: Dalkery Archive, 1998), 192–214.

92. Cooper, *The Prairie*, 950–951, 938.

93. Ibid., 887.

94. Ibid., 925.

95. This notion of Natty Bumppo's journey as culminating in judgment is indebted to Wayne Fields's reading of *The Prairie* in "Beyond Definition: A Reading of *The Prairie*," in *James Fenimore Cooper: A Collection of Critical Essays*, ed. Wayne Fields (Englewood Cliffs, N.J.), 107.

96. The passage that this line is from was not in the first edition, but was added in 1844. The page number cited for it corresponds to the footnotes of the Library of America edition, where they offer the added text. Cooper, *The Prairie*, 1345n.

Coda

1. Lydia Huntley Sigourney, "Indian Names," accessed October 5, 2016, http://www. poetryfoundation.org

2. See Kate Flint, *The Transatlantic Indian, 1776–1930* (Princeton, N.J.: Princeton University Press, 2009), 26–52; Helen Carr, *Inventing the American Primitive: Politics, Gender, and the Representation of Native American Literary Traditions, 1780–1936* (New York: New York University Press, 1996); and David Simpson, "Romantic Indians: Robert Southey's Distinctions," *The Wordsworth Circle* 38 (2007): 20–25.

3. Giambattista Vico, *The First New Science*, ed. Leon Pompa (Cambridge: Cambridge University Press, 2002), XXIV: 307.

4. Hugh Blair, *Lectures on Rhetoric and Belles Lettres* (Philadelphia: Aitken, 1784), 55.

5. Vico, *The First New Science*, XXIV: 180.

6. M. H. Abrams, *The Mirror and the Lamp: Romantic Theory and the Critical Tradition* (New York: Oxford University Press, 1953), 78–84.

7. Vico, "Method," chapter 2, 404, in *The New Science* (New York: Penguin, 1999), 159.

8. Blair, *Lectures on Rhetoric and Belles Lettres*, 123.

9. Abrams, *The Mirror and the Lamp*, 52, 78.

10. *Transactions of the Historical and Literary Committee of the American Philosophical Society*, vol. 1 (Philadelphia: Printed and Published by Abraham Small, 1819), 7, 10.

11. As Heckewelder writes in his chapter on language, "I hope the result of these publications [meaning the Historical Committee of the American Philosophical Society] will be to satisfy the world that the languages of the Indians are not so poor, so devoid of variety of expression, so inadequate to the communication even of abstract ideas, or in a word so *barbarous*, as has been greatly imagined" (*Transactions*, 112).

12. Ibid., xiv.

13. Ibid., 451–464.

14. Ibid., xiv–xv.

15. Ibid., xxiii–xxiv.

16. Peter Du Ponceau, *Memoire sur le systeme grammatical des langues de quelques nations indiennes de l'amerique du nord* (Chicago, 1838), 32–33.

17. Robert Dale Parker, ed., *Changing Is Not Vanishing: A Collection of Early American Indian Poetry to 1930* (Philadelphia: University of Pennsylvania Press, 2011), 64.

18. Natalie Diaz, *When My Brother Was an Aztec* (Port Townsend, Wash.: Copper Canyon, 2012), 22.

{ BIBLIOGRAPHY }

Aarsleff, Hans. *From Locke to Saussure: Essays on the Study of Language and Intellectual History*. Minneapolis: University of Minnesota Press, 1982.

Aarsleff, Hans. "Language, Man, and Knowledge in the 16th and 17th Centuries." Unpublished manuscript, 1971.

Aarsleff, Hans. *The Study of Language in England, 1780–1860*. Princeton, N.J.: Princeton University Press, 1967.

Abnaki Prayer Book. American Indian Vocabulary Collection, Watkinson Library, Trinity College, Hartford, Conn.

Abram, David. *The Spell of the Sensuous: Perception and Language in a More-Than-Human World*. New York: Pantheon, 1996.

Abrams, M. H. *The Mirror and the Lamp: Romantic Theory and the Critical Tradition*. New York: Oxford University Press, 1953.

Acosta, José de. *Natural and Moral History of the Indies*. Edited by Jane E. Mangan, translated by Frances M. López-Morillas. Durham, N.C.: Duke University Press, 2002.

Adair, James. *The History of American Indians*. Edited by Kathryn E. Holland Braund. Tuscaloosa: University of Alabama Press, 2005.

Alexander, Peter. *Ideas, Qualities and Corpuscles: Locke and Boyle on the External World*. Cambridge: Cambridge University Press, 1985.

Allouez, Claude. *Facsimile of Pere Marquette's Illinois Prayer Book*. Edited by J. L. Hubert Neilson. Quebec: Quebec Literary and Historical Society, 1908.

American Indian Vocabulary Collection. American Philosophical Society, Philadelphia, Pa.

Anderson, Emma. "Blood, Fire, and 'Baptism': Three Perspectives on the Death of Jean de Brébeuf, Seventeenth-Century Jesuit 'Martyr.'" In *Native Americans, Christianity, and the Reshaping of the American Religious Landscape*, edited by Joel W. Martin and Mark A. Nicholas, 125–158. Chapel Hill: University of North Carolina Press, 2010.

Andresen, Julie Tetel. *Linguistics in America, 1769–1924*. New York: Routledge, 1990.

Andrew, Edward G. *Imperial Republics: Revolution, War, and Territorial Expansion from the English Civil War to the French Revolution*. Toronto: University of Toronto Press, 2011.

Apter, Emily. *Against World Literature: On the Politics of Untranslatability*. New York: Verso, 2013.

"*Archaeologia Americana: Transactions and Collections of the American Antiquarian Society*, vol 2. (Review)." *North American Review* 45, no. 96 (July 1837): 34–35.

Aristotle. *The Rhetoric and Poetics of Aristotle*. Translated by Ingram Bywater. New York: Modern Library, 1954.

Armstrong, Robert L. *Metaphysics and British Empiricism*. Lincoln: University of Nebraska Press, 1970.

Ash, Anna, Jessie Little Doe Fermino, and Ken Hale. "Diversity in Local Language Maintenance and Restoration: A Reason for Optimism." In *The Green Book of Language Revitalization in Practice*, edited by Leanne Hinton and Ken Hale, 19–35. San Diego: Academic Press, 2001.

Assmann, Jan. "Translating Gods: Religion as a Factor of Cultural (Un)Translatability." In *The Translatability of Cultures: Figurations of the Space Between*, edited by Sanford Budick and Wolfgang Iser, 25–36. Stanford, Calif.: Stanford University Press, 1996.

At a Conference Held at Deerfield in the County of Hampshire. Boston, 1735.

Aubrey, John. *Brief Lives, Chiefly of Contemporaries.* Edited by Andrew Clark. Oxford: Clarendon, 1898.

Augustine. *Earlier Writings.* Edited and translated by John H. S. Burleigh. Philadelphia: Westminster, 1953.

Axtell, James. "Babel of Tongues: Communicating with the Indians in Eastern North America." In *The Language Encounter in the Americas, 1492–1800*, edited by Edward G. Gray and Norman Fiering, 15–60. New York: Berghahn, 2000.

Axtell, James. *The Invasion Within: The Contest of Cultures in Colonial North America.* New York: Oxford University Press, 1985.

Bacon, Francis. *The Instauratio Magna, Part II: Novum Organum and Associated Texts*, vol. 11, edited by Graham Rees and Maria Wakely. *The Oxford Francis Bacon*, edited by Graham Rees and Lisa Jardine, 134–135. Oxford: Clarendon, 2004.

Banner, Stuart. *How the Indians Lost Their Land: Law and Power on the Frontier.* Cambridge, Mass.: The Belknap Press of Harvard University Press, 2005.

Barton, Benjamin Smith. *New Views of the Origin of the Tribes and Nations of America.* Philadelphia: Printed for the Author by John Bioren, 1797.

Bass, Althea. *Cherokee Messenger.* Norman: University of Oklahoma Press, 1936.

Bauman, Richard, and Charles L. Briggs. *Voices of Modernity: Language Ideologies and the Politics of Inequality.* Cambridge: Cambridge University Press, 2003.

Baxter, Joseph. "Journal of the Rev. Joseph Baxter, of Medfield, Missionary to the Eastern Indians in 1717." *New England Historical and Genealogical Register* 21 (1867): 45–60.

Bayard, John. *Charter of the American Philosophical Society.* In *Laws and Rules of the Administration and Order.* Philadelphia: Printed for the American Philosophical Society, 1910.

Beautiful Beyond: Christian Songs in Native Languages. Produced by Howard Bass, National Museum of the American Indian, Smithsonian Folkways Recordings, 2004, compact disc.

Behmen [Böhme], Jacob. *Signatura Rerum; or, The Signature of All Things....* London, 1651.

Bejan, Teresa M. "'The Bond of Civility': Roger Williams on Toleration and Its Limits." *History of European Ideas* 37, no. 4 (2011): 409–420.

Bell, David A. *The Cult of the Nation in France: Inventing Nationalism, 1680–1800.* Cambridge, Mass.: Harvard University Press, 2001.

Bellenger, Joseph. *Grammar of the Mikmaque Language of Nova Scotia, Edited from the Manuscripts of the Abbé Maillard by the Rev. Joseph Bellenger.* New York: Cramoisy, 1864.

Bellenger, Joseph, ed. *Instruction sur la langue Mickmaque.* Philadelphia, 1814.

Bennett, Jim, and Scott Mandelbrote. *The Garden, the Ark, the Tower, the Temple: Biblical Metaphors of Knowledge in Early Modern Europe.* Oxford: Museum of the History of Science, 1998.

Bent, Margaret. "The Late-Medieval Motet." In *Companion to Medieval and Renaissance Music*, edited by Tess Knighton and David Fallows, 114–119. New York: Schirmer, 1992.

Black, Mary B. "Ojibwa Power Belief System." In *The Anthropology of Power: Ethnographic Studies from Asia, Oceania, and the New World*, edited by Raymond D. Fogelson and Richard N. Adams, 141–151. New York: Academic Press, 1977.

Blair, Hugh. *Lectures on Rhetoric and Belles Lettres*. Philadelphia: Aitken, 1784.

Blakemore, Steven. "Strange Tongues: Cooper's Fiction of Language in *The Last of the Mohicans*." *Early American Literature* 19, no. 1 (1984): 21–41.

Boggs, Colleen Glenney. *Transnationalism and American Literature: Literary Translation, 1773–1892*. New York: Routledge, 2007.

Bono, James J. *The Word of God and the Languages of Man: Interpreting Nature in Early Modern Science and Medicine*. Vol. 1, *Ficino to Descartes*. Madison: University of Wisconsin Press, 1995.

The Book of Common Prayer... Translated into the Mohawk Language. Translated by Joseph Brant. London, 1787.

Boullenger, Antoine-Robert Le. *French and Miami-Illinois Dictionary*. John Carter Brown Library, Brown University, Providence, R.I.

Bowden, Henry Warner. *The American Indians and Christian Missions*. Chicago: University of Chicago Press, 1981.

Boyle, Robert. Preface to the Irish Testament, 1681, Boyle Papers, 1/4/16, Royal Society, London.

Brainerd, David. *Mirabilia Dei Inter Indicos, or the Rise and Progress of a Remarkable Work of Grace Amongst a Number of the Indians in the Provinces of New-Jersey and Pennsylvania*. Philadelphia: Printed and Sold by William Bradford in Second-Street, 1746.

Brasser, T. J. "Mahican." In *Handbook of North American Indian*. Vol. 15, *Northeast*, edited by Bruce G. Trigger, 198–212. Washington, D.C.: Smithsonian Institute, 1978.

Bremmer, Rolf H., Jr., and P. G. Hoftijzer. "Johannes de Laet (1581–1649): A Leiden Polymath [introduction]." *Lias: Special Issue* 25, no. 2 (1998): 135–136.

Brickhouse, Anna. *The Unsettlement of America: Translation, Interpretation, and the Story of Don Luis de Velasco, 1560–1945*. New York: Oxford University Press, 2015.

Bridenbaugh, Carl. *Cities in the Wilderness: The First Century of Urban Life in America, 1625–1742*. New York: Capricorn, 1964.

Brooks, Lisa. *The Common Pot: The Recovery of Native Space in the Northeast*. Minneapolis: University of Minnesota Press, 2008.

Bross, Kristina. *Dry Bones and Indian Sermons: Praying Indians in Colonial America*. Ithaca, N.Y.: Cornell University Press, 2004.

Brown, Wendy. *Walled States, Waning Sovereignty*. New York: Zone, 2010.

Browne, Thomas. *Pseudodoxia Epidemica*. London, 1646.

Bruyneel, Kevin. *Third Space of Sovereignty: The Postcolonial Politics of U.S.–Indigenous Relations*. Minneapolis: University of Minnesota Press, 2007.

Bryant, William Cullen. "An Indian at the Burial-Place of His Fathers." Quoted in James Fenimore Cooper, *The Leatherstocking Tales*, vol. 1. New York: Literary Classics of the United States, 1985.

Bryant, William Cullen. "The Prairies." In *Nineteenth-Century American Poetry*, edited by William C. Spengemnn and Jessica F. Roberts. New York: Penguin, 1996.

Burke, Peter. "The Jesuits and the Art of Translation in Early Modern Europe." In *The Jesuits II: Cultures, Sciences, and the Arts*, edited by John W. O'Malley, SJ, Gauvin Alexander Bailey, Steven J. Harris, and T. Frank Kennedy, SJ, 24–32. Toronto: University of Toronto Press, 2006.

Burkhart, Louise M. *The Slippery Earth: Nahua-Christian Dialogue in Sixteenth-Century Mexico*. Tucson: University of Arizona Press, 1989.

Burnet, Thomas. *The Theory of the Earth.* London: Printed by R. Norton, 1684.

Byrd, Jodi A. *The Transit of Empire: Indigenous Critiques of Colonialism.* Minneapolis: University of Minnesota Press, 2011.

Calloway, Colin G. *The Abenaki.* New York: Chelsea House, 1989.

Calloway, Colin G. *The Western Abenakis of Vermont, 1600–1800: War, Migration, and the Survival of an Indian People.* Norman: University of Oklahoma Press, 1990.

Calvert, Mary R. *Black Robe on the Kennebec.* Monmouth, Me.: Monmouth, 1991.

Campbell, Lyle. *American Indian Languages: The Historical Linguistics of Native America.* Oxford: Oxford University Press, 1997.

Cannon, Christopher. *The Grounds of English Literature.* Oxford: Oxford University Press, 2004.

Carey, Daniel. *Locke, Shaftesbury, and Hutcheson: Contesting Diversity in the Enlightenment and Beyond.* Cambridge: Cambridge University Press, 2006.

Carey, Daniel. "Travel, Geography, and the Problem of Belief: Locke as a Reader of Travel Literature." In *History and Nation,* edited by Julia Rudolph, 97–136. Lewisburg, Pa.: Bucknell University Press, 2006.

Carr, Helen. *Inventing the American Primitive: Politics, Gender, and the Representation of Native American Literary Traditions, 1789–1936.* New York: New York University Press, 1996.

Chase, Stuart. Foreword to *Language, Thought, and Reality: Selected Writings of Benjamin Lee Whorf.* Edited by John B. Carroll. Cambridge, Mass.: MIT Press, 1956.

Clark, William A. "The Church at Nanrantsouak: Sebastian Rale S.J., and the Wabanaki of Maine's Kennebec River." *Catholic Historical Review* 92, no. 3 (2006): 225–251.

Cmiel, Kenneth. "'A Broad Fluid Language of Democracy': Discovering the American Idiom." *Journal of American History* 79, no. 3 (1992): 913–936.

Codignola, Luca. *Guide to Documents Relating to French and British North America in the Archives of the Sacred Congregation "de Propaganda Fide" in Rome, 1622–1799.* Ottawa: National Archives of Canada, 1991.

Cohen, Charles L. "The Colonization of British North America as an Episode in the History of Christianity." *Church History* 72, no. 3 (2003): 553–568.

Cohen, Matt. *The Networked Wilderness: Communicating in Early New England.* Minneapolis: University of Minnesota Press, 2010.

Cohen, Matt, and Jeffrey Glover, eds. *Colonial Mediascapes: Sensory Worlds of the Early Americas.* Lincoln: University of Nebraska Press, 2014.

Cohen, Patricia. "Indian Tribes Go in Search of Their Lost Languages." *New York Times,* April 5, 2010.

Cohen, Paul. "L'Imaginaire d'une langue nationale: l'État, les langues et l'invention du mythe de l'ordonnance de Villers-Cotterêts à l'époque moderne en France." *Histoire Épistémologie Langage* 25, no. 1 (2003): 19–69.

Cohen, Paul. "Was There an Amerindian Atlantic? Reflections on the Limits of a Historiographical Concept." *History of European Ideas* 34, no. 4 (2008): 388–410.

Colden, Cadwallader. *The History of the Five Indian Nations.* Ithaca, N.Y.: Cornell University Press, 1958.

Colley, Linda. *Britons: Forging the Nation, 1707–1837.* New Haven, Conn.: Yale University Press, 1992.

Collingwood, R. G. *The Idea of History: With Lectures, 1926–1928.* Edited and with an introduction by Jan van der Dussen. New York: Oxford University Press, 1994.

Condillac, Etienne Bonnot de. *Essay on the Origin of Human Knowledge*. Translated and edited by Hans Aarsleff. Cambridge: Cambridge University Press, 2001.

Cooper, James Fenimore. *The Leatherstocking Tales*, vol. 1. New York: Literary Classics of the United States, 1985.

Cordova, V. F. *How It Is: The Native American Philosophy of V. F. Cordova*. Edited by Kathleen Dean Moore, Kurt Peters, Ted Jojola, and Amber Lacy. Tucson: University of Arizona Press, 2007.

Costa, David J. *The Miami-Illinois Language*. Lincoln: University of Nebraska Press, 2003.

Cotton, John. *Christ the Fountaine of Life*. London, 1651.

Cotton, Josiah. *Vocabulary of the Massachusetts (Or Natick) Indian Language*. In Collections of the Massachusetts Historical Society, 3rd ser., 2. Cambridge, Mass.: Printed by E. W. Metcalf and Company, 1830.

Coudert, Alison. "Some Theories of a Natural Language from the Renaissance to the Seventeenth Century." In *Magia Naturalis und die Entstehung der modernen Naturwissenschaften: Symposion der Leibniz-Gesellschaft Hannover, 14. Und 15. November 1975*, edited by Kurt Müller, Heinrich Schepers, and Wilhelm Totok, 56–114. Wiesbaden, Germany: Steiner, 1978.

Crain, Patricia. *The Story of A: The Alphabetization of America from the New England Primer to the Scarlet Letter*. Stanford, Calif.: Stanford University Press, 2000.

Cram, David. "Linguistic Eschatology: Babel and Pentecost in Seventeenth-Century Linguistic Thought." *Language and History* 56, no. 1 (May 2013): 44–56.

Cranston, Maurice. *John Locke: A Biography*. London: Longmans, 1957.

Crosby, Constance A. "From Myth to History; or, Why King Philip's Ghost Walks Abroad." In *The Recovery of Meaning: Historical Archaeology in the Eastern United States*, edited by Mark P. Leone and Parker B. Potter, 183–210. Washington, D.C.: Smithsonian Institution, 1988.

Daviault, Diane. *L'algonquin au XVIIe siècle: Une édition critique, analysée et commentée de la grammaire algonquine du Père Louis Nicolas*. Quebec: Press of the University of Quebec, 1994.

Davis, James Calvin. *The Moral Theology of Roger Williams: Christian Conviction and Public Ethics*. Louisville, Ky.: Westminster John Knox Press, 2004.

Dawson, Hannah. *Locke, Language and Early-Modern Philosophy*. Cambridge: Cambridge University Press, 2007.

Day, Gordon M. *The Western Abenaki Dictionary*, vol. 1. Quebec: Canadian Museum of Civilization, 1994.

De Beer, E. S., ed. *The Correspondence of John Locke*. Oxford: Clarendon, 1981.

Dekker, George. *The American Historical Romance*. New York: Cambridge University Press, 1987.

Déléage, Pierre. *La croix et les hiéroglyphes: Écritures et objects rituels chez les Amérindiens de Nouvelle-France, XVIIe–XVIIIe siècles*. Paris: Rue d'Ulm, 2009.

Deloria, Philip J. *Playing Indian*. New Haven, Conn.: Yale University Press, 1998.

Deloria, Vine, Jr. *Red Earth, White Lies: Native Americans and the Myth of Scientific Fact*. New York: Scribner, 1995.

Deserontyon, John. "A Mohawk Form of Ritual Condolence." Translated and with an introduction by J. N. B. Hewitt, *Indian Notes and Monographs* 10, no. 8 (1920): 86–110.

Dew, Nicolas. *Orientalism in Louis XIV's France*. Oxford: Oxford University Press, 2009.

Diaz, Natalie. *When My Brother Was an Aztec*. Port Townsend, Wash.: Copper Canyon Press, 2012.

Dickason, Olive Patricia. "Amerindians Between French and English in Nova Scotia, 1713–1763." *American Indian Culture and Research Journal* 10, no. 4 (1986): 31–56.

Dillon, Emma. "Unwriting Medieval Song." *New Literary History* 46, no. 4 (Autumn 2015): 595–622.

Dorsey, Peter A. "Going to School with the Savages: Authorship and Authority Among the Jesuits of New France." *William and Mary Quarterly* 55, no. 3 (July 1998): 399–420.

Douglas Anderson. "Subterraneous Virginia: The Ethical Poetics of Thomas Jefferson." *Eighteenth-Century Studies* 33, no. 2 (2000): 233–249.

Droixhe, Daniel. "Adam ou Babel? Théorie du signe et languistique biblique de Descartes à Leibniz." In *Language Philosophies and the Language of Sciences: A Historical Perspective in Honor of Lia Formigari*, edited by Daniele Gambarara, Stefano Gensini, and Antonino Pennisi. Münster: Nodus Publikationen, 1996.

Droixhe, Daniel. *La linguistique et l'appel de l'histoire (1600–1800): Rationalisme et révolutions positivistes*. Geneva: Droz, 1978.

DuBois, Laurent. "The Jesuit Relations." In *A New Literary History of America*, edited by Greil Marcus and Werner Sollors, 50–54. Cambridge, Mass.: The Belknap Press of Harvard University Press, 2009.

Du Ponceau, Peter. *A Discourse on the Necessity and the Means of Making Our National Literature Independent of That of Great Britain*. Philadelphia, 1834.

Du Ponceau, Peter. *Mémoire Sur Le Système Grammatical Des Langues de Quelques Nations Indiennes de L'Amérique Du Nord*. Paris, 1838.

Du Ponceau, Peter. "Report of the Corresponding Secretary to the Committee." In *Transactions of the Historical and Literary Committee of the American Philosophical Society*, vol. 1. Philadelphia, 1819.

Durston, Alan. *Pastoral Quechua: The History of Christian Translation in Colonial Peru, 1550–1650*. Notre Dame, Ind.: University of Notre Dame Press, 2007.

Eccles, W. J. *Canada Under Louis XIV, 1633–1701*. Toronto: McClelland and Steward, 1964.

Edwards, Jonathan. "Drafts of Professions of Faith." The Jonathan Edwards Collection, f. 1245, Beinecke Rare Books Library, Yale University.

Edwards, Jonathan. *A History of the Work of Redemption*. The Works of Jonathan Edwards, vol. 9, edited by John F. Wilson. New Haven, Conn.: Yale University Press, 1989.

Edwards, Jonathan. *Letters and Personal Writings*. The Works of Jonathan Edwards, vol. 16, edited by George S. Claghorn. New Haven, Conn.: Yale University Press, 1998.

Edwards, Jonathan. *The Life of David Brainerd*. The Works of Jonathan Edwards, vol. 7, edited by Norman Pettit. New Haven, Conn.: Yale University Press, 1985.

Edwards, Jonathan. *Sermons and Discourses, 1743–1758*. The Works of Jonathan Edwards, vol. 25, edited by Wilson H. Kimnach. New Haven, Conn.: Yale University Press, 2006.

Edwards, Jonathan. *Typological Writings*. The Works of Jonathan Edwards, vol. 11, edited by Wallace E. Anderson and Mason I. Lowance. New Haven, Conn.: Yale University Press, 1993.

Edwards, Jonathan, Jr. *Observations on the Language of the Muhhekaneew Indians*. London, 1788.

Edwards, Nancy. "Edward Lhuyd and the Origins of Early Medieval Celtic Archaeology." *The Antiquaries Journal* 87 (2007): 165–196.

Eliot, John. *Communion of Churches; or, The Divine Management of Gospel Churches by the Ordinance of Councils....* Cambridge [Mass.], 1665.

Eliot, John. *The Eliot Tracts: With Letters from John Eliot to Thomas Thorowgood and Richard Baxter.* Edited by Michael P. Clark. Westport, Conn.: Praeger, 2003.

[Eliot, John]. *Indian Dialogues, for Their Instruction in That Great Service of Christ, in Calling Home Their Country-men to the Knowledge of God....* Cambridge [Mass.], 1671.

Eliot, John. *The Indian Grammar Begun; or, An Essay to Bring the Indian Language into Rules, for the Help of Such as Desire to Learn the Same, for the Furtherance of the Gospel Among Them.* Cambridge, Mass., 1666.

Eliot, John. *The Indian Primer; or, The First Book by Which Children May Know Truely to Read the Indian Language. And Milk for Babes.* Boston, 1720.

E[liot], J[ohn]. *The Logick Primer: Some Logical Notions to Initiate the INDIANS in the Knowledge of the Rule of Reason; and to Know How to Make Use Thereof....* [Cambridge, Mass.], 1672.

Eliot, John. *Tears of Repentance.* London, 1653.

Elmer, Jonathan. "The Archive, the Native American, and Jefferson's Convulsions." *Diacritics* 28, no. 4 (1998): 5–24.

Emerson, Ralph Waldo. *Emerson: Essays and Lectures.* New York: Literary Classics of the United States, 1983.

Erben, Patrick M. *A Harmony of the Spirits: Translation and the Language of Community in Early Pennsylvania.* Chapel Hill: University of North Carolina Press, 2012.

Errington, Joseph. *Linguistics in a Colonial World: A Story of Language, Meaning, and Power.* Malden, Mass.: Blackwell, 2008.

Essick, Robert N. *William Blake and the Language of Adam.* Oxford: Clarendon, 1989.

Fabian, Johannes. *Time and the Other: How Anthropology Makes Its Object.* New York: Columbia University Press, 1983.

Ferguson, Arthur B. *Utter Antiquity: Perception of Prehistory in Renaissance England.* Durham, N.C.: Duke University Press, 1993.

Fiedler, Leslie A. *Love and Death in the American Novel.* Champaign, Ill.: Dalkey Archive, 1998.

Field, Margaret C. "Metaphor, Mythology, and a Navajo Verb: The Role of Cultural Constructs in Lexicography of Endangered Languages." *Anthropological Linguistics* 51, nos. 3/4 (Fall and Winter 2009): 296–302.

Fields, Wayne. "Beyond Definition: A Reading of *The Prairie.*" In *James Fenimore Cooper: A Collection of Critical Essays,* edited by Wayne Fields, 93–111. Englewood Cliffs, N.J.: Prentice-Hall, 1979.

Fisher, Linford D. *The Indian Great Awakening: Religion and the Shaping of Native Cultures in Early America.* Oxford: Oxford University Press, 2012.

Flint, Kate. *The Transatlantic Indian, 1776–1930.* Princeton, N.J.: Princeton University Press, 2009.

Foley, Denis. "Iroquois Mourning and Condolence Installation Rituals: A Pattern of Social Continuity." In *Preserving Tradition and Understanding the Past,* edited by Christine Sternberg Patrick, 34–35. Albany, N.Y.: New York State Education Department, 2010.

Ford, Paul Leicester, ed. *The New-England Primer: A History of Its Origin and Development with a Reprint of the Unique Copy of the Earliest Known Edition....* New York, 1897.

Frantzen, Allen J. *Desire for Origins: New Language, Old English, and Teaching the Tradition.* New Brunswick, N.J.: Rutgers University Press, 1990.

Frazier, Patrick. *The Mohicans of Stockbridge.* Lincoln: University of Nebraska Press, 1992.

Frégault, Guy. *Canada: The War of the Conquest.* Translated by Margaret M. Cameron. Toronto: Oxford University Press, 1969.

Fumaroli, Marc. "The Fertility and Shortcomings of Renaissance Rhetoric: The Jesuit Case." In *The Jesuits: Cultures, Sciences, and the Arts, 1540–1773,* edited by John W. O'Malley, SJ, Gauvin Alexander Bailey, Steven J. Harris, and T. Frank Kennedy, 90–106. Toronto: University of Toronto Press, 1999.

Gagliano, Joseph A., and Charles E. Ronan, eds. *Jesuit Encounters in the New World: Jesuit Chroniclers, Geographers, Educators and Missionaries in the Americas, 1549–1767.* Rome: Institutum Historicum Societatis Jesu, 1997.

Galissonnière, M. De La. "Memoir on the French Colonies in North America." In *Documents Relative to the Colonial History of the State of New York,* vol. 10, edited by E. B. O'Callaghan. Albany, N.Y.: Weed, Parsons, 1858.

Garland, P. S. *The History of the City of Ogdensburg.* Ogdensburg, N.Y.: M. J. Belleville, 1927.

Gaustad, Edwin S. *Liberty of Conscience: Roger Williams in America.* Grand Rapids, Mich.: W. B. Eerdmans, 1991.

Geary, James. *I Is an Other: The Secret Life of Metaphor and How It Shapes the Way We See the World.* New York: HarperCollins, 2011.

Gibbon, Edward. *The History of the Decline and Fall of the Roman Empire, Volume I.* Edited by David Womersley. New York: Penguin, 2005.

Goddard, Ives. "'I Am a Red-Skin': The Adoption of a Native American Expression (1769–1826)." *European Review of Native American Studies* 19, no. 2 (2005): 15–16.

Goddard, Ives, and Kathleen J. Bragdon, eds. *Native Writings in Massachusett.* 2 vols. Philadelphia: American Philosophical Society, 1988.

Goddard, Peter A. "Canada in Seventeenth-Century Jesuit Thought: Backwater or Opportunity?" In *Decentering the Renaissance: Canada and Europe in Multidisciplinary Perspective, 1500–1700,* edited by Germaine Warkentin and Carolyn Podruchny, 186–199. Toronto: University of Toronto Press, 2002.

Goldman, Shalom. *Hebrew and the Bible in America: The First Two Centuries.* Hanover, N.H.: University Press of New England, 1993.

Goodman, Glenda. "'But They Differ from Us in Sound': Indian Psalmody and the Soundscape of Colonialism, 1651–75." *William and Mary Quarterly* 69, no. 4 (October 2012): 793–822.

Gradish, Stephen F. "The Establishment of British Seapower, in the Mediterranean, 1689–1713." *Canadian Journal of History* 10, no. 1 (1975): 1–16.

Gravier, Jacques. *Dictionary of the Algonquian-Illinois Language.* Watkinson Library, Trinity College, Hartford, Conn.

Gray, Arthur. *Jesus College.* London: F. E. Robinson, 1902.

Gray, Edward G. *New World Babel: Languages and Nations in Early America.* Princeton, N.J.: Princeton University Press, 1999.

Greenblatt, Stephen J. *Learning to Curse: Essays in Early Modern Culture.* New York: Routledge, 1992.

Greene, John C. "Early Scientific Interest in the American Indian: Comparative Linguistics." *Proceedings of the American Philosophical Society* 104, no. 5 (1960): 511–517.

Greenfield, Bruce. "The Mi'kmaq Hieroglyphic Prayer Book: Writing and Christianity in Maritime Canada, 1675–1921." In *The Language Encounter in the Americas, 1492–1800,* edited by Edward G. Gray and Norman Fiering, 189–211. New York: Berghahn, 2003.

Greengrass, M. M. Leslie, and M. Hannon, eds. *The Hartlib Papers*, electronic edition. Sheffield, UK, 2013, http://www.hrionline.ac.uk/hartlib/context.

Greer, Allan, ed. *The Jesuit Relations: Natives and Missionaries in Seventeenth-Century North America*. Boston: Bedford/St. Martin's, 2000.

Gruzinski, Serge. *The Mestizo Mind: The Intellectual Dynamics of Colonization and Globalization*. Translated by Deke Dusinberre. New York: Routledge, 2002.

Guggisberg, Hans R. "Religious Freedom and the History of the Christian World in Roger Williams' Thought." *Early American Literature* 12, no. 1 (1977): 36–48.

Gundaker, Grey. *Signs of Diaspora/Diaspora of Signs: Literacies, Creolization, and Vernacular Practice in African America*. New York: Oxford University Press, 1998.

Gustafson, Sandra M., and Gordon Hutner, eds. "Projecting Early American Literary Studies." Special issue, *American Literary History* 22, no. 2 (2010).

Haan, Richard L. "Covenant and Consensus: Iroquois and English, 1676–1760." In *Beyond the Covenant Chain: The Iroquois and Their Neighbors in Indian North America, 1600–1800*, edited by Daniel K. Richter and James H. Merrell, 41–57. Philadelphia: Pennsylvania State University Press, 2003.

Haefeli, Evan, and Kevin Sweeney. *Captors and Captives: The 1704 French and Indian Raid on Deerfield*. Amherst: University of Massachusetts Press, 2003.

Haffenden, Philip S. "France and England in North America, 1689–1713." In *The New Cambridge Modern History: Vol. 6. The Rise of Great Britain and Russia, 1688–1715/25*, edited by J. S. Bromley, 480–508. Cambridge: Cambridge University Press, 1970.

Hale, Horatio. *The Iroquois Book of Rites*. Philadelphia: D. G. Brinton, 1883.

Hale, Matthew. *The Primitive Origination of Mankind, Considered and Examined According to the Light of Nature*. London: Printed by William Godbid, 1677.

Hallowell, A. Irving. "Ojibwa Ontology, Behavior, and World View." In *Culture in History: Essays in Honor of Paul Radin*, edited by Stanley Diamond, 19–52. New York: Columbia University Press, 1960.

Hamilton, Raphael N. "Who Wrote *Premier Établissement de la Foy dans la Nouvelle France?*" *Canadian Historical Review* 57, no. 3 (1976): 265–288.

Hanzeli, Victor Egon. *Missionary Linguistics in New France: A Study of Seventeenth-and Eighteenth-Century Descriptions of American Indian Languages*. The Hague: Mouton, 1969.

Harkin, Michael E., ed. *Reassessing Revitalization Movements: Perspectives from North America and the Pacific Islands*. Lincoln: University of Nebraska Press, 2004.

Harrison, John, and Peter Laslett. *The Library of John Locke*. Oxford: Clarendon, 1965.

Harrison, Regina. *Signs, Songs, and Memory in the Andes: Translation Quechua Language and Culture*. Austin: University of Texas Press, 1989.

Hart, William B. "Mohawk Schoolmasters and Catechists in Mid-Eighteenth-Century Iroquoia: An Experiment in Fostering Literacy and Religious Change." In *The Language Encounter in the Americas, 1492–1800*, edited by Edward G. Gray and Norman Fiering, 230–257. New York: Berghahn, 2000.

"The Hartlib Papers,". University of Sheffield Library, Sheffield, United Kingdom.

Hartog, Francois. *The Mirror of Herodotus: The Representation of the Other in the Writing of History*. Translated by Janet Lloyd. Berkeley: University of California Press, 1988.

Harvey, Sean P. " 'Must not their languages be savage and barbarous like them?': Philology, Indian Removal, and Race Science." *Journal of the Early Republic* 30, no. 4 (Winter 2010): 506–532.

Harvey, Sean P. *Native Tongues: Colonialism and Race from Encounter to the Reservation.* Cambridge, Mass.: Harvard University Press, 2015.

Havard, Gilles, and Cécile Vidal. "Making New France New Again." *Common-Place* 7, no. 4 (2007), http://www.common-place-archives.org/vol-07/no-04/harvard/.

Hawkins, Benjamin. *The Collected Works of Benjamin Hawkins, 1796–1810.* Edited by Thomas H. Foster. Tuscaloosa: University of Alabama Press, 2003.

Hawley, Gideon. *Gideon Hawley Journal and Letterbook.* Congregational Library, Boston.

Haycock, David Boyd. *William Stukeley: Science, Religion and Archeology in Eighteenth-Century England.* Woodbridge, UK: Boydell, 2002.

Heckewelder, John Gottlieb. *An Account of the History, Manners and Customs of the Indian Nations Who Once Inhabited Pennsylvania and the Neighbouring States.* In *Transactions of the Historical and Literary Committee of the American Philosophical Society,* vol. 1. Philadelphia, 1819.

Heckewelder, John Gottlieb. Letters, 1816–1822, to Peter Stephen Du Ponceau. American Philosophical Society, Philadelphia, Pa.

Heckewelder, John Gottlieb. "Words, Phrases, and Short Dialogues in the Language of the Lenni Lanape, or Delaware Indians." In *Transactions of the Historical and Literary Committee of the American Philosophical Society,* vol. 1. Philadelphia, 1819.

Hinton, Leanne. *Bringing Our Languages Home: Language Revitalization for Families.* Berkeley, Calif.: Heyday, 2013.

Hinton, Leanne, and Ken Hale. *The Green Book of Language Revitalization Movements in Practice.* San Diego, Calif.: Academic Press, 2001.

Hinton, Leanne, Matt Vera, and Nancy Steele. *How to Keep Your Language Alive.* Berkeley, Calif.: Heyday, 2002.

Hobbes, Thomas. *Leviathan.* Edited by Noel Malcolm. Oxford: Clarendon, 2012.

Hobbs, Catherine L. *Rhetoric on the Margins of Modernity: Vico, Condillac, Monboddo.* Carbondale: Southern Illinois University Press, 2002.

Holifield, E. Brooks. *The Covenant Sealed: The Development of Puritan Sacramental Theology in Old and New England, 1570–1720.* New Haven, Conn.: Yale University Press, 1974.

Hooke, Robert. *The Posthumous Works of Robert Hooke…, Containing His Cutlerian Lectures, and other Discourses, Read at the Meeting of the Illustrious Royal Society.* London: Sam Smith and Benj. Walford, 1705.

Hopkins, Samuel. *Historical Memoirs, Relating to the Housataunnuk Indians.* Boston: Printed and Sold by S. Kneeland, 1753.

Hornborg, Anne-Christine. *Mi'kmaq Landscapes: From Animism to Sacred Ecology.* Burlington, Vt.: Ashgate, 2008.

Howard, James H. "The Nanticoke-Delaware Skeleton Dance." *American Indian Quarterly* 2, no. 1 (1975): 1–13.

Hsia, Florence C. *Sojourners in a Strange Land: Jesuits and Their Scientific Missions in Late Imperial China.* Chicago: University of Chicago Press, 2009.

Humboldt, Wilhelm Von. *On Language: The Diversity of Human Language-Structure and Its Influence on the Mental Development of Mankind.* Translated by Peter Heath and with an introduction by Hans Aarsleff. New York: Cambridge University Press, 1988.

Humphreys, David. *An Historical Account of the Incorporated Society for the Propagation of the Gospel in Foreign Parts.* London: Printed by Joseph Downing in Bartholomew-Close near West-Smithfield, 1730.

Hunter, Michael, Antonio Clericuzio, and Lawrence M. Principe, eds. *The Correspondence of Robert Boyle*. 6 vols. London: Pickering and Chatto, 2001.

Hutton, Ronald. *Blood and Mistletoe: The History of the Druids in Britain*. New Haven, Conn.: Yale University Press, 2009.

Iannini, Christopher. *Fatal Revolutions: Natural History, West Indian Slavery, and the Routes of American Literature*. Chapel Hill: University of North Carolina Press, 2012.

Iannini, Christopher. "*Notes on the State of Virginia* and the Natural History of the Haitian Revolution." *Clio: A Journal of Literature, History, and the Philosophy of History* 40, no. 1 (2010): 63–85.

"Imagines seu Figurae variorum Inscriptionum praecipue Sepulchralium." Stowe MS 1023, British Library, London.

Inglis, Stephanie. "400 Years of Linguistic Contact Between the Mi'kmaq and the English and the Interchange of Two World Views." *Canadian Journal of Native Studies* 24, no. 2 (2004): 389–402.

Jackson, Gregory S. "A Game Theory of Evangelical Fiction." *Critical Inquiry* 39, no. 3 (Spring 2013): 451–485.

Jaenen, C. J. "Germain, Joseph-Louis." In *Dictionary of Canadian Biography*, vol. 2, accessed Februrary 12, 2014, http://www.biographi.ca/en/bio/germain_joseph_louis_2E.html.

James, Edwin. *Account of an Expedition from Pittsburgh to the Rocky Mountains*, vol. 1. Philadelphia, 1822.

James, Edwin. "Part of a Manuscript Note Book of Dr. Edwin James, Comprising a Comparative Vocabulary & Phrases, Menomini & Ojibway, and a Sioux-Dakota Vocabulary Tr(anslated). Written About 1825–6." American Indian Collection, Watkinson Library, Hartford, Conn.

Jefferson, Thomas. *Notes on the State of Virginia*. Edited by William Peden. Chapel Hill: University of North Carolina Press, 1955.

Jefferson, Thomas. *The Papers of Thomas Jefferson*. 42 vols. Princeton, N.J.: Princeton University Press, 1950–.

Jefferson, Thomas. *Papers of Thomas Jefferson*, electronic edition. Edited by Barbara Oberg and Jefferson J. Looney. Charlottesville: University of Virginia Press, 2009.

Jehlen, Myra. "History Before the Fact; Or, Captain John Smith's Unfinished Symphony." *Critical Inquiry* 19, no. 4 (1993): 677–692.

Jennings, Francis. *The Invasion of America: Indians, Colonialism, and the Cant of Conquest*. Chapel Hill: University of North Carolina Press, 1975.

Jones, G. Lloyd. *The Discovery of Hebrew in Tudor England: A Third Language*. Manchester: Manchester University Press, 1983.

Jones, Sir William. "A Dissertation on the Orthography of Asiatick Words in Roman Letters." *The Works of Sir William Jones*, vol. 3. London: John Stockdale, 1807.

Jong, J. A. de. *As the Waters Cover the Sea: Millennial Expectations in the Rise of Anglo-American Missions, 1640–1810*. Kampen: Kok, 1970.

Keenan, SJ, James F. "Jesuit Casuistry or Jesuit Spirituality? The Roots of Seventeenth-Century British Puritan Practical Divinity." In *The Jesuits: Cultures, Sciences, and the Arts, 1540–1773*, edited by John W. O'Malley, SJ, Gauvin Alexander Bailey, Steven J. Harris, and T. Frank Kennedy, SJ, 627–640. Toronto: University of Toronto Press, 1999.

Kelley, Donald R. *Foundations of Modern Historical Scholarship: Language, Law, and History in the French Renaissance*. New York: Columbia University Press, 1970.

Kennedy, Archibald. *Serious Considerations on the Present State of the Affairs of the Northern Colonies*. New York, 1754.

Kidd, Thomas S. *The Protestant Interest: New England after Puritanism*. New Haven, Conn.: Yale University Press, 2004.

Kilarski, Marcin. "Cherokee Classificatory Verbs: Their Place in the Study of American Indian Languages." *Historiographia Linguistica* 36, no. 1 (2009): 39–73.

Kling, David W., and Douglas A. Sweeney, eds. *Jonathan Edwards at Home and Abroad, Historical Memories, Cultural Movements, Global Horizons*. Columbia: University of South Carolina Press, 2003.

Knapp, Samuel L. *Lectures on American Literature*. New York: Elam Bliss, 1829.

La Chasse, Pierre-Joseph de. "Une Relation Inédite de la mort du P. Sébastien Racle, 1724." *Nova Francia* 4 (1929): 342–350.

Lafitau, Joseph François. *Customs of the American Indians Compared with the Customs of Primitive Times*. Edited and translated by William N. Fenton and Elizabeth L. Moore. Toronto: Champlain Society, 1977.

Lahise, Robert. "Picquet, Francois." In *Dictionary of Canadian Biography*, vol. 4, accessed March 3, 2016, http://www.biographi.ca/en/bio/picquet_francois_4E.html.

Latour, Bruno. *Science in Action*. Cambridge, Mass.: Harvard University Press, 1987.

Latourette, Kenneth Scott. *A History of Christian Missions in China*. New York: Macmillan, 1932.

Lauzon, Matthew. *Signs of Light: French and British Theories of Linguistic Communication, 1648–1789*. Ithaca, N.Y.: Cornell University Press, 2010.

Law, Jules David. *The Rhetoric of Empiricism: Language and Perception from Locke to I. A. Richards*. Ithaca, N.Y.: Cornell University Press, 1993.

Lawrence, D. H. *Studies in Classic American Literature*. Edited by Ezra Greenspan, Lindeth Vasey, and John Worthen. Cambridge: Cambridge University Press, 2003.

Le Clercq, Chrestien. *New Relation of Gaspesia with the Customs and Religion of the Gaspesian Indians*. Edited and translated by William F. Ganong. Toronto: Champlain Society, 1910.

Le Clercq, Chrestien. *Nouvelle Relation de la Gaspesie, qui contient Les Mœurs and la Religion des Sauvages Gaspesiens Porte-Croix, adorateurs du Soleil, and d'autres Peuples de l'Amerique Septentrionale, dite le Canada*. Paris, 1691. Bodleian Library Oxford University, Locke 7.80c.

Le Clercq, Christian. *First Establishment of the Faith in New France*. Edited and translated by John G. Shea. New York: John G. Shea, 1881.

Leahey, Margaret J. "'Comment peut un muet prescher l'évangile?' Jesuit Missionaries and the Native Languages of New France." *French Historical Studies* 19, no. 1 (Spring 1995): 105–131.

Leavelle, Tracy Neale. "'Bad Things' and 'Good Hearts': Meditation, Meaning, and the Language of Illinois Christianity." *Church History: Studies in Christianity and Culture* 76, no. 2 (2007): 363–394.

Leavelle, Tracy Neal. *The Catholic Calumet: Colonial Conversions in French and Indian North America*. Philadelphia: University of Pennsylvania Press, 2012.

Lepore, Jill. *The Name of War: King Philip's War and the Origins of American Identity*. New York: Knopf, 1998.

Leroy-Turcan, Isabelle. *Introduction à l'étude du "Dictionnaire étymologique ou origines de la langue françoise*. Lyon: Centre d'études linguistiques Jacques Goudet, 1991.

Lévis, Chevalier De. *Journal des campagnes du chevalier de lévis en canada de 1756 a 1760*. Montreal: C. O. Beuchemin & Fils, 1889.

Lévis, Chevalier De. *Lettres du chevalier de lévis concernant la guerre du canada*. Montreal: C. O. Beuchemin & Fils, 1889.

Lewis, Rhodri. *Hamlet and the Vision of Darkness*. Princeton, N.J.: Princeton University Press, forthcoming.

Lewis, Rhodri. *Language, Mind and Nature: Artificial Languages in England from Bacon to Locke*. Cambridge: Cambridge University Press, 2007.

Lhwyd, Edward. *Archaeologia Britannica: Texts and Translations*. Edited by Dewi W. Evans and Brynley F. Roberts. Aberystwyth, UK: Celtic Studies Publications, 2009.

Lhwyd, Edward. "Part of a Letter from Mr. Edward Lhwyd to Dr. Martin Lister." *Philosophical Transactions* 20, no. 243 (1698): 279–280.

Libby, Sam. "Tribes to Revive Language." *New York Times*, October 18, 1998.

Locke, John. *An Essay Concerning Human Understanding*. Edited by Peter H. Nidditch. Oxford: Clarendon, 1975.

Lodwick, Francis. *A Common Writing*. [London,] 1647.

Losonsky, Michael. *Linguistic Turns in Modern Philosophy*. Cambridge: Cambridge University Press, 2006.

Lowth, Robert. *Lectures on the Sacred Poetry of the Hebrews*. Translated by G. Gregory. Boston, 1815.

Lukacs, Georg. *The Historical Novel*. Translated by Hannah Mitchell and Stanley Mitchell. Boston: Beacon, 1963.

Luther, Martin. *Lectures on Romans*. Edited and translated by Wilhelm Pauck. Philadelphia: Westminster, 1961.

Lydekker, John Wolfe. *The Faithful Mohawks*. Cambridge: Cambridge University Press, 1938.

Lyons, Scott Richard. "There's No Translation for It: The Rhetorical Sovereignty of Indigenous Languages." In *Cross-Language Relations in Composition*, edited by Bruce Horner, Min-Zhan Lu, and Paul Kei Matsuda, 127–141. Carbondale: Southern Illinois University Press, 2010.

Maaka, Roger C. A., and Chris Andersen, eds. *The Indigenous Experience: Global Perspectives*. Toronto: Canadian Scholars Press, 2006.

MacCormack, Sabine. *On the Wings of Time: Rome, the Incas, Spain, and Peru*. Princeton, N.J.: Princeton University Press, 2007.

MacLeod, D. Peter. *The Canadian Iroquois and the Seven Years' War*. Toronto: Dundurn, 1996.

Maddison, R. E. W. "Robert Boyle and the Irish Bible." *Bulletin of the John Rylands Library* 41, no. 1 (September 1958): 81–101.

[Maillard, Pierre]. *An Account of the Customs and Manners of the Micmakis and Maricheets Savage Nations, Now Dependent on the Government of Cape-Breton, from an Original French Manuscript-Letter; Never published*. London: Printed for S. Hooper and A. Morley, 1758.

Maillard, Pierre. "Lettre de M. l'abbé Maillard sur les missions de l'Acadie et particulièrement sur les missions micmaques." In *Les Soirees Canadiennes*, vol. 3, 289–426. Quebec: Brousseau, 1863.

Malcolm, David. *An Essay on the Antiquities of Great Britain and Ireland*. Edinburgh: Printed by T. and W. Ruddimans, 1738.

[Malcolm, David, and Edward Lhwyd]. "A Letter to Archimedes." In *A Collection of Letters, in Which the Imperfection of Learning, Even Among Christians, and a Remedy for It, Are Hinted*. Edinburgh, 1739. John Carter Brown Library, Brown University, Providence, R.I.

Malcolm, Noel. "Comenius, Boyle, Oldenburg, and the Translation of the Bible into Turkish." *Church History and Religious Culture* 87, no. 3 (July 2007): 327–362.

Mannheim, Bruce. *The Language of the Inka Since European Invasion*. Austin: University of Texas Press, 1991.

Manuel, Frank E. *The Broken Staff: Judaism Through Christian Eyes*. Cambridge, Mass.: Harvard University Press, 1992.

Maracle, David Kanatawakhon. *One Thousand Useful Mohawk Words*. Guilford, Conn.: Audio-Forum, 1992.

Markley, Robert. *Fallen Languages: Crises of Representation in Newtonian England, 1660–1740*. Ithaca, N.Y.: Cornell University Press, 1993.

The Massachusett Psalter: Or, Psalms of David...in Columns of Indian and English. Boston: Printed by B. Green and J. Printer, 1709.

Masta, Henry Lorne. *Abenaki Indian Legends, Grammar and Place Names*. Victoriaville, P.Q.: La Voix des Bois-Frances, 1932.

Mather, Cotton. *Another Tongue Brought in, to Confess the Great Saviour of the World*. Boston: B. Green, 1707.

Mather, Cotton. *Biblia Americana*. Vol. 1, *Genesis*. Edited by Reiner Smolinski. Grand Rapids, Mich.: Baker Academic, 2010.

Mather, Cotton. *Magnalia Christi Americana: Or, the Ecclesiastical History of New-England....* Edited by Thomas Robbins. Hartford, 1853.

Mather, Cotton. *Psalterium Americanum*. Boston: Samuel Kneeland, 1718.

Mather, Cotton. *Selected Letters of Cotton Mather*. Edited by Kenneth Silverman. Baton Rouge: Louisiana State University Press, 1971.

Mayhew, Experience. *Indian Converts: A Cultural Edition*. Edited and with an introduction by Laura Arnold Leibman. Amherst: University of Massachusetts Press, 2008.

Mayhew, Experience. *Observations on the Indian Language*. Edited by John S. H. Fogg. 1722; reprint, Boston: D. Clapp & Son, 1884.

Mayhew, Experience. Sermons, Papers of Experience Mayhew. Massachusetts Historical Society, Boston.

McClymond, Michael J., and Gerald R. McDermott. *The Theology of Jonathan Edwards*. New York: Oxford University Press, 2012.

McDermott, Gerald R. "Missions and Native Americans." In *The Princeton Companion to Jonathan Edwards*, edited by Sang Hyun Lee, 258–273. Princeton, N.J.: Princeton University Press, 2005.

McDermott, Gerald R. *One Holy and Happy Society: The Public Theology of Jonathan Edwards*. University Park: Pennsylvania University Press, 1992.

McGann, Jerome. "Fenimore Cooper's Anti-aesthetic and the Representation of Conflicted History." *Modern Language Quarterly* 73, no 2 (2012): 123–155.

McGiffert, Arthur Cushman, Jr. *Jonathan Edwards*. New York: Harper & Brothers, 1932.

McGinness, Frederick J. "Preaching Ideals and Practice in Counter-Reformation Rome." *The Sixteenth Century Journal* 11, no. 2 (1980): 109–127.

McNeil, Kent. *Common Law Aboriginal Title*. Oxford: Clarendon, 1989.

McShea, Bronwen Catherine. "Cultivating Empire Through Print: The Jesuit Strategy for New France and the Parisian *Relations* of 1632–1672." PhD diss., Yale University, 2011.

"Meet the Masters: Mohawk Choir of St. Regis." Feb. 28, 2000, North Country Public Radio, http://www.northcountrypublicradio.org/news/story/3581/20000228/meet-the-masters-mohawk-choir-of-st-regis.

Merleau-Ponty, Maurice. *Phenomenology of Perception*. Translated by Colin Smith. London: Routledge and Kegan Paul, 1962.

Merritt, Jane T. "Metaphor, Meaning, and Misunderstanding: Language and Power on the Pennsylvania Frontier." In *Contact Points: American Frontiers from the Mohawk Valley to the Mississippi, 1750–1830*, edited by Andrew R. L. Cayton and Fredrika J. Teute, 60–87. Chapel Hill: University of North Carolina Press, 1998.

Mignolo, Walter D. *The Darker Side of the Renaissance: Literacy, Territoriality, and Colonization*. Ann Arbor: University of Michigan Press, 2003.

Mignolo, Walter D. "Nebrija in the New World: The Question of the Letter, the Colonization of Amerindian Languages, and the Discontinuity of the Classical Tradition." *L'Homme* 32, no. 122/124 (1992): 185–207.

Millar, Robert. *History of the Propagation of Christianity, and the Overthrow of Paganism*. 2 vols. London: Printed for A. Millar, 1731.

Miller, Charles. *Jefferson and Nature: An Interpretation*. Baltimore, Md.: Johns Hopkins University Press, 1988.

Miller, Perry. *Roger Williams: His Contribution to the American Tradition*. 1953; repr., New York: Atheneum, 1962.

Minkema, Kenneth P. "East Windsor Conversion Relations, 1700–1725." *Connecticut Historical Society Bulletin* 51 (1986): 9–63.

Mochon, Marion Johnson. "Stockbridge-Munsee Cultural Adaptations: 'Assimilated Indians.'" *Proceedings of the American Philosophical Society* 112, no. 3 (1968): 182–219.

Modarelli, Michael. "The Struggle for Origins: Old English in Nineteenth-Century America." *Modern Language Quarterly* 73, no. 4 (2012): 527–543.

Momaday, N. Scott. *House Made of Dawn*. 1968; repr., New York: Harper & Row, 2010.

Monaghan, E. Jennifer. *Learning to Read and Write in Colonial America*. Amherst: University of Massachusetts Press, 2005.

Monboddo, James. *Of the Origin and Progress of Language*. Edinburgh: Printed for J. Balfour, 1773–1792.

More, Henry. *An Antidote Against Atheisme*. London, 1653.

More, Henry. *The Immortality of the Soul*. London, 1659.

More, Henry. *Philosophicall Poems*. Cambridge, 1647.

Morgan, Prys. "From a Death to a View: The Hunt for the Welsh Past in the Romantic Period." In *The Invention of Tradition*, edited by Eric Hobsbawm and Terence Ranger, 43–101. Cambridge: Cambridge University Press, 1992.

Morin, Maxime. "L'abbé Pierre Maillard: Une figure missionaire emblématique du XVII siècle acadien." *Études d'histoire religieuse* 75 (2009): 39–54.

Morrison, Kenneth M. "The Cosmos as Intersubjective: The Native American Other-than-human Persons." *Indigenous Religions: A Companion*, edited by Graham Harvey, 23–36. New York: Cassell, 2000.

Morrison, Kenneth M. *The Embattled Northeast: The Elusive Ideal of Alliance in Abenaki-Euramerican Relations*. Berkeley: University of California Press, 1984.

Morrison, Kenneth M. "Sharing the Flower: A Non-supernaturalistic Theory of Grace." *Religion* 22, no. 3 (1992): 207–219.

Morrison, Kenneth M. *The Solidarity of Kin: Ethnohistory, Religious Studies, and the Algonkian-French Religious Encounter.* Albany: State University of New York Press, 2002.

Morrissey, Robert M. "'I Speak It Well': Language, Cultural Understanding, and the End of a Missionary Middle Ground in Illinois Country, 1673–1712." *Early American Studies* 9, no. 3 (2011): 617–648.

Morse, Jedidiah. Appendix to *Report to the Secretary of War…on Indian Affairs.* New Haven, Conn., 1822.

Mullet, Michael A. *The Catholic Reformation.* New York: Routledge, 1999.

Mungello, D. E. "European Philosophical Responses to Non-European Culture: China." In *The Cambridge History of Seventeenth-Century Philosophy,* vol. 1, edited by Daniel Garber and Michael Ayers, 87–100. Cambridge: Cambridge University Press, 1998.

Murr, Sylvia. *L'Inde Philosophique entre Boussuet et Voltaire.* Paris: École française d'Extrême-Orient, 1987.

Murray, David. *Forked Tongues: Speech, Writing, and Representation in North American Indian Texts.* Bloomington: Indiana University Press, 1991.

Murray, David. *Matter, Magic, and Spirit: Representing Indian and African American Belief.* Philadelphia: University of Pennsylvania Press, 2007.

Murray, Laura J. "Joining Signs with Words: Missionaries, Metaphors, and the Massachusett Language." *New England Quarterly* 74, no. 1 (2001): 62–93.

Myles, Anne G. "Dissent and the Frontier of Translation: Roger Williams's *A Key into the Language of America.*" In *Possible Pasts: Becoming Colonial in Early America,* edited by Robert Blair St. George, 88–108. Ithaca, N.Y.: Cornell University Press, 2000.

Nebrija, Antonio de. *Gramática castellana: Texto establecido sobre la ed. "princeps" de 1492.* Edited by Pascual Galindo Romeo and Luis Ortiz Muñoz. Madrid: Edición de la Junta del Centenario, 1946.

Nicolas, Louis. "Grammaire Algonquine, ou des sauvages de l'Amérique septentrionnale." Manuscrits Américains 1, *Bibliothéque National.* Paris, France.

Nussbaum, Martha. *Liberty of Conscience: In Defense of America's Tradition of Religious Equality.* New York: Basic, 2008.

O'Brien, Jean M. *Firsting and Lasting: Writing Indians Out of Existence in New England.* Minneapolis: University of Minnesota Press, 2010.

O'Domhnuill, Huilliam. *Tiomna Nuadh ar dTighearna agus ar Slanuigheora Iósa Criosd.* London, 1681.

Ogg, David. "The Emergence of Great Britain as a World Power." In *The New Cambridge Modern History: Vol. 6. The Rise of Great Britain and Russia, 1688–1715/25,* edited by J. S. Bromley, 254–283. Cambridge: Cambridge University Press, 1970.

O'Malley, John W. *The First Jesuits.* Cambridge, Mass.: Harvard University Press, 1993.

O'Malley, SJ, John W., Gauvin Alexander Bailey, Steven J. Harris, and T. Frank Kennedy, eds. *The Jesuits: Cultures, Sciences, and the Arts, 1540–1773.* Toronto: University of Toronto Press, 1999.

O'Neill, Charles E. "Gravier, Jacques." In *Dictionary of Canadian Biography,* vol. 2, accessed February 20, 2014, http://www.biographi.ca/en/bio/gravier_jacques_2E.html.

Ong, Walter. *Orality and Literacy: The Technologizing of the Word.* New York: Methuen, 1988.

Owen, Edward, ed. *A Catalogue of Manuscripts Relating to Wales in the British Museum,* part 4. London: Issued by the Honorable Society of Cymmrodorion, 1922.

Pagden, Anthony. *European Encounters with the New World.* New Haven, Conn.: Yale University Press, 1993.

Palmer, Randall. "Freeman, Bernardus." In *American National Biography Online*, accessed August 7, 2016, http://www.anb.org/articles/08/08-00504.html.

Parmenter, Jon. "After the Mourning Wars: The Iroquois as Allies in Colonial North American Campaigns, 1676–1760." *William and Mary Quarterly* 64, no. 3 (2007): 39–76.

Pastoureau, Mireille, Annie Chassagne, and Pierre Gasnault. *Le Dictionnaire de l'Académie françoise, 1694–1994: Sa naissance et son actualité*. Paris: Institut de France, 1994.

Patrides, C. A., ed. *The Cambridge Platonists*. Cambridge, Mass.: Harvard University Press, 1970.

Paxman, David B. "Language and Difference: The Problem of Abstraction in Eighteenth-Century Language Study." *Journal of the History of Ideas* 54, no. 1 (1993): 19–36.

Pearson, Diane. "Medical Diplomacy and the American Indian." *Wicazo Sa Review* 19, no. 1 (2004): 105–130.

Peckham, Howard H. *The Colonial Wars, 1689–1762*. Chicago: University of Chicago Press, 1964.

Perley, Bernard C. "Aboriginality at Large: Varieties of Resistance in Maliseet Language Instruction." *Identities: Global Studies in Culture and Power* 13, no. 2 (2006): 187–208.

Peters, Edward. *Heresy and Authority in Medieval Europe*. Philadelphia: University of Pennsylvania Press, 1980.

Pezron, Paul Yves. *The Antiquities of Nations, More Particularly of the Celtæ or Gauls, Taken to Be Originally the Same People as Our Ancient Britains...Englished by Mr. Jones*. London, 1706.

Philbrick, Thomas. "Cooper's *The Pioneers*: Origins and Structure." In *James Fenimore Cooper: A Collection of Critical Essays*, edited by Wayne Fields. Englewood Cliffs, N.J.: Prentice-Hall, 1979.

Pickering, John. *An Essay on a Uniform Orthography for the Indian Languages of North America*. Cambridge: Hilliard and Metcalf, 1820.

Picquet, François. "Prayer Book." Ruggles Collection, Newberry Library, Chicago, Ill.

Poole, William. "The Divine and the Grammarian: Theological Disputes in the Seventeenth-Century Universal Language Movement." *Historiographia Linguistica* 30, no. 3 (2003): 273–300.

Poole, William. *The World Makers: Scientists of the Restoration and the Search for the Origins of the Earth*. Oxford: Peter Lang, 2010.

Porter, David. *Ideographia: The Chinese Cipher in Early Modern Europe*. Stanford, Calif.: Stanford University Press, 2001.

Powicke, F. J., ed. "Some Unpublished Correspondence of the Rev. Richard Baxter and the Rev. John Eliot, 'The Apostle to the American Indians,' 1656–1682." *Bulletin of the John Rylands Library* 15, no. 1 (January 1931): 138–176.

Quantin, Jean-Louis. *The Church of England and Christian Antiquity: The Construction of a Confessional Identity in the Seventeenth Century*. Oxford: Oxford University Press, 2009.

Rasles [Rale], Sebastian. *A Dictionary of the Abnaki Language, in North America*. In *Memoirs of the American Academy of Arts and Sciences* I, new series, edited by John Pickering. Cambridge: Printer to the University, 1833.

Rasmussen, Birgit Brander. *Queequeg's Coffin: Indigenous Literacies and Early American Literature*. Durham, N.C.: Duke University Press, 2012.

Reading, Philip. *The Protestant's Danger and the Protestant's Duty*. Philadelphia: B. Franklin and D. Hall, 1755.

Rebok, Sandra. "Enlightened Correspondents: The Transatlantic Dialogue of Thomas Jefferson and Alexander von Humboldt." *Virginia Magazine of History and Biography* 116, no. 4 (2008): 328–369.

"Rev. John Ogilvie, Albany NY, July 27, 1750." 102.3, Society for the Propagation of the Gospel Papers, Rhodes House, Oxford, England.

Rivett, Sarah. "Empirical Desire: Conversion, Ethnography, and the New Science of the Praying Indian." *Early American Studies* 4, no. 1 (2006): 16–45.

Rivett, Sarah. *The Science of the Soul in Colonial New England*. Chapel Hill: University of North Carolina Press, 2011.

Roberts, Brynley F. "The Discovery of Old Welsh." *Historiographia Linguistica* 26, nos. 1/2 (1999): 1–21.

Ronda, James P. "The European Indian: Jesuit Civilization Planning in New France." *Church History* 41, no. 3 (September 1972): 385–395.

Rosenmeier, Jesper. "The Teacher and the Witness: John Cotton and Roger Williams." *The William and Mary Quarterly* 25, no. 3 (1968): 408–431.

Rossi, Paolo. "La religion dei geroglifici e le origini della scrittura." In *Le sterminate antichità e nuovi saggi vichiani*, 80–131. Scandicci: La Nuova Italia, 1999.

Round, Philip H. *Removable Type: Histories of the Book in Indian Country, 1663–1880*. Chapel Hill: University of North Carolina Press, 2010.

Rousseau, Jean-Jacques. "Essay on the Origin of Languages." In *Collected Writings of Rousseau*, vol. 7. Translated and edited by John T. Scott. Hanover, N.H.: University Press of New England, 1998.

Rousseau, Jean-Jacques, and Johann Gottfried Herder. *On the Origin of Language*. Translated by John H. Moran and Alexander Gode. New York: Frederick Ungar, 1966.

Rush, Benjamin. *The Selected Writings of Benjamin Rush*. Edited by Dagobert D. Runes. New York: Philosophical Library, 1947.

Rushforth, Brett. *Bonds of Alliance: Indigenous and Atlantic Slaveries in New France*. Chapel Hill: University of North Carolina Press, 2012.

Ruyl, Albert Cornelisson, Jan van Hasel, and Justus van Heurne. *De vier Heylighe Euangelien, Beschreven door de vier Euangelisten, Matthaeus, Marcus, Lucas, Johannes. Ende het Boeck van de Handilingen der H. Apostelen, Beschreven door Lucam*. Amsterdam, 1651.

Sadosky, Leonard J. *Revolutionary Negotiations: Indians, Empires, and Diplomats in the Founding of America*. Charlottesville: University of Virginia Press, 2009.

Sagard, Gabriel. *Le Grand Voyage du Pays des Hurons*. Paris, 1632.

Salmon, Vivian. "Thomas Harriot (1560–1621) and the English Origins of Algonkian Linguistics." *Historiographia Linguistica* 19, no. 1 (1992): 25–56.

Salvucci, Claudio R. Introduction to *Elements of a Miami-Illinois Grammar*. Edited by John Gilmary Shea. 1890; repr., Bristol Pa.: Evolution, 2005.

Sayre, Gordon M. "The Mound Builders and the Imagination of American Antiquity in Jefferson, Bartram, and Chateaubriand." *Early American Literature* 33, no. 3 (1998): 225–249.

Scancarelli, Janine. "Cherokee." In *Native Languages of the Southeastern United States*, edited by Heather K. Hardy and Janine Scancarelli, 351–384. Lincoln: University of Nebraska Press, 2005.

Schmidt, David L., and Murdena Marshall, eds. *Mi'Kmaq Hieroglyphic Prayers: Readings in North America's First Indigenous Script*. Halifax, N.S.: Nimbus, 1995.

Schoolcraft, Henry R. "Considerations on the Art of Picture Writing, and the System of Mnemonic Symbols of the North American Indians." In *Oneóta, or Characteristics of the Red Race of America*, New York: Wiley & Putnam, 1845.

Schreyer, Rüdiger. "'Savage' Languages in Eighteenth-Century Theoretical History of Language." In *The Language Encounter in America*, edited by Edward G. Gray and Norman Fiering, 310–326. New York: Berghahn, 2000.

Sedgwick, Sarah Cabot, and Christina Sedgwick Marquand. *Stockbridge, 1739–1974.* Stockbridge, Mass.: Berkshire Traveller, 1974.

Seeman, Erik R. *The Huron-Wendat Feast of the Dead: Indian-European Encounters in Early North America*. Baltimore, Md.: Johns Hopkins University Press, 2011.

Selections from the Catholic Prayer Book. MS 1627, Ayer Collection, Newberry Library, Chicago, Ill.

Sergeant, John. *A Letter from the Rev'd Mr. Sergeant of Stockbridge, to Dr. Colman of Boston.* Boston: Printed by Rogers and Fowle, for D. Henchman in Cornhill, 1743.

Shapiro, Barbara J. *John Wilkins, 1614–1672: An Intellectual Biography*. Berkeley: University of California Press, 1969.

Sheehan, Bernard W. *Seeds of Extinction: Jeffersonian Philanthropy and the American Indian.* Chapel Hill: University of North Carolina Press, 1973.

Sheehan, M. "The Development of the British Theory and Practice of the Balance of Power Before 1714." *History* 73, no. 237 (1988): 24–37.

Shelley, Percy Bysshe. *A Defence of Poetry*. In *The Major Works*. Edited by Zachary Leader and Michael O'Neil. New York: Oxford University Press, 2003.

Shepard, Thomas. *The Clear Sun-Shine of the Gospel Breaking Forth upon the Indians in New-England*. London: R. Cotes, 1648.

Shepard, Thomas, Jr. Letter, Sept. 9, 1673, Wod. Qu. CV, fols. 105–112. Woodrow Collection, National Library of Scotland, Edinburgh.

Sher, Richard B. "Millar, Robert (1672–1752)." In *Oxford Dictionary of National Biography*, accessed May 17, 2014, http://www.oxforddnb.com/view/article/67754.

Sigourney, Lydia Huntley. *Poems*. Philadelphia: Key and Biddle, 1834.

Silverberg, Robert. *Mound Builders of Ancient America: The Archaeology of a Myth.* Greenwich, Conn.: New York Graphic Society, 1968.

Silverman, David J. "Indians, Missionaries, and Religious Translation: Creating Wampanoag Christianity in Seventeenth-Century Martha's Vineyard." *William and Mary Quarterly* 62, no. 2 (2005): 141–174.

Silverstein, Michael. "Old Wine, New Ethnographic Lexicography." *Annual Review of Anthropology* 35 (2006): 481–496.

Simms, William Gilmore. *Views and Reviews in American Literature, History and Fiction.* New York: Wiley and Putnam, 1845.

Simpson, David. *The Politics of American English, 1776–1850*. New York: Oxford University Press, 1986.

Simpson, David. "Romantic Indians: Robert Southey's Distinctions." *The Wordsworth Circle* 38, nos. 1/2 (2007): 20–25.

Slotkin, Richard. *Regeneration Through Violence: The Mythology of the American Frontier, 1600–1860*. Middletown, Conn.: Wesleyan University Press, 1973.

Smith, Adam. *Theory of Moral Sentiments. To Which Is Added a Dissertation on the Origin of Languages*. London: Printed for A. Millar, A. Kincaid, and J. Bell in Edinburgh, 1767.

Society for the Propagation of the Gospel Papers. Rhodes House, Oxford University.

Spengemann, William C., and Jessica F. Roberts, eds. *Nineteenth-Century American Poetry.* New York: Penguin, 1996.

Sprat, Tho[mas]. *The History of the Royal-Society.* London, 1667.

Spruit, Leen. *Species Intelligibilis: From Perception to Knowledge,* vol 1. Leiden: Brill, 1994.

Stanwood, Owen. "Unlikely Imperialist: The Baron of Saint-Castin and the Transformation of the Northeastern Borderlands." *French Colonial History* 5 (2004): 43–61.

Steckley, John. "Huron Carol: A Canadian Cultural Chameleon." *British Journal of Canadian Studies* 27, no. 1 (2014): 55–74.

Steckley, John. *A Huron-English/English-Huron Dictionary (Listing Both Words and Noun and Verb Roots).* Lewiston, N.Y.: Edwin Mellen, 2007.

Steckley, John L. "Brébeuf's Presentation of Catholicism in the Huron Language: A Descriptive Overview." *Revue de l'Universite d'Ottawa/University of Ottawa Quarterly* 48, nos. 1/2 (1978): 93–115.

Steckley, John L. *Words of the Huron.* Waterloo, Ont.: Wilfrid Laurier University Press, 2007.

Steele, Brian. *Thomas Jefferson and American Nationhood.* New York: Cambridge University Press, 2012.

Steele, Ian K. "Exploding Colonial American History: Amerindian, Atlantic, and Global Perspectives." *Reviews in American History* 26, no. 1 (1998): 70–95.

Stoddard, Solomon. *Question Whether God Is Not Angry with the Country for Doing So Little Towards the Conversion of the Indians?* Boston: Printed by B. Green...And Sold by Samuel Gerrish, 1723.

Sugirtharajah, Sharada. "Max Muller and Textual Management: A Postcolonial Perspective." In *Hermeneutics and Hindu Thought: Toward a Fusion of Horizons,* edited by Rita Sherma and Arvind Sharma, 33–45. New York: Springer, 2008.

Swadesh, Morris. "Lexicostatistic Dating of Prehistoric Ethnic Contacts." In *Proceedings of the American Philosophical Society,* 96 (1952): 452–463.

Swenson, John F. *Letters Re Gravier Dictionary.* American Indian Vocabulary Collection, Watkinson Library, Trinity College, Hartford, Conn.

Swift, Jonathan. *Conduct of the Allies.* London, 1711.

Swift, Jonathan. *A Proposal for Correcting, Improving and Ascertaining the English Tongue.* London, 1712.

Sylvester, Matthew[, ed.]. *Reliquiæ Baxterianæ; or, Mr. Richard Baxter's Narrative of the Most Memorable Passages of His Life and Times.* London, 1696.

Taylor, Alan. *William Cooper's Town: Power and Persuasion on the Frontier of the Early American Republic.* New York: Alfred A. Knopf, 1995.

Teunissen, John J., and Evelyn J. Hinz. "Roger Williams, Thomas More, and the Narragansett Utopia." *Early American Literature* 11, no. 3 (1976/1977): 281–295.

Thompson, Peter. "'Judicious Neology': The Imperative Paternalism in Thomas Jefferson's Linguistic Studies." *Early American Studies* 1, no. 2 (2003): 187–224.

Thomson, Keith Stewart. *Jefferson's Shadow: The Story of His Science.* New Haven, Conn.: Yale University Press, 2012.

Thoreau, Henry David. *The Maine Woods: A Fully Annotated Edition.* Edited by Jeffrey S. Cramer. New Haven, Conn.: Yale University Press, 2009.

Thorowgood, Thomas. *Jews in America, or Probabilities That Those Indians Are Judaical.* London: Henry Brome at the Gun in Ivie-lane, 1660.

Thrush, Coll. *Indigenous London: Native Travelers at the Heart of Empire.* New Haven, Conn.: Yale University Press, 2016.

Thwaites, Reuben Gold. *The Jesuit Relations and Allied Documents.* 73 vols. Cleveland: Burrows Brothers, 1896–1901.

Tilghman, William. "Report of the Historical and Literary Committee to the American Philosophical Society." In *Transactions of the Historical and Literary Committee of the American Philosophical Society,* vol. 1. Philadelphia, 1819.

Tomalin, Marcus. *Romanticism and Linguistic Theory: William Hazlitt, Language, and Literature.* New York: Palgrave Macmillan, 2009.

Tomlinson, Gary. *The Singing of the New World: Indigenous Voice in the Era of European Contact.* Cambridge: Cambridge University Press, 2007.

Tooker, William Wallace. "John Eliot's First Indian Teacher and Interpreter Cockenoe-De-Long Island and the Story of His Career from the Early Records." In *Languages and Lore of the Long Island Indians,* edited by Gaynell Stone Levine and Nancy Bonvillain, 176–189. Lexington, Mass.: Ginn, 1980.

Townsend, Camilla, ed. and trans. *Here in This Year: Seventeenth-Century Nahuatl Annals of the Tlaxcala-Puebla Valley.* Stanford, Calif.: Stanford University Press, 2010.

Tracy, David. *The Analogical Imagination: Christian Theology and the Culture of Pluralism.* New York: Crossroad, 1981.

Tracy, Patricia J. *Jonathan Edwards, Pastor: Religion and Society in Eighteenth-Century Northampton.* New York: Hill and Wang, 1980.

Trask, William Blake, ed. *Letters of Colonel Thomas Westbrook and Others Relative to Indian Affairs in Maine, 1722–1726.* Boston: George E. Littlefield, 1901.

Trautman, Thomas R. *Languages and Nations: The Dravidian Proof in Colonial Madras.* Berkeley: University of California Press, 2006.

Trevor-Roper, Hugh. "The Invention of Tradition: The Highland Tradition of Scotland." In *The Invention of Tradition,* edited by Eric Hobsbawm and Terence Ranger, 15–43. Cambridge: Cambridge University Press, 1992.

Trigger, Bruce G. *The Children of Aataentsic: A History of the Huron People to 1660.* 2 vols. Montreal: McGill-Queen's University Press, 1976.

True, Micah. *Masters and Students: Jesuit Ethnography in Seventeenth-Century New France.* Montreal: McGill-Queens University Press, 2015.

Trumbull, James Hammond. *Natick Dictionary.* Washington, D.C.: US Government Printing Office, 1903.

Trumbull, James Hammond. *Natick Dictionary: A New England Indian Lexicon.* Lincoln: University of Nebraska Press, 2009.

Twain, Mark. "Fenimore Cooper's Literary Offenses." *North American Review* 161, no. 464 (July 1895): 1–12.

Vajda, Edward. "A Siberian Link with the Na-Dene." *Anthropological Papers of the University of Alaska,* New Series, 5 (2010): 31–99.

Vastokas, Joan M. "History Without Writing: Pictorial Narratives in Native North America." In *Gin Das Winan: Documenting Aboriginal History in Ontario,* edited by Dale Standen and David McNab, 48–65. Toronto: Champlain Society, 1996.

Vaugelas, Claude Favre de. *Remarques sur la langue françoise.* Paris, 1647.

Venuti, Lawrence. *The Scandals of Translation: Towards an Ethics of Difference.* New York: Routledge, 1998.

Vico, Giambattista. *The First New Science*. Edited by Leon Pompa. Cambridge: Cambridge University Press, 2002.

Vico, Giambattista. *New Science*. New York: Penguin, 1999.

Vizenor, Gerald. *Manifest Manners: Narratives on Postindian Survivance*. Lincoln: University of Nebraska Press, 1999.

Vizenor, Gerald, ed. *Survivance: Narratives of Native Presence*. Lincoln: University of Nebraska Press, 2008.

Volney, Constantin Francois. *View of the Climate and Soil of the United States of America*. London: Printed for J. Johnson, 1804.

Wagner, R. L. *Les Vocabulaires français*. Paris: Didier, 1967.

Waldstreicher, David. Introduction to *Notes on the State of Virginia*, edited by David Waldstreicher. Boston: Bedford St. Martin's, 2002.

Walker, Willard, and James Sarbaugh. "The Early History of the Cherokee Syllabary." *Ethnohistory* 40, no. 1 (1993): 70–94.

Wallace, Anthony F. C. *Jefferson and the Indians: The Tragic Fate of the First Americans*. Cambridge, Mass.: The Belknap Press of Harvard University Press, 1999.

Wallis, Wilson D., and Ruth Sawtell Wallis. *The Micmac Indians of Eastern Canada*. Minneapolis: University of Minnesota Press, 1955.

Walsham, Alexandra. *Reformation of the Landscape: Religion, Identity, and Memory in Early Modern Britain and Ireland*. Oxford: Oxford University Press, 2011.

Warkentin, Germaine. "Dead Metaphor or Working Model? The 'Book' in Native America." In *Colonial Mediascapes: Sensory Worlds of Early America*, edited by Matt Cohen and Jeffrey Glover, 47–75. Lincoln: University of Nebraska Press, 2014.

Warkentin, Germaine. "In Search of 'The Word of the Other': Aboriginal Sign Systems and the History of the Book in Canada." *Book History* 2 (1999): 1–27.

Washington, George. *The Writings of George Washington*, vol. 30. Edited by John C. Fitzpatrick. Washington, D.C.: US Government Printing Office, 1931.

Weaver, Jace. *The Red Atlantic: American Indigenes and the Making of the Modern World, 1000–1927*. Chapel Hill: University of North Carolina Press, 2014.

Wellenreuther, Hermann, and Carola Wessel, eds. *The Moravian Mission Diaries of David Zeisberger, 1772–1781*. Translated by Julie T. Weber. University Park: Pennsylvania State University Press, 2005.

Wenzel, Siegfried. *Preachers, Poets, and the Early English Lyric*. Princeton, N.J.: Princeton University Press, 1986.

Weslager, C. A. *The Nanticoke Indians: Past and Present*. Newark: University of Delaware Press, 1983.

Wheeler, Rachel. *To Live upon Hope: Mohicans and Missionaries in the Eighteenth-Century Northeast*. Ithaca, N.Y.: Cornell University Press, 2008.

Wheeler, Rachel M. "Edwards as Missionary." In *The Cambridge Companion to Jonathan Edwards*, edited by Stephen J. Stein, 196–214. Cambridge: Cambridge University Press, 2007.

Wheeler, Rachel M. "'Friends to Your Souls': Jonathan Edwards' Indian Pastorate and the Doctrine of Original Sin." *Church History* 72, no. 4 (2003): 736–765.

White, Bruce M. "Encounters with Spirits: Ojibwa and Dakota Theories About the French and Their Merchandise." *Ethnohistory* 41, no. 3 (1994): 369–405.

Whitehead, Ruth Holmes. *Elitekey: Micmac Material Culture from 1600 AD to the Present*. Halifax: Nova Scotia Museum, 1980.

Whitehead, Ruth Holmes. "A New Micmac Petroglyph Site." *Occasional: An Occasional Journal for Nova Scotia Museum* 13, no. 1 (1992): 7–12.

Whitehead, Ruth Holmes. *Nova Scotia: The Protohistoric Period, 1500–1630.* Halifax: Nova Scotia Museum, 1993.

Whorf, Benjamin Lee. "An American Indian Model of the Universe." In *Language, Thought, and Reality: Selected Writings of Benjamin Lee Whorf,* edited by John B. Carroll, 57–64. Cambridge, Mass.: MIT Press, 1956.

Wilkins, John. *An Essay Towards a Real Character and a Philosophical Language.* London, 1668.

Williams, Eleazar. *Papers, 1758–1858.* Box 2, fol. 15, Ayer Collection, Newberry Library, Chicago, Ill.

Williams, Roger. *Christenings Make Not Christians: Or a Briefe Discourse Concerning That Name* Heathen, *Commonly Given to the Indians.* In *The Complete Writings of Roger Williams,* vol. 7. Edited by Perry Miller. New York: Russell & Russell, 1963.

Williams, Roger. *A Key into the Language of America.* In *The Complete Writings of Roger Williams,* vol 1. Edited by J. Hammond Trumbull. New York: Russell and Russell, 1963.

Wilson, Douglas L. "The Evolution of Jefferson's *Notes on the State of Virginia.*" *Virginia Magazine of History and Biography* 112, no. 2 (2004): 98–133.

Winiarski, Douglas L. "A Question of Plain Dealing: Josiah Cotton, Native Christians, and the Quest for Security in Eighteenth-Century Plymouth County." *New England Quarterly* 77, no. 3 (2004): 368–413.

Winslow, Edward. *The Glorious Progress of the Gospel, Amongst the Indians in New England.* London, 1649.

Wiseman, Frederick Matthew. *The Voice of the Dawn: An Autohistory of the Abenaki Nation.* Hanover, N.H.: University Press of New England, 2001.

Woodward, John. *An Essay Toward a Natural History of the Earth.* London: Printed for Ric. Wilkin at the Kings Head in St. Paul's Church-yard, 1695.

Worcester, Thomas, ed. *The Cambridge Companion to the Jesuits.* New York: Cambridge University Press, 2008.

Wyss, Hilary E. *English Letters and Indian Literacies: Reading, Writing, and New England Missionary Schools, 1750–1830.* Philadelphia: University of Pennsylvania Press, 2012.

Wyss, Hilary E., and Kristina Bross, eds. *Early Native Literacies in New England: A Documentary and Critical Anthology.* Amherst: University of Massachusetts Press, 2008.

Zeisberger, David. *A Grammar of the Language of the Lenni Lenape or Delaware Indians.* American Philosophical Society, Philadelphia, 1827.

Zupanov, Ines G. "Aristocratic Analogies and Demotic Descriptions in the Seventeenth-Century Madurai Mission." *Representations* 41 (Winter 1993): 123–148.

Note: Page numbers in italics indicate figures.